Wall Street

and the

Russian Revolution

1905-1925

Richard B. Spence

WALL STREET AND THE RUSSIAN REVOLUTION, 1905-1925
COPYRIGHT © 2017 RICHARD B. SPENCE

Published by:
Trine Day LLC
PO Box 577
Walterville, OR 97489
1-800-556-2012
www.TrineDay.com
publisher@TrineDay.net

Library of Congress Control Number: 2017936719

Spence, Richard B.
–1st ed.
p. cm.

Epud (ISBN-13) 978-1-63424-124-3
Mobi (ISBN-13) 978-1-63424-125-0
Print (ISBN-13) 978-1-63424-123-6
1. United States -- Foreign economic relations -- Russia. 2. United States -- Foreign economic relations -- Soviet Union. 3. Russia -- History -- Revolution, 1905-1917. 4. Soviet Union -- History -- Revolution, 1917-1925. 5. International economic relations. 6. Investments, American. I. Spence, Richard B. II. Title

FIRST EDITION
10 9 8 7 6 5 4 3 2 1

Printed in the USA
Distribution to the Trade by:
Independent Publishers Group (IPG)
814 North Franklin Street
Chicago, Illinois 60610
312.337.0747
www.ipgbook.com

Publisher's Foreword

Who Cares?

Who cares, who cares?
My head is full of snot, snot, snot, snot ...

– Watt's Acid Test, 2/12/66

Thy glass will show thee how thy beauties wear,
Thy dial how thy precious minutes waste;
The vacant leaves thy mind's imprint will bear,
And of this book, this learning mayst thou taste.
The wrinkles which thy glass will truly show
Of mouthed graves will give thee memory;
Thou by thy dial's shady stealth mayst know
Time's thievish progress to eternity.

– William Shakespeare, Sonnet L LXXVII

One day in the late 1990s an email from Antony Sutton flashed on my computer screen. First, I wondered if it was a hoax, but no it was really him. It was exciting. I had tried to reach him many years before, even writing to his publisher in Montana. Nothing. And now he was writing to me. Wow!

I had written an article on the Order of Skull & Bones that had been picked up by Parascope, an early AOL attempt to foster content providers on the Internet. The article spread far and wide and was always in the top position in search engines, including the number one Google pick for "George W. Bush." The listing helped to raise the question of whether W's membership in Bones would hold him back in 2000?

Time and tide soon buried the article, but Antony had contacted me. I wrote him back, we talked on the phone, communicated and had fun. I asked to visit, he said no, and the only people that he had seen in years were "folks from three-letter agencies." He had dropped political research, in favor of his first love, technology. He had become tired of going to "banquets" and being sandwiched in between UFO's and the John Birch Society. The Internet and events, it seemed, were drawing him back in.

It took some time before Antony allowed a personal visit. It was wonderful. After all, this was the man, who had authored the book, *America's Secret Establishment* in 1986 that I read in 1988, and helped me understand what my recalcitrant ex-CIA father had told me in 1969. Tony also informed me his publisher was going out of business.

When he had first published his four pamphlets on the Order, which were later combined into *America's Secret Establishment*, Tony printed them in Australia, because he could not find anybody here. Many of these pamphlets were stolen off the docks, and interestingly, at this time, George HW Bush was denying any involvement with a secret society. In these pre-Internet days Tony had a newsletter. One of his subscribers, a mom and pop print shop in Montana, became his publisher and produced his book for many years. They were retiring and moving to Arizona.

"Tony, that can't happen," I said. "Your book has never been in hard cover, and is rarely found in libraries."

So, I borrowed $5,000 and started TrineDay. Our first book being Tony's *America's Secret Establishment*. But tragically, three weeks after the printing, Tony fell dead in his kitchen. Yes, it was suspicious, but all the county coroner would tell us – was "natural causes."

A great and wonderful researcher was lost that day. Tony knew how, and what to ask for. His years in academia had honed his skills. You want first person sources and documents, Tony supplied them.

Tony's "Wall Street" books were prompted by his experience at the Hoover Institute at Standford. He had been contracted to write *Western Technology and Soviet Economic Development*. He had finished his writing in 1970, but the "powers-that-be" wouldn't publish the last book of the three volume series. It seemed that Antony had stumbled on a deeply hidden secret conspiracy: American interests were supplying some of the armaments being send by the USSR to North Vietnam to be used against Americans. Tony protested, they said, "Don't break your rice bowl." Tony persisted, eventually taking his research and publishing, *National Suicide: Military Aid to the Soviet Union (1973)* thereby forcing the Hoover Institue to publish their final volume. Tony was "let go," and real history was buried.

Tony looked around to find out who was responsible. This led to *Wall Street and the Bolshevik Revolution (1974)*, *Wall Street and FDR (1975)*, *Wall Street and Hitler (1976)*. A relative of a member of the secret society Skull & Bones then sent Tony a membership list, which led to his magnum opus *America's Secret Establishment: An Introduction to The Order of Skull & Bones*.

Tony would love Richard Spence's new well-researched book, *Wall Street and the Russian Revolution*, another author that knows how to find first person sources and documents that tell an "interesting" story.

Onward,
Peace,
RA Kris Millegan
Publisher
TrineDay
May 1, 2017

TABLE OF CONTENTS

The Empire of the Tsar
The Russian Revolutionaries
The Russian Liberals
The "Jewish Question"
The Empire of the Trusts
American Business in Russia
Regime Change and American Interventionism

Charles R. Crane: The "Outsider-Insider"
Jacob H. Schiff: The "Jewish Avenger"
The Warburgs
The House of Morgan
The Friends of Russian Freedom

The Road to Bloody Sunday
The Day
Hero of the Revolution
The American Reaction
The Tsar Resurgent
Trotsky and Parvus
The Underside of the Revolution
The Lessons of 1905

Friends
The Gorky Mission
The Matyushenko Affair
Apostles of Revolutions
Money and Martyrs

To: Antony Cyril Sutton
1925-2002

ACKNOWLEDGMENTS

M any people, knowingly or unknowingly, assisted me in the writing of this book. First and foremost, I should thank "Bina Tiferet" whose curiosity, constant questioning and encouragement finally got me to commit to this project. Elena Chavchavadze and the Russian Cultural Foundation were also of invaluable assistance. I also want to extend heartfelt thanks, in no special order, to Abbie Venner of the Long Lake, NY, Historical Society, Harry and Marjorie Mahoney, Stan Vaughan, Jeff Spencer, Yuri Totrov, Svetlana Chervonnaya, Phil Tomaselli, Ron Basich and the Hoover Institution Archive, the staffs of the Bakhmetev Archive, Columbia University and Sterling Library, Yale University. Last, but by no means least, thanks to Kris Millegan and Trine Day Press. If I have forgotten anyone, I humbly beg your pardon.

ABBREVIATIONS
USED IN FOOTNOTES

BA	Bakh'metev Archive, Columbia University.
BI	U.S. Department of Justice, Bureau of Investigation (precursor to the FBI), U.S. National Archives and Records Administration (NARA), M1085.
CAC	Churchill Archive, Cambridge
CSA	Chief Special Agent files, U.S. Department of State, NARA.
FO	Foreign Office, UK.
GARF	State Archive of the Russian Federation, Moscow
HIA	Hoover Institution Archive, Stanford University.
MID	Military Intelligence Division, U.S. Army, NARA.
NAC	National Archives of Canada, Ottawa.
ONI	Office of Naval Intelligence, U.S. Navy, NARA.
RGASPI	Russian State Archive of Socio-Political History, Moscow
RIP	Ralph Isham Papers, Sterling Library, Yale University.
SIS	Secret Intelligence Service (MI6) Records, UK.
TNA	The National Archives, UK.
USDS	United States Department of State, NARA.
WWP	Sir William Wiseman Papers, Sterling Library, Yale University.

Introduction

If the dedication doesn't make it clear enough, I owe an immense debt of gratitude to Antony C. Sutton and his original, groundbreaking, *Wall Street and the Bolshevik Revolution*. The present book almost certainly would not have been written without Sutton paving the way. My original idea, which goes back almost twenty years, was to obtain the rights to Sutton's book and produce an updated, annotated edition. For a variety of reasons, that didn't pan out, and it's just as well. Among other things, it forced me to re-imagine the entire subject and how it might be presented. That took some time, and a few false starts.

Wall Street and the Russian Revolution fundamentally differs from Sutton's work in two key respects, both centering on context. First, as *Russian Revolution* suggests, it takes a broader chronological approach. Sutton basically focused on the years 1917-1920. The present book treats the Russian Revolution not as a single event but as a movement, a process, unfolding as series of events over roughly twenty years. Second, Sutton really only looked at the American end of the equation. This book adds the critical Russian dimension. Russian radicals were not passive actors in their dealings with American capital. The book gives much attention to people and personalities. Understanding who men like Charles Crane, Jacob Schiff, Sidney Reilly and Leon Trotsky were, and not just what they did, is a key part of this larger picture. Ultimately, it's about connections, and the most important of those connections were between people.

None of this is meant to fault Sutton. There is much more information accessible today than in the 1970s. This isn't to say that he wasn't wrong about a few things, and where I've found mistakes I've tried to correct them. Doubtless I've made a few of my own. It also doesn't mean I don't differ with Sutton on some points. For instance, Sutton seemed to believe that the main thing impelling Wall Street capitalists to lend support to the Bolsheviks was a shared "globalist" mentality. I accept that, to a point. The idea of a Socialist or Communist International does have a kind of mirror image in the notion of a Capitalist International or *Capintern*. According to Carol Quigley "the powers of financial capitalism had another far reaching aim, nothing less than to create a world system of financial control in private hands able to dominate the political system of each country and the economy of the world as a whole."[1] To do so without Russia would be impossible.

However, Quigley proposed that the "apex" of this system was the Bank for International Settlements in Switzerland. The BIS did not come into being until 1930, a detail that fits my contention that the Wall Street and competing capitalist efforts to manipulate and exploit the Russian Revolution were a groping, imperfect and ultimately failed effort in pursuit of the grand goal. A failed experiment that demanded, and created, improved methods. One learns through ones mistakes, assuming one doesn't perish from them.

There also was an ideological factor. As we'll see, "socialist-capitalist" is not an oxymoron. But the true believers, while often useful tools, weren't the driving force either. That, in my humble opinion, was simple greed. Wall Street capitalists, like any others, invested in search of profit. Investing in a revolution was fundamentally no different from investing in anything else.

So, *Wall Street and the Russian Revolution* isn't intended to replace or negate Sutton's work, but expand it. In addition to context, it simply provides more information. This isn't to claim that there is nothing more to be said on the subject. Far from it. This, too, is only a gateway to more research and further discovery.

To a great extent, the book you are about to plunge into is a giant exercise in connect the dots. Some dots will occur over and over again, others only once, but there is no getting around the fact that there are a lot of them. While I have tried to craft the narrative to be readable, getting the most out of it will require attention and some patience. The story unfolds through the layering of people and events. Flow is basically chronological, but it will sometimes be necessary to pause, to jump ahead, or to go back before we can go forward. One word that will come up with almost annoying frequency is coincidence. They are everywhere. Some are just that, random coincidences. But the repetition of coincidence becomes something else, a pattern, and that it what we will be most interested in.

Some dots will form neat, definite lines. Others will not, and some will stand starkly alone. This book does not and cannot explain everything. Mysteries abound. For every question answered, at least one will be raised. Very often, we will be discussing *possibilities* as opposed to *certainties*. But that's what real history is like.

Two predictable criticisms of this book will be that it indulges in speculation and conspiracy theory. "Speculation" is commonly used to imply empty theorizing in the absence of evidence. That is not what is going on here. This is an historical detective story. Much of the evidence is circumstantial. Such evidence may not be sufficient to prove anything beyond

---

1. Carol Quigley, *Tragedy and Hope: A History of the World in Our Time* (1966), 323-324.

a reasonable doubt, but it may be sufficient to raise serious questions and suggest possible answers. Speculation, as *educated guesswork*, is the driving force of investigation. One has to imagine what might be or what might have been before one can set out to prove or disprove it. Every new discovery begins with a hunch.

As for conspiracy *theory*, what this book emphasizes is conspiracy *fact*. The Russian Revolution, like every revolution, was by nature conspiratorial. You cannot organize the overthrow of a regime without conspiracy, or you won't be organizing very long. Business is no different. As good old Adam Smith observed in *The Wealth of Nations*, "People of the same trade seldom meet together, even for merriment and diversion, but the conversation ends in a conspiracy against the public...." A trust is a conspiracy, and so are stock raids and corporate takeovers. Conspiracy begets conspiracy. Simply put, conspiracy is not the exception in human behavior, it is the norm.

The book admittedly contains a rather large number of notes. Feel free to ignore them if you like, but they are provided to show where information came from; i.e., that it's not just speculation conjured out of thin air. Wherever possible, I have tried to rely on primary documents and contemporary accounts. Newspapers are a very important source. This doesn't mean that everything that appeared in them, or in any official document, is necessarily accurate. Hardly. But they do show what people, or some people, believed to be true at the time, and it's that belief that shaped their reality and their actions. Old newspapers also contain many details that the Mighty Wurlitzer of official history has chosen to forget or ignore.

Believe it or not, in an effort to reduce the number of notes, there were some things I decided not to cite meticulously, mainly travel and immigration records. There will many references to dates of arrival or departure, the issuance of passports, etc. Unless otherwise noted, these are all gleaned from digitized public records available through Ancestry.com or similar sites.

The book references many Russian names, some commonly familiar, others not. As a general rule, I've stuck to the anglicized versions of Russian personal names; Leon not Lev, Paul not Pavel, Alexander not Aleksandr, etc. But I've made some exceptions, Nikolai Bukharin, for example. I've also used the simplified –y ending for names and words like Trotsky, Kerensky, and Novy, as opposed to –ii, -ij, -yi, etc. Just so you purists know.

I hope, above all, that you will find the book interesting whether or not you agree with everything it has to say. I hope it answers some questions, and makes you think about others. And I also hope that, maybe, you'll actually enjoy it.

PROLOGUE

On 13 May 1917, peripatetic Russian revolutionary Leon Trotsky arrived in Christiania (Oslo), Norway. He was about to start the last leg of a long-anticipated return to Russia, a homeland he had not set foot in for a decade. His first stop, however, was the Christiania telegraph exchange were he fired off a terse message to Petrograd: "After a month of English captivity, I come to Petrograd with family 5/18 May."[1] The message's recipient was one Abram L'vovich Zhivotovsky.

Trotsky had indeed spent the better part of the previous month cooling his heels in a Canadian-run POW/internment camp in Amherst, Nova Scotia. British authorities released him and a small group of companions on 21 April, but they then had to wait more than a week for a liner to carry them on to Scandinavia. Trotsky's wife and two young sons, meanwhile, waited patiently in a Halifax hotel.

Back in early January, the little family had arrived in New York City. While they lived there little more than two months, Trotsky's New York stay would be an important milestone in his career, arguably a critical one. It was there he received the electrifying news that revolution had come again to Russia. The Tsar had fallen. A Provisional Government had taken his place. Trotsky, like many other exiles, was determined to get home and join a revolution that he was certain was only just beginning. Now that goal was almost within reach. Destiny or chance awaited him in Petrograd.

But who was Abram Zhivotovsky, and why did Trotsky pick him of all people to inform of his arrival? Why did the British interrupt his homeward journey, and why did they later cut him loose? How had Trotsky ended up in New York in the first place, and what did he do there and who did he meet? And why would Trotsky's presence there have any bearing on the connection of Wall Street interests to the Russian Revolution? All those questions, and many, many more, will be addressed in the chapters ahead.

---

1. RGASPI, Fond 4, opis3, delo 39, 14.

Tsar Nicholas II in Balmoral castle, 1896, with (from left to right) Tsarina Alexandra Fedorovna, Grand Duchess Tatiana, Queen Victoria, and Edward, Prince of Wales

CHAPTER ONE

TWO EMPIRES

THE EMPIRE OF THE TSAR

In his famous 1835 work, *Democracy in America*, Alexis de Tocqueville observed that "There are ... two great nations in the world which seem to tend toward the same end, although they started from different points: I allude to the Russians and the Americans."[1] "Their starting-point is different, and their courses are not the same," he added, "yet each of them seems to be marked out by the will of Heaven to sway the destinies of half the globe." Thus, America and Russia represented parallel, and inevitably rival, Manifest Destinies. Historically, that has proven to be absolutely true.

The always-quotable Winston Churchill famously described Russia as "a riddle, wrapped in a mystery, inside and enigma." The reality is more a set of paradoxes. In 1900, the Russian Empire was the largest country on Earth. Only the far-flung British Empire could claim more territory. Like the British Empire, Russia ruled over a bewildering array of nationalities, languages and religions. Russians, per se, made up less than half the population. Eleven percent was Muslim of one stripe or another and 5% Jews. Millions of Poles, Finns, Latvians and others lived under the rule of the Romanov Dynasty, some contentedly, others despairingly. Russia was counted among the Great Powers and boasted the largest army on earth. Nevertheless, in 1904-05 it was unable to defeat small, upstart Japan.

Inside Russia's immense expanse, nearly three times the area of the continental U.S., was a vast treasure house of natural wealth. By merit of these resources, the Tsar's domain should have been among the most prosperous anywhere. It was blessed with abundant human resources. In the twenty years between 1897 and 1917 its population burgeoned to almost 180 million, nearly twice that of the United States. Some 85% of those people, however, were crammed into the 20% of the Empire that constituted European Russia. Instead of general prosperity there was pervasive poverty. Three quarters of the population eked a living from the soil. Poverty and frustration bred discontent.

---

1. Alexis de Tocqueville, *Democracy in America*, Vol. 1, trans. by H. Reeve (1959), 286-287.

It was not surprising that many inside and outside Russia regarded it as a "backward" country and this image was magnified by its political system. Until 1906, the Russian Empire was an autocracy, the Tsar its sole source of authority. There was no constitution, no parliament, and no political parties – at least no legal ones. When the Revolution of 1905 created a constitutional order with an elected Duma (parliament), the Tsar still retained the absolute power to dismiss it and veto its laws.

Tsar Nicholas II

Thus, it followed to many that the cause of the country's backwardness was the Tsarist system itself. It equally followed that the overthrow of this antiquated regime would not only free Russia from tyranny, but also open the vast country to efficient development. What was good for the masses would be good for business, including foreign business. This attitude especially resonated with the American reformist mindset which had coalesced around abolitionism in the early 19th century and became the driving force behind prohibition and Progressivism in the early 20th. American Progressives tended to see every social problem as a moral crusade, a crusade that could justify violence, revolution, even war. From this perspective, Tsarism was not just backward, but evil. The American Progressive link to the Russian Revolution would be most clearly embodied in the Society of the Friends of Russian Freedom (SFRF), which will feature prominently in the coming discussion.

The central conceit of the Russian revolutionaries and their foreign supporters was that the Tsar's rule was irredeemably tyrannical and cruel. The reality, of course, was not quite so black and white. Between 1876 and 1905, the Russian justice system executed some 500 persons. Per capita, this was less than half of those put to death in Britain and, more significantly, a mere fraction of the 2,700 judicially killed in the United States from 1880-1905, and America's population was only 60% of Russia's.[2] Put another way, the US executed nine citizens to every one put to death in Russia. No aspect of the Russian penal apparatus aroused more indignation than the Siberian exile system which was widely held up as the "embodiment of brutality."[3] It was an American, journalist George Kennan, who popularized this view in his 1891 *Siberia and the Exile System*. The book portrayed Russia as an "amalgamation of villainy, frozen wastes and hound packs."[4]

---

2. Jonathan Daly, "Russian Punishments in the European Mirror," in Susan P. McCaffrey and Michel Melancon (eds.), *Russia in the European Context: A Member of the Family* (2005), 165-166.

3. Mikhail Nakonechny, "The Forgotten Success of Penal Transportation Reform in Late Imperial Russia…," http://staffblogs.le.ac.uk/carchipelago/2016/06/08/the-forgotten-success-of-penal-transportation-reform-in-late-imperial-russia-the-lowering-of-prisoner-mortality-in-the-transfer-system-1885-1915/. (Posted 8 June 2016).

4. G. L. Owen, *American-Russia Relations, 1910-1917*, MA Thesis, University of Nebraska (1963),

Again, the reality was rather different. During 1904-13, years of rebellion and mass repression, almost 30,000 persons were dispatched to Siberia for political offenses, but only 14% received the harshest punishment (prison labor).[5] By 1913, amnesties left a mere 1051 political prisoners in custody.[6] Adjusted for population, the American and Russian prison systems held roughly the same proportion of inmates in 1910. On an index of human misery and degradation, it is doubtful that much distinction could be drawn between a Siberian labor camp and a Louisiana chain-gang. The point here isn't that the Tsar's regime was some shining beacon of tolerance and mercy. It could be arbitrary, oppressive and cruel. But in that regard it was not drastically different from any other government of the day.

"Backward" Russia began to industrialize in the 1890s under the guidance of Imperial Minister of Finance, Sergius Witte. Witte believed that the expansion of Russia's transportation system would open the country's vast resources and facilitate the migration of millions to the virgin lands of Siberia. Witte achieved considerable success: prior to 1904 Russia's economic growth has been estimated at an astounding 8% per annum, and after the chaos of 1905, it rebounded to 6-7% before the next war arrived. Between 1880 and 1913, Russia's "Industrial Potential" tripled.[7] By the latter year its share of world manufacturing output exceeded 8% and it had overtaken France in that and in steel production and was 60% of Britain's levels in both.[8] Russia could also boast being the world's second biggest producer of oil (after the U. S.). Russian productivity was still only about a quarter of America's, but it was a dynamic economy seemingly on the cusp of a great break-out.

Witte

Of course, a Russia that realized its full economic potential would constitute a major competitor to every other industrial power, including the U.S.A. Russia was the only country that had the resources to displace America as the world's dominant economy. From the standpoint of Wall Street, it was a potential rival that needed to be co-opted, controlled, or eliminated.

THE RUSSIAN REVOLUTIONARIES

The first effort to overthrow the Tsarist regime was the so-called Decembrist Revolt of 1825. Disgruntled elite intelligentsia, inspired by

---

Table XII: "Russian Revolutionary Party Membership, 1906-1917, 37, n. 101.

5. Daly, 85.

6. *Ibid.*, 84.

7. Paul Kennedy, *The Rise and Fall of the Great Powers* (1989), 201.

8. *Ibid.*, 200, 202.

the ideas of the French Revolution, coalesced into two societies, a moderate one that envisioned a constitutional monarchy and a more radical clique that advocated the abolition of the Monarchy and its replacement with a collectivist republic. In late 1825, these elitist rebels tried to incite mutiny against the new Tsar Nicholas I. It was a complete fiasco.

In the decades following, scattered political cells kept the spirit of dissent alive. Many of those who fell afoul of the authorities, or simply could not abide the repressive atmosphere, sought freedom abroad. Thus began the phenomenon of the Russian radical émigré, men, and women who would spend their lives plotting revolution in places like Paris, Geneva and New York.

A new revolutionary wave began in the 1870s, a direct result of the liberalizing reforms of Tsar Alexander II. In addition to freeing the serfs, the "Tsar Liberator" permitted several thousand young, overwhelmingly upper class, Russians to seek education abroad.

Tsar Alexander II

Exposed to radical ideas, many returned home, determined to change the system. The result was the so-called *Narodnik* (Populist) movement in which hundreds of starry-eyed activists tried to "raise the consciousness" of the newly-liberated peasants. Their efforts, too, failed. Frustrated by the reactionary mindset of the peasantry, some would-be saviors turned to terrorism and the conviction that they, as an enlightened vanguard, had to make the revolution for the masses. Again, the movement split into factions, some more radical than others. The most militant element, *Narodnaya Volya* ("Peoples' Will") focused on assassinating Tsar Alexander. They succeeded in March 1881. Contrary to their hopes, the Tsarist regime did not collapse.

Around the turn of the century there was a fresh surge of revolutionary activity. Out of this arose the Party of Socialist Revolutionaries, better known as the SRs, which appeared in 1901. Like the earlier Narodniks, the SRs saw themselves as the liberators of the peasantry. They also embraced terrorism and embarked on a campaign of political assassination. The SRs could claim to be the largest revolutionary faction, boasting 50,000 full members by 1907 with another 300,000 supposedly under "party influence."[9] What the SRs never produced was a unified ideology or a charismatic leader.

The SRs' chief competition came from the Social Democrats, or SDs, who sprang into being in 1898.[10] The SDs were Marxists, which meant that

---

9. Maureen Perrie, *The Agrarian Policy of the Russian Socialist Revolutionary Party from Its Origins through the Revolution of 1905-1907* (1976), 186.
10. The full name was the Russian Social Democratic Labor Party (RSDLP).

their brand of socialism fixated on the industrial working class, or prole-tariat. However, while early 20th century Russia had well over 100 million peasants, it had at only 2-3 million factory workers. This sparked doctri-nal debates that came to a head at the 1903 Party Congress in London. The result was two rival factions, Mensheviks and Bolsheviks. The former, taking its cue from Socialist parties in the West, advocated a mass work-ers' party and held that before Russia could embark on a Socialist course, it first had to pass through a bourgeois revolution. For anyone itching to see a communist utopia, this was a frustrating proposition. In contrast, the Bolsheviks, under Vladimir Lenin's dictatorial thrall, advocated a small "vanguard" party dedicated to seizing power and instituting a "dictatorship

Lenin

Stalin

Krasin

of the proletariat" at the first opportunity. Nor were Bol-sheviks and Mensheviks the only factions; there were separate Latvians and Jewish Bundists. Membership fluctuated; in 1906, Bolshevik strength was less than 15,000, but by the 1907 Congress, the total number of SDs had risen to 150,000, of which Lenin's crew counted for about a quarter.[11] However, hard-core revolutionists of all stripes probably numbered no more than 300,000 in 1907. Even 500,000 would represent but a tiny frac-tion of Russia's adult population.[12] Adding "sympathiz-ers" would expand this number significantly, but it's hard to make a case that the Russian revolutionary movement was truly a mass one or even a popular one.

Even more important than numbers was money. Revolutions don't come cheap, and the movement could never have enough. One means to generate funds was *ekspropriatsiya* ("expropriation"), or, more simply, rob-bery. The Bolsheviks showed a special affection for this. On 26 February 1906, a gang of Bolsheviks and Latvian SDs held up the Helsinki State Bank and got away with 170,000 Rubles (@ $85,000). The biggest and bloodiest expropriation, however, was the Tiflis (Tblisi) heist on 26 June 1907 in which Bolshevik gunmen got away with 341,000 Rubles. The robbery was notable for its carnage, forty killed and fifty injured, and the involvement of one Yosif Djugashvili, a.k.a., Stalin. Lenin's financial wiz-ard, Leonid Krasin, was involved in planning the operation and fencing the stolen cash. We will hear much more of him.

Robberies, of course, were hit and miss. More important to revolution-ary finances were the contributions of wealthy sympathizers. A key bene-

---

11. Paul Le Blanc, *Lenin and the Revolutionary Party* (1993), 108. Le Blanc claims as many as 46,000 Bolsheviks in 1907, while the Congress seems only to have credited 33,000.
12. Owen, 122.

factor of the SRs was the Paris chief of the Russian Wissotzky (Vysotsky) Tea Company, Mikhail Tsetlin.[13] Wissotzky was the official supplier of the Tsar's household and, thus, the same company that supplied morning tea to Nicholas and Alexandra funded revolutionaries seeking to kill them. The Bolsheviks found a sugar-daddy in textile tycoon Savva Morozov, at least until he shot himself – or was murdered – on the French Riviera in May 1905. Morozov conveniently left a large insurance policy payable to the left-wing writer Maxim Gorky.[14] From Gorky's hands, the money passed into Lenin's coffers. In this, too, Leonid Krasin played a central role.

Another source of income, by far the most secretive and controversial, was "foreign interests." During 1904-05, Tokyo's agent in Scandinavia, Col. Motojiro Akashi, dished out cash to foment sedition and rebellion across the Russian Empire.[15] The Germans would do the same, on a larger scale, during WWI. But as far back as 1906, Russian authorities also suspected British and *American* hands in financing revolution.[16]

From 1905 to 1910, the Tsarist Government faced a veritable onslaught of revolutionary terrorism. From 1901 to 1917, but overwhelmingly concentrated in the post-1905 years, there were 23,000 acts of revolutionary violence which killed or wounded nearly 17,000 – mostly innocent bystanders.[17] The Imperial authorities responded by putting to death another 7,800 persons, albeit only 214 for official "crimes against the state."[18] The Tsarist regime was forced to fight for its life, and it won. Its most effective weapon was the secret police, popularly known as the Okhranka or Okhrana, which riddled the revolutionary parties with informers and agents provocateurs. The Okhranka was a ruthlessly effective organization but frequently seemed to follow some sinister agenda all its own. Tsar Nicholas was also

13. Richard B. Spence, *Boris Savinkov: Renegade on the Left* (1991), 399 n. 39.

14. Yuri Felshtinsky, *Lenin and His Comrades: The Bolsheviks Take over Russia, 1917-1924* (2010), 11.

15. On this see: Dmitrii B. Pavlov, "Japanese Money and the Russian Revolution, 1904-1905," *Acta Slavica Iaponica*, #11 (1993), 79-87.

16. TNA, HD3/132, Spring Rice to Hardinge, 1 March 1906.

17. Anna Geifman, *Death Orders: The Vanguard of Modern Terrorism in Revolutionary Russia.* (2010), 15.

18. HIA, Paris Okhrana Records File XXIVi, Vol. 2, "Introduction to Terrorism an Anarchism, 1, and Daly, 84.

ably served by his Prime Minister, Peter Arkadyevich Stolypin, who combined an iron fist with pragmatic reforms. Stolypin's 1911 assassination was a loss from which the regime never fully recovered. That his killer was a revolutionary, employed as a police informer, says much about the murky politics and loyalties of the time.

Stolypin

By 1909, terror was all but throttled and the radical cadres decimated, defeated and demoralized. In 1914, active membership for all parties dropped below 100,000, with the Bolsheviks numbering less than 20,000.[19] They would be half that by early 1917. The simple fact was that the revolutionaries did not have the power to topple the Tsar, and they never would. That would be the handiwork of the Liberals.

THE RUSSIAN LIBERALS

In the Russian context, "Liberal" basically referred to those who favored a constitutional monarchy or broad-based republic, but not a social revolution. The main embodiment was the Constitutional Democratic Party, popularly known as the Kadets, which came together in 1905. The outstanding personality of the Kadets was a lawyer, Paul (Pavel) Milyukov, a man who had very important connections in the United States. The Kadets could claim 50,000 members, drawn mostly from the professions, but in 1906 they too split into factions. The more conservative one, dubbed the Party of 17th October, or the Octobrists, was led by an ambitious millionaire industrialist, Alexander Guchkov.

Guchkov

While the Kadets and Octobrists touted themselves as the safe and sane alternative to revolution, there was always communication across the political divide. While liberals usually postured as supporters of the monarchy, many were as much Nicholas's enemy as any Bolshevik. The SR terrorist mastermind Boris Savinkov admitted that he received secret funding from the same Alexander Guchkov.[20]

THE "JEWISH QUESTION"

Perhaps no aspect of the Russian Revolution has generated more controversy and mythology than the role played by Jews in its origins, character and leadership. Since we will be making many, many references to persons of Jewish background, it is a question best confronted head-on and as objectively as possible. On one extreme lies the assertion, eagerly

---

19. Owen, 122.
20. Spence, *Renegade*, 45, 85, 399 n.41.

embraced by the likes of the Nazis, that not only did Jews play a dominant role in the Russian Revolution, but also that they gave it a peculiar Jewish agenda. On the other side is the contention that despite the significant number of Jews in the movement, there was absolutely no disproportionate or definable "Jewish influence" and to suggest otherwise is a crude anti-Semitic canard. Between these poles of damnation and denial the truth remains elusive.

The Russian Empire only acquired a significant Jewish population in the late 18th century when Catherine the Great annexed most of the former Kingdom of Poland. Catherine restricted Jews to the so-called Pale of Settlement, basically freezing them where they already lived. A century later, Russia ruled over more than half the world's Jews, most still dwelling within the Pale. The late 19th century saw more irksome and discriminatory restrictions, most notably the May Laws or Temporary Regulations Regarding the Jews enacted in 1882. These forbade Jews from moving into villages, from holding deeds or mortgages,

Catherine the Great

and from doing business on Sundays and Christian holy days. A few years later, the Government imposed Jewish quotas in higher education and in the early 1890s there was the humiliating spectacle of mass expulsions of "illegal" Jews from Moscow and St. Petersburg.

All this was compounded by outbreaks of anti-Jewish violence, the infamous pogroms, which erupted like wildfire in the 1880s and again, with greater virulence, during 1903-05. These attacks were mostly localized, but the fear they generated spread far beyond the areas directly affected. Incidents such as the Kishinev (1903) and Odessa (1905) Pogroms received widespread coverage in the American press.[21] So, too, did the 1911 arrest and resulting trial of Kiev brick-works employee Mendel Beilis for alleged ritual murder ("Blood Libel") of a Christian boy. Regime critics, including radical writer Maxim Gorky and crusading liberal Paul Milyukov, cited these outrages as further proof of the hatefulness and backwardness of the Romanov Regime.

Accumulated insult and tribulation inculcated a pervasive sense of mistrust and insecurity among Russian Jews, and fueled suspicion that the Tsar himself was to blame. Nevertheless, while many Russian officials tolerated or even instigated anti-Jewish excesses, there was no grand Tsarist conspiracy at work. The notorious *Protocols of the Learned Elders of Zion*, with its lurid tale of a Judaeo-Masonic plot to overthrow all existing order, was, and is, commonly laid at the feet of the Russian secret police. In fact, they had no demonstrable part in its creation or promotion.[22]

21. "Scores of Jews Killed," *New York Times* (26 April 1903).

22. Cesare G. De Michaelis, *The Non-Existent Manuscript: A Study of the Protocols of the Sages of*

Just as revolutionary and liberal political groups coalesced at the start of the 19th century so, too, did anti-Semitic, ultra-nationalist factions commonly referred to as the "Black Hundreds." It was in one of their publications, *Znamya*, that the *Protocols* first appeared.[23] As early as 1881, anti-Semites latched onto the notion that Jews were behind the murder of the Tsar Liberator which then morphed into the claim that they ran the whole revolutionary movement, and ultimately blossomed into the *Protocols*.

Conversely, the more Jews became identified with revolution, the more it appealed to some as a means to strike back against oppression. If one has already been convicted of the crime, there is little to be lost by committing it. By the start of the 20th century, a deep gulf of ill-will and suspicion separated most Russian Jews from their government. If the revolution promised to change things, then it somehow had to be good for Jews.

An essential point in most anti-Semitic propaganda is that Jews are, in some mysterious way, all in on it together. Anti-Semitism, at bottom, is really an inversion of the Chosen People idea. The idea of some over-arching Jewish solidarity flies in the face of the many factors dividing Jews from one another. As an old saying goes, "get three Jews together and you will get four opinions. Let them argue for and hour and your will get five." To traditional Orthodox believers, who constituted the great majority of Russia's Jews, the only things that mattered were the Torah, the Talmud and rabbinical authority. They generally viewed with disdain assimilated or secular Jews, not to mention atheist radicals. Conversely, those "enlightened," assimilated types looked down on the traditionalists as backward and ignorant. Zionists, who commonly espoused socialistic beliefs, generally took scant interest in religion or making revolution in Russia; they were focused on creating a new home in Palestine and getting as many Jews as possible to move there.

In America, Russian Jewish immigrants encountered a Jewish establishment dominated by assimilated German Jews who shunned Orthodoxy and who looked upon the new arrivals with a mixture of sympathy, condescension and disgust. Jews, like human beings generally, exploited, betrayed, cheated and abused each other on a regular basis.

All that being said, despite the many sectarian differences, there remained among many Jews an almost reflexive solidarity. If centuries of living among *Goyim* (non-Jews) had inculcated anything, it was that the latter were generally hostile, unpredictable and seldom gave Jewish interests a second thought. Fellow Jews, whatever their faults and peculiarities, at least offered the illusion of sympathy and brotherhood. Thus, a Marxist revolutionary like Trotsky, who outwardly did his best to reject or ignore

---

Zion (2004), 120-123, and *passim*.
23. *Ibid.*, 7.

his Jewish background, still often found himself dealing with and relying on other Jews, even across ideological lines.[24]

Jews played almost no part in the Russian revolutionary movement prior to the 1890s. They only gravitated there with the rise of Socialism, and its siren call was strongest among the sons and daughters of assimilated and well-to-do families. For example, Trotsky's father was a prosperous landowner and entrepreneur, that of Gregory Zinoviev a successful dairy farmer, Maxim Litvinov's a banker.[25] They saw in Socialism not a way to affirm Jewishness, but a way to erase it. The Marxian future promised a world without class, race, nation or religion, in effect, a world without Jews. Jewish revolutionaries were, by definition, apostates. To embrace a faith in internationalism, class, materialism, and atheism was to abandon anything smacking of traditional Judaism. Thus, Jews may have been drawn to political radicalism because they were Jews, but within the movement there was no place for a "Jewish agenda."

So, how many Jewish radicals were there? One Okhranka report rather hysterically claimed that Jews made up 90% of radicals.[26] In 1903, Russian Minister of Finance Sergius Witte told the Zionist leader Theodore Herzl (not a Russian) that while Jews made up only some 5% of the population they comprised 50% of the revolutionaries.[27] At the same time, Witte conceded that the Government's own policies were to blame. However, his estimate is certainly an exaggeration. Statistics on arrested radicals show that 13% of those apprehended between 1880 and 1890 were Jewish, but the percentage jumped to 25% in 1899.[28] In early 1905, a survey of political exiles in Siberia found 37% were Jews.[29] This roughly fits Soviet historian M. N. Pokrovsky's later estimate that a quarter to a third of the revolutionary parties' organizational cadres was Jewish.[30]

24. Joseph Nedava, *Trotsky and the Jews* (1972), 10-11.

25. Of course, since Kamenev's mother was an Orthodox Christian, no traditional Jew would have considered him one at all.

26. Nedava, 22, and Harry T. and Marjorie L. Mahoney, *The Saga of Leon Trotsky: His Clandestine Operations and His Assassination* (1998), 16.

27. Leonard Schapiro, "The Role of Jews in the Russian Revolutionary Movement," *The Slavonic and East European Review*, Vol. 40, #94 (1961), 148.

28. Iu. Larin, *Evrei i antisemitizm v SSSR* (1929), 31.

29. "Iz istorii bor'by s revoliutsiei v 1905 g.," *Krasnyi Arkhiv*, Vol. 29 (1929), 229.

30. *Kratkaya Evreiskaya Entsiklopedia*, Vol. 7 (1976), 398.

By any calculation, Jews were heavily over-represented in revolutionary ranks and they attained prominent and influential roles. But, again, this is not the same as saying they played a consciously *Jewish* role or that they ran the show. Remember that the revolutionary cadre numbered only a few hundred thousand in the pre-1917 years. A third of this would amount to roughly 100,000-200,000 persons, a very, very small portion of Russia's 7,000,000 Jews.

After 1881, Jews responded to the deteriorating conditions in Russia by emigrating *en masse*, mostly to America. More that 2,000,000 Jews left the Tsar's domain between 1880 and 1920, three quarters ending up in the States. In 1910, the U.S.A. counted nearly 2,600,000 residents with origin or ancestry in the Russian Empire, slightly more than half of them Jews, and 2/3 of them born in the Tsar's domains.[31] Jews congregated in and around New York City; its Jewish population jumped to nearly 1,500,000 by 1918, with the vast majority of Russian origin. At the same time, the entire Jewish population of the USA rose from a quarter million to some 3,300,000.[32] Thus a large community of people broadly hostile to the Tsarist regime and widely sympathetic to the revolution was established on American shores and in its most important economic center.

Inevitably, these immigrants included some professed revolutionaries, and many of these found their way into American radicalism. In 1912, the Socialist Party of America formed a special Jewish Socialist Federation that attracted about 3,000 comrades, mostly former Bund members. Other Russian Jews, including Trotsky, joined a separate, smaller Russian Socialist Federation that appeared in 1915. Active revolutionaries represented a tiny fraction of Jewish immigrants, but there was a larger number who broadly sympathized with their aims.

The Tsarist Government was more than happy to see disaffected subjects depart the realm, and it did not welcome them back. Between 1905 and 1910, Russian authorities refused visas to seven American passport-holders, all naturalized Russian Jews, on the ground that they were convicted revolutionists. This provoked a diplomatic spat with the U.S. Government which insisted that all its citizens must be treated equally. While most Jewish returnees experienced no problems, these denials were trumpeted as proof of the Russian regime's knee-jerk anti-Semitism and general arbitrariness.

Russian immigration changed the whole profile of American Jewry. The pre-1880 population was largely composed of German Jews, men like Jacob Schiff. German Jews saw themselves as more modern and sophisticated than their eastern brethren, and as the latter swamped them in

---

31. *The World Almanac and Encyclopedia for 1919* (*New York World*, 1918), 275. Other groups from the Russian Empire were Poles (655,000), German (245,000) and Lithuanians (204,000). "Russians," per se, were only 65,000.

32. *Ibid.*, 302.

numbers, the German elite sought to preserve its influence and leadership by making the Russian Jews' cause its own. That inevitably involved some collaboration with the revolutionary element. Just how far that went will be a key question.

However, most Russian Jews did not leave the Empire and many of them not only survived but prospered. A listing of the Russian Empire's "business elite" in 1914 reveals roughly 15% Jews, also well above their 5% of the population.[33] The ranks of Russian bankers were replete with Jews such as Kamenka, Rafalovich, Rubinstein and Rothstein. The last, German-born Adolf Rothstein, the "Great Jewish financier," played an important role not only as an executive of the St. Petersburg International Commercial Bank, but also as foreign representative of the Tsarist Ministry of Finance.[34] Plus, he was father-in-law to one of the French Rothschilds. Even the Tsar's physician, Dr. Samuel Hirsch, was Jewish. At the tip of this elite stood the widely esteemed figure of Baron Horace (Goratsii) Günzburg, a wealthy philanthropist who occupied a position not unlike that of Jacob Schiff in America. The elite also included the previously mentioned Wissotzkys, kings of the Russian tea trade, the Brodskys with their empire of sugar refining and brewing, not to mention Trotsky's father and uncles.

However, a successful Jewish bourgeoisie did not mean a bourgeoisie that felt any deep gratitude or loyalty to the Tsarist system, the Wissotzkys being an excellent case in point.[35] It was easy for Russian Jews to believe that they had succeeded in spite, not because of, the regime. Revolution, while a risky proposition, might offer even better opportunities, especially a revolution that had your nephew at the helm.

THE EMPIRE OF THE TRUSTS

At the opening of the 20th century the United States prided itself on being the Great Republic and the Land of Opportunity. Between 1900 and 1917, its population swelled from 76 million to 105 million, fueled by the steady influx of immigrants. The U.S.A. also possessed, hands down, the most productive economy on Earth. In 1913, America's share of "World Manufacturing Output" was 32%, more than the next two biggest producers, Britain and Germany, combined.[36] Between the turn of the century and 1912, American national wealth surged from $100 billion to $187 billion, almost equal to that of Britain, Germany *and* France.[37]

---

33. A. N. Bokhanov, *Delovaya elita Rossii 1914 g.* (1994).

34. F. Cunliffe-Owen, "Some Influential Russian Jews," *New Era Illustrated Magazine*, Vol. 5 #11 (June 1904), 493-496.

35. "The Socialist Revolutionaries Maximalists," https://libcom.org/forums/history/social-ist-revolutionaries-maximalists-srs-maximalists-24092014.

36. Kennedy, 202.

37. *1919 Almanac*, 449.

The United States was the world's richest country and the world's largest democracy, but its riches were not shared democratically. In 1913, America's top 1% controlled an astounding 45% of total wealth.[38] A key factor in the concentration of money and power was the trusts. In 1904, financial analyst John Moody identified more that 440 of these de facto cartels.[39] Trusts endeavored, with varying degrees of success, to control the production, pricing and competition of just about everything made, bought, sold and consumed. Trust apologists argued, with some validity, that such combines eliminated "wasteful" competition and fostered standardization in quality and pricing. Opponents countered that they throttled free trade and benefited only the big stockholders. By Moody's calculation, seven mega-trusts – *oil, steel, shipping, smelting, copper, sugar and tobacco – ruled the economy.*

Moody

The real issue was who controlled these trusts. In 1911, Moody and fellow muckraker George Turner identified seven "Masters of American Capital."[40] Leading the pack, to no surprise, were John D. Rockefeller, chief of Standard Oil, and John Pierpont Morgan (after 1913, J. P. Morgan, Jr.), head of the nation's largest investment banking house. Closely allied with Morgan were railroad tycoon James Hill and George F. Baker, head of the First National Bank. Rockefeller's circle included his brother William and nephew Percy, James Stillman of National City Bank and Jacob H. Schiff, kingpin of the Kuhn Loeb investment house. By Moody's reckoning, these seven were the real rulers of America.[41]

John D. Rockefeller

The Rockefeller Empire, besides oil, extended into railroads, metals, communications and banking. Both Western Union and AT&T were under Rockefeller dominance, as was the National City Bank (which will be very important in our story) and the Equitable and Mutual Insurance Companies. The Morganites held the commanding position in coal and

38. Dr. Aidan Regan, "Lecture 14: The Inequality of Capital Ownership in Europe and the U.S.A.," Figure 10.5., https://capitalistdemocracy.files.wordpress.com/2014/10/lecture-14.pdf. See also, Emanuel Saez and Gabriel Zucman, "Wealth Inequality in the United States since 1913: Evidence from Capitalized Income Tax Data," http://gabriel-zucman.eu/files/SaezZucman2015.pdf.
39. John Moody, *The Truth about the Trusts: A Description and Analysis of the American Trust Movement* (1904).
40. John Moody and George Kibbe Turner, "The Masters of Capital: The Seven Men" *McClure's Magazine*, Vol. 37, (1911), 418-428.
41. *Ibid.*, 425.

steel, plus big shares of railroads and insurance, but their real strength lay in their power over credit, i.e., money. The Chase and First National Banks were in Morgan's pocket as were the Bankers and Guaranty Trust Companies.

This "dictatorship of the trusts" did not go unchallenged. President Theodore Roosevelt (1901-08) styled himself a "trust-buster" and in 1911 Federal action forced mighty Standard to dissolve into thirty–odd independent firms. Of course, this made little difference so long as the same people held the stock and sat on the boards. A year later, an investigation in the US Senate, the so-called "Pujo Committee," revealed what many already knew: a small group of Wall Street

Theodore Roosevelt

financiers, headed by the troika of Morgan, Stillman and Baker, still dominated the American economy.[42] Also singled out were Jacob Schiff and his partners at Kuhn Loeb, notably the Warburg brothers, Paul and Felix.

The Zeus-like reputation of the elder Morgan was underlined by the fact that he not once, but twice, intervened to save the United States Government from economic ruin, or that's the way he saw it. During the Panic of 1893, Morgan staved off the default of the US Treasury by teaming up with the London Rothschilds to offer a bail out of gold bullion. He made a tidy profit, of course. When a similar panic gripped Wall Street in 1907, King Morgan summoned fellow capitalists and demanded they pump money into the market. They did. A suspicious mind might wonder whether Morgan and his cronies instigated the very crises to which they offered solutions.

The 1907 Panic was the stimulus, or excuse, for a hush-hush gathering convened in November 1910 at the exclusive Jekyll Island Club on the coast of Georgia. Nick-named the "Millionaire's Club," the secluded island was a summer get-away for the Morgans, Rockefellers and other big names of America's Capitalist aristocracy. On this occasion, its privacy was utilized to lay plans for an American central bank, what would eventually emerge as the Federal Reserve. Present at the creation was a constellation of the stars of Wall Street. Drawing up the draft bill was Kuhn Loeb's Paul Warburg, while Frank Vanderlip (National City Bank), Henry P. Davison (Morgan & Co.), and Charles Norton (First National) were on hand to hash out the details. The Federal Reserve Act, finally enacted in 1913, created a government-sanctioned consortium of private banks which did not simply control the money supply but created it. A cynic might call it the ultimate trust, and as H. L. Mencken observed, the cynics are almost always right.

---

42. Named for its chairman, Louisiana Senator Arsene Paulin Pujo.

Wall Street's influence over the national economy inevitably extended to politics. Then, as now, organized capital provided the big money to fund campaigns. Politics, after all, was merely another realm of investment, and as with every investment there was expectation of return. The Republican Party, which had dominated the presidency and national politics since the Civil War, was widely seen as the Party of Wall Street. However, the Democratic alternative was just the Other Party of Wall Street. The American political system was itself a trust with the same trustees pulling the strings. When Woodrow Wilson took the White House in 1912, and subsequently ushered in the Federal Reserve, he did so under the guidance of Col. Edward M.  House, a man, we shall see, intimately linked to Big Business. And the man who organized the financing of Wilson's campaign was millionaire industrialist Charles R. Crane, someone who also will play a very important part in our story.

American capitalists viewed themselves as a force above politics, and in large measure they were. They were used to getting their way. If a politician or a government proved an impediment to business, they could be replaced. If a means to accomplish that did not exist, money could create one.

Wall Street's America was not immune to Socialism or radical terrorism. The "labor wars" that raged in American mines and mills between 1890 and 1920 were the most violent in the nation's history. In 1892, Alexander Berkman, an anarchist, and a Russian Jew, shot steel magnate Henry Clay Frick in revenge for the failed Homestead Steel Strike. In 1901, another anarchist gunman, Leon Czolgosz, shot and mortally wounded President William McKinley. That same year, the Socialist Party of America emerged on the scene. By 1912 it boasted 118,000 dues-paying members and drew nearly a million votes at the ballot box.[43] 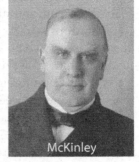 However, the same doctrinal schism between proponents of evolution versus revolution led to the rise of a more radical faction, the Industrial Workers of the World (IWW). Nicknamed "Wobblies," the IWW mustered 100,000 followers by 1916, while the main Socialist Party fell to below 90,000.[44]

---

43. "The Socialist Party of America (1897-1946)," https://www.marxists.org/history/usa/eam/spa/socialistparty.html.
44. *Ibid.*

Per capita, there were more Socialists in America than Russia, and more Wobblies than Bolsheviks. Yet if the masters of capital were frequently perturbed by revolutionary socialism, they could also reckon it constituted no mortal threat. Like everything else, it was dominated by men who could be reasoned with, bought off or eliminated. The SPA and IWW were dwarfed by the non-Marxist American Federation of Labor (AFL) which claimed 2,000,000 members in 1914 and twice that by 1920. Labor, after all, was a commodity, and as with any commodity there was a perceived advantage to organizing it as a trust. The idea of running labor as one big union as opposed to many small ones made perfect sense, and the same logic applied whether that Big Union was the AFL, the IWW or the Communist Party.

AMERICAN BUSINESS IN RUSSIA

The Russian economy was organized along lines like America's. In 1914, there were 2,303 joint stock companies in the Tsar's domain. Some 1,500 persons comprised a Russian "business elite."[45] At the tip of this small pyramid sat men like the "Russian Morgan" Alexis Ivanovich Putilov, who by 1914 put himself at the head of Russia's largest bank, the Russo-Asiatic, its biggest industrial concern, the mammoth Putilov metallurgical works in St. Petersburg, as well as being a major stockholder and director in forty other companies.[46] Russia even had its own "Hearst" in the person of press and publishing baron Alexis Suvorin whose holdings included forests and pulp and paper mills. Russia had its own trusts which dominated metals, coal, textiles, oil, and sugar. Concerns employing 1,000 or more workers controlled 40% of the industrial labor force.[47]

Suvorin

Something else the American and Russian economies shared was a heavy reliance on foreign investment. Witte aggressively courted foreign investment and between 1890 and by the turn of the century increased it from $100 million to $500 million. By 1914, that had doubled or even tripled. The U.S. held $7 *billion* in foreign money, much of which had financed America's railroads.[48] Ten-percent of Russia's stock companies were foreign owned and 10% of its business elite were foreigners.[49] The

---

45. Bokhanov, 66.
46. Interestingly, Putilov was not related to the founders and namesake of the Putilov Works.
47. Penelope C. Buessing, "The House of Morgan and Its Investments in Russia, 1905-1918," MA Thesis, History, Texas Tech University (1974), 18.
48. Alexei Bayer, "1913-2013: How Russia Botched an Entire Century: Could Russia have been as successful as the United States?" The Globalist (5 Sept. 2015). http://www.theglobalist.com/1913-2013-russia-botched-entire-century/.
49. Bokhanov, 66.

French controlled over a third of Russia's foreign investments, Britons about 25% and Germans almost as much. French money constituted 79% of the investment in metallurgical industries while British money was half of that in oil and 70% in mining. Germans dominated in the electrical and chemicals spheres.[50] Thus, there wasn't much room left for American investment which amounted to no more than 5%. Likewise, the United States was the source of only 5% of Russian imports and a market for a mere 1% of its exports.

If it seems that Russia and America just weren't that interested in each other economically, the reality was quite different. In the imagination of American capitalists like Charles Crane, the only place U.S.-Russian economic relations could go was up. The question was on whose terms. As noted, in the long run Russian economic development constituted a challenge to American interests. But in the short term, it offered huge opportunities for American expansion. By the beginning of the 20th century, the struggle for control of America's economy had largely been decided. While there were still railroads and factories to be built, just about everything worth owning was already owned by someone. The big opportunities lay abroad: in Latin America, China, the Middle East – and Russia.

In 1904, American railroad tycoon E. H. Harriman formed a syndicate to pursue construction of a railway tunnel under the Bering Strait.[51] This would connect the Trans-Siberian to the American-Canadian system. Included in the plan were provisions for a 99-year lease and mineral rights along a wide rail corridor. Budgeted at $300 million, the plan was ambitious and expensive, but behind Harriman were the deep pockets of men like Rockefeller and Schiff. In August 1906, the New York Times trumpeted that "Czar authorizes syndicate to begin work," but suspicious minds in St. Petersburg saw the scheme as a wedge for further concessions and the flooding of Siberia with American products and capital.[52] Such opposition, and mounting technical problems, ultimately killed the scheme. However, Harriman and friends almost immediately hatched a new plan to finance a Chinese takeover of the Russian-and Japanese-controlled rail lines in Manchuria. They touted the advantages of "neutralizing" Manchuria's lines to eliminate future friction between Russia and Japan, but the scheme was another springboard for the Yankee penetration of Siberia. In 1910, both St. Petersburg and Tokyo vetoed the plan.[53] To many on Wall Street, this typified the antiquated thinking and narrow-minded obstructionism of the Tsarist Regime. Something had to change.

A serious wrinkle in American-Russian economic relations arose when the U.S. Congress unilaterally canceled the Russian-American Commercial

50. Buessing, 21.
51. V. V. Lebedev, Russko-Amerikanskie ekonomicheskie otnoshenie, 1900-1917 gg. (1964), 94-109.
52. "For Bering Strait Bridge," New York Times (1 Aug. 1906).
53. Owen, 4.

Treaty in 1911. This, as we will see, was largely the work of one man, Jacob Schiff. The declared aim of Schiff and his supporters was to force the Russian Government to remove all restrictions on its Jewish subjects. Viewing this as a blatant attempt to meddle in its internal affairs (which it was), in 1913 the Russian Duma responded by passing a bill that slapped a double tariff on American goods and double duties on anything carried on U.S.-flagged vessels.[54] Beyond this, the

post of American Ambassador to Russia fell vacant, and would remain so for almost two years as Washington and St. Petersburg bickered. Thus, on the eve of the First World War, Russo-American relations were, not to put too fine a point on it, a mess.

These frictions aside, men like Sergius Witte, and many others in the Russian technical and industrial sphere, warmly embraced the notion of *Amerikanizm* ("Americanism") or *Amerikanizatsiya* ("Americanization") as "a metaphor for speedy industrial tempo, high growth, productivity and efficiency."[55] The same ideas would appeal to the Bolsheviks. As historian Richard Stites has written, "American efficiency and Russian revolutionary sweep was rooted in Bolshevism from the very beginning."[56]

On the eve of the First World War, the biggest American investment in Russia, about $35 million, was held by Chicago-based International Harvester.[57] A third of IH's foreign exports went to Russia making the Tsar's Empire its biggest overseas customer.[58] Next was Singer Sewing Machine Company's $25 million investment. Singer operated a large plant near Moscow employing 30,000 people. A smaller, but not insignificant, stake was held by another Chicago outfit, the Crane-Westinghouse Company. American insurance giants Equitable Life and New York Life also did significant business. By 1912, they held 11.5% of all foreign insurance issues in Russia and 18.5% of all *private* loans to the Russian Government.[59] Sensing a coming bonanza, in 1913 the National Association of Manufacturers formed a new Russian Division.[60]

---

54. Owen, 27, n.84.

55. Richard Stites, *Revolutionary Dreams: Utopian Vision and Experimental Life in the Russian Revolution* (1989), 149.

56. *Ibid.*

57. Lebedev, 143.

58. Buessing, 27.

59. Richard B. Fisher, "American Investments in Pre-Soviet Russia," *The American Slavic and East European Review*, Vol. 8, #2 (April 1949), 94-95.

60. *Ibid.*, 97.

Compared to manufacturers, American financiers were more cautious in dealing with Russia. Between 1889 and 1904, eleven small Russian bond issues were floated on Wall Street, with London-based N. M. Rothschild & Sons acting as agent for five of them.[61] Thereafter, however, access to American capital virtually dried up for Russia, again due mostly to the efforts of Jacob Schiff. Even Schiff, though, couldn't stop the Morgan behemoth from sticking its toes into the Russian pond. In 1905, Morgan toyed with the idea of backing a big Russian loan, but ultimately backed off over concerns about the Empire's stability. Morgan did put money into firms doing business there, including a machine-building trust organized in 1910 and the British-dominated mining conglomerate, Russo-Asiatic Corporation.[62] Morgan's hand also was behind the 1912 appointment of a new American manager for Russo-Asiatic, Herbert Hoover, a future dealmaker with the Bolsheviks and future President of the United States.

Hoover

In the view of historian G. L. Owen, in the decade prior to WWI, Russia was under nothing less than a persistent, multi-pronged "economic assault" by American commercial and financial interests aimed at penetrating its markets and gaining control of its resources.[63] The assault failed because the Tsarist Government proved itself more resistant and more resilient than anticipated. The solution, therefore, rested not on diplomacy but on *regime change*.

Regime Change and American Interventionism

Russia's revolutionary upheavals between 1905 and 1917 were not isolated cases. Very similar disturbances occurred in Persia (Iran), Turkey, Mexico and China. In each case, foreign interests, including American, funded or encouraged the revolutionary movements. The natural resources and economic assets of these countries came up for grabs, and grabbed they were.

At the beginning of the 20th century, all the above states were governed by "backward" authoritarian regimes. Each possessed natural wealth that foreign capitalists were eager to exploit. As in Russia's case, the existing regimes were held to be obstacles to "progress" and "democracy." The revolutions created nominally democratic governments that quickly degenerated into chaos, civil war and dictatorships. In the process, the afflicted nations were rendered almost helpless against foreign penetration and exploitation.

---

61. *Ibid.*, 95.
62. Lebedev, 113-114.
63. Owen, 132-133.

A "Constitutionalist Revolution" swept oil-rich Persia in 1906. Four years later, the desperate Persians appealed to Washington for help which appeared in the form of "economic advisers" led by W. Morgan Shuster, a corporate lawyer and former U.S. Customs official who had recently overseen the "Americanization" of Cuba and the Philippines. Viewing him as a cat's paw for U.S. business and financial interests (and, thus, a threat to their own), the British and Russians forced the Persians to send him home.[64]

In 1908-09 a military-political conspiracy dubbed the "Young Turk" Revolution came to power in the Ottoman Empire which then controlled much of the Middle East. The American minister in Constantinople during this tumult was John G. A. Leishman, ex-president of Carnegie Steel.[65] His successor, in 1909, was Jacob Schiff's bosom friend, Oscar Straus.

Mexico's turn came in 1910, when another revolution toppled the country's aging dictator, Porfirio Diaz. The result was ten years of chaos and civil war in which American, British, German and even Japanese interests backed the factions vying for power. Encouraged by Wall Street, Woodrow Wilson dispatched a personal agent to south of the border, journalist William Bayard Hale.[66] The sidelined U.S. Ambassador, Henry Lane Wilson, identified Hale as the leader of a group of conspirators who included representatives of "an American oil company," "a large banking firm of New York," and "one of the largest American land-holding interests in Mexico."[67] These same men, alleged the Ambassador, had financed the revolt against Diaz.

---

64. After returning to the States, Shuster wrote a self-aggrandizing, anti-Russian account of his experience, *The Strangling of Persia*, and settled down as president of the Century Publishing Co. Century, interestingly enough, had been the publisher of Kennan's Siberia book.

65. Leishman was a card-carrying member of the Eastern Establishment whose close friends included steel baron Henry Clay Frick, banker Andrew Mellon and lawyer-banker-steel executive Philander Knox who served as Secretary of State from 1909-1913.

66. Harry T. and Marjorie L. Mahoney, *American Prisoners of the Bolsheviks: The Genesis of Modern American Intelligence* (2001), 160-161. Among other things, Hale had also served as President Wilson's official biographer and speech-writer.

67. Henry Lane Wilson, *Diplomatic Episodes in Mexico, Belgium and Chile* (1927), 306-307.

In 1911, revolution came to China. Sun Yat-sen launched a rebellion that ended the Manchu Dynasty. An influential American in China during this period was Willard D. Straight who served as U.S. Consul in Manchuria before going to work for J. P. Morgan and the "American Group" that bankrolled Sun's revolution. We'll meet Straight again as an officer of the future American International Corporation. Sun's republican experiment quickly degenerated into warlordism, foreign intervention and civil war which did not end until Mao and his Communists seized control in 1949.

Russia's revolution conformed to the same template. The 1905 episode compelled concessions but failed to topple the regime. That took another twelve years and a bigger war to accomplish. What followed, though, was more of the same: a failed democratic interlude, the establishment of a ruthless dictatorship, civil war and a free-for-all by foreign interests vying for loot and influence.

It is a common misconception that prior to World War One the U.S. was an isolationist nation with little political or economic interests outside its borders. Nothing could be further from the truth. The roots of American interventionism go back as far as the 1823 Monroe Doctrine which effectively proclaimed an American protectorate over the Western Hemisphere. The pervasive notion of "American Exceptionalism" proposed a messianic American mission to democratize the world. In 1904, the "Roosevelt Corollary" asserted Washington's *moral obligation* to intervene against American governments deemed guilty of persistent or flagrant wrongdoing.

In the 1890s, American business interests first overthrew the Kingdom of Hawaii and then stage-managed its annexation into the budding American Empire. The 1898 victory over Spain secured Washington's, and Wall Street's, control of Cuba, Puerto Rico and the Philippines. In 1903, another ginned-up revolution in Panama secured American possession of the planned canal route. Over the next fifteen years, American troops intervened no less than sixteen times in Central America and the Caribbean, establishing de facto rule over Haiti and Nicaragua and twice invading Mexico. In almost every case, the underlying justification was defense of American "economic interests."[68] The bottom line is that well before 1917 the U.S. Government and Wall Street were well-versed in instigating revolutionary upheavals to achieve economic and political aims. Russia would offer the biggest opportunity of all.

---

68. Gen. Smedley D. Butler, *War Is a Racket* (1935).

"DEE-LIGHTED!"

CHAPTER TWO:

WALL STREET
DRAMATIS PERSONAE,
AND OTHERS

D ue to their prominent roles in the coming discussion, there are several individuals, mostly American capitalists, and at least one organization that deserve special attention.

CHARLES R. CRANE, THE "OUTSIDER-INSIDER"

I n the first two decades of the 20th century, arguably no American businessman had greater influence on Russian-American relations than Charles Richard Crane (1858-1939). He did so, furthermore, without

Charles. R. Crane

having any formal connection with the U.S. Government. Capitalist, philanthropist and serial causist, Crane was the eldest son of wealthy Chicago industrialist Richard Teller Crane. Charles Crane took only a marginal role in the family business, but used the fortune it provided him to indulge in travel, philanthropy and intrigue. He became an international *"eminence grise"* with his fingers in many events of the early 20th century, the most important being the Russian Revolution.[1] His money and political connections made him a player on Wall Street and an influencer right up to the White House.

1. Two biographies of Crane are Norman Saul's, *The Life and Times of Charles Crane, 1858-1936* (2013) and David Hapgood, *Charles Crane: The Man Who Bet on People* (2000). Saul's is arguably the better, but both leave certain aspects of his career unexplored.

Crane was a director of the Chicago National Bank of the Republic and had many friends in high finance, notably George F. Roberts of National City Bank. Another close friend (and occasional rival) was press tycoon William Randolph Hearst. Crane was a charter member of the ultra-exclusive Jekyll Island Club, where he rubbed elbows with the Morgans, Rockefellers and Vanderbilts. Politically, Crane styled himself a Progressive. He personally eschewed socialism, but was willing to befriend, promote and subsidize those who embraced it. He had close personal relations with left-wing reformers like Jane Addams, Lincoln Steffens and Lillian Wald. The last was also an associate and beneficiary of Jacob Schiff. Crane cultivated Socialist journalists like Walter Lippmann and Norman Hapgood. That duo plus Addams and Wald were members of the Society of Friends of Russian Freedom, a group Crane never formally joined, but carefully monitored through these acquaintances. We'll have more to say about that group later.

Another Crane intimate was Canadian political economist James Mavor.[2] A member of the Fabian Society, the Socialist League and the Social Democratic Federation, Mavor authored a two-volume *Economic History of Russia* (1914), the second part of which has been described as "virtually a history of the revolutionary movement" and an exposé of the "devious and deceitful ways of the autocracy."[3]

A long-time Republican, in 1912 Crane bolted to the Democrats, became vice president of the Party's finance committee and a key backer of Woodrow Wilson's presidential campaigns. In fact, Crane's $50,000 personal contribution made him Wilson's single biggest donor in the 1912 election.[4] He counted both Wilson and the President's Svengali-like adviser Col. Edward House as personal friends. Journalist Joseph Herrings aptly described Crane as a man "dominated by the idea that his money has been given him to play the role of a world-wide liberator," and he used his wealth "for organizing a revolution throughout the world on strictly business principles."[5]

In the 1890s, Charles Crane developed a fascination, some might call it a love affair, with Russia. He made his first trip there in 1887 and visited the country more than

Col. Edward House

---

2. James Mavor, *My Window on the Street of the World*, Vol. II (1923), 103.

3. Sidney B. Fay, "The Economic History of Russia," *The American Economic Review*, Vol. 5. #3 (1915), 586-589.

4. Owen, 59, n.164. Another American involved in Russian business, International Harvester's Cyrus McCormick, was the second biggest at $25,000.

5. "Novel Built Around Crane," *New York Times* (15 Oct. 1909).

twenty times by 1917. An early and lasting in-fluence on Crane's view of Russia was journalist George Kennan, author of the famous and inflam-matory exposé of the Siberian exile system.

An early Russian acquaintance was Jacob "James" Nikolaevich Rostovtsev who Crane met at the 1893 Chicago World's Fair. The Oxford educat-ed Rostovtsev held high positions in the Tsarist ad-ministration, including state councilor and private secretary to the Empress Alexandra.[6] Three years later, Crane met another Russian, Prince Michael Ivanovich Khilkov who was Tsar Nicholas's new-ly-appointed minister of communications.[7] Most importantly, Khilkov and Rostovtsev were Russian liberals, men willing to serve the Tsar but dedicated to the idea of modernization and reform and fascinated by the image of *Amerkanizm* that Crane represented.

Another of Crane's Russian associates was a woman, Zinaida Alexievna Ragozina. She came to the United States in the 1870s with her Narodnik husband and returned to Russia in 1900 where she became an historian and author of popular articles on American history and culture.[8] She became one of Crane's growing stable of informants and agents-of-influence.[9] Crane subsequently made it a point to cultivate relationships with leading Rus-sian liberals, most notably Paul Milyukov.

In the late 1890s, Richard Crane took his company into the manufac-ture of air brakes for railway cars, a move that put him into direct compe-tition with the leading air brake maker, Westinghouse. Westinghouse con-trolled vital patents and was sure to fight Crane tooth and nail. In a typical trust-like move, Charles came up with plan that avoided competition. In 1897, Crane visited St. Petersburg where, with the help of Khilkov, he se-cured exclusive rights to supply air brakes to Russian passenger trains. With the Trans-Siberian under construction, this promised to be a gold mine. He then brokered a deal with George Westinghouse by which Crane & Co. abandoned the American market in return for a joint venture with West-inghouse in Russia.[10] Thus was born the Crane-Westinghouse Russian Co. which Charles treated as his baby and whose operations he oversaw until its nationalization by the Soviets in 1925. That's right, not 1917, but 1925.

6. Shay McNeal, *The Plots to Rescue the Tsar* (2002), 27.

7. Saul, 51.

8. Saul, 46-48.

9. Alexandre Andreyev, *The Myth of the Masters Revived: The Occult Lives of Nikolai and Elena Ro-erich* (2014), 51.

10. Saul, 50.

William R. Harper

Crane was a big benefactor to the University of Chicago and a bosom friend of its long-time president, William R. Harper. Under Crane's guidance, Harper's son, Samuel N. Harper, studied Russian language and culture and came to head America's first Russian Studies program at the University. But the relationship between Crane and the younger Harper went beyond academics. Samuel Harper became a key agent and recruiter for Crane's private intelligence organization that acted in close coordination with the U. S. State Department.[11] In that regard, it's important to note that Crane's own son, Richard Crane, would serve as Secretary of State Robert Lansing's confidential secretary in 1917.[12]

Crane's penchant for political intrigue was not limited to Russia. In 1903-04, he showed up in the Balkans where a guerrilla war was brewing in the Ottoman-ruled province of Macedonia. Journalist Herrings encountered him in Bulgaria in the spring of 1904. Crane was busy ingratiating himself with Macedonian rebel leaders and was "lavish in the distribution of money."[13] In Ottoman Macedonia, violence soon escalated, tipping the whole region into crisis. Herrings recounted the story that the rebels planned to kidnap Crane and hold him for ransom, a scheme in which the American was "not altogether an unwilling party."[14] The real aim was to provide the U. S. Government a pretext to intervene in the Balkans. Curiously, at almost the same time an almost identical scenario played out in Morocco where a rebel chieftain, Mulay Ahmed er-Raisuli, snatched a presumed American citizen, Ion Perdicaris. This gave President Theodore Roosevelt the bully opportunity to dispatch a U. S. Navy flotilla across the Atlantic and issue his famous demand of "Perdicaris alive or Raisuli dead!"[15] Was the Crane plot inspired by this, or was it the other way around? In 1909, Herrings announced that he had penned a novel, *The Golden Peril*, based on Crane's Balkan intrigues in which the central character was "an eccentric American plutocrat obsessed with the idea of freeing the oppressed peoples of all lands."[16]

In was also in the spring of 1904, amid these Macedonian machinations, that Crane forged a personal alliance with Russian liberal dissident Paul Milyukov. As we will discuss further, Crane's extended visit to Russia that summer and his reunion with Milyukov in Paris that fall, may also have its own covert political agenda.

---

11. Mahoney, *American*, 57.
12. *Ibid.*, 41.
13. "Novel Built Around Crane," *Ibid.*
14. *Ibid.*
15. Perdicaris, of course, turned out not to be an American citizen at all, a fact carefully concealed at the time.
16. *Ibid.*

Crane also took a special interest in China where revolution was organizing against the decrepit Manchu Dynasty. Indeed, revolution or the threat of revolution was a common denominator in most of Crane's foreign travels. In 1909, President Taft named Crane American Minister to China, but his appointment was abruptly canceled before it began. Not incidentally, his nomination coincided with railway tycoon E. H. Harriman's scheme to engineer an American buy-out of the Manchurian railways.

E. H. Harriman

Sensing a connection, the Japanese Government mounted a fierce objection to Crane's appointment. Their suspicions were not unjustified. Crane had cultivated ties to Chinese revolutionaries and he was one of the financial angels of Sun Yat Sen's Tong Meng Hui secret society that initiated the overthrow of the Manchu's just two years later.[17]

Crane, however, smelled another rat, Jacob Schiff and his "Jewish friends" in New York. Schiff, as we will see, bankrolled Japan in its war with Russia while Crane supported the latter.[18] This doubtless played into Crane's creeping anti-Semitism, an attitude that emerged full-blown after WWI when he latched on to the Arab cause. In the 30s, Crane became an outspoken defender of Adolf Hitler. In a 1933 conversation with the newly-appointed American Ambassador to Berlin, William E. Dodd, Crane opined that German Jews "deserved what they were getting."[19] It was Dodd who recollected that Crane "did much to bring on the Kerensky revolution [in Russia] which gave way to communism."[20]

In late 1913, Woodrow Wilson offered Crane the empty ambassador's post in St. Petersburg. Crane toyed with the idea, but ultimately turned it down.[21] The reason was that Crane, and others, knew he was more useful as a private citizen. In 1915, one of Crane's friends and admirers, Charles McCarthy, warned Col. House *not* to bring Crane into the government because the interests of the country were better served by keeping him "doing just what he is doing now."[22] And what, exactly, was that?

JACOB SCHIFF, "THE JEWISH AVENGER"

The only man who could give Charles Crane a run for his money where Russian-American relations were concerned was Jacob Henry

17. Yong Zhang Volz, "Transplanting Modernity: Cross-Cultural Networks and the Rise of Modern Journalism in China, 1890s-1930s." Dissertation; University of Minnesota (2006), 178, n.11. and Saul, 200 and 210-211, n. 128.

18. Saul, 94.

19. Saul, 239.

20. Mahoney, *American*, 41.

21. Owen, 56, n. 154.

22. Saul, 110, quoting McCarthy to House, 9 Nov. 1915.

Schiff. What Schiff lacked in Crane's insider connections in Washington and St. Petersburg, he made up for in sheer determination, financial clout and the creation of America's early "Jewish Lobby." He directed this lobby towards a single goal: the ending of the inequality and persecution of Russia's Jews, and the ruination of the government that abused them.

J. Schiff

Schiff was born in Frankfurt-am-Main in 1847, one of four sons of Moses Jakob Schiff, a minor banker and broker affiliated with the Rothschilds. While by no means as rich or as well known as the latter, the Schiffs were an old Frankfurt family with roots going back to the 14th century. Through marriage, they were linked to other German-Jewish families such as the Adlers, Oppenheimers, and Wertheimers. These connections are not trivial. Generations of intermarriage and the creation of interlocking "cousinhoods" formed a *Mishpocha*, or extended family that connected people in ways not apparent to an outsider.

Continuing in the family business, young Jacob first came to the U.S. just after the Civil War and became a partner in the short-lived firm of Budge & Schiff. He became an American citizen in 1870, but returned to the newly-unified Reich the following year. In 1874, he came back to New York at the behest of Solomon Loeb, one of the founding partners of Kuhn, Loeb & Co, a mercantile enterprise that had morphed into an investment bank. Schiff's initial rise in the firm was mostly due to one, simple fact: he married Loeb's daughter. With Solomon Loeb's retirement in 1885, Schiff became the dominant force. Until his death in 1920, he guided Kuhn Loeb to great success using acumen, guts and, when necessary, an iron fist.

While he could be affable and hugely generous, Schiff's management style, in the office and at home, tended to the autocratic. Some saw him as "a disagreeable character who ceaselessly badgered members of his family" and pretty much everyone else.[23] Others called him "formidable."[24] While he avoided anything patently illegal in business, his ethics were "sometimes ambivalent."[25] Put another way, when he was determined to do something, he found a way to do it.

Schiff and his Kuhn Loeb partners "were instrumental in bringing European funds into the new enterprises on the American continent."[26] Schiff has been described as a member of a "small international fraternity" that included Max Warburg (Hamburg and Berlin), Ernest Cassel (London), Wertheim and Gumpertz (Amsterdam), Eduard Noetzlin (Paris), and

23 Milton Goldin, "Goldin on Cohen, 'Jacob A. [sic] Schiff: A Study in American Jewish Leadership,'" *H-Antisemitism* (Oct. 2000).

24. Priscilla Roberts "Jewish Bankers, Russia, and the Soviet Union, 1900-1940: The Case of Kuhn, Loeb and Company," *American Jewish Archives Journal*, Vol. 94, # 1-2 (1997), 12.

25. Goldin.

26. *Investment Banking through Four Generations* (1955), 17-18.

Cassel

Franz Philippson (Brussels). Cassel's biographer Brian Connell, said these men "maintained between them an incredibly accurate network of economic, political and financial intelligence at the highest level."[27] Cassel, who professed great admiration for the lot, added that "the web of their communications quivered at the lightest touch." "They could withdraw support here, provide additional funds there," he added, and "move immense sums of money with lightning rapidity and secrecy from one corner of their financial empires and influence the political decisions of a score of countries."

It perhaps goes without saying that Schiff, Warburg, Cassel, et al, were not just international bankers but, by origin at least, international *Jewish* bankers. Thus, we seem to be getting perilously close to anti-Semitic conspiracy theories of world Jewish financial control. While Connell's description may (or may not) be exaggerated, his observations were made in the context of admiration, not condemnation, and the fact is that Schiff did, indeed, have connections to every one of these fellow financiers, most importantly, the Warburgs. These connections offered Schiff resources and reach that many of his competitors, even Mighty Morgan, could not equal. For our purposes, imagine how the ability to "move immense sums" with "rapidity and secrecy" could aid in the fostering and support of revolution in Russia – or anywhere else.

By 1901, Schiff had built Kuhn Loeb into the second largest investment bank in the United States, mostly by underwriting the expansion of America's railroads. "While essentially conservative," Schiff "often went in where others feared to tread."[28] Success made him "a member of Big Business's Our Crowd as well as of New York's German Jewry's Our Crowd."[29] It followed that like other members of the Wall Street elite he "exerted considerable political influence," which included reminding presidents of the "strategic importance of the Jewish vote."[30] He then "used his political connections and prestige to promote the interests of Judaism in the United States and overseas."[31] Politically, Schiff long identified himself as a Progressive Republican, but he, just like Crane, went over to the Wilson camp in 1912 when the Democrat seemed more likely to support his private war on Russian autocracy. Still, Schiff's contribution to Wilson's war chest was less than a third of Crane's.[32]

While most of Schiff's friends and collaborators were fellow businessmen, he was closely associated with the likes of Felix Adler, the reformist

27. Brian Connell, *Manifest Destiny: A Study in Five Profiles on the Rise and Influence of the Mountbatten Family* (1953), 60.

28. *Investment Banking*, 8.

29. Goldin.

30. Roberts, 15.

31. Ibid., 11.

32. Owen, 59, n. 164.

and anti-capitalist founder of Ethical Culture, and he had a special soft spot for left-wing social worker Lillian Wald whose Henry Street Settlement House in the Lower East Side was a favorite gathering place for "radical intellectuals and activists."[33] Wald is significant because she provided Schiff with a discreet entrée into Gotham's vibrant subculture of political and cultural radicals.

Wald

Schiff made himself the uncrowned king of Jewish America, and he did so largely through the wide-spread and abundant use of philanthropy. He reportedly donated no less than 10% of his substantial income to charities, by no means exclusively Jewish. But in that sphere his fingers were in virtually everything. He was one of only two people who belonged to every major Jewish charity in New York City.[34] For instance, in 1909 alone Schiff bestowed $400,000 on assorted "Hebrew charities."[35] In 1906, he spearheaded the creation of the American Jewish Committee, and during WWI, he was a major force in the formation of the American Jewish Relief and Joint Distribution Committees which would aid the plight of Russian (and other) Jews before and after the Bolshevik Revolution. He was "among only a few rich and powerful men ever trusted and admired by nearly all of his coreligionists."[36] And probably a little feared as well. It is certainly fair to say that "no Jewish leader today has anywhere near his influence."[37]

Schiff's philanthropic impulse wasn't unique. Conspicuous charity was a favorite pastime of America's plutocratic elite, as men like Carnegie and Rockefeller attest. And it wasn't altogether unselfish; behind it was a self-serving desire for adulation and influence.

Schiff's zeal to aid his brethren in Russia is generally attributed to his deep religious convictions. Like most German Jews, he adhered to the "modernized" Reform branch of Judaism, but his personal faith has been described as "a strange mixture of orthodoxy and ritualistic liberalism he had concocted for himself."[38] It wasn't until around 1890 that Schiff started to take an interest in the conditions of Russia's Jews. This probably was stimulated by the recent pogroms and the May Laws and other restrictions enacted in the Tsar's domain. Another factor, doubtless, was

---

33. Michael Reisch and Janice Andrews, *The Road Not Taken: A History of Radical Social Work in the United States* (2002), 25.

34. "Jacob Schiff," Jewish Encyclopedia, http://www.jewishencyclopedia.com/articles/13266-schiff.

35. *World Almanac and Fact Book, 1909*, 345. Of course, in the same year John D. Rockefeller lavished over $13,000,000 on his favored charities and causes (*Ibid.*, 343).

36. Goldin.

37. *Ibid.*

38. Roberts, 13.

the mounting wave of immigrants this persecution brought to New York. Once begun, Schiff's anti-Tsarism more and more took on the flavor of a personal vendetta. He slammed the Russian Government as the "enemy of mankind."[39] Tsar Nicholas, a man he had never met, he condemned as "this most hated and inhuman of rulers."[40] In 1905, he even urged President Teddy Roosevelt to "employ military force against Russia."[41] Nor was he above involving his beloved charities in the fight. In 1907 he committed the American Jewish Committee "to use all feasible means to alleviate the sufferings of East European Jewry."[42]

Schiff was not Russian. He never set foot in the country, nor did he have any relations there. He did, however, carefully cultivate connections, mostly through the Jewish philanthropic nexus. Perhaps the most important of these was the "Grand Old Man" of Russian Jewry, Baron Horace (Goratsy) de Günzburg. Günzburg was the preeminent figure in Russia's Jewish elite, a kind of "Russian Schiff," who maintained a close connection to the Tsar's court. In November 1905, Schiff triumphantly displayed a telegram from Günzburg in which

de Günzburg

he begged Schiff's help in aiding the sufferers of the raging pogroms.[43]

Usually ignored by those obsessing over Schiff's Jewishness was his *Germaness*. He retained strong familial, emotional and financial ties to the *Vaterland*. Two of his brothers, Ludwig and Phillip Schiff, were bankers in Germany with connections to the Kaiser's Court. The same went for Schiff's friend and key business partner Max Warburg, head of M.M. Warburg & Co., a friend of Kaiser Wilhelm and a financial mainstay of the future German war effort. As discussed below, Kuhn Loeb directly employed two more Warburg brothers, Felix and Paul. A *mishpocha* if there ever was one.

This raises the question of whether Schiff's animus against Tsarism, in effect an animus against Russia, was rooted as much in German political and financial interest as Jewish solidarity. Was this *quid pro quo* for the support Warburg and other German financiers lent him? Russia was an ally of France and Britain and a potential enemy of the Kaiser. By obstructing Russia's access to American capital, Schiff was not just serving his own interests, or Jews', but Germany's.

In early February 1904, Schiff invited, or summoned, Jewish leaders to his home. "Within seventy-two hours," he declared, war will break

---

39. *Investment Banking*, 18
40. Roberts, 19.
41. *Ibid.*, 15.
42. *Ibid.*
43. *The Menorah*, Vol. 39 (July-December 1905), 249.

out between Japan and Russia."[44] And it did, which begs the question of how he knew. Leaving aside psychic powers, the best bet is that Schiff had been actively encouraging the Japanese to attack. His inducement was simple: money. He quickly added that "the question has been presented to me of undertaking a loan to Japan. I would like to get your views as to what effect my undertaking of this would have upon the Jewish people in Russia," i.e., would the Tsar's Government take it out on their Jews if they found out Schiff and other Jewish financiers were financing their enemies? The English Rothschilds thought yes, and refused to touch the matter. Regardless, Schiff was positive that the best way to pressure the Russians was with financial blackmail.[45] He did not let down the Japanese. Pulling out the stops, Schiff helped raise $535 million for Tokyo, half its total war expenditure.[46] Sixty-percent of this was marketed in Europe, largely through M. M. Warburg. Schiff fervently hoped that a Russian defeat "might lead to revolution" and the installation of a government that would remove discrimination against Jews.[47]

Takahashi

Japan could not have fought or won the war without Schiff's help and Tokyo proved most appreciative, lavishing the New York banker with praise and honors. He formed an especially close bond with Baron Korekiyo Takahashi, the Mikado's special financial adviser and head of Yokohama Specie Bank. In 1906, Takahashi's daughter returned to the U.S. with the Schiffs and lived with them while attending school.[48]

But Jacob was only getting started. He boasted that he blocked every attempt by the Russians to raise a loan in the U.S. from 1904-1916. He also rebuffed every effort by St. Petersburg to extend an olive branch. As early as 1900, Witte dispatched St. Petersburg banker Adolf Rothstein, himself a Jew, to New York to pursue loans and win over Schiff. Rothstein offered to make Kuhn Loeb Russia's exclusive financial agent in U.S. and added that Witte would work to rescind the hated May Laws.[49] Schiff flatly refused any accommodation with the "fiercest Jew-hater of nations."[50] In

---

44. Naomi W. Cohen, *Jacob H. Schiff: A Study in American Jewish Leadership* (1999), 134. The war commenced with a Japanese surprise attack on 8 February.

45. "Russo-Japanese War – financed by Jacob Schiff," The Strange Side of Jewish History (12 Dec. 2012), http://strangeside.com/russo-japanese-war-financed-by-jacob-schiff/. See also: "Financing a Foreign War: Jacob H. Schiff and Japan, 1904-05." American Jewish Historical Review, # 61 (1971/1972).

46. Roberts, 18.

47. *Ibid.*, 16.

48. *Investment Banking*, 18.

49. "Financier of Russia," *Chicago Tribune* (8 July 1900), 34, and Morgan, 130.

50. *Ibid.*

June 1904, The Tsar's minister of the interior, the notably anti-Semitic Vyacheslav von Plehve, privately offered to meet face-to-face with Schiff to work out some resolution. Schiff responded that if Plehve "really wants me to come ... he must not say ... that he is *prepared* to see me; he must say that he *wishes* to see me – and the invitation must be addressed to me directly."[51] No such invitation ever came because soon after Plehve fell victim to an SR assassin, a deed Schiff hailed as "divine justice."[52]

Finally, in August 1905, during the Russo-Japanese peace negotiations in Portsmouth, New Hampshire, Schiff headed a delegation of "Jewish bankers" that met face-to-face with Witte. In fact, the group contained three financiers, Schiff, Isaac Seligman and Adolph Lewisohn, the others being Oscar Straus and Adolph Kraus, chairman of the Chicago B'nai B'rith.[53] Witte, whose wife was Jewish, expressed his personal sympathy for the grievances of Russian Jews, but admitted that it was beyond his power to do much about them.[54] Still, he offered to try, if in return his visitors used their influence to discourage Jews from taking up revolutionary activity. Kraus tried to strike a conciliatory tone, but an irate Schiff pounded the table and seemed determined to scuttle any chance of accord.

Schiff had other weapons up his sleeve. In the spring of 1905, American anti-Tsarist George Kennan arrived in Japan as a war correspondent. The war was going badly for Russia and Japanese POW camps were packed with 70,000 prisoners. Kennan saw a marvelous chance to proselytize this literally captive audience. He conveyed this to his comrades in the Friends of Russian Freedom who promptly dispatched a veteran revolutionary, Nicholas Sudzilovsky. The latter was now an American citizen living in Honolulu under the name Dr. Nicholas Russel.[55] In Tokyo, Russel organized the production of an estimated "ton and a half" of propaganda which, if Kennan is to be believed, found its way into the hands of 50,000 Russian officers and men.[56] Later reports claimed that "all of these had become liberals and three-quarters of these revolutionaries."[57] As always, though, the most important thing wasn't who wrote the propaganda but who paid for it.

Sudzilovsky

51. Cohen, 135-136.

52. *Ibid.*

53. *Ibid.*, 137-138.

54. Also at the meeting was Witte's aide and translator, Gregory Vilenkin, also a Jew, which only seemed to antagonize Schiff. At one point he demanded to know why a man like Witte should enjoy all the rights and one like Vilenkin, none.

55. Ronald Hayashida and David Kittelson, "The Odyssey of Nicholas Russel," https://evols.library.manoa.hawaii.edu/bitstream/10524/110/2/JL11116.pdf.

56. "Kennan Retells History," *New York Times* (24 March 1917), 1.

57. Hayashida and Kittelson, 121.

Kennan later publicly proclaimed that "the movement was financed by a New York banker you all know and love," Jacob Schiff.[58] Thus, while Schiff was meeting with Witte in Portsmouth, revolutionary propaganda he paid for was being handed out to Russian prisoners. For his part, Russel later became a "wholehearted" champion of the Soviet regime.[59] So, capitalist Schiff was perfectly willing to subsidize revolutionary sedition when it suited his purposes.

Another avenue of attack was trade. As previously mentioned, in 1910, Schiff put together a "pressure group," including friends Louis Marshall, Cyrus Sulzberger, and Oscar Straus (the latter a former Commerce Secretary) to push for the unilateral abrogation of the 1832 trade agreement with the Russian Empire.[60] A point of attack was that the Russian Government discriminated against American passport holders of Jewish origin.[61] Propaganda spun out by the Friends of Russian Freedom helped tip the scales, but Schiff's financial and political clout weighed heavily. On 13 December 1911, the House approved abrogation by an astounding 300-1 vote.[62] This prompted the Tsar's new Minister of Finance, Vladimir Kokovtsev, to confess that "our government will never forgive or forget what the Jew Schiff did to us.... He was one of the most dangerous men we had against us abroad."[63]

As a Russophile, Charles Crane opposed Schiff's actions and increasingly saw the banker as his nemesis. Crane "developed a grudge against Jacob Schiff and other Wall Street Jewish bankers for their active support of Japan," and the attack on the Trade Treaty, naturally, threatened Crane's personal interests.[64] As noted, Crane also held the Japanese and their "Jewish friends," i.e., Schiff, responsible for the failure of his Chinese appointment.[65] Their mutual friend Lillian Wald offered to host a *tête-à-tête* where the two men could hash out their differences but Schiff, as usual, haughtily declined.[66] However, their personal feud should not obscure this: while Crane and Schiff were divided on tactics, they were united in the ultimate goal of disposing of Tsarism and replacing it with a "democratic" regime.

THE WARBURGS AND OTHERS

Kuhn, Loeb & Co. was very much a family enterprise. All but one of the partners were either blood relatives or in-laws. Until his death in

---

58. "Kennan Retells History," *Ibid.*

59. Hayashida and Kittelson, 122.

60. Owen, 10.

61. Herman Bernstein, "Russia Is Hoodwinking Us about Passports for Jews," *New York Times* (2 July 1911).

62. Owen, 11, n. 32.

63. Cohen, 134.

64. Saul, 86.

65. *Ibid.*, 94.

66. *Ibid.*, 86.

1920, Jacob Schiff lorded over everyone, but other partners were not insignificant. Schiff's son, Mortimer, was more interested in chasing showgirls and playing Boy Scouts than banking. Jerome Hanauer, the only non-relative in the bunch, was a former office boy who never stood on equal footing with the others.[67]

The Warburg brothers, Felix and Paul, were quite another story. Both were German immigrants and both retained close ties to their big brother Max in Germany. As a banker, Felix reputedly was a lightweight, but his marriage to Schiff's only daughter earned him the Old Man's acceptance. Felix further ingratiated himself with his father-in-law by throwing himself into the philanthropic activities so dear to Schiff's heart.

Felix Warburg

Paul Warburg

But that was not all there was to Felix Warburg. Wartime reports from the U.S. military attaché in Stockholm, ground zero for Russian revolutionary intrigues, pegged Felix as one of a "group of Germans" financing "Russian disorganization."[68] Another report, from 1920, noted mention of Felix in a telegram from veteran Russian anarchist Emma Goldman, then in Soviet Russia, to leftist American journalist Herman Bernstein. Goldman advised him that their mutual friend Henry G. Alsberg, who was coming out of Russia, should stop in Paris to meet Warburg "for conference."[69] Alsberg, another left-wing writer, had been in Moscow as agent for the Jewish Joint Distribution Committee whose activities Warburg oversaw on behalf of Schiff. Owen Young, the State Department's high commissioner in the Baltic States regarded Alsberg and the Committee's activities as "very suspicious."[70] Other reports noted that "Felix Warburg ... handles all matters of Jewish Charities for Schiff," and "under the guise of these charities many anti-Ally movements have been helped financially by Schiff through Warburg."[71] Felix and Schiff (along with fellow Jewish bankers James Speyer and Henry Goldman) allegedly "were behind the Jewish Anti-War movement

67. "Jacob H. Schiff Left $34,426,282 Subject to New York Taxes," *New York Times* (3 March 1922).

68. MID, #10087-22, I/O Philadelphia, 20 Feb. 1918.

69. MID, #10058-450, 4, MOB 1 #332, 28 Sept. 1920.

70. MID, #10058-450, 6: MOB #722, 21 Dec. 1920.

71. RIP, 2/5, "Information Gathered in America and Sources of Such Information," (c. July 1919).

on behalf of the present [Bolshevik] Russian Government to whom they furnished funds."[72]

All this, of course, can be airily dismissed as just so much anti-Semitic conspiracy mongering, but the persistence of the accusations from a variety of sources argues that there was some fire beneath all the smoke. The real story may be that much of the pro-German skullduggery, including the financing of Russian revolutionaries, laid at Schiff's doorstep was the handiwork of the Warburgs. With that in mind it's worth mentioning that a 1917 report from a British agent in Russia, flatly labeled big brother Max as the "chief German agent in Russia."[73]

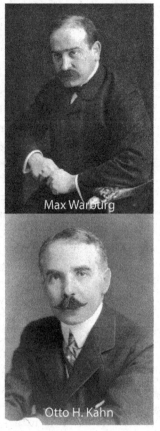

Max Warburg

Otto H. Kahn

The same suspicions attached themselves to Paul Warburg, architect of the Federal Reserve and widely regarded the best brain at Kuhn Loeb. His tenure at the firm was rather brief. Joining in 1902, he resigned in 1914 when President Wilson appointed him to the Federal Reserve Board. He retained, of course, personal ties to the firm through his brother and brother-in-law, Jacob Schiff. A 1918 report from the U.S. War Trade Board put Paul W. "in touch with Bolshevik Chief Secret Service agent, Col. Malinowsky, in NYC."[74] The same Malinowsky reportedly received money from Warburg brother Fritz in Stockholm.[75]

Then there was Otto Hermann Kahn, also of German Jewish origin, but unrelated to the Schiffs or Warburgs. Like Schiff, he entered the firm by marrying a senior partner's daughter. Relations between him and Schiff were never close. Kahn was indifferent to religion and let it be thought by many that he had converted to Christianity. Before coming to New York in 1896, he worked for years in England and was a British subject. He would not acquire American citizenship until 1917. In fact, Kahn was a staunch anglophile, which made him odd man out at the otherwise very German firm. His British sympathies weren't a casual affectation. Nor-

---

72. *Ibid.*

73. WWP, Box 10, File 257 (10/257), "Summary of Reports Received from Agent in Petrograd under Date of September 11, 1917," 3. The author of this and like reports was Wiseman's special agent, William Somerset Maugham. See also: MID, #10080-342/II, Capt. Bruff, 5 June 1918.

74. MID, #10080-342-38, War Trade Board, Aug. 1918.

75. RIP, *Ibid.*

man Thwaites, the #2 man in British intelligence's wartime operation in New York, wrote that Kahn "was definitely and whole-heartedly pro-Ally, especially pro-British."[76]

Kahn, an unabashed bon-vivant, indulged his philanthropic impulse as a generous patron of the arts, an activity that brought him into contact with Gotham's bohemian community, including political radicals. This led some to suspect that he entertained similar sympathies, though it probably would be truer to say that he was a political agnostic. In a 1917 address to the New York Stock Exchange, Kahn argued that capitalists and radicals had "neither horns, nor claws, nor hoofs" and the seemingly unbridgeable gulf between them could be overcome through dialog and recognition of mutual humanity.[77]

THE HOUSE OF MORGAN

Much has already been said about the power and reach of the Morgan enterprise, but it is worthwhile to take a closer look at some key members who will pop up in a variety of roles. Unlike his rival Kuhn Loeb, Morgan & Co. wasn't a *mishpocha* but a machine. As much as Schiff's firm was a German one, Morgan's was devotedly English.

Junius S. Morgan

The man who got the whole ball rolling was Junius Spencer Morgan (1813-1890), a Massachusetts dry-goods broker who ventured to London in the 1840s where he founded the investment banking house that became Morgan Grenfell & Co. Junius earned a rapacious "take no prisoners" reputation in business. His son, John Pierpont Morgan (1837-1913), demonstrated the same traits plus an intense desire for privacy and a mania for collecting things like art, books, and companies.

J. P. Morgan

As the "Bull of Wall Street," J. P. perfected what came to be called "Morganization."[78] Basically, a targeted company was attacked to drive down its value and then the lowered stock scooped up. With a controlling interest established, the victim was ruthlessly "reorganized" to insure dividends for investors and whole thing rolled into a cartel ruled by a voting trust. Wasteful competition was eliminated and profit assured. Of course, what could be done to a company could, with a little imagination and a lot

76. Norman G. Thwaites, *Velvet and Vinegar* (1932), 255.
77. *Editor and Publisher*, Vol. 49 (31 March 1917), 8.
78. Buessing, 44.

of money, be done to a country. Morgan complemented his business style with a well-funded private intelligence service.[79]

Looking for new worlds to conquer, the elder Morgan ventured into Russia, but cautiously. In 1900, he dickered with Witte's agent Rothstein about underwriting a loan for St. Petersburg, but pulled out at the last moment, and did so again after prolonged negotiations during 1905 and 1906. Morgan didn't bail out over fear of Schiff's retaliation. When negotiations first began in the fall of '05, the revolutionary momentum had reached its peak, the Imperial treasury was empty and the Russian banking system on the verge of collapse. Morgan ruthlessly pressed his advantage by demanding that the Russians grant preferential terms to Morgan-controlled firms that would have handed him control over Russian purchases of American machinery. The Tsar's finance minister, Kokovtsev, balked at the terms in which he saw ruination of Russia's growing industry and the threat of "exploitation [by] American capitalists and imperialists."[80]

However, in March 1906, when it came time for everyone to sign on the dotted lines, Morgan suddenly backed out. Witte suspected the Germans were behind it, but the main factor was that in the interim Russia's politics and economy had stabilized. From the standpoint of Morganization, Russia was no longer a plum investment. Interestingly, one of the French bankers involved in the deal was Edouard Noetzlin, part of the same "small fraternity" as Schiff. It was Noetzlin (or was it Schiff?) who gave Witte a heads-up on Morgan's withdrawal.[81] At bottom, Morgan really didn't like or trust Russians, whom he placed more or less on the same level as the Chinese.

Old Man Morgan didn't avoid Russia entirely. He poured millions into the Empire through companies he controlled, like International Harvester, and even those in which he held a minor stake, like Crane-Westinghouse. J. P. Morgan Jr., better known as Jack, inherited most of his father's business acumen, but he was regarded as "more mysterious and much quieter."[82] Under his watch, Morgan's Russian holdings quietly grew; by 1917 New York Life had an office in St. Petersburg as did Guaranty Trust, a firm that became the centerpiece of Jack's operations. The New York Life branch, not incidentally, was run by Frederic M. Corse, who would work very closely with American diplomatic and intelligence personal come 1917-18.[83]

J. P. Morgan Jr.

79. Ron Chernow, *The House of Morgan: An American Banking Dynasty and the Rise of Modern Finance* (1990), 211, 315.

80. Buessing, 57.

81. *Ibid.*, 58.

82. *Ibid.*, 62.

83. Mahoney, *American*, 37, 50, 108.

Like his father, Jack Morgan was a thorough anglophile. Also like his father, he harbored a mistrust of Russians and regarded most of the Tsar's representatives in New York as glorified grafters.[84] He also wasn't overly fond of Jews, especially foreign ones.[85] As soon as the European War started in 1914, Morgan aligned himself with the Allies. On 15 January 1915, he signed an agreement making him London's exclusive agent.[86] The deal included a modest $12 million credit to finance Russian purchases in America.

Young Morgan, like his father, was ably assisted by a brace of partners at least as single-minded and ruthless as himself. At the top of the list was Henry P. Davison who joined the firm in 1902 and made senior partner seven years later. Davison was deeply loyal to Morgan *Pere* and, it may be recalled, represented the company at the Jekyll Island conclave. To Jack he was a valued mentor, and in some respects, the real brains of the firm. In 1917, Davison nominally resigned from Morgan to take charge of the American Red Cross. That job, as we will see, had very little to do with charity.[87]

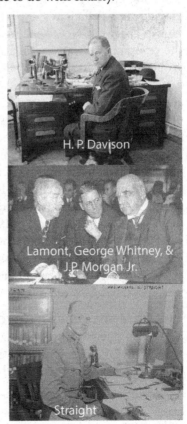

H. P. Davison

Lamont, George Whitney, & J.P. Morgan Jr.

Straight

In 1903, Davison recruited an up-and-coming "financial problem-solver," Thomas W. Lamont, to head up the new Bankers Trust, and in 1911, Lamont joined Morgan as a full partner. Early jobs working for the *New York Tribune* and other papers left Lamont bitten by the journalism bug and in 1918 he bought the *New York Evening Post* and financed other publications. Dwight Morrow, Charles Lindbergh Jr.'s later father-in-law, was a Wall Street layer until he joined the House of Morgan in 1913. During the War he would head up the Military Board of Allied Supply and later served as ambassador to Mexico.

Willard D. Straight, whose tenure with Morgan was short-lived both figuratively and literally, started out as a U. S. diplomat in the Far East. He was a newspaper correspondent during the Russo-Japanese War and in 1906 became American Consul in Mukden, Manchuria where he became a front man for E.

84. John D. Forbes, *J. P. Morgan, Jr., 1867-1943* (1981), 57-58.

85. *Ibid.,* 116-117.

86. *Ibid.,* 89-90.

87. For what it may be worth, one of Davison's sons, F. Trubee, became director of personnel at the CIA. The other, Henry, was an executive at *Time Magazine* (and a member of Skull & Bones!).

H. Harriman's Manchurian railway scheme. The next year he was working for Morgan. He was also interested in publishing, and in 1914, along with his socialite activist wife Dorothy Payne Whitney Straight, started the *New Republic* which became an important voice of the Progressive movement. A year later he officially left Morgan to become vice president of the new American International Corporation. Joining the Army in 1917, Straight went to Paris where he succumbed to complications of the Spanish Flu in December 1918.[88]

Last, but by no means least, there were George W. Perkins and Edward R. Stettinius. Perkins was a crony of J. P. senior and, curiously enough, his caricature is prominently featured in radical artist Robert Minor's 1911 cartoon showing a gaggle of beaming Wall Street tycoons (Morgan and Rockefeller included) greeting a grinning Karl Marx.[89] Hailed as an "efficiency expert," Morgan put Perkins in charge of New York Life where he oversaw the company's expansion in Russia. Perkins was a go-between for Morgan and Witte during the loan negotiations in 1905.[90] Politically, Perkins was yet another capitalist Progressive and a big backer of Teddy Roosevelt. Stettinius was a workaholic match company executive hired by Morgan at the beginning of WWI to lead its new Export Department.[91] As such, he was the head buyer for all Allied war purchasing, including Russian, handled by Morgan. In 1917, like other Morganites, he shifted to government service and in 1918 became assistant secretary of war.[92]

Perhaps the most important thing to notice in all of this is the seamless way Morgan men moved back and forth within the "triangle of power" – finance, government and media.

THE FRIENDS OF THE REVOLUTION

While never a large organization, the Society of the Friends of Russian Freedom (SFRF) was the public face of pro-Russian Revolutionary advocacy in the United States for a quarter century and the key

88. Straight's son, Michael Whitney Straight, attended Cambridge University in the 1930s where he joined the infamous Apostles secret society and, in due course, became a secret Communist and Soviet spy.

89. Robert Minor, "Dee-lighted!," *St. Louis Post-Dispatch* (1911).

90. Lebedev, 85, 87.

91. "Edward Reilly Stettinius." *Dictionary of American Biography, Supplement 4* (1974).

92. Stettinius's son, Edward R. Jr., was later part of FDR's regime and briefly Secretary of State at the close of WWII.

front organization for collecting and channeling funds. It achieved little success until someone on Wall Street took an interest.

The original Society coalesced in London in 1890 under Sergius Stepniak (Kravchinsky), a revolutionary exile who had sensationally stabbed to death the Tsar's chief of gendarmes in 1878. Stepniak penned *Underground Russia,* one of the first books about the Russian revolutionary movement to appear in English and which included sections addressing Propaganda and Terrorism.[93] In London he met or re-united with revolutionary comrades Felix Volkhovsky and Wilfrid Voynich. Voynich, the husband of British radical feminist Ethel Boole, was an early a friend and mentor of Sidney Reilly.

The heart of the Society of the Friends of Russian Freedom was an admiring coterie of British liberal intellectuals. Most held progressive or radical views and literary pretensions abounded, but they were above all well-heeled and respectable. The Society's long-time president, Robert Spence Watson, was a Quaker attorney who "spent his life championing the oppressed and the working man."[94] Another prominent member, writer Edward Pease, joined the Fabian Socialist Society, and yet another, publisher William P. Byles, was an outspoken pacifist.

In 1891, Stepniak arrived in Boston and inaugurated an American branch of the SFRF.[95] Here, too, the Society drew its members from the wealthy liberal intelligentsia. One early adherent was George Kennan, whose ubiquitous exposé of Tsarist beastliness, *Siberia and the Exile System* (1891), became a kind of bible for the Society. Other early members included Thomas Wentworth Higginson, a member of the Secret Six cabal that had backed John Brown's infamous uprising, journalist Edmund Noble, poets James Russell Lowell and John Greenleaf Whittier, plus feminist-pacifist Julia Ward Howe and, most famously, Samuel Clemens, a.k.a., Mark Twain. Twain had visited Russia in the late 1860s and came away with a positive view of the country and Tsar Alexander II. After reading Kennan's book, however, he was transformed into a militant opponent of Tsarism and happily suggested that one ought to "knife a Romanov wherever you find him."[96]

---

93. *Underground Russia* (1883) https://archive.org/details/undergroundruss00lavrgoog.

94. "Robert Spence-Watson (1837-1911)," *Bensham Grove,* http://www.benshamgrove.org.uk/history/the-spence-watsons/.

95. "Friends of Russian Freedom," *Boston Evening Transcript* (15 Feb. 1892), 6. Back in London, Stepniak was run over and killed by a train in 1895. Whether it was a simple accident or murder remains an intriguing question.

96. Philip Foner, *Mark Twain: Social Critic* (1958), 316.

Most of the leading members had a past connection to abolitionism, and there was a strong influence of Quakerism and Unitarianism. The Society produced a newsletter, *Free Russia*, but it had little impact outside Boston and New York and membership never topped 200. In 1894, the American SFRF suspended active operation due to lack of interest and the death of several of its elderly leaders.

The Society remained moribund until late 1903 when Bostonian Alice Stone Blackwell set out to revive it. The forty-six-year-old Blackwell was a parlor socialist steeped in the self-righteous idealism of the suffrage and temperance movements. In early June 1904, the *Boston Evening Transcript* announced the "Friends of Russian Freedom" as a "new society" dedicated to helping Russian political exiles and informing the American public about the "evils of Russian autocracy."[97] The earlier noted Emma Goldman, who collaborated closely with the new SFRF, described its mission "to aid by all moral and legal means the Russian patriot in their efforts to obtain for their country political freedom and self-government."[98]

Breshko-Breshkovskaya

Over the next dozen years, in addition to perpetual fund-raising, the Society translated and published works extolling the revolutionary movement and hosted a cavalcade of anti-Tsarist visitors. The first was the "Grandmother of the Revolution" and founding member of the newly-born Socialist-Revolutionary (SR) Party, Ekaterina Breshko-Breshkovskaya, who arrived in October 1904. The following year the Society secured Jacob Schiff's all-important financial support, and backed Kennan's scheme to distribute revolutionary propaganda among Russia prisoners-of-war in Japan.

The revived, Schiff-financed SFRF eventually grew to 500 members, most still concentrated in Boston and New York, but the make-up was broader than the old one. The first president was William Dudley Foulke, poet, journalist and progressive reformer. His lieutenants included George Kennan, Julia Ward Howe, and William Lloyd Garrison II, all holdovers form the original society, plus newcomers William G. Ward, Rabbi Charles Fleischer and Meyer Bloomfield, who served as secretary.[99] Ward, a professor at Boston's Emerson College, gave a talk in October 1906 in which he offered that nothing uttered by the Tsar or his officials should ever be believed and that half the peasant population was dying of

97. "To Help Exiles from Russia," *Boston Evening Transcript* (3 June 1904), 9.
98. Candace Falk (ed.) *Emma Goldman: A Documentary History of the American Years*, II, 555.
99. "To Help Exiles from Russia," *Ibid.*

scurvy or some other preventable disease. However, he conceded that the recent reforms granted by Nicholas II might signal that the "worst tyranny is permanently ended and better times are in sight."[100]

Both Bloomfield and Fleischer were Jews, an element lacking in the old leadership. Bloomfield, born in Romania and raised in the squalid tenements of New York's Lower East Side, was a social worker at Boston's Civic Service settlement house but later became a labor lawyer, "industrial expert," and banker.[101] After 1917 he would make several trips to Soviet Russia and in 1922 he sat with American Communists in Moscow as they listened to Trotsky speak in Red Square.[102] German-born Rabbi Fleischer headed Boston's leading Reform synagogue, Temple Israel. An important member of America's Jewish establishment, he was well-acquainted with Jacob Schiff. In December 1905, for instance, Fleischer and Schiff shared the stage at a gala event in Carnegie Hall honoring the 250th anniversary of the "coming of Jews to the America."[103] The evening's festive mood was dampened by news of pogroms in Russia, something that Fleischer and other speakers made sure to mention.

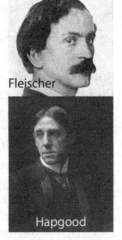

Schiff was himself a member of the Society. In 1917 he sat on its National Committee alongside Chicago social activist Jane Addams, AFL president Samuel Gompers, Sears and Roebuck executive Julius Rosenwald, Rabbi Stephen Wise, Schiff's longtime friend Cyrus Sulzberger, and two of Charles Crane's pals, muck-racking journalist Norman Hapgood, and crusading editor Oswald Garrison Villard.

It seems no accident that the SFRF's revival coincided almost exactly with the outbreak of the Russo-Japanese War and the revolution soon to follow. On 23 January 1905, barely 24 hours after the events of Bloody Sunday, the New York branch of the "Friends of Russian Freedom" organized a mass rally "to spread the propaganda of the revolution in Russia," aided by "agents of the Russian Revolution ... now here directing propaganda."[104] At the same time, in Chicago, Jane Addams convened a meeting featuring Breshko-Breshkovskaya and initiated a petition drive demanding that Tsar Nicholas accede to the revolutionaries' demands.[105] Also on

100. *Boston Evening Transcript* (17 Oct. 1906), 8.

101. Bertrand M. Patenaude, *The Big Show in Bololand: The American Relief Expedition to Soviet Russia in the Famine of 1921* (2002), 638.

102. "An American in Moscow on November 7," *Soviet Russia Pictorial* (March 1923), 48.

103. "New York Jews in Celebration," *Boston Globe* (1 Dec. 1905), 5.

104. "Will Aid the Movement," *The Pittsburgh Press* (24 Jan. 1905), 1.

105. *Ibid.*

hand was Rabbi Emil G. Hirsh, head of Chicago's Sinai congregation and, as might be expected, another collaborator of Schiff.

Another branch of the SFRF popped up in San Francisco in early 1905, organized by Russian-born "Girl-Socialist" Anna Strunsky and her leftist  comrades, William English Walling and writer Jack London.[106] In November 1905, as the revolution in Russia approached its final stage, Walling determined to see things first hand and lend his hand "stirring the masses to revolt."[107] He urged Strunsky and her sister to join him, and using fraudulent American passports (probably supplied by Society members) they reached St. Petersburg in December. Whether the Strunsky sisters also carried literature or money is an interesting, if unanswerable, question.

By 1917, the nominal chief of the SFRF was Herbert Parsons, a Wall Street lawyer and former U.S. Congressman, the very one, in fact, who had introduced the 1911 bill to abrogate the Russo-American Commercial Treaty. Parsons, naturally, was a friend of Schiff.[108] Parsons later enlisted in the U.S. Army as an intelligence officer and served in the "counter-espionage" section of General Pershing's staff in France.[109] The Society's vice-presidents included another Schiff intimate, lawyer and social activist Louis Marshall and New York Episcopal Bishop David Greer, both of whom had been prominent campaigners against the Russian treaty.

Despite later claims that the Society closed-up shop with the fall of the Tsar, more than a month later, 28 April 1917, it still labored "to raise a great fund in America" to aid Russian revolutionary exiles.[110] The money was entrusted to a special committee in Russia headed by Crane's friend Paul Milyukov.

It seems clear enough that the Society of the Friends of Russian Freedom was co-opted by Schiff after 1904 and became another tool in his relentless battle with Tsarism. Schiff's dominating role may have been

---

106. John Hamilton Gilmour, "Girl Socialist of San Francisco," *San Francisco Examiner* (3 Oct. 1897).

107. John Simkin, "Anna Strunsky," *Spartacus International* (Aug. 2014), http://spartacus-educational.com/USAstrunsky.htm.

108. Parsons was also a director of the Metropolitan Trust Co.

109. Sixty-Sixth Congress, First Session, "Hearings on the Reorganization of the Army," (1919), 553.

110. "Just a Word," *The Independent* (28 April 1917), 189.

one of things that made Charles Crane keep his distance from the Society, though he was always lurking on its periphery and counted among his friends and associates many of its members and collaborators, among them Jane Addams, Norman Hapgood, Lincoln Stephens and, of course, Milyukov.

—BUT HIS SOUL GOES MARCHING ON.

CHAPTER THREE:

THE FAILED
REVOLUTION OF 1905

THE ROAD TO BLOODY SUNDAY

The Revolution of 1905 generally gets short shrift in historical accounts, and the basic story usually follows the same line.[1] In January of that year, the Tsar's troops fired on protesting workers in St. Petersburg, an event duly immortalized as "Bloody Sunday." This ignited a wave of strikes that spread like wildfire from city to city. In the months following, radicals of every stripe, disgruntled liberals, dissident nationalities and angry peasants leapt on the insurrectionary bandwagon. By summer, mutiny appeared in the armed forces. The crest of the wave came in October when liberals joined revolutionists in a general strike. But at the end of that month, Tsar Nicholas saved the day, and probably his throne, by reluctantly promising a package of reforms, most notably a constitution and elected parliament. Having got what they wanted, or believing that they had, the liberals broke ranks and cheered on Imperial troops as they crushed the radical soviets (councils) in Petersburg and Moscow. There is much more to the story, but what we are interested in is how the uprising shaped American perceptions of and policies toward Russia and what role some Americans played before, during and after the fact.

An essential point is that the revolutionary upheaval of 1905 occurred against the backdrop of the Russo-Japanese War. That contest, raging since early 1904, had gone disastrously for Russia. At the center of the conflict was the Russian naval bastion of Port Arthur, the "Gibraltar of the East," which the Japanese vigorously besieged for months. On 20 December 1904 (2 January 1905, New Style), the dismal news reached St. Petersburg that Port Arthur had fallen.[2] This defeat, compounding earlier failures, was a major blow to Nicholas' prestige and that of his regime. It created an atmosphere of confusion and vulnerability that his enemies

---

1. For a detailed history see: Abraham Ascher, *The Revolution of 1905*, Vols. I and II (1994).

2. Russia was on the Julian Calendar until early 1918. This put Russian dates thirteen days behind the Western Gregorian Calendar and explains, among other things, why the later October Revolution is today commemorated in November.

were quick to exploit. The war also fueled inflation which eroded the already meager earnings of Russian workers, heating up their simmering discontent.

Arguably, the first step towards revolution took place in Paris in late September-early October 1904. At the instigation of Finnish nationalist Konrad "Konni" Zilliacus, eight revolutionary, liberal and nationalist parties assembled in the City of Light to concoct a common battle plan.[3] Not coincidentally, the same Zilliacus was a Japanese agent dispensing Tokyo's money among the revolutionaries.[4] The result of the gathering was a declaration

Zilliacus

calling for the overthrow of the autocracy and its replacement with some sort of "democratic regime."

One of the signatories of this declaration was liberal luminary, and Charles Crane's bosom friend, Paul Milyukov.[5] Crane and Milyukov rendezvoused in the Balkans that spring. Crane then spent most of that summer in Russia with his protégé Samuel Harper, before linking up once more with Milyukov in Paris that fall.[6] Whether Crane was present for the anti-Tsarist conclave is not clear, but in December he and Milyukov headed back across the Atlantic to the States. A more intriguing question is whether Crane, while in Russia, acted as a secret representative and intelligence gatherer for Milyukov and his comrades. It also would have been an excellent opportunity to discreetly distribute money, something with which Crane had more than a little experience.

The next step occurred in Russia. From 19-22 November 1904, St. Petersburg hosted a self-proclaimed Congress of Zemstvos, the latter being the elected district and municipal councils that handled public works, welfare and education. As such, the Zemstvos were a bastion of Russian liberalism. The more than one hundred delegates to the Congress saw themselves as a prototype Russian legislature, or Duma. Also present were the editors of the "principal newspapers."[7] Among the leading lights, were Prince George L'vov and Michael Rodzianko, both of whom would go on to play important roles in 1917. Participants took as a heartening sign the fact

Rodzianko

that the conclave, something previously forbidden, was happening at all. It seemed further evidence of the Tsar's weakening power.

---

3. Dmitrii B. Pavlov, "Japanese Money and the Russian Revolution," *Acta Slavica Japonica*, #11 (1993), 83.

4. *Ibid.*, 79.

5. Edward Crankshaw, *The Shadow of the Winter Palace* (1976), 334.

6. Saul, 86.

7. "Zemstvos Modify Memorial to Czar," *New York Times* (23 Nov. 1904).

The Zemstvo Congress received notice and praise in the American press where it was hailed as a "fateful meeting," a "turning point in Russian history" from which "no retreat is possible."[8] The visible fruit of the assembly was a letter or "memorial" addressed to Nicholas "setting forth the evils of the bureaucratic government and demanding comprehensive reforms."[9] The key word was "demand." Topping the list were a parliament and constitution followed by guarantees of equal rights and freedom of speech and religion, plus a general political amnesty and civilian control of justice.[10] The letter ended up in the hands of the Minister of the Interior, Prince Peter Sviatopolk-Mirsky (another liberal), who passed it to the Emperor. On 25 November, the Tsar even received four of the Zemstvo leaders at his residence at Tsarskoe Selo south of Petersburg. But nothing further happened, or at least nothing appeared to.

Mirsky

There was plenty going on behind the scenes. Prince Khilkov, one of Charles Crane's friends, noted that the Zemstvo meeting "had results that were not apprehended by the government."[11] Most notably, this included the establishment of secret communication between the liberals and the revolutionists which resulted in an escalating campaign of agitation against the government. In the wake of their Congress and right up to the eve of Bloody Sunday, the liberals held thirty-eight public "banquets" that were thinly disguised political forums.[12] The terroristic SRs offered their support.[13] Something that looked very much like a conspiracy was being laid against Nicholas and his government.

Khilkov

Nevertheless, the Tsar, whether from stubbornness, confusion or simple indifference, failed to offer the slightest concession. Clearly, another shoe needed to drop, and a big one. At the start of the 20th century, the generally accepted template for revolution was still the French one and its events were seen as textbook lessons to be studied and emulated. The conceit of liberals and revolutionaries alike was that Russia now stood on the cusp of its own 1789. A pivotal event in that year was the Parisian mob's storming of the Bastille on 14 July. Three days later a chastened King Louis appeared in Paris to accept a tricolor cockade and, whether he realized it or not, symbolically bow to the new order. A few months later,

8. "Czar Opposes Zemstvos?," *New York Times* (24 Nov. 1904).

9. "Russia Enslaved by Bureaucracy," *Chicago Tribune* (25 Jan. 1905), 1.

10. "Zemstvos Demand Parliament," *New York Times* (22 Nov, 1904), 1.

11. "Russia Enslaved by Bureaucracy," *Ibid.*, 3.

12. Florence Brooks, "New York End of the Russian Uprising," *New York Times* (29 Jan. 1905).

13. "Zemstvos Modify Memorial...," *Ibid.*

another mob forced its way into the royal residence at Versailles. Louis in due course found himself and family forced to move to Paris as virtual prisoners of the new government. By forcing Tsar Nicky into a similar act of submission, the Russian Revolution might at last gain momentum.

The man at the center of the coming storm, nominally at least, was Father George Apollonovich Gapon, a thirty-five year-old Russian Orthodox priest from Ukraine. Gapon has been variously described as a naïve idealist, a cunning peasant, a con-man, mentally unbalanced and a "politically illiterate."[14] For a brief time, some even imagined him a saint. He was most clearly a vain, unscrupulous and ambitious man who envisioned himself a populist demagogue. That made him an ideal tool for even more ambitious, unscrupulous and smarter men. His fondness for women, liquor and gambling smacked just a bit of another "holy man" destined to play an important part if the decline and fall of the Romanov regime, Rasputin.

Arriving in St. Petersburg in 1902, Gapon ministered to the workers of the huge Putilov plant and the following year formed the Assembly of Russian Factory and Mill Workers, which boasted about 10,000 members by 1905. The organization wasn't a proper labor union, something still illegal, but an ostensibly apolitical benevolent aid society. As such, it was tolerated by management and by the Okhranka. In fact, the secret police

Gapon

subsidized Gapon's Assembly as a antidote to revolutionary agitation. The good father scrupulously excluded socialists and Jews and passed along information regarding radical agitation among the workers. At the same time, he was courted by Marxists, SRs and liberals for the simple reason that he commanded influence among the working class. All this convinced Gapon that he was a very important person.

THE DAY

In December 1904, four Putilov workers got the sack allegedly because of conflict with a foreman. All were members of Gapon's Assembly. As labor disputes went, this was a minor affair and surely could have been resolved without much fuss. Instead Gapon, on his own initiative (or at someone's urging?), seized upon it as pretext to mount a general campaign for worker rights, one markedly more political than material. At the resulting meetings, "workers were motivated not so much by considerations of a material character, as by purely moral aspirations to settling everything 'according to justice' and to force employers to atone for their

14. Adam B. Ulam, *The Bolsheviks* (1998), 205.

past sins."[15] And if the factory bosses could be made to atone, so might the ultimate boss, the Tsar. On 16 January, Gapon called a walk-out of over 13,000 workers at Putilov. By Saturday the 21st sympathy strikes in and around St. Petersburg swelled the number to as many as 200,000.

Meanwhile the Father drafted and circulated a petition of grievances he planned to present to the Tsar. How much of it was his personal handiwork is uncertain. The SRs "elaborated" its contents and one report claimed that "some of the guiding minds of the Zemstvo agitation are at work through the instrumentality of the Social Labor Party."[16] Gapon's petition was essentially a slightly more radical version of the earlier Zemstvo letter. Along with demands for an eight-hour workday and better pay, it demanded an end to the war, legislative representation, universal suffrage, freedom of speech and assembly, separation of church and state and political amnesty. As many 150,000 persons supposedly signed it. Whether that was true hardly mattered.

On Thursday, 19 January Gapon announced that come Sunday he would lead a mass procession to the Tsar's residence in the Winter Palace to deliver the petition in person. He demanded that His Majesty appear in person to receive it promptly at 2:00 PM. Despite boilerplate affirmation of monarchical devotion, Gapon's pronouncements carried a clear threat. "If you do not appear, he warned Nicholas, "then the moral bonds between you and the people, who trust you, will disappear because innocent blood will now flow between you and the people."[17] In another interview, he pointedly warned that if the Tsar refused to come and "receive a reception for a constitution" … "there will be a terrible uprising."[18] Gapon wasn't offering compromise, he was delivering an ultimatum; if Nicholas did not acquiesce there would be violence. These dire warnings echoed far and wide, even in America. An exclusive to the *Los Angeles Herald* breathlessly warned that the march could ignite "the bloodiest day even in Russia's annals."[19] The *Pittsburgh Press* predicted that a "general uprising or horrible slaughter may occur," if Nicholas proved stubborn.[20]

Gapon magnanimously promised to guaranty the safety of the Imperial Person. Of course, if there was nothing to fear, why was a guaranty necessary? One report claimed that a picked force of 400 workman had been formed to "surround and protect" the Emperor.[21] By the same means, of course, he also would become their prisoner. Gapon expressed

15. "Bloody Sunday 1905," quoting Menshevik organizer I. A. Peskin (Somov), http://alphahistory.com/russianrevolution/bloody-sunday-1905/.

16. "Russian Tells Story of Sunday's Massacre," and "The Crisis in Russia," *New York Times* (25 Jan. 1905).

17. "Czar's Subjects Arm for Revolt," *New York Times* (23 Jan. 1905), 1.

18. "Rioting Begun at St. Petersburg, *Pittsburgh Press* (21 Jan. 1905), 1.

19. "Emperor Besieged in Palace," *Los Angeles Herald* (22 Jan. 1905), 1.

20. "General Uprising of Horrible Slaughter May Occur," *Pittsburgh Press* (21 Jan. 1905), 1.

21. "Rioting Begun at St. Petersburg," *Ibid.*

confidence that when push came to shove, the soldiers would not obey any order to fire on their brothers, and many of his followers convinced themselves the same.[22] As one commenter put it, "if Father Gapon, the mastermind of the movement, aimed at open revolution, he managed the affair like a genius."[23]

Whether Gapon was the mastermind of anything is questionable. In the aftermath of Bloody Sunday a cryptic headline in the *Minneapolis Journal* proclaimed that in Russia "Mysterious Power Furnishes Sinews of War."[24] It may have been journalistic hyperbole, but the strikes, the petition, the march and the command performance in Palace Square do suggest choreographed political theater aimed at forcing Nicholas into a corner. If he acceded to the Father's demands, he would be following in the footsteps of Louis XVI. Or else bloodshed, for which Nicholas would bear the blame.

The strikes and walk-outs had all but shut down normal life in the capital. In response, the government flooded Petersburg with troops. Palace Square, where Gapon planned to make his grand appearance, was an army camp full of tents and field kitchens. St. Petersburg's prefect of police issued a warning against "gatherings and processions" but otherwise made no effort to interfere with the strikers.[25] Meanwhile, Gapon dutifully provided his Okhranka handlers with an advance copy of the petition and plans, and they raised no objections. However, troops took up positions at key bridges and junctions with standing orders to prevent marchers from reaching the city center. The potential, even likelihood, of violence was obvious.

Saturday night some two hundred journalists and liberal "professional men" met to discuss plans to avoid bloodshed, to no result. That same night a delegation of writers, including Maxim Gorky, appeared at the home of Prince Sviatopolk-Mirsky with the same aim, only to be told it was too late. They next descended on the abode of ex-finance minister and liberal sympathizer Witte, to be told there was nothing he could do. One could almost get the impression that what was going to happen, had been pre-determined.

Almost everyone knew what was coming, even in America. In January 1905, Paul Milyukov sat comfortably ensconced in Chicago as the guest of Charles Crane. He was being subsidized by Crane to deliver a series of lectures and articles on Russian politics. It was excellent timing, indeed. On 21 January, Milyukov sat for an interview in Crane's home where he was asked about developments in his homeland. "There will be bloodshed in Russia within two days," he asserted, and "If the great gath-

---

22. "Emperor Besieged in Palace," *Ibid.*
23. "Civil War Threatened," *New York Times* (23 Jan. 1905), 1.
24. "Mysterious Power Furnishes Sinews of War," *Minneapolis Journal* (24 Jan. 1905), 1.
25. "Rioting Begun at St. Petersburg, *Ibid.*

ering of masses before the Winter Palace Sunday afternoon is in some way prevented it will take place in some other part of St. Petersburg and I do not see how a clash can be avoided."[26] "To all intents and purposes a revolution is already in progress, he continued, and what "All Russia" desired was the "abolishment of autocracy and inauguration of a constitution and establishment of an assembly elected by the people." Milyukov's words were eerily prophetic or he knew more than he let on. He, and others, not only anticipated violence but seemed to welcome it. Milyukov, after all, had signed a declaration calling for nothing less that the overthrow of the autocratic regime. A scenario in which Nicholas bowed to the petitioners' demands would leave him humbled, but still on the throne. Bloodshed alone would provide the necessary pretext to get rid of him altogether.

Whether out of luck, cunning or caution, Nicholas left St. Petersburg on Saturday for the relative security of Tsarskoe Selo, some fifteen miles south. The basic reasoning was that if he was not in town to receive the petition, then Gapon would cancel the march. However, Nicholas did not go so far that he could not easily return.

As the standard story goes, the next day Father Gapon led his faithful followers to the Winter Palace only to be unexpectedly and maliciously fired on by soldiers resulting in hundreds killed and wounded. The actual course of events is rather different and, as one eye-witness put it, "it is impossible to know what occurred in many places widely apart."[27] There were several different processions starting from different parts of the city. The main one, variously estimated at 3,000 to 8,000 people, was personally led by Gapon, bearing the precious petition, from the Putilov factory. It never got anywhere near the Winter Palace, being halted at the Nar-

va Arch a few miles south. Gapon tried to hand the petition to an officer of the Ismailovsky Guards Regiment who refused it because he had no authority to accept anything. By one account, after a few minutes of befuddlement, Gapon urged the marchers forward and received a "sharp order" to halt and disperse.[28] The procession pushed forward and soldiers fired a volley of blanks, followed by another command to halt. As the crowd pressed on, two volleys of live rounds followed the first over their heads. Another account claims that "several times an officer called upon the procession to

---

26. "Russian Predicts Great Bloodshed," *Los Angeles Herald* (22 Jan. 1905), 1.

27. "Day of Terror in Czar's Capital," *New York Times*(23 Jan. 1905).

28. *Ibid.*

stop, but Gapon did not falter."[29] As the bullets began to strike people in the front ranks, the rest turned and fled trampling those in their path. "Some who had revolvers fired as they fled," which seems odd for what was supposed to be a peaceful, unarmed march.[30] A charge by mounted Cossacks scattered the remnants the crowd. It was all over before noon.

Nearly identical, if smaller, scenarios played out across the city, with the same result. The number of dead and wounded became an immediate bone of contention. Government figures of 96 killed and 333 injured are certainly lowball, but anti-Tsarist claims of 5,000 – which appeared with hours of the shootings – are even more fanciful.[31] In the end, it didn't really matter; innocent blood had been spilled and Nicholas, as predicted, was held accountable. The revolution now had a bloody shirt to wave and did so with vigor.

What happened was a tragedy; innocent people did die. Nicholas, seemingly incapable of acting in a timely or decisive manner, bore responsibility in that he preferred to run away from a crisis rather than face it head on, and because his officers were left with orders that only allowed them to shoot when faced with mass disobedience. Politically, Nicholas was damned if he did and damned if he didn't. But Father Gapon and those who guided and egged him on were responsible for willfully leading the lambs to slaughter.

As for Gapon, aided by the revolutionary underground, he slipped out of the country and made his way to Geneva. There, he proclaimed himself an SR an expected to be anointed king of the revolution. He wasn't. Gapon retained his connection to the Tsar's secret police and he began reporting on his new acquaintances, including Lenin and the SR terrorist Savinkov. The latter took an immediate dislike of the priest and began nosing into the "dark rumors" about the Father's relations with the police.[32] The ugly truth ultimately came out, and in April 1906 Gapon went to a remote house in Finland where he was murdered by fellow SR and erstwhile admirer Pinchas Rutenberg. Gapon certainly had become an inconvenient man who probably knew a bit too much about things that were never intended to be known.

HERO OF THE REVOLUTION

Gorky would fare much better. The writer eagerly took up the Gapon's mantle as the "champion of downtrodden Russia," penning a diatribe in which he described Bloody Sunday as a "premeditated massacre" for which Tsar Nicholas bore personal responsibility.[33] More interesting,

---

29. *Ibid.*

30. *Ibid.*

31. *Ibid.*

32. Spence, *Savinkov*, 44-46, 62-63.

33. "Maxim Gorky's Trial," *Evening Post* [New Zealand] (1 July 1905), 9.

Gorky's name surfaced as a member of a "provisional government" set up to take power if and when Nicholas's rule collapsed.[34] Someone was thinking ahead. The source of this story was the London *Daily Telegraph's* man in St. Petersburg, E. J. Dillon.[35] An eighteen-year veteran of the Russian beat, Dillon was well-informed and well-connected; he counted both Gorky and Witte among his intimate acquaintances. According to the story, "a kind of Jacobin Club has sprung suddenly into existence" based around an earlier liberal-radical discussion group connected with *Pravo* (not *Pravda*) magazine. At meetings held on 20 and 21 January, that is, in *advance* of Bloody Sunday, the suggestion of an "obscure individual" led to a resolution proposing the provisional government. It is, of course, interesting that no one later could recall who made such a momentous proposal. Gorky's comrades in the proposed government were Nicholas Annensky and Constantine Arseniev, both liberal intellectuals and both delegates to the earlier Zemstvo Congress.[36]

Largely because of his association with this "plot," Tsarist authorities arrested Gorky (and the others) on charges of sedition and treason, igniting fears in Russia and abroad that he would face execution. In New York, a body of "distinguished literary men" led by editors Richard Watson Gilder (*Century Magazine*), Henry M. Alden (*Harper's*) and publisher Charles Scribner led the charge to save the great artist and "leader of the revolutionary movement."[37] All were connected to the Friends of Russian Freedom. Gorky soon gained release from custody and the threat of prosecution evaporated. In July he turned down an offer to give lectures in the United States. But another offer would come soon enough.

THE AMERICAN RESPONSE

Nowhere was Tsar Nicholas II damned more loudly and consistently than in the American press. The first contact between revolutionary St. Petersburg and the Stateside media was provided by the same Maxim Gorky. Following the debacle at the Narva Gate, from which he somehow managed to escape without a scratch; Father

The Evening News, Detroit, MI, 1/24/1905.

---

34. "Liberal Russian Leaders Join to Form Provisional Government," *The Minneapolis Journal* (24 Jan. 1905), 1.

35. *Ibid.*

36. "Russian Reformers," *Los Angeles Times* (18 Feb. 1905), 2.

37. "Trepoff Did Not Order the Execution of Gorky," *Albuquerque Morning Journal* (4 Feb. 1905), 1-2.

Gapon took refuge at Gorky's flat and offered his version of what happened. That evening Gorky made his way to the telegraph office and cabled the *New York Evening Journal* with the message "Today inaugurated Revolution in Russia."[38] Picked up by the Associated Press, Gorky's words were splashed across pages from sea to sea. It was also Gorky who relayed Father Gapon's new outlook. "There is no God and no Tsar!" he reportedly lamented and soon after issued an appeal for the death of the Emperor and his "whole reptilian brood."[39] The "miscreant Czar" and his "malicious officials" had "deliberately resolved to massacre our unarmed brothers," he howled, "death to them all!"

A very interesting question is why, of all the newspapers in the world, did Gorky send his 22 January cable to the *Journal*? The basic answer is that the *Journal* was William Randolph Hearst's flagship and Gorky was Hearst's St. Petersburg correspondent. This arrangement was made in 1903 when Gorky encountered Hearst reporter and Irish republican-socialist Michael Davitt. The later had come to Russia to investigate the Kishenev Pogrom. Davitt's subsequent book, *Within The Pale: The True Story Of Anti-semitic Persecutions In Russia*, drew attention to the plight of Jews in the Russian Empire and naturally earned the warm appreciation of Schiff. Hearst, as noted, was a political simpatico and friend of Charles Crane. It would be

Davitt

through Hearst that Crane later would meet and befriend Socialist writer Lincoln Steffens.[40]

Hearst papers were hardly the only ones baying for Romanov blood. Condemnation was almost universal. The *Chicago Tribune*, with which Crane had a close connection, ran headlines proclaiming "Death to Czar!"[41] Even the front page of the Huntington, Indiana *Evening Herald* screamed "Streets of St. Petersburg Are Soaked in Human Blood" and "Russia Now Is Facing Red Revolution."[42] The *Minneapolis Journal* ran a rogue's photo gallery of the "Cabal of Grand Dukes" whose "insolent abuses of power" was bringing about the fall of the Romanovs, and quoted an unnamed Russian diplomat in Washington who opined that the same

38. "Civil War Threatened," *New York Times* (23 Jan. 1905), 1. Often paraphrased "Today the Russian Revolution began."

39. "Russia Enslaved by Bureaucracy," *Chicago Tribune* (25 Jan. 1905), 1.

40. Saul, 84.

41. "Death to Czar," *Chicago Tribune* (25 Jan. 1905), 1.

42. "Russia is Now Facing Red Revolution," Huntington Evening Herald [IN] (23 Jan. 1905), 1.

men "should be taken out and hanged at once."[43] A prize for over-the-top reporting might have gone to the *Scranton Republican* for its announcement of "thousands slaughtered," "men, women and children, shot down in cold blood by merciless soldiers," and squadrons of marauding Cossacks ordered to "kill without mercy."[44]

Even the usually staid *New York Times* trumpeted accusations of "wholesale massacre" and "helpless, inoffensive crowd shot down by troops."[45] It editorialized that "gunpowder is His Imperial Majesty's only argument with his protesting people" and "the autocracy, of course, rules only by force and terror over its subject people."[46] The writer asserted that "the proclamation put forth by the Social Democratic Labor Party contains nothing that a sensible and right-thinking American could not approve, sanction and sign."[47] "This is not socialism," the piece continued, "it is common sense and political wisdom." It was abundantly clear which side of the barricades the good guys were on. Any "besotted loyalty" to the despicable regime was nothing but base "superstition."[48]

Also roused to indignation was the grand old man of the Friends of Russian Freedom, Mark Twain. On 2 February he penned: "The Czar's Soliloquy," a none-too-subtle appeal for the assassination of Nicholas and his whole clan.[49] In it, he portrays Russia as a land where "there is no such thing as law" and his fictional Nicholas proclaims of himself and his kin: "Our common trade has been crime, our common pastime murder, our common beverage blood." To Twain, the Romanovs were "a family of cobras, set over a hundred and forty million  rabbits, whom we torture and murder and feed upon all our days."

Twain

With the press and well-known writers taking sides, it was inevitable that politicians should weigh in. The day following Bloody Sunday, Congressman Robert Baker, representing New York's 6th Congressional District interrupted House proceedings in an "excited manner" to demand adjournment to demonstrate "our indescribable horror at the wanton

---

43. "Hang Grand Dukes Urges Diplomat," *The Minneapolis Journal* (24 Jan. 1905), 1.
44. "Thousands Slaughtered," *Scranton Republican* (23 Jan. 1905), 1.
45. "Russian Tells Story of Sunday's Massacre," *New York Times* (25 Jan. 1905).
46. "The Crisis in Russia," *New York Times* (25 Jan. 1905).
47. *Ibid.*
48. "Russian Riots and the War," *New York Times* (26 Jan. 1905).
49. Published March 1905 in the *North American Review*.

massacre that has taken place in Russia."[50] No one supported his proposal, but his histrionic display made the papers. Another outraged politico was New York Supreme Court judge (and future Gotham mayor), William J. Gaynor. Addressing a meeting of the Hebrew Education Society, a Schiff charity, he blasted the Tsar as the "tool and victim of a corrupt and avaricious church and aristocracy," and thundered that such a regime "should not be permitted to exist."[51] In a comment that would warm the heart of a modern-day neocon, Gaynor added that if the Russian people could not

Gaynor

end this tyranny, "the combined civilizations of the world would have to interpose as did the United States in the case of Cuba." Official Washington kept diplomatically silent, but "unofficially every man of prominence in the government, from the president down, is showing the keenest interest in today's happenings."[52] As for Wall Street, Russian events reportedly kept the markets "in a state of nervous tension," behaving "erratically," but displaying "no pronounced weakness."[53] Everyone was waiting to see which way the cat would jump.

But what about the ordinary street; what reaction did Russia's turmoil provoke there? Given its large Russian-Jewish population, New York was the epicenter of reaction. On 23 January, the *Times* reported East Side cafes "ablaze" with eager thousands flocking to newspaper offices for the latest news. Members of the Bund (the Russian-Jewish Social Democrats) pointed out that the uprising had coincided with the opening of their annual convention. Their aim now was to raise funds for "their brethren who are fighting for the cause in Russia."[54] One Bundist proudly noted that over the past six years they had sent $500,000 to Russia to fund revolutionary propaganda. This supposedly had been collected among people with very little disposable income. The issue of money also came up in a 29 January *Times* piece about the "New York End of the Russian Uprising."[55] In it, a Gotham revolutionist recounted that "money is collected which is sent to secret agents in Russia."[56] Just how it got to them was tactfully ignored along with where it came from. Passing the hat surely was part of it, but

---

50. "House Refuses to Adjourn," *New York Times* (24 Jan. 1905).

51. "Gaynor Denounces Czar," *New York Times* (23 Jan. 1905).

52. "Intense Interest in Washington," *Scranton Republican* (24 Jan. 1905), 1.

53. "Topics on Wall Street," *New York Times* (24 Jan. 1905).

54. Revolution Party Here Hails News With Joy," *New York Times* (23 Jan. 1905), 2.

55. Florence Books, "New York End of the Russian Uprising," *New York Times* (29 Jan. 1905).

56. *Ibid.*

was that all? If Schiff was willing to bankroll radical propaganda put out by the Friends of Russian Freedom, was that because he was already in the habit of doing so?

As the Bundists mobilized for action, another Russian-Jewish meeting convened. On 23 January, an estimated 1,000 people crammed into Clinton Hall where, among others, they listened to the "impassioned address" of Chaim Zhitlovsky, the "accredited agent of the Russian Revolutionary Society."[57] In fact, Zhitlovsky represented the Socialist Revolutionary Party whose central committee had dispatched him and veteran radical Ekaterina "Babushka" Breshko-Breshkovskaya to the U. S. in October 1904 on a mission to raise money and spread propaganda. Sometimes a cigar is just a cigar, but the timing of their
mission was certainly fortuitous. Afterwards a special committee met at the home of another émigré, Social Democrat Dr. Sergius Ingermann. That same evening, at the Universalist Club, Rabbi Joseph Silverman told the assembled that "the revolution of today is the natural expression of oppressed humanity" and "right will conquer."[58] Silverman's regular job was presiding over New York's most exclusive Reform Synagogue, Temple Emanu-El, the synagogue attended by Jacob Schiff, Oscar Straus and other of the City's (and Wall Street's) Jewish elite.

Meanwhile, in Chicago, "Babushka" Breshkovskaya, convened a meeting of SR sympathizers to plot strategy. In addition to raising money, they initiated a petition campaign to demand that the Tsar grant reforms and end the violence. Hosting and assisting Breshkovskaya was Charles Crane's good friend Jane Addams and the local branch of the Friends of Russian Freedom.[59]

THE TSAR SURVIVES

Despite the fervent hopes of Russian dissidents and their American supporters, the Romanov regime did not go belly up, but neither did it quickly regain control of the situation. In February the Russian Army sustained yet another defeat in Manchuria (the Battle of Mukden) and in May the Russian Baltic Fleet, sent half way around the world, was all but annihilated by the Japanese in the Strait of Tsushima.

It was also in May that President Theodore Roosevelt offered his good offices to broker a peace conference, and in June both Tokyo and St. Petersburg accepted. Roosevelt, in fact, had long been in contact with the Japanese and knew their proposed peace terms as far back as February.[60]

---

57. "Will Aid the Movement," *Pittsburgh Press* (23 Jan. 1905), 1.
58. *Ibid.*
59. *Ibid.*
60. "Japan Begins Hardest Task," *Democrat and Chronicle* [Rochester, NY] (25 Feb. 1905), 1.

TR's personal sympathies were squarely on Tokyo's side. His "diploma-cy was always calculated to advance American interests," and this was no exception.[61] The main issue was American trade and influence in China, and wherever such matters were involved, so was Wall Street. Remember, Harriman and Morgan soon would make a big push to expand American interests there, specifically in Manchuria. Roosevelt convinced himself that the Japanese represented less of a threat to American interests in the Far East. Defeat, hopefully, would chasten the Tsar and internal unrest distract him. It was no coincidence that with the negotiations underway, Morgan suddenly invited Witte to his yacht to discuss a loan.

In June 1905, President Roosevelt took the unusual step of person-ally appointing a third secretary to the U.S. Embassy in St. Petersburg. This was Paxton Hibben, a twenty-five year old Princeton and Harvard Law grad who had somehow earned TR's confidence. In making the appointment the President re-portedly "has in mind the gathering of a good deal of useful, and probably interest-ing, information."[62] In other words, Hibben was an intelligence agent. As such, he was a prototype for Maddin Summers, DeWitt Poole and other American diplomat-spies who would operate in Russia before and after the Bolshevik seizure of power. Roo-

Hibben

sevelt's decision to post Hibben to St. Petersburg at this critical juncture was certainly not a casual one. However, Hibben's tenure in St. Petersburg was short-lived. He quickly gravitated to the revolutionary movement, and probably acted as a *sub rosa* contact between the Embassy and U.S. Government and the anti-Tsarists. This inevitably provoked complaints from the Russians, and the State Department pulled Hibben from St. Pe-tersburg in late 1905. His radical sympathies would survive, however, and he later emerged as an outspoken advocate of the Soviet regime.

In early August, a Russian peace delegation helmed by Witte arrived at Portsmouth, New Hampshire, and the process of working out a treaty began. Formal signing took place of 5 September and the Russo-Japanese War at last was over. But Tsar Nicholas's problems were not.

Back in early February1905, Charles Crane's houseguest Milyukov vanished from Chicago.[63] Until Friday the 3rd he had made daily visits to Professor Harper's home to lecture a select group of students on the latest developments in Russia. Crane "refuses to discuss his disappearance," but

61. "Theodore Roosevelt and the Russo-Japanese War," *The Russo-Japanese War Society*, http://www.russojapanesewar.com/TR.html.

62. "Appointment without Pull," *The Washington Post* (4 June 1905), 8.

63. "Czar's Foe Is Missing," *The Inter Ocean* [Chicago] (8 Feb. 1905), 1.

one can be sure he knew more than he was saying. With Crane's financial, and probably diplomatic, intervention, Milyukov reached Russia in April and soon became a founding member and head of the new Union of Unions. This was an association of liberal professionals, but also encompassing some "semi-proletarians" like office clerks and railway workers. It was the core of the future Constitutional Democrat (Kadet) Party. In October, the Union made common cause with St. Petersburg Workers' Soviet and other radical groups to launch the general strike that would finally break Nicholas' resistance to substantive reforms.

TROTSKY AND PARVUS

Milyukov was by no means the only political returnee to have a hand in this. Back on 23 January, revolutionary Leon Davidovich Bronshtein, better known under his pseudonym, Leon Trotsky, returned to Geneva following a lecture tour in Germany. He picked up some old papers mentioning Gapon's planned march, and initially assumed it had failed to come off. Learning the truth, he determined to go home and join the fight. At this point, Trotsky was a Social Democrat but neither a Menshevik nor Bolshevik. He first rushed back to Munich to the flat of his comrade and mentor Alexander Helphand (Gel'fand), who had his own pseudonym, "Parvus." The Russian-born Parvus, a kind of freelance Marxist ideologue, was a man aptly described as "one of the most extraordinary political figures of the Twentieth century."[64] While Trotsky later overshadowed him and downplayed their relationship, even he acknowledged Parvus as "one of the most important Marxists at the turn of the century."[65]

Trotsky

Parvus

It was Parvus, for example, who first formulated the concept of Permanent Revolution which Trotsky later made his own. Roughly speaking, this posited that in a "backward" or semi-feudal society like

---

64. M. Asim Karaömerioğlu, "Alexander Helphand and His Impact on Turkish Intellectual Life," www.academica.edu, 145. For a complete biography see: Z.A.B. Zeman and W.B. Scharlau, *The Merchant of Revolution: The Life of Alexander Israel Helphand (Parvus), 1867-1924* (1965).
65. Trotsky, *My Life*, Chapter XIII, https://www.marxists.org/archive/trotsky/1930/mylife/ch13.htm.

Russia's the bourgeoisie lacked the strength or resolve to carry through a genuine Democratic Revolution as a transitional step towards Socialism. Likewise, the revolutionary proletariat lacked the power to take power on its own. However, a Socialist revolution might be immediately induced through an alliance of the revolutionary workers and insurrectionary peasantry, and the whole bourgeois-democratic business bypassed.

Of course, the same result might be achieved through the tactical alliance of the revolutionary proletariat (or, really, the party acting in its name) and elements within capitalism itself. Parvus hinted at the possibility when he observed that capitalism represented a "universal system" that contained important lessons, and a functional model, for future international socialism. The latter's destiny, after all, was to assume management over what capitalism had built. Parvus also believed that a world war would ignite world revolution. Russia, as the "weakest link" in the imperialist order, was bound to collapse first. It was again quite prophetic. Trotsky noted that Parvus displayed an unusual trait for a socialist revolutionary, "an amazing desire to get rich."[66] And so he would.

As for Trotsky, a very important figure in events to come, the single most important thing to understand is that he always considered himself the smartest person in the room. Most of the time, he was right. Today, Trotsky is still often regarded as the "Great Red Hope," the man who, had it not been for the villainous Stalin, would have led Soviet Russia, and the world, into the true Communist paradise. To his admirers, Trotsky "is both the hero of the Russian Revolution ... and its Job."[67] He was indeed "an enthralling orator, a brilliant writer and a born leader," but he also was colossally vain and arrogant and possessed of a savage vindictiveness towards perceived rivals.[68] For him, "the revolution was a vehicle of self-expression."[69] Put another way, revolution was the stage and he was determined to make himself its star. Whatever Trotsky did, it ultimately was all about him.

Trotsky reached Kiev in February where he waited around for several weeks. While doing so, he met the Bolsheviks' financial genius, Leonid Krasin, who was busy buying arms and explosives. Trotsky recalled that Krasin was well-connected to certain "liberal Moscow industrialists" who supplied the funds.[70] One of these was the aforementioned – and soon dead – Savva Morozov, but another may have been the wily Alexander Guchkov. By May, Trotsky was in St. Petersburg, but now under the eyes of the Okhranka. He went into hiding and back to waiting. In October he popped up in Petersburg as the general strike took shape. Reunited

66. Ibid.
67. Robert Singer, "The Prophet Vulgarized," The Nation (25 March 1996).
68. Ibid., and Dmitri Volkogonov, Trotsky: The Eternal Revolutionary (1996), 39.
69. Volkogonov, 21.
70. Trotsky, Ibid.

with Parvus, they established themselves as the dynamic duo of the Worker's Soviet, a body that claimed to represent 200,000 revolutionary workmen. They orchestrated a new propaganda campaign with the aim of igniting a fresh rising come January and the first anniversary of Bloody Sunday. It was not to be. The Tsar's October Manifesto and the liberals' resulting defection,

Parvus and Trotsky in St. Petersburg.

left the Soviet and Trotsky-Parvus high and dry. Tsarist authorities arrested them in early December and duly tried, convicted and sentenced them to exile. Trotsky, just as duly, promptly escaped, returned to the West, and went back to waiting. Parvus too escaped, but he would take a somewhat different path. He went to the Balkans, became a businessman, and made himself rich.

THE UNDERSIDE OF THE REVOLUTION

What was Lenin doing while the Revolution reared its glorious head? Where was the great hero of 1917 amidst all the drama? Unlike Trotsky, Lenin did not rush home. From the safety of Switzerland, he took up the "rivers of blood are flowing" chorus and adjusted his polemics to call for violent revolution and unrestricted terrorism. Only in November did he set a toe back in Petersburg, briefly met Trotsky, and then slipped away again as things fell apart.

In the meantime, the earlier-mentioned Finn radical Konni Zilliacus was still trying to rally revolutionary and nationalist elements under the Japanese banner. In the spring of 1905, the Japanese General Staff ponied-up a million Yen to subsidize an armed uprising in Russia. Among the revolutionaries, only the SRs signed on and to little effect.[71] Interestingly, Zilliacus tried to disguise the source of his funds by claiming they came from America.[72] This was at least a half truth since he used American banks to launder the funds.

Durnovo

But might there have been money originating in the States? The Tsar's new minister of the interior, Peter Durnovo, thought so. He was convinced that besides the Japanese, "Jews and revolutionaries" were being backed by the Americans and

---

71. Antii Kujala, "Attempts at Fostering Collaboration among the Russian Revolutionary Parties during the Russo-Japanese War," *Acta Slavica Yaponica*, #9 (1991), 138.

72. *Ibid.*, 139. Zilliacus's plotting culminated in August-September 1905 in the so-called *John Grafton* Affair in which a ship loaded with arms and ammunition was run aground and scuttled off the coast of Finland.

British, and he instigated break-ins at the British and U.S. embassies in an effort to prove it.[73] Durnovo must have had some basis for his suspicions. Where the Americans were concerned the activities of Paxton Hibben must have played a role and, maybe, those of Charles Crane.

THE LESSONS OF 1905

Trotsky accurately dubbed "the year 1905 … a preparation for the year 1917."[74] From his standpoint, it seemed clear enough what had happened; as Permanent Revolution predicted, the Russian bourgeoisie failed to follow through and betrayed the workers and peasants.

As a revolution, 1905 was a half-baked affair, but it was not an accident or a mistake. It was precipitated by a manufactured crisis aimed at forcing the Tsar into sweeping concessions or, better still, igniting a violent confrontation that would cause his government's collapse. It did succeed in discrediting the regime and compelling limited concessions, but it failed by leaving Nicholas firmly in control and capable of rolling back any of the reforms he'd granted. Its failure can be attributed to four main factors:

> 1. The military remained loyal. Despite isolated mutinies, most notably in the Navy, soldiers, and more importantly, officers, remained obedient to the Tsar. While Milyukov, on the eve of Bloody Sunday, may have believed that "revolutionary propaganda has gained a strong foothold among the soldiers," that proved to be a gross overestimation.[75]

> 2. Gapon was a lousy leader. While popular in St. Petersburg he had little influence elsewhere. He was untrustworthy, ideologically unfocused and temperamentally unsuited to lead a revolution. That required cooler and more ruthless heads. His position as a Christian religious figure made him unpalatable to many liberals and revolutionaries, especially Jewish ones. Gorky, too, proved incapable of bearing the revolutionary banner. Professional revolutionaries like Parvus, Trotsky and Lenin came along too late.

> 3. Tsar Nicholas remained at large and free to act. By refusing to meet with Gapon he avoided the possibility of capture (or assassination) or being bottled up in the Winter Palace. In 1917, revolutionary plotters would be sure to take him into custody.

> 4. Finally, and perhaps most importantly, there was inadequate preparation and planning, the prime example being the above fail-

---

73. TNA, Spring-Rice to Hardinge, 1 March 1906, HD3/132, UK National Archives.
74. Trotsky, *Ibid.*
75. "Russian Predicts Great Bloodshed," *Los Angeles Herald* (22 Jan. 1905), 1.

ure to neutralize the military. Prep and planning required money, and there was too little of that as well.

For the revolution to succeed, all these factors would need to be addressed, especially money. And they would be.

CHAPTER FOUR

THE REVOLUTIONARY
ROAD SHOW

FRIENDS

If the aftermath of 1905 saw Russia's revolutionaries defeated and demoralized, it did not mean that they gave up the fight. Far from it. Those that hung on were the core of the hard-core. As their numbers and influence within Russia weakened, foreign countries became more important as places of refuge and support. Nowhere was this more the case than in America. In the decade preceding the beginning of the First World War, the United States welcomed a steady stream of refugees, many of them facing criminal charges in Russia, as well as a cavalcade of radical emissaries bent on mobilizing American support for the struggle against Tsarism.

Russian political exiles on U.S. shores were not a new phenomenon. Michael Bakunin made a brief visit to America in the 1860s and in the decades following, it served as a short or long-term refuge for the likes of Nicholas Sudzilovsky-Russel, Sergius Stepniak-Kravchinsky (founder of the Friends of Russian Freedom) and future SR Yegor Lazarev, who unsuccessfully tried to start a pan-revolutionary newspaper.[1] For our purposes, the "revolutionary road show" really got its start with the visits of venerable anarchist Prince Peter Kropotkin around the turn of the century. The first, in 1897, was instigated by Canadian socialist academic James Mavor, a close friend of Charles Crane. After attending a scientific conference in Toronto, the 55-year-old Kropotkin headed south  of the border for a series of lectures, mostly to anarchist audiences, but

---

1. Alfred E. Senn, "The Russian Revolutionary Movement of the Nineteenth Century as Contemporary History," *Wilson Center Occasional Paper #250* (1993), 23.

in November he gave an address in New York hosted by the Friends of Russian Freedom whose local leaders included Ernest Howard Crosby (a mutual friend of Crane and Mazor) and Columbia professor Franklin Giddings.[2] Apparently, the SFRF wasn't quite dead after all. Kropotkin noted how "chic-trés" and well-heeled this crowd was compared to others he had addressed.[3]

Soon after, "one afternoon a prominent New York banker stopped by to invite the Prince to dinner."[4] It's a pity that banker is left unnamed,

Page

but Jacob Schiff might not be a bad guess, or Otto Kahn, or even, at a stretch, Crane. The real question, of course, is what the anarchist and the banker were going to talk about over the meal. The influential *Atlantic Monthly* magazine offered to serialize Kropotkin's autobiography, later published in book form as *Memoirs of a Revolutionist*. The *Atlantic* was run by progressive journalist-turned publisher Walter Hines Page who, naturally, was another Crane associate. He would later be Woodrow Wilson's ambassador to Britain.

The SFRF's New York secretary, Robert Erskine Ely (who, yes, also knew Crane), took a shine to the Prince and was instrumental in arranging his second visit in 1901. This time the host was Boston's Lowell Institute, which was closely affiliated with the Friends of Russian Freedom. Kropotkin next came to Chicago where his host was SFRF member and Crane intimate Jane Addams. Clearly there is a pattern here; if Charles Crane never seems to be in the same room as Kropotkin, he is constantly lurking just outside the door.

The aristocratic and erudite Kropotkin did his bit to polish the image of Russian revolutionaries, especially the much-maligned anarchists. But the effect was surely negated when later that year self-proclaimed anarchist Leon Czolgosz shot and mortally wounded President William McKinley. The upshot, in 1903, was Congressional enactment of the Anti-Anarchist provision to U.S. Immigration law. This barred admission and permitted deportation of anyone advocating the "violent overthrow of the state."[5] Any state. Strictly interpreted this would have made America a forbidden land for Russian revolutionists, even many liberals, but it never was. To Tsarist officials it became a prime example of American hypocrisy.

2. Paul Avrich, "Kropotkin in America," *International Review of Social History*, Vol 25, #1 (1980), 14.

3. *Ibid.*

4. *Ibid.*, 13.

5. Candace Falk (ed.), *Emma Goldman: A Documentary History of the American Years*, II (2005), 17.

The next to appear, in the summer of 1901, was Maxim Maximovich Kovalevsky. A liberal sociologist exiled from Russia since 1886, Kovalevsky was much more Crane's cup of tea and, appropriately enough, it was Crane who sponsored his lectures in Chicago and elsewhere. One of those elsewheres was the Lowell Institute in Boston. Kovalevsky and Crane shared an allegiance to freemasonry, and Kovalevsky was very soon to become a central figure  in the re-animation of Grand Orient masonry in Russia and the founder of the small, left-of-center, Progressist Party.

The following year, Crane brought Czech nationalist Thomas Masaryk to America. It was the beginning of a long and intimate friendship, and one not without implications for Russia. Finally, in the summer of 1903, Crane brought Paul Milyukov to the States. After delivering talks at the University of Chicago, Milyukov and Crane traveled to Europe. As noted in the last chapter, they returned to America the following December where Milyukov worked on a book and gave more lectures in Chicago and at the Lowell Institute. With Crane's help, of course, Milyukov slipped back to Russia in the aftermath of Bloody Sunday.

Once more sponsored by Crane, Milyukov arrived in New York in early January 1908. On the 14th he addressed 4,000 members of the liberal Civic Forum at Carnegie Hall.[6] The chairman of Civic Forum was Robert Erskine Ely, the same SFRF member who had earlier welcomed Kropotkin. On this occasion, Milyukov's speech was titled "Constitutional Government for a Free Russia." The day after, Milyukov, accompanied by Crane, traveled to Washington for a meeting with members of President Roosevelt's cabinet and 100 members of Congress.[7] He then rushed back to New York and immediately sailed for Europe and, ultimately, Russia. This whirlwind visit surely had some purpose beyond delivering a single address. The real business must have been conducted in Washington. Most likely, Crane wanted his visitor to brief members of TR's government on conditions in Russia where the Third Duma (of which Milyukov was a deputy) was about to convene.

The U.S. press lauded Milyukov as "one of the most remarkable men in Russia" and the supreme leader of the "radical forces" in the upcoming Duma.[8] The same article claimed that the "factions under his direction" included both the Social Democrats and the SRs, which would certainly have come as a big surprise to them. Technically, there were no SR dep-

---

6. "Milyoukov Tells of Russian Struggle," *New York Times* (15 Jan. 1908).

7. "Paul Milyukov," *The Outlook*, Vol. 88 (1908), 161.

8. "Prof. Milyukoff Here," *The Brooklyn Daily Eagle* (13 Jan. 1908), 1.

uties in the Third Duma and the only SDs represented were Bolsheviks. The only party in which Milyukov exercised any real influence was the Kadets, who held a mere 52 seats out of 465. American coverage, doubtless influenced by Crane, made Milyukov out to be both more influential and more leftist than he really was. Such an image might come in handy for raising money in the right quarters.

Also, as mentioned, in October 1904 "Babushka" Breshko-Breshkovskaya and SR representative Chaim Zhitlovsky arrived in America on what they openly admitted was a fund-raising campaign. They were actively aided by the SFRF, Breshkovskaya staying at the home of its Boston chief, Alice Blackwell. Zhitlovsky would return to the U.S. on similar missions in 1907 and 1910.

In 1906 three more revolutionary emissaries arrived, and all were hosted and supported by members of the Friends of Russian Freedom. The first was Ivan Narodny, who showed up in February. His real name was Jaan Sibul. He was an ethnic Estonian with pretensions of literary greatness and a keen interest in the occult. The *New York Times* extolled him as the "Chief Agent of Russian Revolution."[9] Narodny claimed to be a 19-year veteran of the anti-Tsarist struggle, the "Chief Executive Commissar" of the "Russian Military Revolutionary Party" (whatever that was), and claimed links to Milyukov's Union of Unions and the 1905 mutiny in the Black Sea Fleet.[10] Narodny was at least partly a charlatan. A decade later he would stand accused of being an Okhranka or German agent, while he boasted of being a secret operative of Alexander Kerensky.

THE GORKY MISSION

Most importantly, Narodny helped bring the next radical visitor to New York, the great Maxim Gorky. In March 1906, Gorky was living in semi-exile in Switzerland when he received Narodny's invitation to visit the United States on behalf of the "Committee to Help the Russian Revolutionists."[11] Its membership read like a Who's Who of the American liberal intelligentsia. Among them were Mark Twain, Jane Addams, William Dean Howells, Robert Collier and Arthur Brisbane. The first two we've met. Howells was another Friend of Russian Freedom as well as an avowed Christian Socialist and an editor of *Atlantic Monthly*, the same magazine that published Kropotkin's memoirs.

Addams

9. "Russian Republic Near, Declares Leader Here," *New York Times* (7 April 1906), 1-2.
10. "Gorky to Join Exiles' Colony in Manhattan," *Brooklyn Daily Eagle* (8 April 1906) 10.
11. Milton Klonsky, "Maxim Gorky on Coney Island," in William Smart (ed.), *From Mt. San Angelo: Stories, Poems & Essays* (1984), 130.

Collier was the progressive editor of the influential *Collier's Weekly*. Most interesting, though, Arthur Brisbane was not only a senior editor for the Hearst press but also a chum of the Chief himself, William Randolph Hearst. Brisbane, naturally, also knew Crane.[12]

Gorky arrived on 11 April and was met by a small delegation of American supporters, among them "silver spoon socialist" William English Walling and Anna Strunsky, both representing the Friends of Russian Freedom. Accompanying Gorky was his personal secretary, Nicholas Burenin, and his wife, actress Maria Andreeva. Neither was exactly what they seemed. Burenin was a member of the Bolshevik Central Committee, its "arms agent" and a trusted servant of Lenin. In Gorky, Lenin had found an ideal front man. The "immense royalties" from his writing had made Gorky the Bolsheviks' new cash cow.[13]

The writer contributed generously, but the Revolution could never have enough money. As mentioned, in February 1906, Latvian and Bolshevik "expropriators" stole 170,000 rubles from the State Bank in Helsinki. In Stockholm, Burenin took charge of most of the loot, which he planned to launder in America.[14] Thus, he became Gorky's "secretary." The clean cash might be carried back to Europe, but if Burenin and Lenin had any sense, and they surely did, some would have been deposited in American banks. From there it could be transferred securely and almost invisibly anywhere it was needed, even into Russia. Money raised on Gorky's trip could be handled to same way.

Was Gorky aware of this? Certainly. Remember, just a year before he and Andreeva had served as cut-outs in the transfer of the Morozov insurance money to Bolshevik coffers. Moreover, upon arrival Gorky admitted that his sole purpose was to raise money for the revolutionary cause.[15] The real question is how many of Gorky's American hosts knew what was going on and how many abetted it.

Also meeting Gorky on his arrival was his adopted son, Zinovy Peshkov. Only sixteen years Gorky's junior, his original name was Yeshua Zalman Sverdlov, older brother of Bolshevik, and Lenin's future right-hand-man, Jacob Sverdlov. He was also brother to Benjamin ("Benny") Sverdlov who we'll meet further on. Zinovy immigrated to Canada in 1904, but by the time he was reunited with Gorky he was working in the New

Peshkov

12. Crane and Brisbane later also sat together on the committee of the Russian Famine Fund: *The Literary Digest* (3 Dec. 1921), 59.

13. John Spargo, "With Maxim Gorky in the Adirondacks," *The Craftsman*, Vol. 11, #2 (Nov. 1906), 150.

14. B. I. Nikolaevsky, "K istorii bol'shevistskogo tsentra," in Yury Fel'shtinsky (ed.), *Tainye stranitsy istorii* (2003). http://lib.ru/HISTORY/FELSHTINSKY/tajnye_stranicy.txt.

15. Klonsky, 130.

York office of *Wilshire's Magazine*, a muckraking tabloid run by yet another "millionaire socialist," H. Gaylord Wilshire.[16] It was Wilshire who arranged and paid for Gorky and Andreeva's room at Manhattan's posh Hotel Belleclaire.[17]

The evening of his arrival, Gorky was guest of honor at a dinner at the "A Club" in Greenwich Village. The Club was a writers' and activists' collective and a prime gathering spot for Gotham's fashionably radical. Present at the dinner, besides Gorky, Burenin and Peshkov, were Twain, Ivan Narodny, Arthur Brisbane, Robert Collier and several other socialist and progressive intellectuals.[18]

After dinner, Gorky, accompanied by Brisbane, attended a reception at the home of Gaylord Wilshire. This was in honor of another foreign visitor, author and Fabian Socialist H. G. Wells. While there, Wilshire inveigled Gorky to sign a letter of support for jailed Wobblies William Haywood and Charles Moyer, then on trial for murder in Idaho. This immediately provoked controversy when reported in the *New York Times*. Gorky acquired an American lawyer and literary agent in the person of well-known East Side attorney, labor organizer and Socialist Party activist, Morris Hillquit.[19] Hillquit was a friend of the above William Dean Howells, who probably made the introduction.

Wilshire

H.G. Wells

Three days into his visit, Gorky's triumphal procession hit a huge snag. Andreeva, as it turned out, was not actually his wife, at least not in the proper American sense. The legal Mrs. Gorky and kiddies were back in Russia. The story broke in Pulitzer's *New York World*, Hearst's chief rival. The dirt was probably leaked to the *World* by the Russian Embassy which was, as one might suppose, not exactly thrilled by Gorky's visit. Narodny later claimed that he was warned about the pending scandal by a mysterious "Russian banker."[20] Why revo-

Hillquit

---

16. Gaylord Wilshire made much of his fortune in real estate and had a well-deserved reputation as an eccentric. Among other things, Los Angeles's Wilshire Boulevard is named for him.

17. Zinovy Peshkov would go on to a very interesting career becoming both a French general and intelligence agent.

18. The full roster included economist Dr. Walter Weyl, writer-journalists David Graham Phillips, Leroy Scott, Ernest Poole and sociologist Robert Hunter.

19. Born Moishe Hilkowitz in Riga, in 1887.

20. Narodny identified the banker as "V. Zakharov." While he was neither a banker nor Russian,

lutionist Narodny was in secret communication with this or any banker is unexplained. However, Gorky's cardinal sin was being in bed with Hearst (as he had been since 1905), the *World's* big rival. The writer had signed an exclusive deal with the Hearst syndicate which doubtless explains Brisbane's attentiveness.

Once the news hit the streets, Gorky and Andreeva found themselves unceremoniously booted from the Belleclaire and no other "decent" hostelry would have them. The speaking engagements were canceled. Many American supporters, including the oddly priggish Twain, suddenly made themselves scarce. A few however, remained steadfast. A pair of wealthy New Yorkers, John and Prestonia Martin,

Gorky & Andreeva

first sheltered the Russians in their Staten Island mansion and then hustled them off to a secluded retreat in the Adirondacks. Leftist writer John Spargo identified the Martins as "the leaders of the Fabian Movement in this country."[21] It was at this rustic get-away, encouraged by the Martins, that Gorky wrote *Mother*, his novel about revolutionary sacrifice and transformation. On arrival in the States, the writer had declared complete disinterest in new literary projects. However, with his speaking tour dead, a new novel seemed the best alternative to raise money and promote sympathy for the cause. With help of the Martins and others, *Mother* first appeared, in English, in *Appleton's Booklovers Magazine* and later, as a book, by the affiliated D. Appleton publishers.

Burenin

Gorky, Andreeva and Burenin quietly slipped out of the U.S. in November, by which time Burenin had remitted back to the Bolshevik Center in Stockholm a large amount of "American money."[22] Gorky soon settled down into a rented villa on the sun-drenched island of Capri. He may have given his soul to the Revolution, but he liked to live in style and comfort. He turned part of the villa into a "Party School" for the Bolsheviks where comrades could brush up on the finer arts of propaganda and bomb-making.[23] Among his guests were Lenin as well as American radicals William Walling and Anna Strunsky.

In 1907, Gorky played intermediary in the transfer of money from another rich American to Russian revolutionaries, this time in London.

---

it is tempting to imagine some connection between this man and millionaire international arms broker Basil (Vasily) Zaharoff.

21. Spargo, 149.

22. Nikolaevsky, *Ibid.*

23. Luciano Mangiafico, "The Night Train for Naples: Gorky in Italy," *Open Letters Monthly* (1 April 2013). http://www.openlettersmonthly.com/the-night-train-for-naples-gorky-in-italy/.

The American was millionaire soap magnate and leftist philanthropist Joseph Fels ("Fels-Naptha") and the beneficiaries were the Russian Social Democrats, more specifically, Lenin and his Bolsheviks.[24] In the spring of that year, the SD's held a conference in London but came up short of cash to pay the bills. Fels, a "financial angel of revolutionary groups" stepped up to provide the cash.[25] Fifteen years later, in an atypical gesture, Lenin paid the money back to Fels' widow, albeit without interest.

THE MATYUSHENKO AFFAIR

Gorky's visit to America was intertwined with the travels, and perhaps the fate, of another revolutionary celebrity, Afanasy Matyushenko. In the summer of 1905, Matyushenko gained notoriety as leader of the infamous *Potemkin* mutiny which seized control of one of the Tsar's bat-

Matyushenko (in white shirt)

tleships in the Black Sea. This made him both a revolutionary celebrity and a wanted man. Matyushenko first took refuge in Romania and later made his way to Switzerland and England. From the latter, he sailed to the U.S. in June 1906. His arrival, unlike Gorky's, was unheralded and left no traces in passenger or immigration records. Matyushenko, after all, was a man with a price on his head. But his presence in the States did not go unnoticed. Aided by the same American friends, he met Gorky in the Adirondacks where the writer encouraged him to write up the story of the mutiny.

In a later anarchist account, Matyushenko lived on the Lower East Side and worked in a Singer Sewing Machine factory.[26] There he "organized a group of Russian revolutionaries" in New York.[27] Who were they? Nevertheless, "he felt driven to return to Russia," and sailed back to London in late 1906, and from there moved to Paris where he "organized in an anarcho-syndicalist group among the unemployed."[28] Despite the efforts

---

24. Arthur P. Dudden and Theodore H. von Laue, "The RSDLP and Joseph Fels: A Study in Intercultural Contact," *The American Historical Review*, Vol. 61, #1 (Oct. 1955).

25. Alan Moorehead, *The Russian Revolution* (1958), 81 and George Lansbury, *My Life* (1928), 246. Fels didn't claim any allegiance to socialism but to the single-tax doctrine of Henry George. However, he is supposed to have contributed to the Fabian Socialist cause in Britain and America.

26. Anarchist Federation, "Matiushenko, Afanasy Nikolaevich, 1879-1907," (2007). https://libcom.org/history/matiushenko-afanasy-nikolaevich-1879-1907.

27. *Ibid.*

28. *Ibid.*

of his comrades to dissuade him, Matyushenko was determined to return to Russia in order to "carry out anarchist communist activity in the city of Odessa." The same source claims that he secretly entered Russian in June 1907 and was arrested in Nikolayev on 3 July. Following his conviction by a military court, he was hanged on 20 October in Sevastopol.

The above account is at odds with earlier reports in American newspapers. In the anarchist version, Matyushenko could have lived in the USA for no more that six months – from June to December 1906. But the others are unanimous that he lived in New York City for "two years" or "most of the intervening two years" and had spent the time working in an "iron foundry," not a sewing machine factory.[29] This, too, must be in error. By any reasonable calculation, Matyushenko could not have lived in America for more than a year.

Stranger still, American press reports of Matyushenko's capture and death appeared in August 1907, not October. Moreover, they consistently reported that he was apprehended not in Nikolayev, but in Odessa and not 3 July but either on the 15th or 25th of August. The same reports also asserted that Matyushenko was hanged in Sevastopol on 29 August. Quite obviously, no one was sure what happened.

The first American report of Matyushenko's arrest, dated 27 August, notes that he carried a "false passport" and "large sum of money" and that he had "come from America" to "spread revolutionary propaganda."[30] He also was "arrested with other members of a revolutionary organization which had been formed under his leadership."[31] If true, who gave him the passport and the money? Could the latter have been part of Burenin's loot? Matyushenko's American sojourn is unique and puzzling because of the secrecy surrounding it. Essentially, he arrived in America anonymous and penniless and left equally anonymous but armed with sufficient funds to launch a new organization and propaganda campaign in Russia.

APOSTLES OF REVOLUTION

Next up was Nicholas Chaikovsky who appeared in the USA in early January 1907, followed by Alexis Aladin in February. The U.S. press glowingly hailed the former as the "Father of the Russian Revolution" and latter as the "Apostle of Russian Freedom."[32] Chaikovsky was an SR and one who had happily pocketed Japanese yen back in 1905. He and Aladin, representing the SR-aligned Trudovik (Labor) faction, now teamed up to raise money and, more importantly, set up

Aladin

29. "Homesickness Leads Russian to Death," *Los Angeles Herald* (31 Aug. 1907), 1.
30. "Famous Mutineer Caught," *New York Times* (27 Aug. 1907), 3.
31. "Homesickness ...," *Ibid.*
32. "Aladin Sails," *New York Times* (5 June 1907).

a secret network to transfer it to Europe.[33] They were assisted by a special American committee that was a spinoff of the SFRF. Its members included Jacob Schiff, George Kennan, Robert Ely and other members of the Society and grand old liberal and future U.S. Secretary of State, William Jennings Bryan.[34] The question is to what degree this "secret network" received the active cooperation of American banks or other agencies.

In early March 1907, Aladin and Chaikovsky addressed two meetings in one day at Carnegie Hall, the larger drawing a crowd of 3,000.[35] Both convened under the banner of the Friends of Russian Freedom, and two of its leading members, George Kennan and Lyman Abbot, performed the emcee duties. Charles Crane's political hero, Sen. Robert La Follette, lent his name to the affair. Among those reserving special boxes for the gathering were Jacob Schiff, Mark Twain, Cyrus Sulzberger, Robert Ely and Rabbi Joseph Silverman. The revolutionary duo proclaimed that the Russian Government had unleashed a "reign of terror" and was "dancing on the crater of a volcano." It was too late, they declared, to "avoid violence and bloodshed." The point of the meeting, they emphasized, was to "express indignation" and "encourage the fight for Russian freedom," not just raise funds, though donations were happily accepted. The result was a petition condemning the abuses of the Russian Government to be forwarded to Congress. Schiff's name was prominent among the notable signatories.

Also on Aladin's and Chaikovsky's itinerary were talks at Manhattan's Century and City Clubs, exclusive "gentlemen's clubs" whose membership lists included names from the Wall Street elite like Rockefeller and Vanderlip.[36] A member of both clubs was Charles Crane. The Russian pair followed the same pattern in Philadelphia and other cities. The *New York Times* pointed out their special attention to "professional men, captains of industry, bankers [and] statesmen."[37] Such contacts were critical because in addition to raising funds, the duo declared that they had come "here to shut out Russia from the possibility of floating any loans in America."[38] Any such loans, they warned, would only go towards buying more machine guns to murder more innocent people. Thus, Aladin and Chaikovsky's aim meshed perfectly with Schiff's.

Aladin returned to Europe in June 1907. Chaikovsky, along with Breshkovskaya, took the bold step of returning to Russia where, doubtless as planned, Tsarist authorities arrested them. This ignited a ferocious campaign by American supporters, and not just the "usual suspects" of the SFRF. In December 1909, the *New York Times* announced that "500

---

33. HIA, Paris Okhrana Records, File XXVa, #2, 12 June 1907.
34. *Ibid.*
35. "Say Czar's Doom is Near at Hand," *New York Times* (4 March 1907).
36. Aladin Appeals to United States," *New York Times* (5 March 1907).
37. "Mr. Aladin's Mission," *New York Times* (6 June).
38. "Aladin Talks of Duma," *New York Times* (15 March 1907).

prominent men petition Stolypin for a fair trial" for the revolutionaries.[39] In their letter to the Russian Prime Minister, dated 24 November, the petitioners demanded that the "trial will necessarily be open and public in accordance with the time-honored principles of justice in all nations."[40] The SFRF recruited veteran missionary and social reformer Isabel Barrows to carry the petition to St. Petersburg.[41] She also carried $25,000 bail money put up by Chaikovsky's American friends. He soon went free for lack of evidence. Breshkovskaya, on the other hand, was banished to Siberia for life.

Among the petition's signers were the expected array of progressive activists, leftist literati, liberal clergy and grandstanding politicians, but there were at least two bona fide Wall Street bankers. The first, George Foster Peabody, had long association with Edison Electric Co. and J. P. Morgan. Like Charles Crane, he was an important figure and financial *mainstay of the Democratic Party.* While he nominally retired in 1906 to pursue his interests in social causes, in 1914 Peabody became a director of the new Federal Reserve Bank in New York where he associated with Paul Warburg and William Boyce Thompson. The other financier, Henry Clews, was not only a fifty-year veteran of Wall Street investment banking

Clews

but an outspoken Fabian Socialist.[42] In a 1908 address he described socialism as "a state of affairs tending to improve the general condition of all our citizens" and looked forward to the appearance of a "real Moses" who will "lead the captains of industry and the army of laborers in one triumphal procession."[43] Clews believed that this socialist utopia could be achieved "without social revolution" and longed for the day it would be "a fact and not a theory." Other signers of the petition, though they did not advertise it, were Schiff and Crane.

MONEY AND MARTYRS

In June 1907, a Bolshevik gang including Stalin and directed by Krasin carried out the bloody Tiflis Robbery. A large part of the swag consisted of two-hundred 500-ruble notes whose serial numbers were in the hands

39. "Americans Active for Tchaykovsky," *New York Times* (2 Dec. 1909).
40. *Ibid.*
41. Isabel Barrows, "The Island Palace," *The Outlook,* Vol. 92 (1909), 887.
42. In 1908 Clews published the appropriately titled *Fifty Years in Wall Street.*
43. "Banker Henry Clews Writes on Socialism," *San Francisco Call* (16 April 1908), 1.

of Tsarist authorities. Krasin's problem was laundering these notes, which largely proved unsuccessful. In 1909-10, another member of the Bolshevik Center, Alexander Bogdanov, enlisted two agents with the aim of passing some of the notes in America.[44] A Latvian Bolshevik, Julius Wezozol, using the name Andrew Rullow, first tried to pass fifteen of the bills at a small Boston bank, H. Slobodkin & Co.[45] A suspicious manager tipped off the U.S. Secret Service, who nabbed Wezozol and the rubles. The second operative was Vyacheslav Menzhinsky, a Polish Bolshevik later to become Soviet Commissar of Finance and head of the OGPU secret police.[46] He landed in New York in May 1910 and headed for Chicago where he failed to exchange the notes but managed to get away. An interesting detail is that, upon arrival, Menzhinsky gave his local contact as Frank J. Mather of the *New York Post*. Mather was a writer and editor for the *Post* and *The Nation*, both of which were run by Friends of Russian Freedom member and Crane pal, Oswald Garrison Villard.

It was also in 1909 that members of the SFRF welcomed to New York the "Sherlock Holmes of the Revolution", Vladimir Burtsev. He had made a career of exposing Okhranka spies infesting the revolutionary ranks. He had achieved stunning success the year prior by outing the SR terrorist chief Yevno Azef. His mission in America was to similarly expose the "wealthy revolutionist" publisher Alexander Evalenko. Burtsev claimed he was tipped-off to Evalenko's perfidy by a "well-known American socialist" visiting Paris a few weeks prior.[47]

Evalenko, who was guilty as charged, vigorously denied the accusation and demanded a revolutionary "court of honor" to clear his name. Among those he wanted to sit on the court were Jacob Schiff, Cyrus Sulzberger and Louis Marshall, interesting choices, since none were revolutionaries, but it says something about the clout Schiff's and the others' names had in those circles.[48] Nevertheless, they

Menzhinsky

Burtsev

Azef

44. Nikolaevsky, *Ibid.*
45. "Held as Russian Robber," *The Altoona Tribune* (15 Aug. 1910), 4.
46. "To Let US Punish Rullow," *New York Times* (21 Sept. 1910).
47. "Russian 'Red' Calls Evalenko Spy," *New York Times* (4 Sept. 1909).
48. *Ibid.*

declined. Evalenko next slapped Burtsev with a $100,000 slander suit, and the case dragged its way through New York courts for the next three years.[49] The SFRF raised funds for Burtsev's defense and he was ably represented by Friends president and Schiff intimate Herbert Parsons.

The court case provided another opportunity to expose the evils of the Tsar's regime. Among the witnesses summoned to back up Burtsev's claim was Leonid Menshchikov, a turncoat Okhranka officer who testified that the plaintiff had been a police agent for at least twenty years.[50] In November 1912 Evalenko, still proclaiming his innocence, abandoned the suit and fled to Russia.

Burtsev's was not the only legal case to draw America's attention to the Russian revolutionary struggle. During 1908-09 two extradition cases involving "Russian revolutionists" ignited nationwide campaigns in their defense. The first, Jan Pouren, stood accused of committing robbery, arson and murder during the upheaval of 1905.[51] The Russian Government demanded his extradition for these criminal, not political, offenses. Russian officials pointed out that the United State's own Anarchist Exclusion Act made Pouren, as an advocate of the violent overthrow of a

Pouren

government, ineligible for residence. The extradition at first seemed likely to succeed, but the New York Friends of Russian Freedom led the charge against it, forming a "Pouren Defense Conference" that claimed the support of more than 200 societies across the country.[52] Pouren remained in the U.S.

Next was Chicago resident Christian Rudowitz, also wanted by the Tsar's men for crimes relating to 1905. He, too, initially found himself slated for extradition. However, progressive activist and Friends of Russian Freedom stalwart Jane Addams organized the American Political Refugee Defense League, which eventually counted 185 branches in twenty-seven states.[53] Among the attorneys representing Rudowitz was Clarence Darrow. The defense portrayed Rudowitz not as a violent criminal but just a "penniless, obscure and humble Russian

Rudowitz

49. "Boutzeff Is Sued by Man He Accused," *New York Times* (26 April 1910).
50. "Shows Russian Black Book," *New York Times* (12 June 1912).
51. William Appleton Williams, *American-Russian Relations, 1781-1947* (1952), 80-81.
52. Frederick G. Giffin, "The Rudowitz Extradition Case," 65
53. *Ibid.*, 63.

farmhand."[54] In the end, Rudowitz's order for extradition was overturned by Roosevelt's Secretary of State, the eminent Elihu Root.[55]

A prominent member of Addam's Chicago League was a wealthy mining promoter turned into a "cross between a religious and political evangelist," Raymond Robins.[56] At mass meetings for Rudowitz, Robins, never one to mince words, stirred the crowd by proclaiming that "every man who is not a revolutionist in Russia is a traitor" and anyone expressing any sympathy with the Tsar was a "traitor to human freedom."[57] Robins hoped that the campaign would create a climate in which "not a single banking house in New York or anywhere else in America" could "dare to offer a Russian loan in the United States." Again, this precisely echoes Schiff's agenda. Was Robins' wish coincidental, or was it part and parcel of a single campaign? The Pouren and Rudowitz cases also aided Schiff by stirring up anti-Tsarist sentiment just as the vote on the Russian-American Trade Treaty was coming to a head.

Robins

Charles Crane also took an interest in the Rudowitz case, though as usual not publicly. Jane Addams, recall, was his friend and her Hull House, where the Political Refugee Defense League originated, one of his favored charities. Beyond that, a prominent member of the League was Crane's factotum Prof. Samuel Harper.

What did all this coming and going, plotting and propagandizing amount to? From the turn of the century, and especially in the wake of 1905, the American public and political establishment was subjected to a constant drumbeat of anti-Tsarist propaganda. True, most of this went over the head of the average citizen, but in intellectual, academic, political and other "thought leader" circles it firmly established the meme that the current Russian Government was evil and its opponents, be they liberals or revolutionaries, were "good guys." Furthermore, the post-1905 years saw the development of a sophisticated American support network for the Russian revolutionary cause, most clearly embodied by the revived

---

54. *Ibid.*

55. *Ibid.*, 72.

56. Buessing, 35-36 and William Hard, *Raymond Robins' Own Story* (1920), 9.

57. Giffin, 65.

Friends of Russian Freedom. Most importantly, the revolutionary cause had the backing of well-heeled friends in high places, preeminently Crane and Schiff. When 1917 came along, the template was already set, the spin and response pre-determined. Nothing was spontaneous. Wall Street, as ever, called the shots, and Wall Street had decided that in Russia, change was good.

5-15

The Evolution of the American Bolsheviki. —By Webster.

(Copyright, 1918, by H. T. Webster.)

CHAPTER FIVE:

THE "AMERICAN BOLSHEVIKI"

While revolutionary celebrities captured the attention of press and public, thousands of political activists were among the immigrants flocking to American shores from the Russian Empire. Some would make their home in the U.S. for years, some for only a brief time. Short or long, in most cases this American experience made a lasting impact and influenced their later careers, for better or worse. Even Lenin, who never set foot in the States, was fascinated by notions of American "efficiency" and "scientific management." In his various attempts to define Socialism, Lenin once proclaimed that it would consist of Soviet power coupled with the "order of the Prussian railways" and "American technology and organization of trusts," as well as "American education."[1]

The following selection is by no means exhaustive, but these "American Bolsheviki" generally share three things in common. First, they engaged in radical political activity in both Russia and America. Second, they went on to hold positions of greater or lesser importance under the Soviet regime. Third, they had some connection to fund-raising or American business and financial interests. Most will show up again as the story unfolds.

To begin, there are a couple of organizations to consider.

THE UNION OF RUSSIAN WORKERS (URW)

The largest political organization founded by Russian radical immigrants was the Union of Russian Workers in 1908. Some estimates put its membership as high as 10,000 by 1914, though it probably was more like half that.[2] The Union published its own newspaper, *Golos Truda* ("The Voice of Labor"), and offered educational and social services in the communities in which is operated. The political orientation of the Union was basically anarcho-communist, and it developed a close relationship with the American IWW. Due to its aggressively anti-war stance, U.S. author-

---

1. Jutta Scherrer, "To Catch up and Overtake: Soviet Discourse on Socialist Competition," in Katalin Miklossy and Melanie Ilic (eds.), *Competition in Socialist Society* (2014) [E-book].

2. For a more complete account of Russian revolutionary émigrés in the U.S., see: A. M. Chernenko, *Rossiiskaya revoliutsionnaya emigratsiya v Amerike: konets XIX v. – 1917 g.* (1989).

ities suppressed the Union of Russian Workers starting in 1917. Of the 249 radicals deported to Russia in 1919 aboard the so-called
"Soviet Ark" (*USS Buford*), an estimated 184
were members of the URW.[3] Many former
members who remained in the U.S. gravitated to the Communist Party.

THE RUSSIAN SOCIALIST FEDERATION (RSF)

This small group, never more than a few hundred strong, formed in New
York City in May 1915 as a Russian eth-
nic section of the American Socialist Party.
In 1916, the RSF started a newspaper on the
Lower East Side, *Novy Mir* ("New World").
The paper and its parent organization became
an important touchstone for future members
of the Soviet regime. At one point or another, Gregory Weinstein, V. V. Volodarsky, Alexandra Kollontai, Nikolai Bukharin and Leon
Trotsky all labored on the publication. Other future Soviet *apparatchiks* affiliated with the RSF were Michael Yanyshev, Michael Gruzenberg, Alexander
Tobelson-Krasnoshchekoff and Samuel Voskoff.

In 1918, the Federation transformed into the "American Bolshevik Information Bureau" which in turn morphed into the "New York Section of
the Russian Bolsheviki" and finally into the "Russian Soviet Government
Bureau" led by Ludwig Martens. In 1919, during the split of the American
Socialist Party, most of the remaining members of the RSF stuck to its left
wing, which became the nucleus of the Communist Party.

ARTHUR ADAMS

The man best known as Arthur Alexandrovich Adams achieved notoriety in the 1940s as one of Stalin's "Atom Spies;" in fact, the one who first
supplied Moscow with details of America's super-secret Manhattan Project.
He lived in the U.S. and Canada for at least a decade prior to 1920 where he
was active in Russian revolutionary and local socialist organizations. Curiously, most of what Adams later wrote about this early part of his life is de-
monstrably false.[4] For instance, he claimed to have been born in Sweden to
a Swedish engineer father and a Russian-Jewish mother, but Swedish birth
records contain no record of him or his father. Likewise, Adams' claims to

---

3. "Red Ark Sails: Anarchist Emma Goldman, 248 Others Deported," *Today in Civil Liberties History*. http://todayinclh.com/?event=red-ark-sails-emma-goldman-248-others-deported.

4. "Artur Adams: Yemu soputsvovala udacha," in Valerii Kochik, *Razvedchiki i rezidenty GRU*.
http://www.xliby.ru/istorija/razvedchiki_i_rezidenty_gru/p3.php#metkadoc20.

have received a degree from the University of Toronto and to have served as an officer in the U.S.
Army are completely bogus. More reliable, perhaps, is his claim to have joined the Bolsheviks
in 1905 and to have followed the usual course of
arrest and exile for revolutionary activities.[5]

The best bet is that "Adams" arrived in New
York in December 1909 as Boris Adamoff, a
Russian-Jewish metal worker. He headed for
Detroit and promptly ceased to exist, at least so
far as vital records are concerned. Three years
later, Arthur Adams made his first definite ap-

pearance in Toronto working for a clothing manufacturer.[6] In September
of that same year, he made his first recorded visit to the U.S. as a Niagara
Falls sightseer. Somewhere around this time, he supposedly worked for
the Ford Motor Co. However, by early 1915 Adams was living on Manhattan's 19th Street. Two years later his civilian draft registration pegged
him as a foreman at the Blair Tool Machine Co. In the 1920 Census, he is
a clerk. In fact, he was director of the "Technical Department" of the Russian Soviet Government ("Martens") Bureau in New York. As such, he
oversaw the Bureau's relations with the Russian Technical Aid Society;
an ostensible private charity that recruited experts and collected food,
clothing and especially money to be forwarded to the Worker's Paradise.[7]
Adams also handled the Bureau's technical espionage operations.

In early 1921, following the demise of the Soviet Bureau, Adams returned to Russia. Over the next several years he worked as an engineer
and manager in Soviet auto and aircraft plants but maintained contacts
in the States. In 1927, he returned to Detroit to study heavy truck production and was back again five years later to purchase aircraft engines.
In 1934, the GRU (Soviet military intelligence) recruited him to set up
a technological spy ring in the USA and the rest, as they say, is history.

BARNETT (BORNETT) BOBROFF

Born in Moscow as Boris L'vovich Bobrov, he immigrated to the U.S. in
1905. His prior political activity in Russia is unknown, but he quickly affiliated himself with the American Socialist Party, first in Chicago and later in
Milwaukee, where he became a successful businessman, heading the Bobroff
Manufacturing Co., which later became the Bobroff Foreign Trading and Engineering Co. In 1919, he established a close relationship with the Soviet Bureau
in New York, especially with its "commercial attaché," Communist businessman Abraham Heller.

5. *Ibid.*
6. *Toronto City Directory*, 1912.
7. BI, #374605, "Russian Technical and Mutual Aid Society," 17 April 1920, 1-2.

In early 1920, Bobroff returned to Moscow, ostensibly as an American private citizen in search of business opportunities. Another American Socialist there at the time, Jacob Rubin, claimed Bobroff "had many friends among the Soviet [commissars]."[8] One was his brother, Gregory Bobrov, who just happened to be working for a "secret service department" run by another "American Bolshevik," Santeri Nuorteva. [9] In early 1921, Lenin briefly considered Bobroff as a

Bobroff

replacement for Ludwig Martens as Soviet representative in the States. Bobroff's main service to the Kremlin was trying to arrange the importation of $6,000,000 in Russian gold to New York, a job in which he had the help of a Wall Street brokerage firm, Flanders & Co.[10] He also cultivated connections in the Commerce Department and served as courier for confidential letters from Moscow to the Soviet Bureau. [11] Bobroff made further visits to Russia in 1922 and 1924, again on "commercial business."

NIKOLAI BUKHARIN

This future Soviet kingpin arrived in New York from Norway on 1 November 1916 under the name Sam Rumbalsky. A student radical in 1905, he joined the Bolsheviks a year later and ran their Moscow organization until his arrest. Escaping abroad in 1911, he lived in Copenhagen and Stockholm, the nerve-centers of German and Bolshevik intrigue. On landing in the States, he listed his local friend as "L. Martins," undoubtedly Ludwig Martens. Bukharin worked at *Novy Mir* alongside Martens, Kollontai, Volo-

Bukharin

darsky, Trotsky and others until his return to Russia in 1917. Bukharin originally intended to return to Russia with Trotsky in March, but accommodations on the ship were booked, so he traveled via Japan and Siberia.

After October, Bukharin became one of the most important figures in the Soviet Government.[12] He was a candidate member of the elite Politburo in 1919 and full member in 1923. Following Lenin's death in 1924, he temporarily aligned himself with Stalin, only to have the latter boot him from the Party in 1929. Bukharin's fall from Bolshevik grace ended with his arrest in 1937 and execution the year following

8. BI, #202600-740-1, MID, "Confidential Weekly Situation Survey #157," 5 Jan. 1921.

9. BI, #202-600/65, Rubin Interview, 11.

10. BI, #202600-740-1, *Ibid.*

11. USDS, #316-119-458/64, Memo, c. Aug. 1920.

12. On Bukharin's career, see Stephen F. Cohen, *Bukharin and the Bolshevik Revolution: A Political Biography, 1888-1938* (1980).

MICHAEL GRUZENBERG (BERG; BORODIN)

Born to a Jewish family in Vitebsk, Gruzenberg joined the revolutionary movement in 1900 and became a Bolshevik in 1903. He fled Russia in the wake of 1905 and landed in the United States about 1907. He settled in Chicago and attended Valparaiso University, the University of Chicago and Kent Law School. He taught English classes at Jane Addams' Hull House, which was subsidized by Charles Crane. Gruzenberg was active in Chicago Socialist politics and got to know both Krasnoshchekoff and Shatoff. Under the name "Michael Berg," he briefly ran his own Progressive Preparatory School.

Gruzenberg did not rush back to Russia in 1917. Instead, he remained in the U.S. until May 1918, when a pro-Bolshevik Russian official, Yury Lomonosov, dispatched him to Moscow to seek Lenin's instructions.[13] That we'll discuss in a future chapter.

Later, Gruzenberg became an important agent of the Communist International (Comintern) and operated in the USA, Mexico and Britain from 1919-1922. When Gruzenberg reappeared in the U.S. in early 1919, the Bureau of Investigation branded him, next to Martens, "the most dangerous propagandist now in the United States."[14] He also is referenced as the "chief financier of the Russian Revolution."[15] Crane, as we'll see, met him in Moscow in 1921. During the 1920s,

Borodin

under the alias Borodin, he became the lead Soviet military and political agent in China.[16] His star faded under Stalin, and in 1949 Gruzenberg found himself a victim of one of the last purges. He perished in prison two years later.

ALEXANDER GUMBERG

The critical question about Alexander Gumberg is whether he was just a well-meaning businessman interested in promoting friendly and profitable trade between the U.S.A. and the Soviets, or a "sinister, very clever, spy" who used his influence with Americans to advance Soviet interests.[17] The truth is certainly much closer to the latter, though few, if any, of his American acquaintances

Gumberg

13. BI, #61-1819.11, BI to Armour, Dept. of State, 22 April 1924.
14. BI, #247149, Brennan to Burke, "In re: Michael Gruzenberg," 8 Sept. 1919, 1.
15. *Ibid.*, "Michael Groosenberg," 26 Sept. 1919, 1.
16. On this phase of his career, see Dan N. Jacobs, *Borodin: Stalin's Man in China* (1985).
17. Mahoney, *American*, 52. The former view predominates in James K. Libbey's *Alexander Gumberg and Soviet-American Relations, 1917-1933* (1977).

would admit it since it left them in rather awkward positions. Gumberg haled from Elizavetgrad, which put his origins in the same neck of the Ukrainian woods as the to-be-discussed Zhivotovskys. He immigrated to the U.S.A. with his family around 1900. He worked as a chemist-druggist in New York, which brought him into contact with Socialist pharmaceutical entrepreneur Julius Hammer. Alexander's two brothers, Benjamin and Sergius, both radically inclined, later returned to Russia and assumed

Zorin

positions in the Soviet government.[18] The latter took the name Sergius Zorin, served for a time as the Communist Party boss in Petrograd and became a devoted follower of Trotsky.[19] In 1916, Alexander and his brothers were all associated with *Novy Mir*, with Alexander briefly acted as its business manager.

Gumberg returned to Russian in the summer of 1917 as the representative of the A. W. Perelstrous Co., a New York import-export firm located at 42 Broadway. The same company did business with Sidney Reilly and Abram Zhivotovsky who will be discussed in the next chapter. In Russia, Gumberg promptly insinuated himself into the American Red Cross Mission and became aide and translator for Raymond Robins. By one description, he made himself Robins' "man Friday" and "alter ego."[20] Gumberg's real job was spy and agent-of-influence for the Bolsheviks. Attached limpet-like to Robins, Gumberg returned with him to the United States in June 1918.

Always presenting himself as a pragmatic businessman, until his death in 1939, Gumberg continued to act as a Soviet agent-of-influence in American business and political circles, advising and befriending the likes of Floyd Odlum, head of the Atlas Corporation, Reeve Schley of Chase National Bank, Morgan's Dwight Morrow and influential Senator William Borah of Idaho.[21]

JULIUS HAMMER

Julius Hammer's historical role has been eclipsed by the flamboyant career of his eldest son, Armand. Along with amassing fame, fortune and influence, the younger Hammer, faithful to his father's ideals, was a devoted servant of Soviet interests.[22] Julius Hammer was a loyal comrade and financial angel of the defunct

J. Hammer

18. Veniamin for a time headed the Soviet chemical trust. He fell victim to the purges of 1930s but survived.

19. Frank E. Smith, "A Deported Emma Goldman Describes Lenin's Russia." (2008). http://www.fsmitha.com/h2/ch11-emma.htm.

20. Mahoney, *American*, 55.

21. *Ibid.*, 53-54.

22. On Armand Hammer's escapades, see Edward Jay Epstein, *The Secret Life of Armand Hammer* (New York: Random House, 1996).

Socialist Labor Party and a founding father of the American Communist movement. He was a sterling example of a radical Marxist *cum* wealthy entrepreneur. Emigrating from Odessa with his family in 1890, Julius worked his way from humble drugstore clerk to become a successful physician and the owner of a chain of pharmacies and his own company, Allied Drug & Chemical. Even these resources strained to support both Hammer's opulent lifestyle and his generous support of radical causes.

Julius gravitated to socialism as a teenager and never looked back. In 1907, he met Lenin in Germany and felt that he had "become part of the elite underground cadre that Lenin would depend on to change the world."[23] Lenin called Comrade Hammer his "American millionaire."[24] With the help of his friend and fellow businessman Abraham Heller, and

Hammer's sons Armand, Harry and Victor, Julius arranged an array of front companies and deals to assist the Soviet cause. The most important of these was Allied American Corporation, or Alamerico. The Hammers' ability to run these enterprises left much to be desired, as did their ostentatious lifestyle, but the Kremlin found them useful for laundering funds going to and from Moscow.[25]

ABRAHAM A. HELLER

L ike his pal Hammer, Heller was a successful capitalist and revolutionary. Born in Moscow and coming to America in 1891, Abraham early on partnered with his father in a lucrative jewelry firm, "L. Heller & Son."[26] From 1906-10 the younger Heller oversaw the outfit's branch in Paris, a stint that allowed him to indulge his true passion, radical politics. While in Paris, he met Lenin and probably took a hand in clandestine revolutionary finances. Heller's expertise with gems certainly came in handy post-1917 when the Bolsheviks used the smuggling and fencing of precious stones to acquire goods and hard currency.[27]

Returning to the States, in 1911 Abraham Heller teamed up with his brothers to found the International Oxygen Company which eventually operated three plants producing compressed gases.[28] The Company had office at 115 Broadway, right across from 120 and just two blocks from

---

23. Epstein, 36.

24. Philip S. Gillette, "Armand Hammer, Lenin and the First American Concession in Soviet Russia," *Slavic Review*, Vol. 40, #3 (Autumn 1981), 357.

25. Epstein, pp. 120-121.

26. Tim Davenport, biographical note to A A. Heller, "A Plan of Reconstruction," *Soviet Russia* (1 Nov. 1922), 230-232. http://www.marxisthistory.org/history/usa/groups/fsr/1922/1101-heller-programreconstr.pdf.

27. On this and related and related methods of fund-raising, see: Sean McMeekin, *History's Greatest Heist: The Looting of Russia by the Bolsheviks* (2009).

28. BI, #40-7017, "Abraham A. Heller," 11 Sept. 1921.

Wall Street. Among his contacts there was bond broker John Barbrick, the Flanders & Co. manager mixed up in Bobroff's earlier mentioned gold scheme. In 1918, Heller bankrolled the radical Rand School and became one of its directors. He cashed out of the oxygen business in 1919 when he became commercial attaché at the new Soviet Bureau. In May 1921, he finally returned to Moscow where the grateful comrades anointed him the American representative of the Supreme Council of the National Economy (Vesenkha).[29] Back in the States he worked closely with Hammer, Gumberg, Bobroff and others to further Soviet and Communist interests. In 1924, he was the money man and chief stockholder in International Publishers, an outfit that would churn out Marxist and pro-Soviet literature for decades to come.

ALEXANDRA KOLLONTAI

The daughter of a Tsarist general, Kollontai took an early interest in radicalism, joining the Social Democrats in 1899. Thereafter, she earned her main reputation as an advocate of women's rights and "free love." She did not formally join the Bolsheviks until 1915. By that time, she was already closely associated with Lenin and the Bolshevik Foreign Bureau in Stockholm. From Scandinavia, she made two trips to the United States, the first in October 1915 and the second in August 1916. The latter trip coincided with the appearance of another person in New York, Swedish socialist banker Olof Aschberg (of whom we will hear much
Kollontai

more). She remained in New York, joined the Russian Socialist Federation and worked at *Novy Mir.*

German-American Socialist Ludwig Lore said Kollontai came to the U.S. "on a secret mission under the direction of Lenin to collect funds for Russian revolutionary purposes."[30] This is echoed in a 1917 report from a Russian official in New York, Nicholas Volgar, who said Kollontai's close friend, Finnish radical Aino Malmberg, dispersed at least $20,000 to Trotsky, Shatoff and other comrades in New York and saw to it that "other larger sums were transferred through the Swedish and Finnish banks to [Kollontai] in Petrograd."[31] Malmberg, indeed, made at least four visits to the United States between February 1915 and January 1917. Kollontai,

29. Davenport, *Ibid.*

30. Ludwig Lore, "When Trotsky Lived in New York," 3, Browne Mss., Manuscripts Department, Lilly Library, Indiana University, Bloomington, IN.

31. USDS, #861.20211, "Memorandum," c. Nov. 1917.

along with Bukharin, greeted Trotsky upon his arrival in 1917. However, she spied on him for Lenin, and Trotsky later accused her of misrepresenting his activities.

After returning to the new Russia in 1917, Kollontai took charge of the "Women's Department (Zhenotdel) of the Communist Party, but later found herself sidelined to diplomatic posts in Scandinavia and Mexico.

ALEXANDER KRASNOSHCHEKOFF

His original name was Avram Moiseevich Krasnoshchyok. He immigrated to the USA in 1903, and was naturalized in Chicago in July 1912 as Abraham Stroller Tobinson. The 1910 census stated that Tobinson was a house painter, but two years later he received a law degree from the University of Chicago and practiced law under the name Alexander Tobinson or Tobelson. Simultaneously, he was an active member of the American Socialist Labor Party, the Russian Socialist Federation and  worked as an organizer and attorney for the American Federation of Labor. In 1913, he defended workers in the bitter Lawrence, Massachusetts textile strike. Fellow Chicagoan Bill Shatoff was among its organizers.

In June 1917, Krasnoshchekoff became superintendent of the "Worker's Institute" in Chicago (an educational organization) connected to the anti-war "American Liberty Defense League." The latter was funded by Edward C. Wentworth, president of the Willamette State Bank and a Chicago real estate magnate. Wentworth was well-acquainted with Charles Crane through both business and political activities. Krasnoshchekoff's association with the University of Chicago also hints at a possible connection to Crane's man there, Samuel Harper.

In August 1917, the Bureau of Investigation reported that Tobinson had obtained a Russian passport in Chicago and had gone to Siberia as a reporter for the *Chicago Labor News*.[32] The same report described him as "always … in sympathy with the Bolsheviki." In Vladivostok, he wasted no time jumping into local politics and soon became chairman of the so-called Far Eastern Soviet.

In April 1920, Lenin named Krasnoshchekoff head of the Far Eastern Republic, a short-lived buffer state set up by the Soviets in eastern Siberia. Shatoff also joined its government. Among other things, it was hoped that the nominally non-Communist regime would serve as a front for dealings with American business interests. In Moscow, Krasnoshchekoff later held a job in the Commissariat of Finance. In 1924, he fell from grace, perhaps the result of his American connections. Convicted of corruption, he was expelled from the Party.

---

32. BI, #279581, "In re: Jacob Krasnoczkow Tobinson," 31 Aug. 1918.

LUDWIG MARTENS

Martens

Born in Russia to German parents, Martens attended the prestigious St. Petersburg Technological Institute and earned a degree in mechanical engineering. In school, he also began to "study Marxian theories" which inevitably led to his arrest and exile.[33] One of those arrested at the same time was Lenin. It was the beginning of a long comradeship. After Martens' release in 1899, Russian authorities deported him to Germany where he served in the Kaiser's army, obtained more schooling, and worked as a mechanical engineer. He maintained involvement in revolutionary activities "so far as concerned Russia."[34] This involved the printing and smuggling of revolutionary literature, an activity that again brought him into direct contact with Lenin. In 1903 Martens joined the Bolsheviks.

Martens' actions and whereabouts during the Revolution of 1905 are hazy. He later claimed to have slipped back to Russia and acted as an "organizer" during 1905-06, but that seems doubtful.[35] One Soviet-era source asserts that he "secretly dispatched ammunition" to Russia from abroad.[36] What is clear is that on 8 December 1905, Ludwig Martens landed in New York from Antwerp.[37] In his passenger record, he came to see his cousin Max F. Abbe, also an engineer and the owner of a successful firm with offices on Broadway just six blocks from Wall Street. Martens later told American investigators that the trip was purely business, which may be true. It certainly was short; Martens returned to Europe before the end of the year.

However, Martens also claimed to have spent a couple of months in Switzerland in 1906, *before* moving to England, though British immigration records show him arriving there directly from New York.[38] Around this time, Lenin was intensely interested in funding, specifically, how to increase it. "Expropriations" and donations were sporadic and unreliable. Lenin wanted *steady* income. Did he dispatch Martens to New York to explore other avenues where Cousin Max might have shown the way? Or, was Martens' visit an advance operation for Gorky's pending mission?

Be that as it may, Martens spent the better part of the next ten years working in London. He kept up his contacts with fellow radical émigrés

33. Joint Legislative Committee of the State of New York to Investigate Seditious Activities [Lusk Committee], "Testimony of Ludwig C.A.K. Martens," (15 Nov. 1919), 14.

34. *Ibid.*, 16.

35. *Ibid.*, 18.

36. I. Andronov, "Lenin's Ambassador in America," *New Times*, #17 (21 Apr. 1970), 28-32.

37. On both entries, 1905 and 1916, his surname is spelled Mertens, not Martens.

38. Martens Testimony, 18, 23.

like Maxim Litvinov and Leonid Krasin but mostly seemed concerned with making a living.[39] Soon after the outbreak of WWI, Martens' status as an enemy alien (oddly, he was not interned) cost him his job. He somehow came in contact with John Henry Gibson, an agent of the big Demidoff iron and steel company in Russia.[40] Like Martens, Gibson had been born and raised in that country. In fact, Gibson, who was Martens' age, had spent his youth in Kursk, exactly as Martens. It seems obvious that the two knew one another from Russia; the question is whether their past acquaintance included a revolutionary dimension.

In December 1915, probably with Gibson's help, Martens secured permission to leave Britain and the day after New Years 1916 he arrived once more in New York. There, he joined the Demidoff agency in Manhattan's McAlpine Hotel where he and Gibson purchased and shipped machinery to Russia.[41] Two companies they used to do this were Traders, Inc. and the Swedish Russo-Asiatic Company, both of which we will hear of again. Interestingly, upon arrival in New York, Martens did not give Gibson as his contact but instead Dr. Sergius Ingermann, dean of Gotham's Russian Social Democrats and a board member of Novy Mir.[42] Clearly, Martens' move wasn't just about business.

Martens ultimately assumed management of the Demidoff agency, but by early 1917 (i.e., just as Trotsky arrived) he suddenly appeared as vice-president of the engineering firm of Weinberg & Posner. The latter was a Russian outfit with offices in Petrograd (the former St. Petersburg) and Odessa and New York digs in the Equitable Building at 120 Broadway.[43] As we will see, among others doing business at the same address were Sidney Reilly and Benjamin Sverdlov. Moreover, the firm's New York manager, Alexander Posner, was reported to be "more or less on friendly terms with the Bolshevik movement" and later acted as Soviet courier in Sweden.[44]

In early 1919, Lenin tapped Martens to be his representative in the United States, something examined more closely in a chapter to come. After returning to Russia in 1921, Martens held various posts under the Supreme Council of National Economy before being shunted off to edit a technological encyclopedia and dying in obscurity in 1948. Many Americans suspected that the Martens was a "mere figurehead" and not the "the real brains of the Soviet Bureau."[45] That honor probably belonged to the following:

---

39. MID, #10110-1194-65, "Ludwig C. A. K. Mertens or Martens," 12 April 1919.

40. Fully, the P.P. Demidoff, Count San Donato Successors Iron & Steel Works, Perm.

41. The Iron Age (11 Nov. 1915), 1150.

42. On Ingerman, see: BI, #202500-199.

43. Machinery (Sept. 1911), 200.

44. BI, #162958, "In Re: Alexander Posner," 28 Feb. 1919. The source of this information was journalist Herman Bernstein who claimed to know Posner well.

45. MID, #9771-145, "Memorandum on British Secret Service Activities in the Country," (2 Nov.

SANTERI NUORTEVA

Born Alexander Nyberg in Russian-ruled Finland, like so many others, he was radicalized by the events of 1905. Soon after, he adopted the "Finnicized" name of Santeri Nuorteva, became a socialist activist and member of the autonomous Finnish parliament. He entered the U.S. in 1911 supposedly to study American education. Instead, he plunged into labor organizing and joined the Socialist Party. By 1913, Nuorteva headed the Finnish Socialist Federation in Astoria, Oregon and worked on various radical Finnish-language publications. In 1918, the short-lived Finnish Socialist Workers' Republic named him its American representative.[46] He set up a propaganda outlet, the Finnish Information Bureau, to influence U.S. public opinion, not without some success. Most notably, he struck a blow against the Finnish "Whites" by "getting their accounts in New York banks frozen."[47] It was a remarkable coup for a mere propagandist. Nuorteva must have had connections in American financial circles. Who were they?

Nyberg & Martens

With the collapse of the Finnish Workers' Republic, Nuorteva threw in his lot with the Bolsheviks. In May 1918, he addressed a crowd of 3,000 at Carnegie Hall alongside Red luminaries John Reed and Morris Hillquit.[48] In short order, Nuorteva lent his organizing skills to the Soviet Russian Recognition League and the Soviet Russian Information Bureau, the latter morphing into the Martens-led Russian Soviet Government Bureau. Officially, Nuorteva functioned as the Bureau's general secretary, but he is also described as "publicity director" or "diplomatic section chief."[49] Evidently, he handled the Soviet Bureau's more sensitive activities.

On 29 January 1919, shortly after Martens received his marching orders from Moscow, Nuorteva, and Americans Harold Kellock and Grenville S. McFarland went to Washington to meet with the State Department's Frank Polk about the possibility of opening a Soviet information bureau in the capital.[50] Kellock, a radical journalist (and friend of Lincoln Steffens) was Nuorteva's aide from the Finnish Bureau. More interesting, McFarland was William Randolph Hearst's friend and personal attorney who somehow had become Nuorteva's friend as well. When and how did that happen? Polk, moreover, was not just any State staffer but the Department's

1920), 4.

46. This "Red" regime seized power in Helsinki in January 1918, igniting a brief but bloody civil war with the Finnish "Whites" and their German allies, and ending with the Reds' total defeat in early May.

47. Auvo Kostiainen, "Santeri Nuorteva and the Origins of Soviet-American Relations." http:// www.genealogia.fi/emi/art/article252e.htm#a5.

48. *Ibid.*

49. MID, #10110-1194/231, "Synopsis of the Case of Ludwig C.A.K. Martens," 4.

50. David W. McFadden, *Alternative Paths: Soviets and Americans, 1917-1920* (1993), 274-275.

counselor, a position that made him head of its hush-hush Bureau of Secret Intelligence. The elephant in the room, if not the prime topic of discussion, was the recent Soviet conviction and pending execution of an American spy, and businessman, Xenophon Kalamatiano. That, too, is a story to be discussed later. The Nuorteva-Polk meeting may have been an attempt to barter Kalamatiano's release in return for American recognition.

Nuorteva's loyalties are not certain. He picked a bitter quarrel with American Communist leader Louis Fraina and accused him of being a U.S. Government agent.[51] Fraina then accused Nuorteva of precisely the same. After leaving the U.S. for Moscow in 1920, Nuorteva briefly became chief of the "Anglo-American Section" in the Commissariat of Foreign Affairs (NKID). However, in May 1921 the Cheka (Soviet secret police) nabbed him as an "American spy" and part of a "gigantic plot" against the Bolsheviks.[52] The U.S. Bureau of Investigation and Military Intelligence long suspected Nuorteva of being in cahoots with the British.[53] Whatever evidence the Soviets had against him apparently didn't stick. Nuorteva regained his freedom in 1922 and resumed working for the Soviet Government, but never regained his former status. He died in 1929, presumably of natural causes.

Boris Reinstein (1881-1947)

As a youth, Reinstein fled Russia because of involvement in a plot to assassinate Tsar Alexander III. He came to the US in October 1892 as a "student," and settled in Buffalo, New York, where he became a successful pharmacist. That, in addition politics, brought him into contact with Julius Hammer. Reinstein joined the Socialist Labor Party, and in 1906 Buffalo police arrested him for making speeches without a permit. In 1912, he was a strike organizer in Detroit and Passaic, New Jersey. He made a trip to Europe (and possibly Russia) in the summer of 1907. Reinstein again returned to Russia in July  1917 where, along with Alexander Gumberg, he attached himself to the American Red Cross Mission as a translator and adviser. He joined the Bolshevik Party in 1918 and later served in the International Propaganda Bureau and the Comintern. He died in the USSR in 1947.

"Bill" Shatoff

Under his real name, Berl Kligerman, he came to New York on 20 Dec. 1907 as a twenty-year old revolutionary fleeing the Tsar's crackdown. He adopted the name Bill (an Americanization of Berl) Shatoff when he became

51. Richard B. Spence, "Catching Louis Fraina: Loyal Communist, U.S. Government Informant or British Agent?," *American Communist History*, Vol. 11, #1 (April 2012), 81-99.

52. "Nuorteva Reported an Anti-Soviet Spy," *New York Times* (24 May 1921).

53. MID, #9944-A-178, "British Espionage in the United States," 15 February 1921, 6.

active in the U.S. labor movement. Shatoff worked his way through many jobs and cities before settling in Charles Crane's Chicago. In 1909 he joined the IWW and roamed the country as an agitator and organizer. He also joined the Union of Russian Workers. Politically, Shatoff then billed himself an anarcho-syndicalist, and he was friends with anarchists Emma Goldman and Alexander Berkman. He went to jail often, fourteen times in Detroit alone. A "breezy, good-natured" guy, some thought Shatoff dishonest; detractors dubbed him "Yusik the Thief."[54]

By 1916, Shatoff was in New York. The Bureau of Investigation suspected him in the bombing of the Union Metallic Cartridge factory in Bridgeport, Connecticut in February of that year.[55] The plant was making munitions for the Russian Army. In January 1917, he was among the throng greeting Trotsky. In May, the Bureau of Investigation received reports that Shatoff was arranging the return of Russian radical émigrés with the help of a private banker, Emil

Shatoff & Haywood

Kiss.[56] Kiss's lower 2nd Avenue office sat barely a block from *Novy Mir* on St. Mark's Place. Kiss was on a list of bankers suspected of illicit dealing with Germany and Austria.[57] Further investigation revealed that Shatoff and Kiss were somehow financing their operation through the Russian Embassy in Washington, a thread American investigators failed to unravel. Shatoff went back to Russia soon after and became a member of the Military Revolutionary Committee formed by Trotsky to carry out the October Revolution.[58]

Aligning himself with the Leninists, Shatoff attained important positions, in part because he represented the "dynamic Americanism" so much in fashion.[59] In 1919, he was a political commissar attached to the 6th Red Army. Later, he managed the Petrograd-Moscow railway, and in 1920 Lenin sent him to Siberia where he became first the war minister then the minister of ways and communication of the puppet Far Eastern Republic. In June 1921, Shatoff greeted Charles Crane upon his arrival in Siberia and was his intermediary in negotiations with Moscow. In 1930, Shatoff scored his biggest assignment when he oversaw construction of the Turkestan-Siberian Railroad. In the end, however, his American ways, his anarchist past and suspicions of Trotskyism doomed him to execution in the 30s.[60]

---

54. Eugene Lyons, *Assignment in Utopia* (1937), 310.

55. BI, #13255, "In re: William Serge Shatoff," 2 May 1917.

56. *Ibid.*

57. USDS, #763-72112/4533, Memorandum for D. H. Miller, 27 July 1917.

58. Chaim Leib Weinberg, *Forty Years in the Struggle: The Memoir of a Jewish Anarchist* (2008), 192 n. 180.

59. Lyons, 310.

60. "Russia Expands Purge," *Chicago Daily Tribune* (19 June 1937), 9.

ALEXANDER SHLYAPNIKOV

Shlyapnikov, Party name "Belenin," was another old Bolshevik, a veteran of 1905 and a trusted confidant of Lenin. Early in the war, he was in England where he met Martens. Later he was in Switzerland and was Lenin's cut-out in dealings with the clandestine Bolshevik Bureaus in Stockholm and Petrograd. In Scandinavia, he worked closely with Parvus and his agent Jacob Furstenberg although he was never officially affiliated with them. In early 1916, Shlyapnikov returned to Russia and met Gorky. The writer gave him material that purported to show mistreatment of Jews by the Russian Army. Shlyapnikov, on Lenin's instructions, tried to sell this information to foreign Jews, first in Stockholm and then in New York.[61]

Shlyapnikov arrived in New York as "Alexander Schlapnikoff" on 8 July 1916 and returned to Copenhagen on 29 September. Among the information he supplied U.S. Immigration, he identified his local contact as the Russian Consulate. That is a bit odd, since as a known revolutionary the Consulate was a place he'd want to avoid. One explanation is that he wanted to shield his true mission from nosy American officials. But at this juncture, there was no reason for the Americans to concern themselves with such things. Other possibilities are that he had an informant at the Consulate or, more provocatively, that Shlyapnikov was himself an agent of the Tsarist Government.

In his memoir, Shlyapnikov avoids mentioning the names of any of the "New York Jews" he met, though he does identify one as the editor of *Vorwarts*.[62] That was Abraham Cahan, another Russian-born Jewish socialist. However, Shlyapnikov lamented that because he arrived in summer he missed the "rich Jews" because they were away at their summer residences. If he is not specifically talking about Schiff he certainly is talking about men like him. Maybe the interesting thing is that Shlyapnikov and Lenin believed that they could deal with these "rich Jews."

In December 1917, Shlyapnikov became the first Commissar of Labor in the Soviet Government and later leader of the Trotsky-affiliated "Workers' Opposition" movement in the Communist Party. That ultimately earned him expulsion from the Party in 1933, arrest in '35 and execution in '37.

BENJAMIN (VENIAMIN) SVERDLOV

He was a younger brother of the afore-mentioned Zinovy Peshkov (Gorky's adopted son) and Jacob (Yakov) Sverdlov, future Secretary

61. Alexander Shlyapnikov, *On the Eve of 1917* (1982), https://www.marxists.org/archive/shliapnikov/1923/eve1917/chap4.html#s2, and Barbara Allen, *Alexander Shlyapnikov, 1885-1937: Life of an Old Bolshevik* (2015), 70-72.
62. Shlyapnikov, *Ibid.*

of the All-Russian Communist Party, Chairman of the Central Executive Committee of the Soviet and, in the words of some, a key figure in the execution of Tsar Nicholas and his family in 1918. Benjamin, in an American report, was "formerly a revolutionary in Russia."[63] He lived in London from around 1911 through 1915 where he met Ludwig Martens, among others. Soon after the outbreak of the war, he went to work for another Russian, Alexander Weinstein, securing Russian war contracts. Weinstein, in turn, was agent for another Russian businessman, Abram Zhivotovsky, the same man Trotsky was so anxious to contact in Norway. Weinstein would end up in New York as a partner of Sidney Reilly.

Sverdlov landed in New York on 15 January 1916, calling himself a "stock broker-agent" and took a desk in the offices of Charles R. Flint and Co. at 120 Broadway. His precise function there was uncertain. Charles Flint was a force to be reckoned with on Wall Street. Nicknamed the "Father of Trusts," he was, among many other things, the founder of what would become IBM. He was also a business associate of Sidney Reilly. In any case, Flint was in an interesting place for a Russian revolutionary to be working. But that wasn't all. Sverdlov ran a private banking operation on the side and acted as agent for the Russian Aksai Machinery Co. He also established close connections to American businessman John McGregor (or Macgregor) Grant and his partner, Swedish financier Olof Aschberg.

Sverdlov was in NYC on 5 June 1917 when he filled out a U.S. draft registration, listing his occupation as "exporter." Later that year, he returned to Russia as a translator attached to the U.S. Russian Railroad Service Corps. In 1918, he re-emerged as chief of the All-Russian Zemstvo Union and president of the Russian Red Cross."[64] Sometime in late 1919, Trotsky appointed him deputy commissar of railways, and by January 1921, all Russian railways were reportedly under his personal direction. All these posts, of course, brought him into contact with American businessmen. During the 20s and 30s, he was variously pegged as a writer for *Izvestiya* and an official of the Scientific-Technical Department of the Vesenkha and the Commissariat of Education. His enemies branded him an "unscrupulous adventurer" and a Trotskyite. The latter proved fatal in 1940.

V. V. VOLODARSKY

A Jewish Bundist agitator in 1905, later a Menshevik, Volodarsky followed the usual pattern of arrest and exile until freed by the Tsar's amnesty in 1913. He left for New York, arriving on 6 October 1913 under his real name, Moishe Markovich Goldstein. He joined his father in Philadelphia where he worked as a tailor, joined the Socialist Party and became

63. USDS, Counselor's Office, Confidential File #215, Sharp to Bannerman, 13 Dec. 1924, 11.
64. Jennifer Ann Polk, "Constructive Efforts: The American Red Cross and YMCA in Revolutionary and Civil War Russia, 1917-1924," Dissertation, University of Toronto (2012), 192, 216.

an organizer for the International Garment Workers Union. By early 1917, he moved to Greenwich Village, and moving further to the left, worked alongside Bukharin and Trotsky at *Novy Mir*.

Volodarsky

After the fall of the Tsar, Volodarsky initially remained in New York, only reaching Russia in May. He was by this time a trusted ally of Trotsky and, following his lead, joined the Bolsheviks in the summer of 1917. During the same period, Volodarsky became a collaborator of radical American journalist John Reed, tipping off Reed to the exact day of Lenin's anticipated seizure of power.[65] After October he rose in the Leninist ranks, becoming a member of the governing Central Executive Committee and chief Red censor.[66] His career was cut short, however, by his assassination at the hands of an SR gunman in June 1918.

GREGORY WEINSTEIN

The son of a rabbi, born in Vilna, Weinstein early on affiliated with the SR Party and the Jewish Bund. Arrested during the 1905 Revolution, he escaped abroad and found refuge in Geneva where he encountered Lenin and became his "passionate advocate."[67] He emigrated to the U.S. in 1913, joining his parents in Brooklyn. That same year, Weinstein became a comrade of the American Socialist Party, and by 1916 he was on the staff of *Novy Mir*. He rose to be the paper's associate editor and business manager and worked closely with Trotsky, Bukharin, Kollontai, etc. As business manager, Weinstein handled funds, both licit and illicit. Perhaps for that reason, Ludwig Martens recruited him as general manager of the Soviet Bureau. Weinstein returned to Russia in 1921 where he joined the Anglo-American section of the Commissariat of Foreign Affairs. During 1926-28 he served in the Soviet consulate in Istanbul and as a Comintern operative. Returning to Russia, he continued working for the Foreign Commissariat until 1940 when he was arrested and shot as a Trotskyite.

65. Eric Homberg, *John Reed* (1990), 143.

66. Anatoly Lunacharsky, "Comrade Volodarsky," *Revolutionary Silhouettes* (1923). https://www.marxists.org/archive/lunachar/works/silhouet/volod.htm.

67. Epstein, 40.

КАПИТАЛ.

№ 47.

Демьян Бедный.

CHAPTER SIX

THE CONSPIRATORS

We now approach the critical events of 1917, and it's time to take a close look at three men – a Russian businessman, a phony Irishman, and a Swedish banker – along with an assortment of associated people, places, firms and events. All of them connect, one way or another, to the Russian Revolution and Wall Street. Most importantly, each was destined to play an important role in things to come.

"Uncle Abram"

Here we answer the question posed in the Prologue: Who was Abram Zhivotovsky and why was Trotsky so anxious to contact him? Abram L'vovich Zhivotovsky was the youngest of four brothers, all born in the Ukrainian river town of Kremenchug. Their sister, Anna, married David Bronshtein and so became the mother of the future Leon Trotsky.[1] Trotsky and Zhivotovsky were family, *mishpocha*, and close family at that. In his autobiography, Trotsky makes various mentions of Uncle Abram.[2] He provides little context, but reading between the lines, it's apparent that Abram made a vivid impression on his nephew. Born in

Anna Bronshtein

1868, Zhivotovsky was only eleven years older that Trotsky, making him a bit more like an older brother than elder uncle. What Trotsky doesn't mention is that their relationship didn't end in childhood. He and Uncle Abram would remain connected for years to come.

Abram and his brothers Tevel (Timothy), David and Illarion would all become members of the commercial Jewish elite in late Tsarist Russia. Starting with a small saw mill, they branched out into sugar refining, contracting, stock speculation and banking. By 1914, at least three of them, including Abram, were ruble millionaires.

In 1897, Abram Zhivotovsky joined the Moscow Merchants' Club.[3] A year later, he headed out East where he remained for most of the next

1. A. V. Ostrovsky, "O rodstvennikakh L.D. Trotskogo po materinskoi linii," *Iz glubny vremena*, #4 (1995), 105-106.
2. Trotsky, *My Life*, 11, 24, 26, 27.
3. Ostrovsky, 117.

decade. Precisely what he did, where he did it, and who he did it with are unclear. Shortly after the turn of the century he surfaced in Vladivostok where he did business with another Jewish entrepreneur, Moisei Akimovich Ginsburg, and his local agent, Sidney Reilly. This would be the beginning of a long and important friendship.

What Zhivotovsky did during the tumultuous revolutionary years of 1905-06 is also a blank. However, in 1908, he appeared in St. Petersburg as a timber merchant. Four years later, he was a director of the Tula Cartridge Works, a big supplier of ammunition to the Russian Army, and around the same time he became connected with the Russo-Asiatic Bank, the largest financial institution in the Empire. The Russo-Asiatic was dominated by the earlier-mentioned industrial magnate Alexis Putilov with whom Zhivotovsky became a friend and business partner.

Zhivotovsky

Zhivotovsky became well known among the Imperial capital's movers and shakers, and his business and social acquaintances included Prime Minister Stolypin, the Grand Duke Alexander Mikhailovich and the Masonic circle around Prince David Bebutov.[4] And, yes, Abram was a Freemason.[5] Prince Bebutov was mixed up in "anti-government political activity" and the Okhranka regarded him a "security risk."[6] Not too strange an environment for the uncle of a well-known revolutionary. How might Zhivotovsky's connections among the high and mighty have benefited his nephew?

When the First World War broke out, Zhivotovsky, still affiliated with the Russo-Asiatic, formed a "syndicate" to exploit foreign opportunities in war purchasing. He set up offices in New York, London, Tokyo and Stockholm and recruited trusted men to run them. Zhivotovsky's foreign business activities quickly drew the attention of the Okhranka and Russian military intelligence, their suspicions doubtless enhanced because among his relations were known revolutionists.

The Okhranka initiated an investigation in March 1915 based on reports that Zhivotovsky was illegally supplying Russian grain to Germany via neutral countries. However, the police didn't quite understand what they were looking at. Zhivotovsky bought and sold commodities using funds passed through foreign banks and companies. This was basically the same thing Alexander Helphand-Parvus was doing in Copenhagen. Parvus, of course, diverted some of those proceeds to support revolutionary subversion in Russia. Was Zhivotovsky doing likewise? Were he and Parvus working together?

---

4. *Ibid.*, 118.

5. N. Svitkov, *Masonstvo v' russkoi emigratsii* (1932), 24.

6. Charles A. Ruud and Sergei A. Stepanov, *Fontanka 16: The Tsar's Secret Police* (1999), 221.

The Okhranka inquiry proved a dead end, but in May 1915 Army counter-intelligence took up the task. This culminated in a search of Zhivotovsky's Petrograd (the recently renamed St. Petersburg) offices on 2 July and his subsequent arrest and imprisonment.[7] Abram remained in custody through January 1916; his release was variously credited to lack of evidence, bribes or political influence. Back in business, he mostly suspended his import-export activities. Entering into a relationship with the Russian Commercial and Industrial (Torgprom) Bank, he began large-scale speculation in stocks and currency. By early 1917, when Trotsky contacted him, he had firmly established himself among Russia's "financial elite."[8]

Whether Zhivotovsky shared his nephew's Marxist views, or whether he assisted Trotsky out of generic anti-Tsarism or simple familial loyalty is uncertain. Probably, it was a combination of factors. If we have learned anything so far, it's that capitalist acumen and revolutionary sympathies are not mutually exclusive. Whatever the reason, Uncle Abram maintained his connection with Trotsky in the years leading up to 1917, and was available to render financial aid when needed. In the case of a professional revolutionary, that was most of the time. There was good reason for Trotsky to wire him upon reaching Christiania.

Nor did the Trostky-Zhivotovsky relationship end in 1917. In December 1918, a State Department circular identified A. L. Zhivotovsky "on a Bolshevik mission to Stockholm" where he was selling stock in Russian companies at rock bottom prices.[9] A report from early 1919 linked him to Soviet "political intrigues" in Copenhagen.[10] And there would be more to come.

It wasn't just Uncle Abram. In August 1918, the U.S. Bureau of Investigation opened a file on elder brother David, "Russian banker," who had applied for a visa to come to the States from Tokyo.[11] He gave Guaranty Trust and Equitable Trust as references and claimed his purpose in the U.S. was to pursue legal action against Guaranty Trust over a disputed account of $473,000. Further investigation revealed that David Zhivotovsky had another $150,000 tucked away with National City Bank. Yet he had never visited America before. So, who set up these accounts and where did the money come from? Was it Trotsky's? The State Department denied the visa, possibly because the Zhivotovsky name recently had come up in connection with the inauguration of "Bolshevist propaganda in Japan."[12]

---

7. Soon after the outbreak of the war, the Government replaced the distinctly Germanic St. Petersburg (*Sankt Peterburg*) with the more "patriotic" and slavicized Petrograd. In 1924, the Soviets would change the name to Leningrad and today it is once again St. Petersburg.

8. Ostrovsky, 123.

9. USDS, #000-999, "Who's Who," 28 Dec. 1918.

10. MID, #9728-459-24, "Political: Contre-Espionage," 15 April 1919.

11. BI, File #255788, "David L. Givotovsky," August 1918.

12. MID, #10058-NN-16, undated report (c. 1918).

SIDNEY REILLY: CONFIDENCE MAN, SPY, REVOLUTIONARY

Sidney George Reilly has earned posthumous fame as the "Ace of Spies" and model for James Bond. Both accolades are undeserved.[13] Most of what has been written about him, including by this author, has erred by taking all, or even part, of the Reilly legend at face value. His story is so larded with half-truths, disinformation and outright fantasy that it is all but impossible to separate the man from the myth. And that is exactly the way he wanted it, and others as well. In 1968, Soviet dissident Revolt Pimenov wrote a reassessment of Reilly's perhaps most famous episode – his involvement in a 1918 conspiracy to topple Lenin's government.[14] The so-called "Lockhart Plot" failed but not because, as the story goes, heroic anti-Bolshevik Reilly did his damnedest to make it succeed. Pimenov found that when that prejudice was set aside, the evidence clearly pointed to Reilly being a Bolshevik operative and the plot's primary betrayer. That assessment was correct.

A fundamental point often overlooked is that Reilly was never Reilly at all; that identity was never more than a convenient fiction. He probably first showed up as Leon Rosenblatt, a radical Jewish student from Odessa who the Okhranka found attending a medical school in Western Europe in 1894.[15] However, the first place he can be positively identified is London in early 1896 where he was elected a Fellow of the Chemical Society.[16] At this point he was calling himself Sigmund Saloman Georgevitch Rosenblum, and claimed to be the son of a "landed proprietor" with academic training in chemistry.[17] With the exception of his knowledge of chemistry, everything else was a lie. Somewhere along the line, he had also become a Freemason.

Rosenblum styled himself a "consulting chemist" and became a partner in an outfit called the Commercial Ozone Syndicate. He registered at least two patents in Britain and the United States.[18] These dealt with the refining of animal and vegetable fats with a particular application to paints

---

13. On the latter point, see: Richard B. Spence, "Aleister Crowley, Sidney Reilly, Basil Zaharoff: Their Influence on the Creation of James Bond and His World," in Robert Weiner, B. Lynn Whitfield and Jack Becker (eds.), *James Bond and Popular Culture: The Films Are Not Enough* (2010), 212-223.

14. Revolt Pimenov, "Kak ya iskal' shpionam Reilli" ["How I Searched for the Spy Reilly"] (1968), Radio Liberty Samizdat Archive, AC 1089 (1972).

15. HIA, Paris Okhrana Archive, XIIIh, Box 182, File #17.

16. Royal Chemical Society, London, *Fellows of the Chemical Society, 1896* (May-June).

17. Marriage certificate of Sigmund Georgjevich [sic] Rosenblum and Margaret Thomas, London, 22 Aug. 1898, Application #18945.

18. U.S. Senate, *Annual Report of the Commissioner of Patents, 1899*, 332.

and pigments.[19] This detail is not insignif-
icant. In London, he also joined the circle
around Polish revolutionary exile Wilfrid
Voynich, who had escaped Siberian exile five years earlier. Voynich was a close
friend of Stepniak, the founder of the
Friends of Russian Freedom. Voynich was
a charter member of same. Small world. In London, Voynich's cell busied
itself printing and smuggling revolutionary literature. They also counter-
feited Russian rubles, which is where an expertise in dyes and pigments
came in very handy. It also served the interests of Voynich's new cover
business, antiquarian book dealer. Starting in 1898, he was amazingly successful in unearthing previously "lost" medieval and renaissance treasures
which he sold for princely sums, the most famous being the bizarre *Voynich Manuscript written in an undecipherable alphabet.*[20] In all likelihood,
he forged most of them.

Rosenblum, meantime, had another job: informer to
Scotland Yard's redoubtable Chief Inspector, William Mel-
ville. In this way, he managed to secure a degree of protection for Voynich's operation. This arrangement blew up in
the spring of 1899 when Rosenblum's name surfaced in
connection to the counterfeiting operation.[21] The Okhranka dispatched a team from St. Petersburg to investigate. This
placed Melville, who maintained valuable collaboration with the Russian
secret police, in a delicate position. In June 1899, he handed Rosenblum a
British passport in the name of Sidney George Reilly, a dead Irish infant,
and packed him off to the Far East.

By 1901, the newly-minted Reilly was in Port Arthur, the Russian
naval bastion, working for the contracting and provisioning firm of M.
A. Ginsburg & Co. The latter, as noted, did business with Zhivotovsky. If
Uncle Abram and Reilly didn't know one another already, they certainly
met here. In late November 1903, just weeks before the outbreak of the
Russo-Japanese War, Reilly vanished while on a routine business trip to
Japan. Suffice it to say there was a woman involved, a wealthy American.[22]
In the spring of 1904, she and Reilly appeared in Rio. In January 1905, as
"Bloody Sunday" unfolded in Russia, he was living alone in Brussels. In
June, he popped up in Vienna where he obtained a fresh passport from
the British Embassy. Armed with that, Reilly headed to St. Petersburg.

19. *The Chemical Trade Journal and Oil, Paint and Colour Review*, Vol. 22 (Jan. 1898), 91.
20. The Voynich Manuscript or Codex is today held in Yale University's Beinecke Rare Book and
Manuscript Library. It has been described as everything from the lost masterpiece of Roger Ba-
con, to a carefully crafted hoax, to evidence of alien visitation. Another possibility is that it grew of
out Voynich's underground revolutionary work and efforts to create an unbreakable code.
21. Andrew Cook, *M: MIS's First Spymaster* (2004), 128.
22. Her name was Irene Gates Dawson.

The Okhranka picked up his scent in August and kept him under surveillance, suspecting him of being a British agent. He was, but that wasn't all.

For the next nine years, Reilly worked in St. Petersburg as a "commission agent" and insinuated himself into Russia's business and political establishment.[23] Meanwhile, he sold information to the British and anyone else who would pay him. He also maintained his links to the revolutionary underground. By 1914 he was a trusted associate of none other than Abram Zhivotovsky. One must wonder exactly why. Was it Reilly's amoral craftiness, his ideological sympathies, or was he, too, part of the *mishpocha*? One detail that suggests the last is Reilly's second wife, Nadine (Nadezhda) Zalessky, who he married in New York in early 1915. Her mother's maiden name was Brodskaya (Brodsky) and she haled from the prominent brewing and sugar refining clan in Kiev. Trotsky mentioned another uncle, Brodsky, the "brewer," probably Alexander Brodsky who was married to a Zhivotovsky.[24] Thus, Reilly ended up wed to a woman who was, to one degree or another, yet another cousin of Trotsky. And maybe his own relation.

In July 1914, as war loomed, Abram Zhivotovsky dispatched Reilly on a munitions purchasing mission to Japan. Accompanying him was another nephew and another Trotsky cousin, Joseph Davidovich Zhivotovsky. He was affiliated with the SRs. In Tokyo, Reilly and Zhivotovsky worked hand-in-glove with a Russian military mission sent to purchase artillery. The head of that mission was Gen. Eduard Karlovich Hermonius, a man whose future association and assistance would come in very handy.[25]

On Zhivotovsky's orders, or on his own initiative, Reilly left Joseph to handle things in Japan and headed to San Francisco, where he arrived on 6 January 1915. Calling himself a "representative of the Russian Government" (which he was not), on the 18th he briefly surfaced in Washington, DC. A few days later he was sitting in the Manhattan office of the Petrograd Trading Company at 120 Broadway. Petrograd Trading was an import-export firm owned by Abram Zhivotovsky.

120 BROADWAY

Reilly's new digs deserve a little elaboration. The Equitable Building, 120 Broadway, was the newest addition to lower Manhattan's skyline and there was no more desirable or prestigious office space in the city. The Equitable sat majestically in Wall Street's "Golden Circle" within two or three blocks of the Stock Exchange and the offices of J. P. Morgan, Kuhn

---

23. *Ves' Peterburg 1906*, 551.

24. Trotsky, *My Life*, 41.

25. Hermonius was an ethnic Finn in Russian service. The best guess is that Reilly and Hermonius had met before Tokyo, but the exact nature of their relationship is a mystery. Reilly later claimed that the General was the uncle of his then-wife, which he was not.

Loeb, and National City. Finishing touches were still being added; the new skyscraper had just opened its doors to tenants. As the name suggests, the building housed the corporate headquarters of the Equitable Life Insurance Co. along with Liberty National Bank, Empire Trust, Guggenheim Bros., Lazard Frères' Bank, Yokohama Specie Bank and the New York branch of the Federal Reserve. In November 1915, it also became the home of the American International Corporation, an entity discussed below. Guaranty Trust sat at neighboring 140 Broadway. The Equitable's top floors were reserved for the Bankers Club, a 100,000 square-foot playground and private get-away for the lords of

financial creation.[26] Charles Crane was a member, and so were Otto Kahn and Jacob Schiff.

AN INTERNATIONAL CROOK OF THE HIGHEST CLASS

For the better part of the next three years, Reilly's day job was contracting for weapons, munitions and other war supplies, an activity that netted him a small fortune in commissions. His business methods, however, raised eyebrows and questions. Reports reaching British intelligence credited him as "very clever" but cautioned that he was devoid of "patriotism or principles," "entirely unscrupulous," and wholly unsuitable for "any position which requires loyalty."[27] Other informants accused him of rampant graft, being "an enemy of the Allies," "employed by enemy agent[s] in propaganda or other activities," and part of a conspiracy "to send bad ammunition to Russia."[28] On Wall Street he earned the reputation of a "most astute criminal."[29] American investigators labeled Reilly and his cronies "international confidence men of the highest class."[30]

Nor was his reputation among the Russians any better. An exposé of the corruption-plagued Russian Supply Committee in New York lumped Reilly, Zhivotovsky, Friede (see below) and Posner (Ludwig Martens' employer) together as a profiteering cabal.[31] The chief of the Supply Committee's "Investigative Commission," Gen. Nicholas Kozlov, recalled a superior

26. "New Bankers Club is World's Biggest," *New York Times* (1 July 1915).

27. SIS, File #2616, CXM201, 13 March 1918 and CX 023996, 30 March 1918.

28. MID, #9140-817, In Re: Sidney G, Reilly, 9 July 1917.

29. BI, #39368, Memorandum for Lt. Irving, 21 Aug. 1918, 1.

30. ONI, #21010-3241, "Weinstein and Reilly," 17 Dec. 1918.

31. M. I. Gaiduk, *"Utiug": materialy i fakty o zagotovitel'noi deiatel'nosti russkikh voennykh komissii v Amerike* (1918), 16, 70.

113

explicitly warning him that Reilly was a "very suspicious man" who "by no means should … be admitted to any dealings with" the Committee.[32]

Yet he was. The explanation for this evidently lay in the "tremendous political backing" Reilly commanded in Russia, which, according to
American businessman Samuel Vauclain (head
of Baldwin Locomotive), led right up to Grand
Duke Alexander Mikhailovich, the Tsar's cousin
and brother-in-law.[33] The connection might have
stemmed from a common interest in aviation,
or the Grand Duke's earlier dealings with Zhi-

Vauclain

votovsky, but there may have been other factors at work. For instance,
Alexander Mikhailovich, Zhivotovsky and Reilly were all Freemasons.

The Grand Duke, not incidentally, had his own connections to Wall
Street. In August 1913, as plain "Mr. Alexander Romanoff," he arrived in
New York on ostensibly personal business. He spent much of the stay at
the palatial Astor estate in Newport, Rhode Island, the Summer capital of
the Eastern Elite.[34] Outwardly, Alexander Mikhailovich appeared loyal to
the Tsar, but he was a man of esoteric interests, and the American press
hinted at friction between him and his Emperor-cousin.[35]

The Grand Duke may have provided a link between Reilly and the
above General Hermonius. By 1915, Hermonius was in London where he
oversaw Russian war purchasing in both England and America. In other
words, he was the man you needed to know if you were after contracts. Reilly played host whenever the General visited New York. In London, Hermonius employed a certain Benjamin Sverdlov as a confidential courier.

Reilly was everything his critics described him as and more. Within
the cutthroat businessman still beat the heart of Rosenblum the revolutionary. His alliance with Zhivotovsky went deeper than mutual profiteering. His recent companion, Joseph Zhivotovsky, was a known revolutionary sympathizer. The above Benjamin Sverdlov, who Reilly helped
set up shop at the Equitable, was also "formerly a revolutionary in Russia."[36] Even closer to Reilly were Alexander Weinstein and Antony Jechalski. Weinstein was Zhivotovsky's agent in London until mid-1916, when
he came over to be Reilly's "right-hand-man." In London, he'd associated with Sverdlov, Ludwig Martens and Maxim Litvinov, Bolsheviks all.

32. USDS, "Ex. A", Memorandum, 4 Sept, 1918, attached to CSA File #215, Sharp to Bannerman, 13 Dec. 1924.

33. MID, #9140-6073, Memorandum #7, 12 Sept. 1918, 2 and Bond to Hunnewell and Smith, 11 Oct. 1918, 1.

34. "Grand Duke Alexander Left Pleasant Memories Here," *New York Times* (5 Oct. 1913), 84. Americans allegedly found him "very democratic and unaffected."

35. "Russian Grand Duke Visiting America, *Washington Post* (20 Aug. 1913), 4.

36. USDS, CSA 215, Sharp to Bannerman, 13 Dec. 1924, 11.

Plus, he was cousin to *Novy Mir's* business manager Gregory Weinstein. Outwardly a "loyal Russian," immediately after the fall of Tsar Nicholas, Weinstein hosted a gala celebratory bash for "Russians and Socialists," and thereafter "clearly identified with the Bolsheviki."[37]

Jechalski, who posed as a Polish nationalist, openly admitted to holding "more or less radical views."[38] American investigators variously labeled him a "notorious German spy," "labor agitator," and all around "suspicious person," so much so that Military Intelligence arrested him in May 1918 and kept him in a Texas lock-up for six months.[39] During 1914-15, Jechalski had worked in London beside Weinstein and Sverdlov. While there, he made trips to Stockholm and Copenhagen, allegedly on behalf of Polish and Jewish relief work. Those same cities, of course, were the headquarters of the Bolshevik Foreign Bureau and Parvus's operation. Most intriguing, back in New York, Jechalski served as the middle-man between *Polish groups and "certain Jewish* leaders."[40] One of those was Schiff intimate Rabbi Judah Magnus, and Schiff himself may have been another. Thus, Sidney Reilly was surrounded by crypto, and not so crypto, revolutionaries. And he was a bird of the same feather.

Even Reilly's old anti-Tsarist co-conspirator, Wilfrid Voynich, may have gotten in on the act. He appeared in New York in November 1914 and soon relocated his antiquarian business to an office in the Aeolian Building on West 42nd Street. The same location housed the Polish nationalist mission frequented by Jechalski. Voynich came to the attention of the U.S. Bureau of Investigation who determined he "professed great distrust of Russia," and was "an ardent student of the Russian revolution and is well-versed in Russian affairs."[41] How so?

Voynich had some sort of relationship with another denizen of the Aeolian, German-Jewish activist Isaac Strauss, publisher of the vehemently anti-Tsarist *American Jewish Chronicle.*[42] Strauss was an unequivocal "German agent and propagandist" later arrested and interned by American authorities.[43] His main job was whipping up "anti-Russian" sentiment among Jewish immigrants, an effort Jacob Schiff could only applaud.[44] Moreover, Strauss took a hand in "charitable work" among Jews in German-occupied Poland "in close contact with" Jacob Schiff, Felix Warburg and Judah Magnes.[45] Wilfrid

---

37. MID, #9140-6073, Memorandum #2, 23 Aug. 1918.

38. MID, #9140-1496, Bureau of Investigation to Office of Naval Intelligence, 23 Sept. 1921, 3.

39. ONI, #20010-3241, Cards associated with Weinstein-Reilly investigation, 1.

40. MID, #9140-1496, Statement of L. Kraevna, 15 May 1918.

41. BI, #33354, In Re: Wilfred Michael de Voynich, 7 July 1917 and In Re: Wilfred de Voynich, 29 July 1918.

42. On Strauss (or Straus) see: BI, #8000-3595.

43. Cohen, 192

44. *Ibid.*

45 *Ibid.*, 193

Voynich also spent time in Chicago where he reportedly "put it over most of the wealthy Chicagoans."[46] Was Charles Crane one of them?

Among Reilly's American business contacts, perhaps the most revealing was John McGregor Grant. As the plain "John McGregor Grant Co." he maintained offices at 120 Broadway, Stockholm and Petrograd. The vice president of this company, and Grant's trusted associate, was Carl Adolf Holstein, a "Russian revolutionist" active as far back as 1905.[47] At the same time, Grant was New York agent of the Russo-Asiatic Bank, which linked him to Zhivotovsky and Weinstein. Grant was co-owner of the Swedish Russo-Asiatic Co. which also had an office at 120. Grant's partner in the latter firm, and many other dealings, was socialist financier and revolutionary money launderer Olof Aschberg, who we will turn to directly. For good measure, Grant also worked with Benny Sverdlov. In 1917 Grant tried to involve the Brooklyn-based State Bank in a suspicious scheme "for transmitting funds to Russia."[48] Any way you turn it, Grant was in bed with Russian revolutionaries.

Wall Street-wise, another important connection was Reilly's "intimate friend and business associate," financial heavyweight Samuel McRoberts.[49] In addition to being vice-president of Rockefeller-dominated National City Bank (NCB), he was head of the American-Russian Chamber of Commerce and director of at least five additional corporations, two banks and the organizer and president of the Allied Machinery Company, also headquartered at 120 Broadway.[50] In 1916, McRoberts hired Reilly to oversee Allied's Russian business. Allied Machinery even had an office in Petrograd run by another Reilly pal, Alexander Mess.

AMERICAN INTERNATIONAL CORPORATION

In 1916 Allied Machinery became a wholly-owned subsidiary of American International Corporation, (AIC) which made Reilly the latter's agent as well.[51] Formed in November 1915, AIC was a speculative consortium of Wall Street high-rollers boasting $50 million in start-up capital. Banks, steel, shipping, construction, oil and railroads were all represented. To accommodate everyone, there were nine vice presidents and twenty-four directors. Among the former were Morgan's Willard Straight, Standard Oil's Richard P. Tinsley and National City's William S. Kies. National City men dominated the board of directors, including NCB president Frank Vanderlip, James A. Stillman, Percy Rockefeller, Robert Lovett, and Chicago meat-packing magnate J. Odgen Armour. Also on

---

46. BI, #33354," In Re: Wilfred Voynich, 22 Nov. 1917.

47. ONI, #20010-3241, Weinstein and Reilly, 11.

48. ONI, #20010-3241, *Ibid.*

49. BI, #39368, "Names in the Weinstein Case," 5.

50. "Official Changes Made at Allied Machinery," *Steel* (29 Nov. 1917), 1151.

51. *The Economist*, #56 (1 July 1916), 30.

board was Otto Kahn, representing Kuhn Loeb, John D. Ryan of Anaconda Copper, William Correy of Midvale Steel, A.A. Wiggin of Chase National, William Woodward of Hanover National, Ambrose Monell of International Nickel, Robert Dollar of Dollar Shipping lines, Charles Coffin of General Electric, George Baldwin of Pacific Mail lines, Theodore Vail of AT&T, and Charles Sabin of Guaranty Trust. AIC was the hottest ticket on Wall Street.

The avowed mission of the Corporation was the "successful promotion of American commerce and business in foreign countries," and its charter allowed it to engage in any type of business – except, oddly, banking.[52] Simply put, it was a vast scheme to invest burgeoning war profits in opportunities created by the same war. American International's attention was focused in three areas: Latin America, China and, of course, Russia. In 1916, AIC dispatched construction executive Frederick Holbrook to Petrograd to set up a branch office and the necessary banking accounts.

OLOF ASCHBERG: THE RED BANKER

Aschberg

Reilly's banker buddy McRoberts also enjoyed a chummy relationship with Olof Aschberg. Nicknamed the "Red" or "Bolshevik Banker," the Swedish Aschberg was a financially successful socialist (surprise!) who in 1912 founded the Stockholm Nya Banken ("New Bank") as a savings and loan institution for the working class.[53] A Swedish subject of Russian-Jewish ancestry, Aschberg was a fully-vested supporter of the anti-Tsarist cause. When the opportunity came to aid it, he rose to that task – and made a nice profit in the bargain.

In his memoirs, Aschberg recalled that he "foresaw great opportunities" in Russia and "had made many connections there" by the time the war broke out.[54] He learned that it was "most important to have good connection with the border guards" and mastered the delicate art of bribing them.[55] By means he does not describe, Aschberg also made friends in high places, among them the Tsar's Foreign Minister, Sergius Sazonov. [56]He and Aschberg "discussed the possibility of economic connection"

52. U.S. Senate, *United States Shipping Board Emergency Fleet Corporation History*, Vol. I (1920).

53. UCLA Library, Special Collections, Roger Mennevee Collection, #899, Box 914, Folder 50, "Olaf Aschberg." This file contains numerous newspaper clippings and other material documenting Aschberg's career from WWI through the 1950s.

54. Aschberg, Olof. *En vandrande jude från Glasbruksgatan*. Stockholm: Bonnier (1946), 114.

55. *Ibid.*, 115.

56. *Ibid.*, 117.

between Russia and the United States. Like some on Wall Street, Aschberg realized that with access to German capital severed and with Britain and France pre-occupied with their own needs, America offered the Russians the only opportunity for unfettered, large-scale borrowing. Through his Russian connections, in late 1915 Aschberg "got the assignment to go to the U.S.A. and negotiate for a loan to Russia."[57]

It was also in wartime Petrograd that Aschberg encountered, allegedly for the first time, Lenin's old comrade, Leonid Krasin.[58] The latter had outwardly abandoned radical politics and worked as manager of an expropriated German firm, Siemens-Schuckert AG. Through his friendship with industrialist Alexis Putilov (and how, exactly, had that come about?), Krasin also sat on the board of the Russo-Asiatic Bank, the same bank, of course, with which Zhivotovsky, Reilly and Weinstein were associated and with which Aschberg's Nya Banken

Krasin

would do much questionable business. There's that small world again.

Add to this that Aschberg's bank was the main vehicle through which Alexander Helpand-Parvus and his right-hand-man Furstenberg conducted their "commercial transactions" with Russia, transactions that deposited German or other funds in Bolshevik-controlled Petrograd bank accounts. Later defending himself and fellow Bolsheviks against the "German libel," Furtstenberg adamantly swore that while he *received* payments via the Nya Banken, he never sent so much as a kopek or pfennig *to* Russia.[59] However, Aschberg confessed that wasn't exactly true.[60] And who was Zhivotovsky's representative in Stockholm? Well, the same Olof Aschberg.

Between April 1915 and July 1916, Aschberg made four visits to the Big Apple. On the first, ostensibly as a tourist, one of his fellow-passengers was Col. Vladimir Nekrasov, a Russian officer of flexible conscience who would become one of Reilly's inside men at the Manhattan-based Russian Supply Committee. Small world strikes again. On his November 1915 visit, Aschberg gave his destination as Grant's Swedish-Russo-Asiatic office at 120 Broadway. He was in fact on a secret mission for the Russian Ministry of Finance with the aim of working out a deal with Guaranty Trust that would bypass the Morgan-British agreement on Allied war purchasing, an arrangement the Russians found both restrictive and costly.[61]

57. *Ibid.*, 118
58. *Ibid.*, 124-125.
59. Futrell, 166-167
60. *Ibid.*
61. Lebedev, 160.

Aschberg realized that the American financial market was "controlled by two competitive groups," Kuhn, Loeb & Co. and Morgan.[62] He knew that the latter was "considerably more powerful," but nevertheless decided to first approach the former. At Kuhn Loeb, he sat down with Felix Warburg who dutifully informed Aschberg that his father-in-law, Jacob Schiff, would never go along with any loan to Russia, at least not under present circumstances. Aschberg received a much warmer welcome at Guaranty Trust, and in the fall of 1915 he returned to Petrograd with one of the firm's officers, Grayson M.-P. Murphy. Aschberg discovered that American capitalists held gold to be "God the Father Almighty" and Murphy pressed the Russians to put up bullion as collateral for a loan.[63] After a three month stay, during which Murphy seemed "very pleased with what he had seen and experienced," he and Aschberg returned to New York.[64] There Guaranty Trust's Charles Sabin hosted a dinner in the swank Met-

Murphy

ropolitan Club where the Swede addressed the firm's assembled directors on the Russian situation and the advantages of advancing a loan. Based on Aschberg's and Murphy's advice, Guaranty Trust proposed a huge $200 million loan and dispatched one of its lawyers, Rolph Marsh, to Petrograd to hash-out the details.[65] However, the Tsar's advisers balked at the terms, and Marsh spent months waiting around the Russian capital without tangible result.

That provided an opportunity for McRoberts and National City Bank to get involved. In March 1916, McRoberts dispatched NCB exec John B. Young to Petrograd for further negotiations. It was a rather abrupt decision. Young's passport application indicated that the NCB board made the decision on the morning of 15 March and Young set the sail the next day. The result, in April, was a modest $11 million loan to the Tsar's Government, the first it had received from an American bank in many years. There would be more to come.

Samuel McRoberts also made the trip to Petrograd, and on 31 July 1916 he arrived back in New York in the company of Aschberg. On the same ship was Alexander Weinstein's good friend, and future Bolshevik activist, Nicholas Kuznetsov.[66] According to the passenger manifest, this time Aschberg was the official representative of the Imperial Ministry of Finance and its chief, Peter Bark. Remember that name.

---

62. Aschberg, 118.
63. *Ibid.*, 119.
64. *Ibid.*, 121.
65. *Ibid.*, 122.
66. BI, #39368, "Names in the Weinstein Case," 2.

In June 1916, the Russians finally agreed to a $50 million loan backed by a consortium of National City and Guaranty Trust as well as the J. P. Morgan, Kidder-Peabody and Lee Higginson banks. During the negotiations, Aschberg quietly arranged a separate loan of $5 million to the Russo-Asiatic Bank, ostensibly for the purchase of American goods.[67] Leonid Krasin, recall, sat on Russo-Asiatic's board.

Another loan soon followed. McRoberts waxed ecstatic about the opportunities awaiting American industries and investment capital in Russia.[68] Something big was on the horizon. Meanwhile, NCB made plans for branch offices in Petrograd and Moscow. With those in place, millions of dollars could flow freely between New

McRoberts

York and Russia. The branches would be ready to go by the end of 1916.

Why would a revolutionary sympathizer like Aschberg help the Tsar by arranging an American loan? More to the point, why would Bark or any Tsarist official engage a man of Aschberg's known affiliations to represent their interests in such a sensitive matter? Despite Felix Warburg's caution that his father-in-law would not be part of any Russian financial deal, these Aschberg-brokered loans encountered no apparent opposition from Jacob Schiff, the man who had stymied Russian borrowing on Wall Street for years. In late February 1916, Schiff came out swinging against a report that Russian credits might be offered on Wall Street.[69] What he smelled was likely the early negotiations between Aschberg and Guaranty Trust. Granting credits to a "master tyrant" and a government that was "brutality and inhumanity … run riot," Schiff thundered, "will be one of the most insidious pieces of financing ever done in this country." Whoever was responsible for such financing, he warned, "will have cause to regret it." Yet the loans subsequently went through without interference.

So, did the Old Man suddenly grow weary of the fight, or were there other reasons he stood down in the face of the Aschberg-McRoberts deal? That Aschberg was a Jew of radical inclination may have given him an entrée with Schiff that others would not have had. Aschberg could assure him that he was no toady of Nicholas II. Might he also have assured Schiff that however much these loans assisted the Russian war effort, they also could be utilized to finance the hated Tsar's downfall? If so, were men like Bark privy to such intentions? Did Nicholas have any real friends anywhere?

THE MANHATTAN NEXUS

Another man doing business at 120 Broadway was the earlier-mentioned Charles R. Flint who employed Reilly and Sverdlov as com-

---

67. Aschberg, 123-124.
68. "Banker Sees Russia as Rich Trade Field," *New York Times* (21 Aug. 1916).
69. "Objects to Russian Loan," *New York Times* (26 Feb. 1916),

mission agents in Russian rifle and ammunition contracts. Some of the most damning comments about Reilly came from executives in the Flint firm. Also in the same building was Marcus S. Friede, a "highly suspicious" Russian-born importer-exporter who just happened to be the exclusive Ford Motor agent for Russia.[70] Friede also was another business associate of Zhivotovsky.[71] Naturally.

Flint

At nearby 116 Broadway was Max Goldsmith whose insurance firm specialized in policies for war contracts. He also was a director of Equitable Life. In 1916, Goldsmith and Reilly became partners in a new import-export concern simply dubbed Traders, Inc., which was involved in sending goods and money to Russia.[72] This, apparently, was to pick up the slack from Zhivotovsky's defunct Petrograd Trading.

At 140 Broadway sat Kurt Orbanowski, a German-born engineer who had worked with Reilly in Russia. He, too, harbored revolutionary sympathies and served as vice-president of the American Steel Export Corporation, which did a good deal of Russian business. Orbanowski was a "particular friend" of a German-American banker, Adolf Pavenstedt.[73] In addition to being a friend and confidant of Berlin's Ambassador Count Johan von Bernstorff, Pavenstedt moonlighted as the "chief paymaster of the German Secret Service" in New York.[74] As even his harshest critics admitted, Reilly was a man with connections, connections that provided him means to acquire, control and move money.

Further evidence of Reilly's Wall Street reach can be seen in a lawsuit he filed in September 1916.[75] Heading the long list of defendants was Thomas Cochran, president of the Liberty National Bank and soon-to-be Morgan partner. Others included William Boyce Thompson of the New York Federal Reserve and future head of the American Red Cross mission to Russia; Charles H. Sabin, the foreign exchange wizard of Guaranty Trust, and the investment banking houses of William Salomon & Co., Luke, Banks and Weeks and Hallgarten & Co. It was nothing less than a frontal assault on the power of American finance. Reilly's complaint ostensibly concerned unpaid commissions and was "very quickly and silently

Cochran

Thompson

---

70. BI, #39368, *Ibid.*, 4.

71. *Ibid.*

72. *New York Export-Import Directory*, 1917.

73. USDS, CSA 215, Sharp to Bannerman, 13 Dec. 1924, 14.

74. "German Codes and Ciphers," *The World's Work*, Vol. 36 (May-Oct. 1918), 150.

75. Supreme Court, New York County, Sidney G. Reilly against Thomas Cochran and Other Defendants, #26606, 1916.

adjusted out of court."[76] Was it about commissions? Or was Reilly putting the squeeze on the bankers over something else?

The secret to Reilly's "power" was the influence he wielded among the legion of Russian inspectors and workers who labored on Russian armaments orders in American factories, orders financed by those same bankers. Among these inspectors and workmen were not a few revolutionary sympathizers and activists. Radical cells existed in every plant and slowdowns, strikes and sabotage were a constant concern. Reilly's basic job was to "keep the obstreperous Russians in line."[77] And so he did, when it suited him. Through the inspectors, he could literally turn production on and off. Much of this he doubtless accomplished with bribes, but thanks to his revolutionary connections he also had political clout.

A case in point is the so-called "Nekrasov Affair," which erupted in the fall of 1917. Recall that Col. Vladimir Nekrasov was one of Olof Aschberg's New York-bound shipmates two years prior. Once attached to the Imperial Russian Supply Committee, and ensconced in an office at 120 Broadway, Nekrasov became chief munitions inspector. In 1917, another New York Russian (actually Estonian), George Lurich, accused Nekrasov of selling information to German and Austrian agents, engineering delays and sabotage in the plants and abetting the distribution of anti-war propaganda.[78] Moreover, Nekrasov allegedly was helped in this by his personal "secretary" – Antony Jechalski. The same Antony Jechalski who was Reilly's crony. The same Antony Jechalski connected to Schiff-sponsored Jewish charities. In the end, Lurich, who claimed to be acting as an agent of the Kerensky regime, was unable to produce any hard evidence. His efforts were also undercut by other Russian officials as well as British intelligence in New York

Wiseman

The latter underscores Reilly's curious relationship with the chiefs of London's intelligence service in New York – Col. Sir William Wiseman and his #2, Maj. Norman Thwaites. In July 1917, Wiseman candidly admitted to the Americans that "it would not be in the least surprising" if Reilly "was employed by enemy agents in propaganda or other activities."[79] Nevertheless, as we'll see in the next chapter, Wiseman and Thwaites not only employed Reilly, Weinstein *and* Jechalski, but also actively shielded them from the prying eyes of the Yanks and Britain's own MI5.

In mid-December 1916, Sidney Reilly abruptly vanished from New York. But he would be back.

---

76. BI, #39368, Reports of 10 Sept. 1918, 2 and 11 Oct. 1918, 2.

77. *Ibid.*, Report of 2 Oct. 1918, 2.

78. HIA, Russia, Posol'stvo, File 370-12, "Col. Nekrasov."

79. MID, #9140-6073, "Sidney G. Reilly," 9 July 1917.

EDDYSTONE

While it jumps us ahead a bit, perhaps no incident better illustrates the threads connecting Reilly, Trotsky, the revolutionary gang at *Novy Mir* and American Big Business than the Eddystone Explosion of April 1917. On the 10th of that month, just four days after the United States joined the war against Germany, a series of violent explosions completely demolished Building F, the shell loading facility, at the Eddystone Ammunition Corporation (EAC) near Chester, Pennsylvania. Eighteen tons of black powder and 10,000 shrapnel shells went up in an inferno of fire and flying metal fragments.[80] One hundred twenty-nine workers, most of them young women, were blown to bits or mortally wounded. At least as many suffered serious injury. EAC management, and investigators, immediately pointed the finger at sabotage.[81] But whose?

Formed in 1915, Eddystone Ammunition was a subsidiary of Baldwin Locomotive Works and the brainchild of its president, Samuel Vauclain.[82] Soon after the start of the war, Vaulclain had gone to Russia in search of munitions contracts. While there, he discovered that his main competitor was none other than Sidney Reilly. Despite Reilly's effort to undercut Vauclain's price, the American secured the deal for 2,500,000 shrapnel shells and EAC was born. However, it was Vauclain who came away with a respect for Reilly's "tremendous political backing." The Russian official in New York with direct oversight of the Eddystone contract was none other than the above dubious Col. Nekrasov. Vauclain soon realized he needed someone who "had influence with the Russian clique" and could keep the shells rolling off the line.[83] Samuel McRoberts recommended Reilly and Vauclain hired him as a "consulting and technical engineer" with a guaranty of 25 cents for every shell passed by the Russian inspectors.[84]

As noted, the ranks of the inspectors included many with revolutionary sympathies. At Eddystone, two such men were brothers Morris and James (Yakov) Voskoff (or Woskoff). Both had also worked at *Novy Mir*, and so had a third brother, Samuel Voskoff, until he sailed for Russia with Trotsky at the end of March.[85] At Eddystone, the Voskoff brothers

---

80. "See Plot in Powder Blow-Up," *New York Times* (11 April 1917), 1, 2.

81. "Baldwin's Official Blames Conspirators for Munitions Blast that Killed 129 Persons," *Philadelphia Evening Ledger*, (11 April 1917), 1-2.

82. *History of the Eddystone Ammunition Corporation, 1915-1917* (c. 1919).

83. BI, #36368, Report of 11 Oct. 1918.

84. *Ibid.*, Report of 10 Sept. 1918, 2.

85. Louise Bryant later encountered Samuel in Russia where he headed the factory committee of

belonged to a revolutionary socialist cell headed by another employee, Michael Lagoda. Lagoda organized a mass "radical meeting" of Russian Eddystone employees on 24 March, and the Voskoff's were there.[86] So, too, said some rumors, was Trotsky himself, though that seems doubtful. Yet another comrade of this group was David Oldfield, sometime managing editor of *Novy Mir*. These were the men Reilly "handled" for Vauclain.

The counsel and lead investigator for EAC, J. Borton Weeks, discovered that barely an hour after the explosion, James Voskoff had wired *Novy Mir* with the message: "Explosion occurred today. Our crowd safe."[87] The Voskoff brothers found themselves under arrest and intense questioning. Their explanation seemed simply enough. James maintained that his message was merely to inform friends in New York that all comrades at Eddystone were safe. No one could produce evidence of anything more.

Weeks was not so easily convinced. He correctly noted that "at the time of the explosion a great many Russians were employed in the Eddystone plant, including a commission of inspectors."[88] He also discovered that Voskoff had fired off a second, almost identical, telegram to a "Meyers" in New York and Weeks became convinced that "Meyers" was a code name for Trotsky and that he somehow had been the mastermind of the whole thing.[89] The aim, Weeks believed, was to undermine the Russian war effort by destroying and delaying Russian munitions. As it turned out, "Meyers" was Bessie Marrias, Voskoff's common-law wife. Trotsky, in any case, was no longer in the U.S. on 10 April, nor was he in Russia. Rather, he was sitting in the Amherst POW camp.

Trotsky almost certainly had nothing to do with the explosion and likely neither did the Voskoffs. But Reilly might have. Not only did he have an old grudge against Vauclain and EAC, but on 17 March the Eddystone board had carried out a surprise reorganization of the company which cut Reilly and other commission agents out of the loop.[90] At the very least, this inspired him to mount

Amherst POW camp

the Sestoretsk plant near Petrograd: Bryant, *Six Red Months in Russia* (1918), 276.

86. BI, #14664, "Eddystone Explosion," Interrogation of Morris Voskoff, 14 May 1917.

87. "Believed Russian Plotters Caused Eddystone Explosion," *Lebanon Daily News* [PA], (27 April 1917), 1.

88. Robert O'Neill, "The Mystery Lives Where 129 Perished," *The Inquirer* [Philadelphia], (19 April 1992). www.philly.com/philly/archives/.

89. *Ibid.*

90. *Eddystone*, 21 and HIA, *Russia: Posol'stvo*, Box 93, File 2, Memo citing 13 March and 28 Aug.

a suit against Baldwin that would drag on until the end of 1924. Through his influence with inspectors and other employees, Reilly had the means to instigate sabotage. He could even justify it as a blow in the service of the Revolution, or on behalf of Comrade Trotsky; evidence of what could happen if he wasn't set free and allowed to get back to Russia.

1917 resolutions of EAC board.

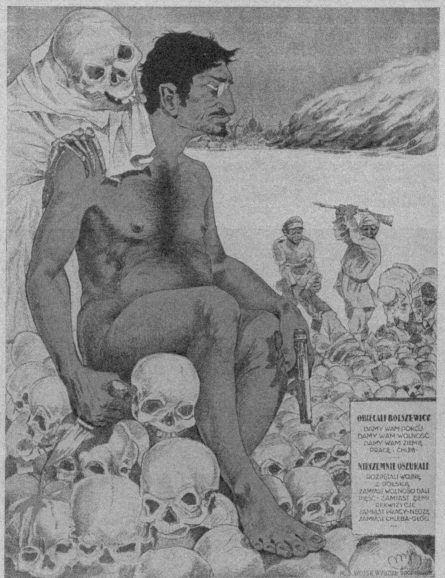

CHAPTER SEVEN

TROTSKY IN NEW YORK

THE WANDERING REVOLUTIONARY

Trotsky's journey to America began with his deportation from France to Spain in the fall of 1916. In 1907, he had slipped Siberian exile and spent most of the next seven years in Vienna. There he passed the time with occasional journalism, meetings and incessant polemics. Lenin was among those with whom he crossed rhetorical swords. Upon the outbreak of war he narrowly avoided internment in Austria and moved next door to neutral Switzerland. In November 1914, he moved again to Paris. Trotsky came under French scrutiny as early as July 1915 when the *Surete* marked him as a "Russian journalist of revolutionary stripe and socialistic tendencies who has association with suspect persons."[1] The same information found its way into British intelligence files.

Trotsky in Siberian exile, 1904

In the City of Light, Trotsky joined a crowd of Russian radicals associated with the Turgenev or Russian Library. He also assumed leadership of an anti-war group, *Comite pour la Reprise des Relations Internationales* ("Committee for the Resumption of International Relations"). For good measure, he joined the editorial board of the radical Russian paper *Nashe Slovo*. French authorities considered the paper "obviously Germanophile," and fretted over its influence among Russian troops sent to the Western Front.[2]

Trotsky later insisted he was the victim of a conspiracy hatched in the Tsarist Embassy and abetted by French President Aristide Briand and his *Ministere de l'Interieur* Louis-Jean Malvy.[3] It was Malvy who signed the 14 September 1916 order for Trotsky's arrest and expulsion to Spain as

---

1. TNA, KV2/502, "Bronstein, Trotsky, Leon," 19 July 1915.

2. *Ibid.*, "Trotzky (Leo Bronshein [sic] & Ianoffsky)," n.d., 1.

3. *Ibid.*, Trotsky to Uritsky, 24 Nov. 1916, 1-2. In the summer of 1917, Malvy found himself accused of treason and later stood trial on the charge. Although acquitted, the court did find him guilty of criminal negligence and exiled him from France. He went to Spain.

an "undesirable." Malvy, however, was a fellow socialist who had long resisted calls for the round-up
or deportation of radicals and other trouble-makers.
Some later accused Malvy of harboring ambitions
to become the "Trotsky of France" in a future revolutionary regime.[4] In October 1917 Malvy did, indeed, face treason charges for his involvement with a
German-subsidized radical paper and German agent
Paul Bolo Pasha. Interestingly, threads in this case
led back to New York. By any measure, Malvy was an
odd choice to be hounding Trotsky out of the country. Was the expulsion part of a plan to first get him
out of France and ultimately to the United States?

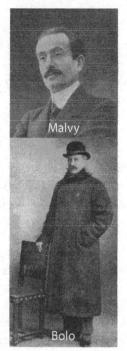

President Briand intervened and granted
Trotsky a month's grace, subsequently extended another fortnight, during which he frantically attempted to secure a visa to return to Switzerland. Trotsky
claimed that he was blocked by more conspiratorial
machinations. The British categorically refused to
grant him passage to Holland or Scandinavia.[5] This
lack of cooperation stands in stark contrast to the attitude of British officials in New York just a few months later.

On 30 October, two plainclothes policemen escorted Trotsky to the
Spanish border crossing at Irun. Temporarily left behind in France were
his spouse, Natalia Sedova, and their two young sons. Trotsky maintained

that his enemies pushed him into Spain in the hope that
reactionary Madrid would ship him off to the wilds of
South America. He initially dismissed the possibility
of passage to New York because there he could still "do
harm to the Ally propaganda."[6] After ten days as a free
man, Spanish police jailed Trotsky as a "dangerous terrorist agitator."[7] Trotsky again saw the long arm of his
powerful tormentors. In fact, he spent a mere three-and-a-half days in a
rather pleasant lock-up with plenty of food and cigarettes.

If Trotsky had enemies out to get him, he also had friends looking out
for him. A mysterious benefactor arranged his release from jail and his
transfer, under police supervision, to the southern port of Cadiz. There he
waited for another month and a half. While there, Trotsky wrote letter after
letter to comrades scattered across Europe. On 24 November, he penned

4. Severance Johnson, *The Enemy Within: Hitherto Unpublished Details of the Great Conspiracy to Corrupt and Destroy France* (1920), 9.

5. Trotsky, *My Life*, 200.

6. TNA, KV2/502, Trotsky to Uritsky, 24 Nov. 1916, 6.

7. *Ibid.*, 5.

a long and revealing one to Moisei Uritsky in Copenhagen.[8] "At Cadiz," wrote Trotsky, "they wanted to put me straight on a steamer bound for Havana, of course in steerage, with a wolf's passport [one bearing a "black mark" against the holder]." Trotsky raised a fuss, and once more the mysterious hand intervened; "There came from Madrid permission for me to be left at Cadiz until the first steamer sailed for New York." As he wrote Uritsky, he was waiting for a New York-bound liner scheduled to leave Cadiz on 30 November. For unknown reasons, that did not come to pass, and he was stuck in Cadiz for another month. He again sought passage to Switzerland, but again without success. The simple fact was that Trotsky lacked the means to travel anywhere. He confessed to Uritsky that when he arrived in Cadiz, "I had only about 40 francs left."[9]

In Copenhagen, Uritsky worked closely with the now familiar Alexander Helphand-Parvus. Uritsky oversaw a clandestine "courier service" which also transferred money.[10] Had Trotsky known that? Trotsky and Parvus, of course, had once been the closest of comrades and "intellectual partners."[11] However, in 1915 Trotsky published an "Epitaph" in *Nashe Slovo* in which he proclaimed Parvus a political dead man.[12] The ostensible reason was Parvus' flaming pro-Germanism. Parvus had reached the conclusion that the interests of International Socialism would be best served by the victory of the nation with the most advanced proletariat, i.e., Germany.[13] In early 1915, he had persuaded the Kaiser's men to fund a subversive offensive against the Romanov regime.

But was Trotsky's feud with Parvus partly an act? Did his denunciation, which stopped short of calling Parvus a German agent, mask ongoing collaboration? Even if Trotsky was through with Parvus, it did not mean that Parvus was through with him. For instance, despite Trotsky's and *Nashe Slovo's* hostility, Parvus channeled German money to the paper to aid its defeatist work.[14]

Trotsky's tale of persecution in Spain does not ring true. At each step of the way, he was treated with kid gloves and despite being officially indigent was never without food, shelter or amenities. He seems to have been purposefully directed to the ship that finally would take him to New York. Moreover, Trotsky knew, or reasonably suspected, that his correspon-

---

8. *Ibid.*

9. *Ibid.*

10. Zeman and Scharlau, 161-162.

11. *Ibid.*, 64-67.

12. *Ibid.*, 155.

13. On this point see also: Heinz Schurer, "Alexander Helphand-Parvus – Russian Revolutionary and German Patriot," *Russian Review*, Vol. 18, #4 (Oct. 1959), 313-331.

14. This money came via another future Soviet luminary, Christian Rakovsky. French and British intelligence were aware of this: KV2/502, "Trotzky," 1. See also: Zeman and Scharlau, 155, and Alfred Erich Senn, "The Myth of German Gold during the First World War," *Soviet Studies*, Vol. 28, #1 (Jan. 1976), 89.

dence was being monitored. It was: French and British intelligence intercepted and read his letters. In another missive to Uritsky, he cautioned that the wording of their correspondence should be "extremely prudent" because of "present circumstances."[15]

Towards the end of December, Trotsky suddenly learned that he was booked to sail for America, not from Cadiz, but from Barcelona all the way on the other side of the country. This was odd, because the same ship would stop in Cadiz a day or two later, and he could have boarded there. Likewise, he could receive both tickets and money in Cadiz. He must have returned to Barcelona to meet *someone*. Most obviously, he was re-united with Natalia and boys, and the happy little family even had time to go sight-seeing before departing. But Natalia, too, could just as easily have met him in Cadiz.

Jack Johnson

Did it mean anything that Allied Machinery, the AIC subsidiary with which Reilly was connected, maintained a branch office in Barcelona? An even more interesting outfit there was "La Informacion – Jack Johnson & Co." an advertising/publicity agency nominally run by fugitive American boxer Jack Johnson. Local scuttlebutt held that the firm was a "cloak for German activities," propaganda and otherwise.[16] More significant, perhaps, was Johnson's partner Moritz Moisevics, like Trotsky, he was a Russian revolutionist deported from France and a known German agent. Did Moisevics also connect to Parvus?

The vessel that Trotsky and family boarded in Barcelona was the *SS Montserrat*. Trotsky remembered that they boarded on Christmas Day, but the ship did not sail until the 28th. He described the *Montserrat* as "an old tub little suited for ocean voyages."[17] The liner surely had seen its better days; at a mere 4,000 tons, it must have provided a lively ride in rough weather. Trotsky also complained about the exorbitant fares charged by the Spanish operators and the "bad accommodations and even worse food."[18] Of course, he wasn't paying for any of it.

If the *Montserrat* was not top-of-the-line in oceanic travel, the Trotskys still had the best it could offer. The ship could haul more than a thousand passengers, but on this crossing she carried fewer than 350. Trotsky and family were among the few score *first-class* passengers. Four first-cabin passages, even with a discount for the minors, would have run at least $250 and possibly more than $400. In either case, this was far beyond the means of a man who only days before had nothing but pocket

15. TNA, KV2/502, Trotsky to Uritsky, 26 Nov. 1916.
16. Randy Roberts, *Papa Jack: Jack Johnson and the Era of White Hopes* (1983), 208-209.
17. Trotsky, *My Life*, 207.
18. *Ibid.*

change. Moreover, American immigration showed that the fares had been purchased *for* him – not *by* him.

HELPING HANDS

This brings us back to that mysterious helping hand. A story that later circulated in Spain held that the "benefactor" was the Marques de Comillas, one of the country's richest men and, in fact, the owner of the shipping company that operated the *Montserrat*. Supposedly, the Marques so feared Trotsky's revolutionary influence that he offered him 5,000 pesetas and a ticket to Mexico just to get him out of Spain.[19] Trotsky, of course, did not go to Mexico. The mystery is solved, in part, by a 1917 French intelligence report from Barcelona. It fingered Trotsky's financial angel as Ernst (Ernesto) Bark, a long-time Russian émigré resident of Madrid.[20] Among his known associates was the above Moritz Moisevics. More revealing, he was a cousin of Russian Minister of Finance Peter Bark, the same man who employed Olof Aschberg and did business with National City Bank and Samuel McRoberts. It was Ernst Bark who provided Trotsky "the money necessary to pay his passage to America."[21] The French report added that Bark also arranged Trotsky's release from the Madrid lock-up and, we may suspect, it was Bark who kept him comfy in Cadiz and safe from a slow boat to Cuba.

The big question is whether Bark provided all this help on his own initiative, or was he was acting for someone else? Bark was a prominent member of Spain's radical community. He came from a Baltic German noble family in what is today Estonia and attended German universities. He had personal connections in Germany and a deep admiration of its culture, traits he shared with Parvus – and Jacob Schiff. Bark also championed the liberation of his Baltic homeland from Tsarist rule, which meshed with Parvus' support of separatist causes.[22] The French dossier indicates that Bark's association with Trotsky continued after the establishment of the Soviet regime; a notation dated 25 January 1919 describes Bark as an "*Agent bolcheviste.*"

But the story has an added twist. On 26 November, Trotsky fired off another letter to Uritsky, it, too, duly intercepted and translated by the French.[23] In it, he tells Uritsky "I received the telegram by which you sent me the money; I thank you." So Uritsky, which is to say Parvus, was helping out to some degree. Trotsky then adds: "Mme J. Sch. has telegraphed

19. "Claudio Lopez Bru" (Marques de Comillas), http://filosofia.org/ave/001/a174.htm.

20. On Bark, see: Dolores Thion Soriano-Molla, *Ernesto Bark: Un Propagandista de la Modernidad* (Valencia: Instituto de Cultura Juan Gil-Albert, 1998).

21. AGF, Deuxieme Bureau (dossiers repatriees), File Z 26610, Report G15 from Barcelona, 26 Dec. 1917.

22. Futrell, 40-42 and 119-151.

23. TNA, KV2/502, *Ibid.*

to Russia that my money be sent to [Cadiz]; I fear encountering the same obstacles that you ran into. If Mme. Sch. obtains enough money, she will also come here with her son and we all go together to New York. The police have advised that she is not permitted to remain (in Spain?) after 1 December." So, Trotsky was looking to get *more* money, apparently from or via Russia and the agent of this arrangement was a Madame J. Sch. She must have been the person he needed to meet in Barcelona. Was her money coming from Uncle Abram or someone else? Was it what Bark used to buy the tickets, or was Trotsky receiving funds from multiple sources?

Obviously "J. Sch." evokes none other than Jacob Schiff, but what could he have to do with this, much less his wife? Like her husband, Therese Loeb Schiff was heavily involved with charities, and so long as he lived Jacob "directed much of his wife's philanthropic activity."[24] Thus, he would have had access to any of her accounts. As the dominant figure in the Joint Distribution Committee and other Jewish relief work in Russia, Schiff could have arranged a discreet diversion of cash from those accounts. But that seems a rather complicated way to handle the matter. This much is certain:

Therese Schiff

Therese Schiff was not in Spain or anywhere outside the U.S. in 1916. She could not have been Madame J. Schiff. So, who was?

Recall that the mystery Madame was accompanied by her son and the pair planned to travel to the States with Trotsky, funds permitting. There was only one mother-son combo aboard the *Montserrat* and they are listed on the manifest immediately following the Trotskys. They were fifty-two year-old Sarah Raiss and her twenty-six year old son, Moise. Sarah Raiss was the widow of Marc Raiss, a businessman, and they had two sons, Moise and David. They were Romanian Jews from Bucharest who had moved to Paris some years earlier. Sarah and Moise had visited New York the previous October, arriving just days after Alexandra Kollontai showed up from Copenhagen. Was this meaningless coincidence or a subtle indication that there was something much bigger going on?

The other Raiss son, David, had also come to New York in 1915, where he worked as a jewelry salesman. Mother and brother were supposedly coming to live with him. It all seems innocent enough. However, David's Manhattan address, 324 E. 9th St. was immediately behind 77 St. Marks Pl., the offices of *Novy Mir*, the very place that became Trotsky's New York headquarters. That seems a bit much to be coincidence. Sarah Raiss must have been the woman Trotsky mentioned to Uritsky, yet nothing in her name or anyone around her can be connected to "J. Sch." The best bet is that Trotsky was being "extremely prudent" and shielding her

24. Idana Goldberg, "Therese Loeb Schiff," *Jewish Women's' Archive Encyclopedia*. http://jwa.org/encyclopedia/article/schiff-therese-loeb.

identity. But why, of all the initials he might have chosen did he pick "J. Sch."? Why not just "Madame X"? Was it to acknowledge to Uritsky who the real source of the money was?

There is one detail that shows a Schiff connection to Spain. A September 1916 report to the U.S. Justice Department quotes an intercepted letter from a former Austrian diplomat in the United States to Alexander von Nuber, a director of the New York Transatlantic Trust Co.[25] In it, the diplomat asks von Nuber to deliver an enclosed letter to "Herr Schiff through Kuhn, Loeb & Co." The second letter, written in Spanish, was addressed to "a Spanish senator in Madrid." and appeared to concern "food conditions in Austria," though most of its content was unreadable. The cooperation of a senator could have come in very handy in pulling strings for Trotsky. "The name Schiff," the report noted, "again appears near the close of the letter." It may have nothing whatsoever to do with Trotsky, but the evident links between Jacob Schiff, an Austrian diplomat and a Spanish senator are definitely intriguing.

Why would Parvus, or Schiff, or anyone have wanted to get Trotsky to America? A partial answer may be found in Parvus' reports to Berlin. He argued that the U.S., with its "enormous number of Jews and Slavs," offered a "very receptive element for anti-Tsarist agitation."[26] A celebrated Russian-Jewish socialist like Trotsky was the ideal man to lead such an effort. Along the same lines, a report to U.S. Military Intelligence from Copenhagen in early 1918 declared that Trotsky "was bought by the Germans" and that he had "arranged [the] Bolshevik movement together with [Parvus]."[27] Equally important, the American scene offered rich new avenues for fund-raising. An early 1917 report to the Russian secret police from their agent in New York claimed that Trotsky came to America with the specific aim of securing funds to support revolutionary activities in Russia and Europe.[28]

PLOTTING A NEW REVOLUTION

Before launching Trotsky on his trans-Atlantic voyage, we need to catch-up on some developments in the U.S. and Russia months earlier. At the beginning of 1916, Parvus believed the time was right to ignite the new revolution in Russia. His target date was 22 January, the eleventh anniversary of Bloody Sunday.[29] A wave of strikes would paralyze production and spark a bank panic that would, hopefully, finish off the Tsarist

25. BI, #8000-449, "Letter in German, dated Vienna, July 16…," 27 Sept. 1916.

26. Zeman and Scharlau, 148 and Alan Moorehead, *The Russian Revolution* (1958), 111-112.

27. MID, #2059-109, 4 May 1918.

28. HIA, Paris Okhrana, XVIIc, folder 2, #99 from Paris, 27 Jan./9 Feb. 1917. Re Patrick, see, *Ibid.*, "Deep Cover Agents – Russian (L-Z)."

29. Zeman and Scharlau, 187-189.

beast once and for all. On 11 January 10,000 workers downed their tools at the naval works at Nikolayev. On the 22nd another 45,000 walked off the job in Petrograd. Despite Parvus' best laid plans, however, the flame failed to ignite. The Second Revolution would clearly need a bigger push.

As if on cue, a meeting reportedly convened in New York's East Side on 14 February. Attending were sixty-two members of the "Russian Revolutionary Party" including fifty veterans of 1905. "A large percentage" were Jews with many belonging to the "intellectual classes" including doctors. "Secret reports" had arrived from Russia proclaiming that "the most favorable moment for [revolution] is close at hand." Was this Parvus asking for help? The topic of conversation inevitably turned to money. Some comrades argued that the whole issue could be solved with the help of "persons in sympathy with the movement." Rich persons, that is. In the report, "the name of Jacob Schiff was repeatedly mentioned." However, the report identified the "soul" of this movement to be not Schiff or Parvus but the German Ambassador in Washington, Count von Bernstorff.

The above report is problematic because the only identifiable source for it is the 1921 book *The World at the Crossroads* by Boris L'vovich Brasol.[30] During 1916-17, Brasol was an investigative officer attached to the Russian mission in New York with offices in the Flatiron Building. Working out of the same Flatiron offices was the alleged author of the report, Col. Nicholas Goleevsky, the Russian military attaché. It is plausible that Brasol would have seen the report and even had a copy. The rub is that Brasol was both a very clever and a very dedicated anti-Semite; he was later instrumental in translating and disseminating the *Protocols of the Elders of Zion* in the United States.[31] Anything he said involving Jews must be approached very carefully. In this case, he is probably quoting a genuine report by Goleevsky. The question is whether he quotes it accurately. Goleevsky effectively monitored Russian radicals in the States – so effectively that some hatched a plot to assassinate him.[32] The report doesn't say anything beyond what might be expected. Any East Side assembly of revolutionaries would include many with links to 1905 and many Jews. Nor would it have been unusual for Schiff's name to come up. After all, if one was looking for a wealthy American who was an avowed enemy of Bloody Nicholas and willing to underwrite propaganda, Schiff was your man.

The *New York Times* noted another curious gathering that took place just a few days later.[33] On 20 February, "a number of prominent persons" attended a "special Masonic service" at Manhattan's Temple Emanu-El.

30. Brasol, *The World at the Crossroads* (1921), 69-70.

31. On Brasol see: Richard B. Spence, "The Tsar's Other Lieutenant, The Anti-Semitic Activities of Boris L'vovich Brasol, 1910-1960: Pt.I, Beilis, the Protocols and Henry Ford," *Journal for the Study of Antisemtism* (June 2012).

32. "Plot Arrest is Likely," *New York Tribune* (30 Nov. 1915), 2.

33. "Advocates a World State," *New York Times* (21 Feb. 1916).

Only members of the Masonic Shakespeare Lodge #750 and invited guests were present. The host was Lodge Master Harry P. Fierst a wealthy (and Russian-born) clothing manufacturer. The service convened in the most exclusive Reform synagogue in the City, and the man delivering the special sermon title "World Brotherhood and World Peace" was its Rabbi, Joseph Silverman. Silverman told his audience that it was the duty of Masonic and kindred orders "to see actual human unity and to make the world see it." He noted that when religion and fraternal societies failed, "men sometimes resorted to force in the effort to create human fellowship. ... There can be no world peace until there is world brotherhood," he explained, and "advo-

Fierst

Silverman

cated a world state as the means for bringing about world brotherhood." Emanu-El, of course, was Schiff's temple and Silverman his friend. Harry Fierst was Schiff's associate in the realm of Jewish charities. If Schiff was not among the "prominent persons" in attendance, many of his friends surely were. There is, of course, nothing tangible to link the upscale Emanu-El service to the previous week's motley assembly of East Side revolutionaries. But if one was looking for well-heeled, broadly sympathetic potential donors, it would have provided an unparalleled opportunity; all within the sanctity and secrecy of the lodge.

Just three days later, who should arrive in town but the earlier-mentioned French conspirator Paul Bolo Pasha. He came to New York to collect German-originated funds which he would use to subsidize defeatist propaganda in France. When he sailed back to Europe in March, he had $1,700,000 secured with the help of "unsuspecting banking houses in New York" in what investigators called a "gigantic financial camouflage."[34] The Wall Street bankers may have been unsuspecting but they weren't unwilling. "International banking houses literally sought [Bolo's] patronage," claimed the report. Most deeply compromised was G. Amsinck & Co., the very same Amsinck soon acquired by American International. The Bolo Pasha case is interesting because it reveals New York to be the center of a financial conspiracy aimed at funding defeatism and subversion. What could be done in France, of course, could be done in Russia.

In early June 1916, Jacob Schiff was back in the news. On the 4th he made a surprise appearance at a meeting of the New York Kehillah (a Jewish community organization).[35] There, in front of 1,000 delegates representing "East Side intellectuals" and "financiers of Wall Street," Schiff, with tears in his eyes, dramatically announced, "I am through forever with Jewish politics," and proclaimed that he would henceforth serve Jews

---

34. "U.S. Operations Will Be Used in Bolo's Trial," *Indianapolis News* (5 Oct. 1917), 6.
35. "Schiff Weeps on Retiring as Jewish Leader," *New York Tribune* (5 June 1916), 1, 11.

purely as a "private individual." As he stalked out of the hall, some of the multitude wept while others, mostly the East Siders, hissed.

While that drama played out in New York, in Petrograd, Samuel McRoberts, Olof Aschberg and Peter Bark put the finishing touches on a big loan to the Russian Government. On 22 June, the *Times* announced that an American syndicate led by National City Bank had just inked a deal for a $50,000,000 loan.[36] Schiff undoubtedly was aware of these negotiations, and so were others. Yet, as noted, he does not seem to have lifted a finger to stop the deal. Is this what his "retirement" was all about? Was he damned by the East Siders because he failed to obstruct the loan or because they feared he might?

Peter Bark

AMERICAN RECEPTION

The *Montserrat* finally left Cadiz on 1 January 1917 and entered New York Harbor very late on the night of the 13th. The passenger manifest prepared for U.S. immigration reveals several interesting details.[37] Trotsky listed his occupation as "Author" and attested that he was neither an anarchist nor a polygamist. He also carried $500, the equivalent of roughly $10,000 today. This belies Trotsky's and Ludwig Lore's claim that the Great Exile arrived "practically penniless."[38] The Trotskys' immediate lodging was the swank Hotel Astor near Times Square. Not only was this one of the most expensive hostelries in the city, it had a reputation as a gathering place for the Wall Street elite – a curious place for a revolutionary socialist to take his rest. Given that Trotsky had no acquaintance with NYC and its amenities, someone surely made the reservation for him. Who? The mysterious generosity clearly did not stop at buying tickets.

Trotsky's appearance coincided (coincidentally or not) with other arrivals in New York. In mid January, Sidney Reilly, who had vanished a few weeks before, suddenly resurfaced at 120 Broadway. The following month he threw a lavish party for all his cronies (and Trotsky?) to celebrate his wedding anniversary with a woman he'd already tired of. Was there another agenda on hand? On 8 January, Antony Jechalski also landed back in New York from Havana. Recall that Trotsky at one point had thought he was headed to Cuba. Was Jechalski there as a contingency? On 21 January three more travelers arrived on the same ship. The first was a Norwegian businessman, Jonas Lied, a man with many business interests in Russia

---

36. "Russians Gratified by American Loan," *New York Times* (22 June 1916).

37. Names in passenger lists, particularly Russian ones, are subject to wide variations in spelling and frequent errors in transcription. In this case, Trotsky's is rendered "Zratsky, Leon."

38. Ludwig Lore, "When Trotsky Lived in New York," 3. University of Indiana, Lilly Library, Special Collections, Browne MSS.

and another associate of Olof Aschberg. Second was Evgeny Kuzmin, who claimed to be an agent of Russian military intelligence. Last was Maria de Victorica, a veteran German operative dispatched to the States to organize a new espionage and sabotage apparatus in anticipation of America joining the war. Was one of her assignments liaising with Trotsky?

Ludwig Lore recalled, "when Trotsky landed here his name was known only to his countrymen and to a handful of German Socialists."[39] Maybe; but his arrival was not unheralded. *Novy Mir* announced it on 6 December. They were tipped off by a wire from Trotsky himself. At the same time, information reaching the Okhranka indicated that, "the majority of Russian and Jewish socialists in New York" eagerly anticipated his arrival and welcomed him with a "grand reception" which attracted delegates from "other cities."[40] Someone had been preparing the ground for Comrade Trotsky.

The Trotskys received a warm welcome on a wet morning when they stepped off the *Montserrat*. The *Novy Mir* crowd was there in force; Bukharin rushed up to give the arrival a bear hug and Kollontai hovered nearby. Someone alerted the press, and the *New York Times* had a reporter on scene. In his account, the "Pacifist editor" and socialist who had been "expelled from four lands" was also greeted on the rain-swept pier by Arthur Concors of the Hebrew Sheltering and Immigrant Aid Society.[41] Concors

acted as Trotsky's translator in a brief interview, which included details at odds with actual events. For instance, Trotsky said he had been "in Berlin editing a Jewish paper," not Vienna, when the war began. Also, he claimed that after his release from the Madrid jail, he went to Seville and only reached Cadiz when taken there by Spanish police and *forcibly* put aboard the *Montserrat*. This was at best creative fiction, and a reminder that Trotsky's self-serving accounts always need to be taken with a grain of salt.

The Hebrew Sheltering and Immigrant Aid Society, which Concors represented, was a charitable organization dedicated to helping Jewish arrivals with food, housing and jobs. It also weeded out undesirables and promoted "Americanization" among the newcomers. Trotsky and family didn't really fit this bill. Nor was Arthur Concors a simple staffer. He was

---

39. Lore, "Leon Trotsky," in *One Year of Revolution: Celebrating the First Anniversary of the Founding of the Russian Soviet Republic: Nov. 7, 1918* (Brooklyn: *The Class Struggle*, 1918).

40. HIA, Paris Okhrana, XVIIc, Folder 2, #99, 27 Jan./9 Feb. 1917.

41. "Expelled from Four Lands," *New York Times* (15 Jan 1917), 2.

"superintendent" of the Society and a member of its board of directors.[42] Someone got Concors out of bed on a dark, chilly morning to play nurse-maid to a wandering revolutionary, a man supposedly unknown outside a narrow political sphere. Who could do that?

Wise

The answer lies in the men Concors answered to. The Society's board boasted several luminaries of the American Jewish establishment, among them Julian Mack, Louis Marshall, Oscar Straus and Rabbi Stephen Wise. The most important though, the Society's main financial backer, and Concors' "boss," was Jacob Henry Schiff.[43]

SCHIFF AND TROTSKY

It has since become a virtual article of faith in some quarters that Schiff not only bankrolled Trotsky, but also acted as a financial mainstay to the subsequent Soviet regime. For instance, Trotsky allegedly had been "seen going in and out of Schiff's New York mansion," and he received "$20 million in Jacob Schiff gold to help finance the revolution."[44] In fact, there are no contemporary references to Trotsky being seen with Schiff or at any of his residences. Of course, if the meetings were clandestine, there should be no

Under Jacob Schiff's portrait, L-R: Gilbert Kahn (Son of Otto Kahn), John M. Schiff, Frederick Warburg (Schiff Grandsons).

record. The "$20 million" appears to be a garbled line from an oft-quoted 1949 column by "Cholly Knickerbocker." In fact it reads: "Today it is estimated by Jacob's grandson, John Schiff, a prominent member of New York Society, that the old man sank around $20 million for the final triumph of Bolshevism in Russia."[45] John Schiff is nowhere on record as saying this anywhere else. Knickerbocker was the pen name of Igor Cassini, a gossip columnist who made a career out of peddling rumors and making things up.[46]

The real question is what would Schiff have gotten out of backing Trotsky? The focus of his interest in Russia was the liberty and welfare of the Empire's Jews. He accepted that revolution was the surest means to end oppression and usher in a brighter future. It followed that a revo-

---

42. BI, #8000-116148, "In re: Leon Bronstein Trotzky (Trotsky) [hereafter, Becker Report]," and *American Jewish Yearbook, 1914-15*, 285.

43. *Jewish Yearbook, Ibid.*

44. David Allen Rivera, *Final Warning: A History of the New World Order* (1994). http://modern-historyproject.org/mhp?Article=FinalWarning&C=7.3.

45. "Cholly Knickerbocker," *New York Journal-American* (3 Feb. 1949). The date is sometimes given as 1 February. The column was syndicated by the Hearst press.

46. Cassini was a grandson of a former Tsarist ambassador to the United States, Count Artur Cassini.

lution influenced by Jews would have an even better chance of achieving that end. Trotsky's was an important name among Russian revolutionists, Jewish and non-Jewish, and he had shown himself to be a man of energy and ability. Was a revolution with Trotsky at its helm a good investment? Schiff's whole career and fortune had been based on sizing up men and seizing – or creating – opportunities.

To be clear, there is absolutely no documentary evidence that Jacob Schiff gave Trotsky a penny. There are, however, several circumstantial threads connecting them. This warrants suspicion, but no more. Again, the whole point of clandestine activity is that it's clandestine. If done right, it is never supposed to be verifiable. Anyone who demands a canceled check made out to Trotsky with Schiff's signature misses this point entirely. Schiff would have been careful about keeping "cut-outs" between himself and Trotsky or any revolutionaries. Concors would have served that role admirably, but he may not have been the only one.

Concors, or someone, reserved the rooms for the Trotskys at the Astor. Staying there at the same time was one Otto Schwarzschild. He recently had returned from Germany and occupied Poland. There he'd represented the "Committee for the East" (*Komitee fur den Osten*), a relief organization set up to aid Jews in war-torn Eastern Europe. However, the Committee also allegedly "disseminated pro-German propaganda among the Jews."[47] Among its main backers, naturally, was Jacob Schiff. Schwarzschild was reliably reported to have "visited Jacob Schiff a number of times during 1916-17."[48] He also happened to be Schiff's kinsman. Schwarzschild was another ideal cut-out, assuming he wasn't representing the Germans outright. But are we simply talking about two side of the same coin?

As noted, Jacob Schiff had strong familial and business ties to Germany. His anti-Russian efforts, while serving Jewish interests, equally served Berlin's. Just how closely did Schiff associate himself with German clandestine operations? Information in the hands of American military intelligence showed that in 1915 he had contact with a "Baron Rapp" who "interested [him] in [a] propaganda movement to overthrow the Czar of Russia to free the Russian Jews."[49] This man was Baron Friedrich von der Ropp, a Baltic nobleman who showed up in New York in April 1915 attached to the Russian Consulate. In 1916 he revealed himself an "agent of the German Government" and a founder of the Stockholm-based *Ligue des Allogenes de l'Empire Russe* which aimed at the liberation of the Tsar's non-Russian subjects. The American report stated, "Jacob Schiff sent several millions of dollars to Berlin for

Ropp

47. Eli Barnavi, "WWI and the Jews," www.myjewishlearning.com/history_community/Modern/Over…, 2.
48. RIP, "Information Gathered in America…."
49. *Ibid.*

this purpose and several men, well known to the U.S. Secret Service agent, were connected with this matter."[50] It should come as no surprise that in Stockholm Ropp dealt with both Fritz Warburg and Parvus. Warburg could have provided the introduction to Schiff. The same Ropp also had dealings with Lenin and even paid some of his printing bills in Switzerland.[51] Was some of that money Schiff's?

Schiff's pro-German activities drew criticism from other Jews in New York. One was Columbia University's Richard Gottheil, who fumed about the banker's money supporting German intrigues and "using East-Side societies to spread pacifist propaganda."[52] One of those "East-Side societies" was *Novy Mir*. Given all this, there is no reason to suppose that Schiff would have been reluctant to lend financial assistance to Trotsky. But that's not the same as insisting he did. Schiff, after all, was not the only game in town.

Professor Gottheil also was one of British intelligence chief William  Wiseman's stable of informants. So, too, was Sidney Reilly. Wiseman even had a spy right in Schiff's board room at Kuhn Loeb – Otto H. Kahn. As mentioned, Wiseman's adjutant Norman Thwaites extolled Kahn as "whole-heartedly pro-Allied and especially pro-British," and "he knew the side on which England ranged herself would win."[53] More intriguing, Kahn "maintained his unshakeable confidence in [British] ability to surmount any crisis with the least possible disturbance...," and Thwaites confessed that he had often consulted Kahn when "delicate decisions hade to be made" and that Kahn's "uncanny foresight as to political and economic tendencies proved very helpful."[54] One could almost be confused about who was working for whom.

Thwaites with Prince of Wales, 1932

SIR WILLIAM WISEMAN: BANKER, SPYMASTER – TRAITOR?

Who, exactly, was Sir William Wiseman? In 1917, he was a thirty-two year-old British Army officer gassed on the Western Front and recent-

50. *Ibid.*
51. Stephan Possony, *Lenin: The Compulsive Revolutionary* (1964), https://archive.org/stream/LeninCompulsiveRevolutionaryPossony1964_201606/Lenin%20Compulsive%20Revolutionary%20Possony%201964_djvu.txt.
52. WWP, 10/255, "Interview with Prof. Gottheil," 29 May 1917.
53. Thwaites, 255.
54. *Ibid.*

ly recruited by the Secret Intelligence Service (SIS: colloquially, MI6) to set up a station in neutral New York. He was about as good an embodiment of secrecy as one could find. Wiseman was a card-carrying member of the British elite, a baronet and Cambridge dropout who gravitated to a career in banking. Early on, this brought him into contact with Americans like insurance tycoon Henry W. Marsh, a man with close ties to Morgan and the Wall Street power elite.[55] Such connections gave Wiseman access and influence in New York, essentials for the success of his intelligence operation. His right hand, Thwaites, had his own connections, having previously worked for the *New York World* and acted as private secretary to its chief, Joseph Pulitzer. While at the *World*, Thwaites met and befriended Frank Polk, the man who was now Counselor of the State Department and head of its intelligence bureau. In turn, it was Polk who introduced Wiseman to Col. Edward M. House, President Wilson's adviser and confidant. House brought Wiseman, a foreign intelligence agent, right into the White House and gave him Wilson's ear.

Gottheil

Wiseman's links to House and Wilson also suggest a connection to Charles Crane. The Chicago tycoon was friend to both House and the President and himself a frequent White House visitor. There is no way he would have overlooked Wiseman's intrusion on that turf. Crane and the Englishman also shared a common link in Richard Gottheil. With Crane's backing, just before the war, Gottheil offered to go to Russia as a "special agent" and hold direct talks with the Tsar.[56] Gottheil and Crane also shared a mutual suspicion of Schiff and his pro-Germanism. Beyond that, Crane knew State's Frank Polk, the man who introduced House and Wiseman, and Crane's son served as personal aide to the Secretary of State. All in all, quite the daisy chain.

However, perhaps Wiseman's and Thwaites' most intriguing dealings were with Sidney Reilly and the gaggle of quasi-revolutionists around him. In sharp contrast to the negative estimations of Reilly that Wiseman's office officially supplied to London and the Americans, Thwaites later praised him for providing "valuable services" and confessed to have "met him several times with Dr. Alexandre Weinstein, one of the nicest Russians I know."[57] Remember Col. Nekrasov, the Russian officer in New York, accused of malfeasance or worse? It was Reilly and Weinstein who

55. Marsh headed Marsh and McLennen, a big Chicago-based insurance firm.
56. Saul, 126.
57. Thwaites, 181.

gave him "a clean bill of health," and Thwaites was content to take their word for it.[58] Why?

Even Antony Jechalski was engaged in "a bit of spy work for the Allies" which ended in his unfortunate arrest in Texas.[59] In late 1917, Thwaites intervened to secure Reilly a commission in the Royal Flying Corps, and he and Wiseman "favorably reported upon" Reilly to London.[60] In dealing with the likes of Reilly and Weinstein, Wiseman was consorting with men widely regarded as crooks or worse and who were entwined with the Russian revolutionary underground. Wiseman got information about intrigues among the New York Russians out of the arrangement and the activities of German agents among them. But what did Reilly and friends glean from the bargain? Presumably, the same thing Rosenblum got from Melville years before: a degree of protection and when needed, a favor or two.

These details and more would later lead State Department Special Agent Robert Sharp to conclude that Reilly was "planted on" the British "through the same secret influence that planted Sir William Wiseman on [them] years ago."[61] Sharp was rather excitable and maybe a touch gullible, but he wasn't crazy. Something strange was going on.

The central question about Wiseman, like so many in this story, is where his true loyalties lay. In London, his "pro-American sentiments" stirred antagonism, and there were those in British intelligence who suspected him of far worse: "treachery and treason during the war."[62] The exact reasons are never made clear but part of it certainly had to do with Wiseman's relationships with the likes of Reilly and Otto Kahn. One example was that in 1916 or 1917 Wiseman and Kahn were present at a reception for Indian poet and nationalist activist Rabindranath Tagore. At the conclave, Tagore, who was associated with the anti-British Friends of Indian Freedom, publicly thanked Kahn and Kuhn Loeb for "furnishing his finances."[63] All this supposedly related to "exploiting Indian unrest to the benefit of Kuhn Loeb."[64] Was there a similar plan to "exploit unrest" in Russia?

Sharp also discovered links between Wiseman and "American millionaire" turned Bolshevik propagandist, John De Kay.[65] The latter was a curious character. He and Wiseman met in pre-war Mexico where both speculated in cattle, land and railroads. Early in the war, De Kay popped up as a German front-man trying to sell phony Mexican rifles to the Bel-

---

58. Ibid.

59. Ibid., 182.

60. USDS, CSA 215, Sharp to Bannerman, 13 Dec. 1924, 6.

61. Ibid.,7.

62. Ibid., 4.

63. USDS, G-2 File 854-56, Sharp to Bannerman, 9 Feb. 1925, 1.

64. Ibid., 13 Feb. 1925.

65. Ibid., 9 Feb. 1925, 2, and "DeKay at Lausanne, a Mysterious Agent," New York Times (26 Nov. 1922), 2.

gians. Dodging the law of several countries, he took refuge in Switzerland where in 1917 British intelligence pegged him as "chief of the murder and sabotage section of the German Secret Bureau."[66] In Switzerland, De Kay subsidized defeatist propaganda and later repackaged himself as an agent of the Comintern. There is evidence suggesting a connection between him and the above Baron von der Ropp, possibly even Bolo Pasha.

De Kay

No wonder someone in London got suspicious. Most damning of all, in Sharp's eyes, was that after the war, Otto Kahn rewarded Wiseman with a job at Kuhn Loeb.

A NEW YORK STATE OF MIND

Trotsky did not linger in the luxury of the Astor. The ever-ready helping hands found him a modern three-room apartment in the Bronx for a very reasonable $18 per month. He coughed up three months' rent in advance – which again contradicts Lore's claim that "the question of meeting expenses was a serious problem."[67] Since the apartment came unfurnished, the Trotskys purchased $200 worth on the installment plan. That required a co-signer. As Trotsky told the story, his only job in New York "was that of revolutionary socialist," and he brushed aside claims that he earned extra money as a film extra or cod-fish cleaner.[68] Lore also dismissed such "fantastic stories."[69] They were indeed fanciful, but there are legitimate questions about the amount of money Trotsky received and from where it came.

After Trotsky became an international figure, New York Deputy Attorney General Alfred Becker decided to investigate what he had been up to in New York and discovered that *Novy Mir* paid him $20 a week.[70] However, Ludwig Lore recollected the pay at a mere $7.[71] Counting up other earnings from writing, speeches and donations, Trotsky visibly took in a bit more than $700 and no more than $1000 during his stay. Of course, this did not account for the $500 he had to start with – something he studiously ignored. Even with that, minus living expenses, he would have been hard-pressed to come up with the $1394.50 he later handed over for 16 second-class and 1 first-class passage on the Norwegian line's *Kristianiafjord*.[72] But Trotsky had not been paying his own way since France, and he wasn't now.

66. TNA, FO 371/5266, "John Wesley de Kay," Feb. 1923.
67. Lore, "When Trotsky…", 6.
68. Trotsky, *My Life*, 209.
69. Lore, "When Trotsky…", 8.
70. BI, Becker Report. Summaries of Becker's report appear in the *New York Times* (18 Jan. 1918), 10, and *New York Call* (21 Jan. 1918), 1.
71. Lore, "When Trotsky…", 6.
72. BI, Becker Report.

Becker's investigators discovered the "steamship agent" from whom Trotsky purchased his return tickets. He was Henry C. Zaro, a *private* banker doing business at 1 Third Avenue.[73] This was close by the *Novy Mir* office, where Zaro was a regular visitor and advertiser.[74] Zaro's "bank" assisted immigrants in sending money to and from Russia, using German or Scandinavian banks as intermediaries. Thus, he controlled a small but practical nexus for the transmitting and laundering of revolutionary funds. And Zaro was anything but apolitical. His was one more Russian-Jewish socialist and the recent author of an anti-Tsarist tract about his travels in war-torn Poland, travels which exactly paralleled those of above-mentioned "German spy" Schwarzschild. In fact, Zaro had returned to the U.S. on the same ship as Schwarzschild. It's hardly a stretch to speculate that they were working together. Lastly, Zaro was friends with Reilly's pal and Wiseman's double-agent, Antony Jechalski.

Another New York "Russian" who took interest in Trotsky was George Raffalovitch. He somehow persuaded the revolutionary to give an interview to radical Anglo-American writer Frank Harris. Raffalovitch was either the son or nephew of Artur Raffalovitch (Rafalovich), an agent of the Russian Finance Ministry and agent of Peter Bark. The U. S. Justice Department determined that George Raffalovitch was not only involved with Russian revolutionaries, but also acted as a "paymaster of German agents."[75] According to the report, "In the month of February [1917], he paid out about \$18,000." Under questioning, Raffalovitch confessed his true loyalty lay with the League for the Liberation of the Ukraine. This was a German-sponsored group subsidized by none other than Parvus.[76] The small world returns. In New York Trotsky was in constant contact with people who were linked with each other and with the Germans and/or Parvus.

G. Raffalovitch

Nevertheless, Becker was forced to declare that "I have been unable to verify any indication of Trotzky [sic] receiving money from any German sources."[77] Maybe he wasn't looking in the right places. As noted, clandestine financiers do not give receipts. Packets of cash are easily hidden. But none of that was necessary. As we have seen, and as Bolo Pasha knew, there were many ways to move money from New York to Russia. American companies and banks like National City, American International, and Allied Machinery (to name but a few) could transfer large sums to Stockholm, Petrograd or just about anywhere else. And then there were "small-fry" operators like Zaro and Sverdlov. It was ridiculously easy.

---

73. BI, #182787, "In Re: Bolshevik Propaganda, Report of V. J. Valjavec, 5 Nov. 1918, and BI #70179, "Various", Eagan to Lansing, 12 June 1917.

74. BI, #182787, *Ibid.*

75. BI, #8000-39583, "In re: George Raffalovitch," 2 Aug. 1917.

76. Zeman and Scharlau, 132-136.

77. *New York Call, Ibid.*

Trotsky later recollected "we lived on 164th Street [in the Bronx], if I am not mistaken."[78] He was. The actual address was 1522 Vyse at 172nd Street.[79] Immediately following the reception at Cooper Union, Lore recalls "a meeting in a private home" in Brooklyn where Trotsky addressed a small group of fellow Russians and other socialists. Trotsky urged them to attack the bourgeois-infested American Socialist Party.[80] An interesting array of Bolsheviki and future Bolsheviki were present, including Bukharin, Volodarsky, and Kollontai. Trotsky joined the staff of *Novy Mir* next

1522 Vyse at 172nd Street, 2016

day. The paper's manager, Gregory Weinstein was also "closely associated with [Trotsky] while the latter was in this country."[81] Also present at this gathering were Julius Hammer and Gregory Chudnovsky, later described as Trotsky's "right-hand man" at *Novy Mir*.[82] Only a short time before, Chudnovsky had been working with Parvus in Switzerland and Copenhagen.[83]

Trotsky cryptically referred to one of his benefactors in New York as "Dr. M.," a man further identified by his wife as "Dr. Mikhailovsky."[84] Among other things, he supposedly lent his car and chauffeur to shuttle the Trotskys around town. There was, indeed, a Dr. Michael Michailovsky, a Russian-born physician and Socialist Party activist who later served as chairman of the Soviet Russian Medical Relief Committee and American representative of the Peoples' Commissariat of Public Health.[85] He undoubtedly met Trotsky in New York. However, again Trotsky either misremembered or deliberately misstated the part about the car and chauffeur. Michailovsky ran a modest practice on the Upper West Side. The man with the car and driver was another doctor – Julius Hammer.[86] It also was Hammer who found the Trotsky's their apartment conveniently close to his own home in the Bronx.

Trotsky's association with Kollontai had special significance. Remember her "secret mission" for Lenin? "It was this money," Lore recalled, "contributed by well-to-do Russian-Americans, who aided the Bolshevik

78. Trotsky, *My Life*, 215.

79. BI, Becker Report, and HIA, Okhrana, XVIIc, Folder 1, #137, 6/22 Feb. 1917.

80. Trotsky, *My Life*, 213.

81. MID, #10110-920/131, 20 January 1919.

82. TNA, FO 371/3009, NID to FO, "Russians Detained at Halifax," 12 April 1917.

83. Zeman and Scharlau, 160.

84. Trotsky, *My Life*, 214.

85. BI, #202600-189, "In re: Soviet Medical Relief Committee," Aug, 1920, 1.

86. Lloyd Ultan, "The Mystery of Trotsky's Bronx Friend," *Bronx County Historical Society Journal* (Fall, 1999), 76.

wing ... to organize its forces in Russia in preparation for the imminent overthrow of the Tsar.[87] Hammer must have been one of the donors, but was it only *Russian*-Americans? Everywhere Trotsky turned in New York he was surrounded by persons willing and able to give him money. That wasn't just a happy accident. Trotsky knew that Kollontai was Lenin's eyes and ears in New York and kept him informed of everything, "my own activities included."[88]

The many threads connecting Trotsky, Lenin, Parvus, Reilly, Schiff and the Germans, all came together in the early months of 1917. Were these all parts of a common plan or competing ones? According to Lore, "Trotsky was convinced ... that the United States was ripe for the overthrow of the capitalist system."[89] He "urged the calling of general strikes against war as a means of undermining the proud structure of our decaying civilization."[90] On 4 March, the *New York Times* noted Trotsky at a Socialist gathering where he introduced a motion calling upon the comrades to foment strikes and resist the draft in event of war.[91] If Trotsky wasn't on Berlin's payroll, he certainly should have been.

UNANSWERED QUESTIONS

In Trotsky's MI5 dossier there is a tantalizing reference to an SIS Report on "Russian Revolutionaries in New York – Activities & Movements of Trotzki – Leon."[92] The actual report has been "weeded." One should wonder why. Nevertheless, it shows that Wiseman was actively monitoring his activities, and Sir William had ample means to do so. In addition to Reilly, Weinstein and Jechalski, Wiseman had other sources of information. One was East Side lawyer Nicholas Alienikoff.[93] Alienikoff described himself as an "intimate" of Trotsky and Chudnovsky, and he was one of those later agitating for Trotsky's release from British captivity.[94] Then there was Ivan Narodny who we've met before. In 1917, he was collaborating with another Russian radical, Ivan Okuntsov, in publishing the anti-Tsarist *Russky Golos*.[95] For personal and ideological reasons, Okuntsov and Narodny cordially hated, and were hated in turn by, the *Novy Mir* bunch, each accusing the other of malfeasance and being German tools.[96]

---

87. Lore, "When Trotsky," 3.

88. Trotsky, *My Life*, 212.

89. Lore, "When Trotsky," 5.

90. *Ibid.*

91. "Socialists Conservative," *New York Times* (5 March 1917).

92. TNA, KV2/502, CX #174440, n.d.

93. ONI, #21010-3241, "Memorandum for Lt. Irving," 21 Aug. 1918, 1-2.

94. *Ibid.*, 1, and "Names in the Weinstein Case," 3.

95. Paul Avrich, *Anarchist Voices: An Oral History of Anarchism in America* (Edinburgh: AK Press, 2005), 367.

96. NAC, C2051, British Military Mission (New York), "In Re: Ivan Okuntzov," 30 July 1918.

Yet another line on Trotsky came from an ex-Scotland Yard and Okhranka informant, Casimir Pilenas. Before the war, Pilenas spied on Russian revolutionaries in London, including Martens and Sverdlov.[97] As a "British S.S. agent of the Scotland Yard detachment" he now worked for Wiseman reporting directly to Thwaites and the British naval attaché, Guy Gaunt.[98] Wiseman expressed complete confidence in Pilenas and was certain that he "worked for no other person but [me]."[99] On 22 March, Wiseman sent London a brief coded telegram stating that Trotsky was being backed by "Jewish funds behind which are possibly German," with the aim of getting himself and other socialist revolutionaries back to Russia. [100] Wiseman noted that Trotsky planned to sail from New York on the 27th. Later, Wiseman identified Pilenas as the source of this information.[101]

Note that Wiseman's initial message gave no specific amount of money, nor did it recommend any action to be taken. "Jewish money," behind which there might German, could describe Schiff or one of his fronts, but that is far from clear. Pilenas was not the only one to say such things. In the weeks and months to come, accusations that Trotsky had gotten money in New York cropped up on a regular basis. For example, in August 1917 Ivan Narodny wired Kerensky that he could prove that Trotsky and other socialists who returned from New York "got money from German agents."[102] Around the same time, two other Stateside Russians, Paul Perov and Nicholas Volgar, insisted that Trotsky shared in funds dispersed by Alexandra Kollontai (on whose orders?) and had bigger sums transferred from the U.S. to Swedish and Russian banks.[103] Volgar claimed that "he could produce in court, proof of the source through which German funds were paid to Leon Trotsky ... which funds financed Trotsky's mission to Russia." It appears no one ever asked him to do so.

Some years later, Charles Crane shared his private thoughts on the "Trotsky money" question, and pointed his finger in both familiar and surprising directions. In a 1921 letter to his friend Dr. Charles Eliot, Crane asserted that Jacob Schiff "had given Trotsky fifty thousand dollars when he started to Russia." The source of this information Crane laid

97. HIA, Paris Okhrana, IIIf, Box 24, File 28, and "Deep Cover Agents – Russian (L-Z)."
98. BI, #105638, "In re: Casimir Pilenas," 18 Dec. 1917.
99. TNA, KV2/502, CX #015649, 19 Jan. 1918.
100. *Ibid.*, CX #625, 22 March 1917.
101. *Ibid.*, CX 015549.
102. *Ibid.*, Special Intelligence Report #654, 26 Aug. 1917.
103. USDS, #861.20211/6, Memorandum (n.d.), attached to Phelps Stokes to Polk, 2 Nov. 1917.

to "the head of our State Department Secret Police in New York."[104] The police official bemoaned the fact that "he was not nearly so well served and had not anything like so important an organization as [Schiff]." Thirteen years further on, Crane elaborated on this in a letter to his son John, saying Schiff had handed the $50,000 to Trotsky at Lillian Wald's house the night before he sailed.[105] Indeed, in Crane's view Wald was the mastermind of the whole affair. Crane proclaimed that "Trotsky was always in touch with her and followed her orders" and "she could always get any amount of money from the Schiff-Warburg family." Wald, he concluded, "played a very important role in bringing about the Russian Revolution" and "when Trotsky and his relatives were in power she could have anything she wanted without hesitation," and she was still an influence in Moscow in 1934. This aside, Crane continued to express great admiration for Lillian Wald and her "fresh, vigorous mind." Was Crane deluded or did he indeed possess insider knowledge? If anyone did, it would be him.

The Schiff-Warburg family

Money or no money, on 25 March Trotsky appeared at the British Consulate at 44 Whitehall St. Under the rules of the British blockade, passengers bound for Scandinavia had to pass inspection at either Halifax, Nova Scotia or the Orkney Islands. Anyone passing through those ports needed the appropriate visa. These were the responsibility of the Passport Control Section of the Consulate. That Section was under the direct supervision of Wiseman and Thwaites. There is no way they would not

104. BA, Charles R. Crane Papers, Crane to Eliot, 5 Feb. 1921.
105. *Ibid.*, C. R. Crane to John Crane, 14 Dec. 1934.

have known who Trotsky was; after all, they had him under surveillance. Trotsky later acknowledged the helpfulness of British officials. They "put no obstacle in the way of my return to Russia," and even allowed him to phone the Russian Consulate to attest that all necessary paperwork was in order.[106] Remember, this was three days *after* Wiseman had received Pilenas' information on Trotsky's plans. Clearly, it didn't seem to trouble him.

---

106. Trotsky, "In British Captivity." (1917), reprinted in *The Class Struggle*, Vol., II, #4 (Dec. 1918), at www.marxists.org/archives/trotsky/works/1917/1917-captivity.htm.

CHAPTER EIGHT:

COME THE REVOLUTION – AGAIN

THE END OF THE ROMANOVS

In early March 1917, Americans were preoccupied with the looming prospect of war with Germany. In response to Berlin's resumption of unrestricted submarine warfare, Wilson had severed diplomatic relations on 3 February. Later that month, the British conveniently handed Washington the infamous Zimmermann Telegram that proposed German-Mexican cooperation in the event of hostilities. Everyone was waiting for the other shoe to drop.

Meanwhile, in Russia, things were going badly for Tsar Nicholas. Despite some victories, the tide of war had mostly gone against the Russian armies. During 1915, the Germans and Austrians overran the whole of Poland and much of the Baltic Provinces. Russian counter-offensives in 1916 failed miserably or clawed back territory at terrible cost. By the beginning of 1917, the Army and the citizenry were exhausted and demoralized. Mounting fuel and food shortages added to the prevailing mood of misery, frustration and uncertainty.

In the summer of 1915, Charles Crane's friend Paul Milyukov became a leading light of the so-called Progressive Bloc in the Duma, an alliance of liberal and moderate left elements. In November 1916, Milyukov caused a sensation in the Duma when he enumerated the Imperial Government's many failings and rhetorically demanded, "Is this stupidity, or is it treason?" It was, in effect, a declaration of war against the Romanov regime and plans for a coup to unseat Nicholas began to coalesce. A further blow to the Monarchy occurred at the end of December when a cabal of monarchists, stage-managed by British intelligence, murdered (with extreme difficulty) Empress Alexandra's notorious and much-despised spiritual adviser, Gregory Rasputin.[1]

From 29 January 1917 through 21 February, Petrograd hosted an inter-Allied conference. Leading the British delegation was the powerful

---

1. See: Richard Cullen, *Rasputin: The Role of Britain's Secret Service in His Torture and Murder* (2010).

and shadowy Lord Alfred Milner, a man who epitomized "a group of managers, behind the scenes and beyond the control of public opinion, who seek efficiently to obtain what they regard as the good for the people."[2] Plus, he was a banker. Also present was London's Ambassador, Sir George Buchanan, another close friend of Milyukov. Milyukov and his fellow-conspirators took advantage of the gathering to reveal their plans to select Allied representatives, and if they did not receive express approval, they were certainly not discouraged.

Milner

The Duma reconvened at the beginning of March and Milyukov, joined by rising leftist star Alexander Kerensky, resumed scathing verbal assaults on the Government.[3] On 7 March, Tsar Nicholas arrived back at Mogilev, base of the Russian High Command, some 450 miles south of Petrograd. That same day, in the capital, workers at the Putilov plant went on strike. The next day, the strikes spread and rumors of food shortages sparked bread riots. By the 9th, 200,000 workers were on the streets. Only on the 10th did officials attempt to restore order,

Kerensky

a seemingly simple task with more than 170,000 troops stationed in or around the city. Unlike 1905, however, the soldiers proved unreliable and the same went for many of their officers. By the 11th, mutiny had spread through the whole garrison.

By 12 March, the Imperial Government had completely lost control of the capital and Milyukov and friends took the cue to proclaim themselves the Provisional Committee of the State Duma. The ranks of the Committee were overwhelmingly dominated by liberals, but there were three bona-fide socialists, including Kerensky. In Mogilev, Nicholas found himself abandoned by almost all his senior commanders. He organized a train and headed back to Petrograd. On the way, he was persuaded to divert to the provincial town of Pskov in hope of restoring telegraphic communication with Petrograd. He rolled straight into a trap. Awaiting him was a delegation of the Provisional Committee with an abdication proclamation ready and waiting for him to sign. Nicholas was a prisoner, and "he did not abdicate absolutely willingly," but it didn't matter. [4] His

---

2. Carroll Quigley, *The Anglo-American Establishment* (1981), 85. Milner, of course, also presided over the Rhodes-Milner or "Round table" Group.

3. "Russia's Will to Conquer, " *New York Times* (5 March 1917).

4. "Was Betrayed, Says the Czar," *New York Times* (18 March 1917).

reign was finished. The Provisional Committee promptly rechristened itself the Provisional Government.

This so-called February Revolution, in reality a carefully orchestrated coup d'état, had achieved in a week what the Revolution of 1905 failed to do in almost a year.[5] The difference was a much longer and more costly war and better preparation. As noted, the principle failure of the revolutionary forces in 1905 was that they did not have control of the military or the Tsar. This time, they had both.

In New York, Trotsky was quite *au courant* with events back home, surprisingly so, in fact. On the evening of 15 March, a *New York Times* reporter interviewed him at *Novy Mir*. He predicted that the new Provisional Government "would probably be short-lived."[6] The regime, he proclaimed, "did not represent the interests or the aims of the revolutionists." It would fall to other men, he added, "to carry forward the democratization of Russia." However, he was quick to add that the revolutionists, his sort of revolutionists anyway, were resolutely *opposed* to a separate peace with Germany. That's something Wiseman and others would have found very interesting.

The Provisional Government immediately issued a general amnesty and called on all expatriates to come home. A week later, 23 March, Trotsky presented himself at the Russian Consulate, along with Volodarsky, Chudnovsky and others, to obtain new passports.[7] Reportedly, only half the émigrés seeking to return got them. Trotsky's success was attributed to the fact that he and his friends supposedly attested willingness to perform military service. He needed to move fast; the liner *Kristianiafjord* was set to depart New York in four days and there would not be another suitable sailing for five weeks.

Charles Crane was also rushing to secure accommodation on the *Kristianiafjord*. His near-obsessive interest in Russian affairs had not slackened. As Schiff made himself the ring-master of Jewish charitable and cultural affairs in America, so Crane did for Russian. He viewed Russia's participation in the war as a positive since it seemed bound to bring political change and because it offered unparalleled opportunities for American business there. Crane saw huge advantages in the rupture of Russia's trade with Germany. Wall Street was poised to replace Berlin's economic influence with its own. Crane buttressed his optimism with the fact that American exports to the Russian Empire had grown from a paltry $40 million in 1913 to more than $550 million in 1917.[8] True, most of this increase was based on war purchasing, but it signaled potential. In

---

5. Deemed the "February Revolution" because under the old (Julian) Russian calendar the events took place over 23 February to 2 March.

6. "Calls People War Weary," *New York Times* (16 March 1917), 4.

7. "Russ Refugees Return," *Washington Post* (23 March1917), 5.

8. *World Almanac, 1919,* 363.

pursuit of this bounty, as early as the fall of 1914 Crane tried to set up a Russian-American bank to underwrite Russian purchases.[9] He even managed to get Morgan on board, but the plan collapsed in the face of British obstructionism. Crane dipped his own toe into Russian war contracts by acting as a lobbyist for Westinghouse. The latter landed a big contract for Russian rifles and built a new plant to manufacture them. Whether he knew it or not, this drew Crane into Reilly's territory. The rifles would never arrive in time to arm the Tsar's troops, but they eventually proved very useful to Trotsky's Red Army.[10]

In November 1914, Crane signed University of Chicago professor Samuel Harper to a four-year contract to act as his representative in Russia. He bought out Harper's time at the school and dispatched him on long "fact-finding" missions in 1915 and 1916. In effect, Harper was Crane's personal spy and destined to become "a central point of contact and liaison in the Russian problem."[11] Among Harper's contacts in Petrograd was his "intimate friend" Frederic Corse, head of the local branch of New York Life.[12]

Through Harper and other "irregular agents" Crane kept himself up to date on developments in the Tsar's domain. In May 1915, he made his own pilgrimage to Petrograd to attend the annual meeting of the Russian Westinghouse Company. Among those he touched base with was Milyukov. One can only imagine what they talked about.

KALAMATIANO

Among other agents keeping Crane informed was a former Chicago academic, turned businessman, Xenophon Kalamatiano. The illegitimate offspring of a Greek-Russian noblewoman, Kalamatiano came to the U.S in 1897 to study at the exclusive Culver Military Academy and later at the University of Chicago where he encountered Harper. In 1904, Kalamatiano returned to Russia as representative of the J. I. Case Threshing Machine Co., eventually overseeing all its Russian and Central European business. In March 1915, he appeared in New York as the agent of the Moscow-based Association of Commerce and Industry whose mission was to "attract attention of foreign businessmen in Russia."[13] Precisely as Crane intended. Interviewed in the *New York Times*, Kalamatiano perfectly echoed Crane's idea of

Kalamatiano

---

9. "Russian-American Bank is Projected," *New York Times* (27 Nov. 1914).

10. Saul, 130.

11. George F. Kennan, *Soviet-American Relations, 1917-1920, Vol. 2, The Decision to Intervene* (1956), 330.

12. *Ibid.*

13. "Here from Russia," *New York Times* (23 March 1915).

American commerce replacing German.[14] The following month, Kalama-tiano was a guest of honor at a luncheon of the Chicago Association of Commerce. If he wasn't already, this is when Kalamatiano became part of Crane's "parallel intelligence organization."[15]

In August 1915, still in Chicago, Kalamatiano became manager of the International Manufacturers Sales Corporation of America, an out-fit representing thirty-five American firms with $300 million in capital. He didn't manage that alone. Crane's hand is evident in Samuel Harper's presence at the outfit's inaugural meeting, and in the financial backing of the National Bank of the Republic.[16] But Kalamatiano had other connec-tions. In early 1917, back in Russia, he signed on as the Russian represen-tative of New York-based Claude M. Nankivel, "commission and selling agent."[17] Nankivel's office was in the familiar confines of 120 Broadway. More than that, Nankivel did business with Reilly's and Aschberg's crony, John McGregor Grant.[18] How's that for a coincidence?

WELCOMING "DEMOCRATIC RUSSIA"

Marye

Francis

Charles Crane's busy hands were active in oth-er areas. In early 1916, he was instrumental in getting President Wilson to recall the "inadequate" American Ambassador in Petrograd, George T. Mar-ye.[19] His replacement by ex-Missouri governor Da-vid Rowland Francis met with the "full approval of Crane" who at once attached Harper to him as an "adviser."[20] Francis had absolutely no qualifications as a diplomat, but he was a banker and director of Kansas City's Merchants-Laclede National Bank and the Missouri Valley Trust Co. Like Crane, Fran-cis was a big investor in National City Bank and the American International Corporation.[21]

In contrast to Trotsky, on 17 March the U.S. State Department was still mostly in the dark about events in Russia.[22] The first news official Washington re-ceived about the regime change in Russia was a terse telegram from Francis on 16 March simply saying that

14. *Ibid.*

15. Mahoney, *American Prisoners*, 261.

16. "Organization to go after Russian Trade," *Federal Trade Reporter*, Vol. 4 (15 Sept. 1915), 531.

17. "New Incorporations," *New York Times* (14 Jan. 1917).

18. "Loans to Foreign Governments," *U.S. Senate Documents*, Vol. I (1921), 256.

19. Saul, 133.

20. *Ibid.*

21. *Ibid.*, 134 and *Moody's Manual of Railroads and Corporate Securities*, Issue 7 (1906), 2391.

22. "Washington Eager for Russian News," *New York Times* (18 March 1917).

Americans there were safe. Secretary of State Robert Lansing turned to his confidential aide, Richard Crane, who, doubtless after consulting his father, turned to Samuel Harper for information on Petrograd's new masters.[23] Crane himself got on the phone to Wilson to urge immediate recognition of the new Russian regime. On 21 March, he arrived in Washington to make the pitch in person. The next day, the United States became the first nation to extend official recognition to the Provisional Government.

Lansing

Most importantly, Wall Street was pleased. On 16 March, the day following the Tsar's abdication, National City banker John B. Young offered his opinion that the regime change in Russia was a "peoples' revolution" and "not a nihilist or anarchist enterprise."[24] Rather, he claimed, it was the handiwork of the "solid, responsible, conservative element of the community." Men like Paul Milyukov. Young spoke with some authority because, it may be recalled, he was the man Samuel McRoberts dispatched to Petrograd almost exactly a year before to negotiate a loan. While there, Young added, "even then the Revolution was talked about ... it wasn't hard to hear it discussed." It's interesting that such things would be freely discussed around a foreign banker. On 16 March, the *New York Times* announced "Bankers Here Pleased at News of Revolution," and quoted several "prominent" (but anonymous) financiers to the effect that the change in Petrograd augured nothing but good for American business and, of course, the Russians. The article also mentioned that certain American financial interests had recently made "heavy private loans to Russian banks to facilitate commercial credits."[25] These "private" loans, possibly as much as $100 million, were completely separate from the ones publicly floated by National City and Guaranty Trust. In other words, persons in New York had been quietly pumping millions into Russia in the months and weeks leading up to the revolution. Just another curious coincidence. Another article vouched that news of the revolution was "by no means unwelcome in more important banking quarters" and opinion there was almost unanimously positive.[26]

Another detail, one of those things that may or may not mean anything, is that on 15 March Paul Warburg suddenly appeared in New York at the home of his brother Felix. While in town, he spent most of the day

23. Saul, 142.
24. "Is a Peoples' Revolution," *New York Times* (16 March 1917).
25. "Bankers Here Pleased at News of Revolution," *New York Times* (16 March 1917), and "Topics on Wall Street," *New York Times* (17 March 1917).
26. "Financial Markets," *New York Times* (16 March 1917).

in meetings at the Federal Reserve offices at 120 Broadway. The papers reported, "It was said his call to the bank had no special significance."[27]

The mainstream press almost universally hailed the fall of the Tsar. The London *Daily Chronicle's* man in Petrograd, Harold Williams, set the tone in a widely syndicated piece that overflowed with phrases like "supreme patriotism," "unflinching purity of devotion," and "nobility" in describing Milyukov, Kerensky and the rest.[28] An avowed socialist and long-time friend of Milyukov, Williams was not exactly an unbiased observer. Jacob Schiff, then relaxing at an Appalachian hot-springs, cabled his "joy" that "a great and good people have at last effected their deliverance from centuries of autocratic oppression."[29]

Nowhere was there greater excitement than in the Lower East Side. Trotsky's *Novy Mir* got into the act by immediately denouncing the Provisional Government as a bourgeois concoction and predicting that the Revolution would soon cast it aside. News of the Revolution sparked mass meetings across the City. On 20 March, at least 10,000 Jews, mostly socialists of one stripe or the other, crammed into Madison Square Garden to hear speakers like Ludwig Lore and Algernon Lee.[30] The latter thought it strange that "capitalist papers that support Wall Street" find the Russian Revolution "magnificent." That same evening, uptown in the Harlem River Casino, Trotsky harangued a smaller crowd of 2,000 "Russian Socialists."[31] They voted to send delegates to Russia and Trotsky was one of them. On 23 March another gathering of thousands took place at Carnegie Hall sponsored by the Friends of Russian Freedom.[32] It was here George Kennan revealed

Algernon Lee

how the Friends, financed by Jacob Schiff, had spread "the gospel of the Russian revolutionists" and "sowed the seeds of liberty" in 1905. SFRF President Herbert Parsons read a message from Schiff in which he hailed the "actual reward of what we had hoped and striven for these long years."

THE INTERRUPTED JOURNEY

Meanwhile, Charles Crane was rushing around Washington meeting with the President, Col. House, the State Department, and others. He decided that he had to see for himself what was happening in Rus-

27. "Paul M. Warburg at Reserve Bank," *New York Times* (16 March 1917).
28. Harold Williams, "Praises Patriotism of Russian Leaders," *New York Times* (16 March), 1.
29. "Jacob H. Schiff Rejoices," *New York Times* (17 March 1917).
30. "10,000 Jews Here Laud Revolution," *New York Times* (21 March 1917).
31. *Ibid.*
32. "Pacifists Pester until Mayor Calls Them Traitors," *New York Times* (24 March 1917), 1-2.

sia. To accompany him, he first enlisted William G. Shepherd, a veteran war correspondent who worked for the *New York Evening Post* and the *United Press* Syndicate. On the 22nd he approached Socialist muckraker Lincoln Steffens who was already working in some capacity for the State Department. Three days before, Steffens had been planning to head to Mexico. Crane needed Steffens because of his radical credentials and contacts. Crane, Steffens explained to his sister, "knows everybody in power

Steffens

[in Russia] now and especially Miliukoff, the head of the new government."[33] The latter, Crane said, "has economic ideas."

Steffens found it "an opportunity too great to miss," and four days later he again wrote his sister from his *Kristianiafjord* stateroom.[34] Crane, he wrote,

Crane

"knows everybody," and "all the great radicals have had his aid." "He (and I with him)," continued Steffens, "will walk into the inner circles of the new government and the new radical party." "And all agree," he added, "that the revolution is in its first phase only, that is must grow. Charles Crane and the Russian radicals on the ship think we shall be in Russia for the re-revolution." Note that this is very close to Trotsky's statement that the present situation was temporary and that the revolution required men "to carry forward the democratization of Russia." Why would Crane believe something like this? Why did so many people seem tapped into the same mysterious wavelength? Steffens also picked up rumors that the "Russian revolutionists plan to *promote* [his italics] a revolution in Germany."

It is likely that Crane's and Trotsky's presence on the same liner was genuine coincidence; the *Kristianiafjord* was the only ship headed to the right port at the earliest opportunity. However, Crane was fully aware Trotsky was on board, and doubtless the reverse was true. Crane bore witness to Trotsky's grand send-off at the pier, complete with band and rain-soaked red flags, and watched his removal from the ship a few days later. [35] On board, Crane kept a discreet distance from the homeward bound revolutionaries, who he estimated at around twenty, but he noted that Steffens "was getting many stories from them."[36] In other words, Steffens was doing his job. Crane dutifully reported everything back to his son at State.[37] However, the Chicago tycoon was a bit concerned that Steffens and Shepherd were getting a little *too* friendly with the radicals.[38]

---

33. *The Letters of Lincoln Steffens*, Vol. I (1938), 395.
34. *Ibid.*, 396-397.
35. Lore, "When Trotsky," 7.
36. Saul, 164, n. 116.
37. *Ibid.*
38. *Ibid.*, 148.

Trotsky and family boarded the *Kristianiafjord* the evening of the 26th. Five other Russian men, most notably Gregory Chudnovsky, were reckoned his "companions," but Trotsky had bought seventeen fares, one of them first class.[39] Trotsky plus family and companions counted nine. Who were the other eight tickets for? And who received the lone 1st class ticket? Trotsky and his party were all in 2nd class. One contender is "Robert Jivotovsky" (Zhivotovsky), another nephew of Uncle Abram and a Trotsky cousin.[40] What a coincidence he was on board. What had he been doing in New York?

There were other passengers of interest as well. One was returning radical Israel Fondaminsky, accused by Trotsky of helping the British "gather information" about him.[41] The most interesting, though, was Russian diplomat/army officer, Andrew Kolpashnikov (Kalpaschnikoff). In New York, Kolpashnikov ran with a familiar crowd. Among his Stateside friends was Vladimir Rogovine, a Russian businessman who simultaneously was a crony of Weinstein and Reilly. More than that, Kolpashnikov worked for John McGregor Grant.[42] The coincidences continue to mount.

On 28 March, with the *Kristianiafjord* at sea, someone at the British Consulate in New York sent a coded wire to London addressed to the chief of Naval Intelligence and MI5. It read: "Trotsky is reliably reported to have $10,000 subscribed by socialists and Germans."[43] Note that this is quite different from what Pilenas originally reported. The message added, "I am notifying Halifax to hold [Trotsky and associates] until they receive your instructions." Although Wiseman later took credit for this, it simply wasn't true. The man who would know, Director of Naval Intelligence Admiral W. R. "Blinker" Hall, identified the sender as Naval Attaché Captain Guy Gaunt.[44]

Hall

Who was Gaunt? Until Wiseman and SIS showed up in early 1916, Guy Gaunt was the top British spook in the U.S.A. and he did not take kindly to being pushed aside.[45] He also maintained a cozy relationship with J. P. Morgan & Co. If he resented Wiseman, Gaunt positively loathed

39. In addition to Chudnovsky, the others were Gregory Mel'nichansky (later an important Comintern official), Nikita Mukhin, Konstantin Romanchenko and Leiba Fishelev, the sole anarchist of the bunch. Two other passengers associated with Trotsky, but *not* arrested, were Gladnovsky and Voskoff. See, National Archives of Canada, RG 24, Vol. 4545, File MD6-73-T9.

40. Robert was the younger son of David Zhivotovsky; Ostrovsky, 110.

41. Trotsky, "In British Captivity."

42. ONI, #21010-3241, "Names in the Weinstein Case," 3, and "Weinstein and Reilly," 4, 9-12, and USDS, CSA 215, Sharp to Bannerman, 13 Dec. 1925, 9-10.

43. NAC, Vol. 2543, File H.Q.C., 2051/1.

44. TNA, FO 371/3009, 86305, 3 April 1917.

45. Thomas F. Troy, "The Gaunt-Wiseman Affair: British Intelligence in New York in 1915," *International Journal of Intelligence and Counter-Intelligence*, Vol. 16, #3 (2003), 42-461.

Reilly, and began to openly defame him in April 1917.[46] While Wiseman and Thwaites, with Reilly's help, quashed the investigation of Russian Col. Nekrasov, Gaunt did everything he could to keep it going. He, not surprisingly, was one of those who later accused William Wiseman of treason. Gaunt had seen the message from Pilenas about Trotsky's supposed "German" money and when Wiseman did not act on it, he did.[47] Gaunt knew that Pilenas' main stoolpigeon was a German-American Socialist named John Lang. Lang was part of Ludwig Lore's circle and, thus, close to Trotsky, which made the information worth taking seriously.[48]

Based on Gaunt's information, on 29 March, Admiral Hall ordered British naval authorities (not Canadian) to arrest Trotsky when the ship stopped for inspection in Halifax. On the morning of 3 April, that's precisely what they did. They also removed his five comrades and wife and sons. Interestingly, the man who stepped forward to act as Trotsky's translator in dealing with the British officers was the earlier-mentioned Andrew Kolpashnikov. Certainly, he was not the only bi-lingual person on board; someone in Trotsky's entourage could have managed that. Kolpashnikov was doing what he had been put aboard the ship to do: keep an eye on Trotsky. The question is who put him there?

Two commonly repeated stories regarding Trotsky's arrest are that the search revealed him to be carrying the $10,000 and an American passport. The actual records reveal no mention of these, nor would it have been a crime if he had possessed them. In terms of financing a revolution, $10,000 – or even $50,000 – is and was chicken feed. The accusation that "Woodrow Wilson, despite the efforts of the British police, made it possible for Leon Trotsky to enter Russia with an American passport," appears, unattributed, on the last page of Jennings C. Wise's Wilson biography published in 1938.[49] All other issues aside, the passport would have been completely unnecessary; Trotsky already had all the paperwork he needed to return home.

---

46. BI, #39368, Agent L.S. Perkins, 3 April 1917. This was, perhaps not coincidentally, the same day as Trotsky's arrest. See also *Ibid.*, "Memo to Lt. Irving," 21 Aug. 1918.

47. On this, see the author's "Englishmen in New York: The SIS American Station, 1915-21," *Intelligence and National Security*, Vol. 19, #3 (Autumn 2004), 511-537, and Thomas F. Troy, "The Gaunt-Wiseman Affair: British Intelligence in New York in 1915," *International Journal of Intelligence and CounterIntelligence*, Vol. 16, #3 (2003), 447-461.

48. BI, #105638, *Ibid.*

49. Jennings C. Wise, *Woodrow Wilson, Disciple of Revolution* (1938), 647. Wise was a DC lawyer, onetime Commandant of the Virginia Military Institute and briefly a special assistant to the U.S. Attorney General. It is possible that Trotsky possessed an altered or stolen U.S. passport as an emergency back-up, but he could easily have attained that from his radical friends in New York.

Whatever Kolpashnikov did or didn't say to the Brits, Trotsky and his friends ended up in an internment camp near Amherst, Nova Scotia for the better part of the month. Trotsky later blamed Milyukov for his arrest (because Milyukov's friend Crane was aboard?), but, in fact, Milyukov almost immediately called for the Halifax detainees' release, believing it would only antagonize radicals in Petrograd.[50] Trotsky's incarceration was entirely the doing of British Naval Intelligence, not Wiseman's SIS. Admiral Hall not only ordered the arrest but twice, on 4 and 10 April, defended it against mounting pressure from the Russian Government and his own. Wiseman's name comes up nowhere in the process. Finally, on 20 April, Hall relented and cabled Halifax that "Russian socialists should be allowed to proceed."[51] A week later they boarded the liner *Helig Olav* bound for Christiania.

Almost certainly Wiseman's intention was that Trotsky return to Petrograd unmolested. He had his reasons. His subsequent cables to London show that he was concerned that "German agents" in the U.S. "are sending Russian-Jewish Socialists back to Petrograd who are either knowingly or unknowingly working in the German cause."[52] Wiseman concocted a scheme to send his own agents from America to "guide the storm" by exerting counter influence. These agents included "international socialists" and even "notorious nihilists."[53] Trotsky, arguably, was his first stab at this. His priorities were that these agents have no perceptible British ties and that they *oppose any move toward a separate peace*. Trotsky had recently proclaimed exactly that in no less than the *New York Times*. The question is whether Wiseman was just hoping that Trotsky would follow through in Russia, or did he make some sort of deal with him? That is not as outlandish as it may seem. Trotsky was a pragmatist. He knew that the British, in the person of Wiseman, had the power to get him home or keep him bottled up in New York. It was no different from the deal Lenin made with the Germans to get out of Switzerland.

Might there have been other factors involved? In facilitating Trotsky's return to Russia, was Wiseman also paying a debt for the assistance of Reilly and Weinstein, the agents of Uncle Abram who was anxiously awaiting his nephew's return? Did that, in turn, earn Wiseman good will, cooperation and ultimate reward in the offices of Kuhn Loeb?

In this regard, the shifting attitude of Jacob Schiff may be significant. With America entering the war on 6 April, he had to distance himself from anything smacking of pro-Germanism no matter what his personal feelings. Moreover, Schiff's professed aim, unseating Tsar Nicholas, had been accomplished. He, too, promptly voiced his opposition to any Rus-

---

50. TNA, FO 371/3009, #70787, DID to Campbell, 4 April 1917.

51. NAC, RG 24, Vol. 3967, NSC 10474-50/1 Navcon Halifax to Naval, Ottawa, 21 April 1917.

52. WWP, 10/255, "Russia," 18 May 1917, 1.

53. *Ibid.*, 3, and 10/261, "Intelligence and Propaganda Work in Russia, July to December 1917."

sian separate peace.[54] Wiseman even enlisted Schiff's help in his "guide the storm" campaign. Or was this just more sleight of hand meant to disguise true loyalties and true intentions?

THE ROOT, RAILWAY AND RUSSIAN DIPLOMATIC MISSIONS

While Trotsky sat waiting in Nova Scotia, Charles Crane and companions reached Petrograd. As chance (?) would have it, they arrived on the same day, 16 April, and likely on the same train, as Lenin.[55]

Regarding Lenin's "sealed train" trip through Germany, there is a story worth noting told by future CIA spymaster Allen Dulles. On Easter weekend 1917, Dulles, then a young secretary-intelligence officer at the U.S. Legation in Bern, Switzerland, answered a telephone call from and "obscure Russian revolutionary named Lenin" who wanted to meet with someone there right away.[56] Given that it was Sunday and Dulles had a pressing tennis date with a pretty girl, he told Lenin to call back on Monday. The Russian regretted that by then he would be on his way elsewhere. To CIA recruits, Dulles used this as an example of how *not* to handle a potential source. Of course, some have questioned whether the incident ever happened at all.

A. Dulles

Lenin

While Dulles likely dramatized things, odds are the story is true. The question, of course, is why Lenin would have reached out to the Americans on the eve of his departure, and what did he hope to get out of it? At the time, Dulles' brother, future Secretary of State John Foster Dulles, was working for the high-powered New York law firm of Sullivan & Cromwell. He also was a protégé of financier Bernard Baruch, who had stepped away from Wall Street to advise Woodrow Wilson. Both Dulles brothers, moreover, were nephews of then-Secretary of State Lansing. By accident or design, Lenin had spoken with probably the best-connected person in the whole Legation. What Lenin may have been fishing for was a backup if his deal with the Germans went sour. In return for passing to the Americans whatever juicy

Root

54. WWP, 10/256, "Copies of Cables," Schiff to Kamenka, 15 April 1917.

55. Saul, 164 n. 117.

56. Central Intelligence Agency, "Secret Intelligence," https://www.cia.gov/library/publications/intelligence-history/oss/art06.htm.

tidbits he gleaned from the Germans, Lenin would expect the Yanks to offer help as needed in Petrograd.

Charles Crane's trip to Russia was also part of a bigger plan. He was the point man of a special American mission, later to be dubbed the Root Commission after its nominal leader, former Senator and Secretary of War Elihu Root. Crane pitched the idea or something like it when he visited Washington in March.[57] Among other things, it would give semi-official cover to his personal and political intrigues. However, the Commission's official origins stemmed from an 11 April 1917 letter from Oscar S. Straus (former secretary of commerce, businessman, diplomat and friend of Jacob Schiff) to Col. House and Secretary Lansing. Straus argued that an American mission should be sent to Russia as a sign of solidarity with the Provisional Government and a means to combat the influence of radical socialist and German agents who were pressing for a separate peace. Wall Street would be well-represented, and the unstated but clear message to the Russians would be "no fight, no loans."

The Root venture has been aptly described as "[a] clandestine intelligence organization ... [which] unofficially and covertly used the infrastructure of the Departments of State and Army. It was closely connected to the Executive Branch (President Wilson and Col. House) and was actively supported by leading American industrialists, academicians and backstopped by a series of quasi-official missions and groups."[58] Put another way, it was a cover for "covert political action, black propaganda, intelligence collection and counter-espionage operations."[59] Root's party departed Washington on 15 May, reached Petrograd on 13 June and remained about a month, returning to the USA on 3 August.

The conceit of the Commission was that it represented a cross-section of American interests. It did, if those interests extended no further than Wall Street and Washington. There was much behind-the-scenes maneuvering to secure appointments or prevent others. Col. House pushed hard for Root to be chief. Root, Wall Street lawyer and Washington insider was a perfect embodiment of American plutocracy.[60] House also insisted on Samuel Reading Bertron, an investment banker with offices at 40 Wall Street and an expert in public financing.[61] Bertron was also a vice-president of Guaranty Trust and chairman of the American-Russian Chamber of Commerce. Besides House, he was a close friend of Herbert Hoover.

Bertron

---

57. Saul, 144.

58. Mahoney, *American Prisoners*, 57.

59. Harry Mahoney and Marjorie Mahoney, *The Saga of Leon Trotsky: His Clandestine Operations and His Assassination* (1998), 40.

60. Root was a long-time associate of steel baron Andrew Carnegie. He later became a charter member of Col. House's Council on Foreign relations.

61. Saul, 145.

Crane insisted on the inclusion of his friend and fellow Chicago industrialist Cyrus H. McCormick who was, of course, president of International Harvester Co., which had huge investments in Russia. For good measure, McCormick was a director of National City Bank, a close associate of J. P. Morgan and another member of the Jekyll Island "Millionaires' Club." Crane also secured the appointment of another pal, John R. Mott, Head of the Young Men's Christian Association (YMCA).

McCormick

Also on the roster were two token lefties, James Duncan, Vice President of the American Federation of Labor (AFL), and Charles E. Russell, a pro-war Socialist journalist. Russell was another Crane "recommendation."[62] Rounding things out were two military men, Admiral James H. Glennon and former Chief-of-Staff General Hugh L. Scott. The outward achievements of the Root Commission were nil. In Russia, its members engaged in speechmaking and sight-seeing. Back in America, Root and the others received official thanks, filed reports that no one read, and made more speeches.

Russell

Crane, of course, was himself a member, yet his connection to the Commission was purely nominal. He went to Russia weeks earlier, stayed much longer, and had virtually nothing to do with the others in the interim. As his factotum, Crane assigned ever-faithful Samuel Harper to the Root crew as shepherd and "adviser." Crane, in the meantime, did his own thing and, as usual, only he knew what that was. He immediately connected with friend Milyukov, now the Provisional Government's foreign minister, and was much dismayed in May 1917 when radical socialists in the Petrograd Soviet of Workers and Soldiers Deputies (who wielded power somewhat equal to the Government), forced his resignation. Crane could only watch as "his" liberal revolution, and the American-clone republic it was supposed to create, was hijacked by Lenin and Trotsky. Or was this the very "re-revolution" he had anticipated?

Almost simultaneously with the Root mission, Wilson dispatched a separate, smaller Railway Mission to study Russia's transportation needs. While the Provisional Government desperately wanted American locomotive and rolling stock, they had no use for meddling American "experts." The U.S. insisted that, if the Railway Mission was not allowed to do its work, there would be no aid of any kind. At the head of the Mission was John F. Stevens, former chief engineer of the Panama Canal and a man with long experience in building and running railroads. Stevens currently operated a

---

62. Saul, 152.

Wall Street consulting and construction firm and was closely connected to the American International Corporation. In Russia, he likely acted as an informal agent for American International by indentifying mineral resources and other potential assets along the Trans-Siberian line. In any case, Stevens recruited four other engineers and departed for Russia in May 1917. He and his team reached Petrograd ahead of Root and remained there until 28 October, just before the Bolshevik takeover. Returning to San Francisco, Stevens rounded up a 300-man corps of railway men with the aim of taking over operation of the Trans-Siberian. Bolshevik officials in Vladivostok initially blocked this, but in 1918, under the mantle of Allied intervention, Stevens and his American Railway Service Corps took control over large sections of the Trans-Siberian. Control of Siberia's railways had been the dream of Wall Street interests for many years.

In the meantime, the Provisional Government sent its own mission to America. The Tsar's ambassador, George Bakhmetev, resigned his post on 17 April 1917. In Petrograd, Milyukov appointed Boris Alexandrovich Bakhmetev (no relation), an assistant minster of trade and industry, to assume the ambassadorial post in Washington. Politically, Bakhmetev was a Menshevik who had proclaimed allegiance to the Kadets. He had visited the USA in 1916 where he met Charles Crane, and it almost certainly was Crane who pressed Milyukov to make him ambassador. Further connection is attested by the fact that Crane assigned Lincoln Steffens to accompany Bakhmetev to America.

Bakhmetev's delegation of almost fifty people left Petrograd in May and he presented his credentials to President Wilson on 5 July. The Russian Diplomatic Mission next went to New York where they were feted at public events and private gatherings. A grand reception at New York City Hall was hosted by none other than Jacob Schiff.[63] Also present were Friends of Russian Freedom stalwarts George Kennan, Walter Lippmann, Oscar Straus, Nicholas Murray Butler (president of Columbia University and a close friend of Elihu Root) and steel magnate Charles Schwab. On 8 July, Bakhmetev addressed an overflow crowd of 12,000, mostly Russian Jews, at Madison Square Garden. The organizer of this event was SR Peter Rutenberg, the same man who eleven years earlier had murdered Father Gapon. Rutenberg was now a recruit in William Wiseman's secret propa-

---

63. "Russian Envoy Thrills East Side," *New York Times* (10 July 1917).

ganda campaign.[64] Bakhmetev also visited the Henry Street Settlement House on the Lower East Side where he was received by Lillian Wald and, again, Jacob Schiff.

Connected to the Russian Mission were railway expert Yury Lomonosov, who would later become a Bolshevik representative in the U.S., and Alexander Postnikov, Xenophon Kalamatiano's partner in the International Manufacturers' Sales Corporation. That old small world kept spinning.

Amidst all the festivities, however, Wall Street had a bone to pick with Bakhmetev. American "commercial interests" felt aggrieved that despite all the war materiel flowing to Russia from U.S. factories, there had been too little "reciprocity" on the part of the Russian Government regarding the export of "raw materials."[65] The Americans wanted "a more liberal export policy," and there was the clear threat that if they did not get one, the flow of war supplies would suffer.

COL. EDWARD M. HOUSE, THE PUPPETMASTER

Since his name has come up several times already, it is worth saying a bit more about Col. Edward Mandell House, President Wilson's "second personality" or Rasputin, take your pick.[66] A successful career as Democratic Party kingmaker in Texas, and investor, brought him to New York around 1908. House's entrée into Wall Street was through an unlikely friend, Boston Brahmin Thomas Jefferson Coolidge, Jr., a partner in Old Colonial Trust which was, in turn, part of the Morgan sphere of influence. Coolidge had close ties to official Washington and has been dubbed a "prototype member of what today we call the foreign policy establishment."[67] In 1912, House guided Woodrow Wilson into the White House and their special relationship began.

About the time he met Wilson, House anonymously penned *Philip Dru, Administrator: A Story of Tomorrow*. This curious book, writes House biographer Godfrey Hodgson, is a "master key to the political beliefs of the Progressive movement and of House in particular."[68] Its titular hero leads a crusade against the evils of "money power," emerges the benign dictator of the Republic, and remolds America into a socialistic paradise. The story is a paean to collectivist authoritarianism, and *Philip Dru* could be as much an idealized vision of Lenin as it is Wilson. In Bolshevism, House encountered a movement with aspirations broadly sympathetic to his own.

---

64. WWP, 10/255, "Russia," 3.

65. "To Ask Reciprocity for Russian Trade," *New York Times* (8 July 1917).

66. John M. Cooper, *Woodrow Wilson: A Biography* (2011), 193.

67. Ernest R. May, *American Imperialism: A Speculative Essay* (1968), 45.

68. Godfrey Hodgson, *Woodrow Wilson's Right Hand: The Life of Colonel Edward M. House* (2006), 43.

Nevertheless, "in spite of his radical streak, the Colonel was not without friends in the dwelling of Mammon," and he acted as "the intermediary between the White House and the financiers."[69] House was on intimate terms with Morgan, Percy Rockefeller, Charles Sabin, Otto Kahn and, of course, fellow Wilson devotee, Charles Crane. The little Colonel assured the Money Trust they had nothing to fear and they, in turn, "put their faith in House."[70]

P. Rockefeller

THE AMERICAN RED CROSS MISSION

By far the most important and controversial of the missions sent to Russia was the American Red Cross Mission. From its founding in 1881, the American Red Cross (ARC) enjoyed the patronage of America's business and financial elite. Indeed, the "ARC depended heavily upon the nation's banks for raising funds for its operations. In order to maintain its financial stability, ARC accepted direction from, and was virtually controlled by, the New York bankers."[71] This is clearly shown in the composition of the ARC War Council formed in April 1917:

Left to right, front row: Robert W. deForest; President Woodrow Wilson; Former President William Howard Taft; and Eliot Wadsworth. Back Row: Henry P. Davison; Grayson M.P. Murphy; Charles D. Morton, and Edward N. Hurley.

AMERICAN RED CROSS WAR COUNCIL, 1917
(Appointed by President Woodrow Wilson, who was also president of the Red Cross)

Henry P. Davison, Chairman. Davison was a partner in J. P. Morgan & Co. and an important financial backer of President Wilson.

Grayson M-P Murphy. A private banker and senior vice-president of the Guaranty Trust Co., closely connected to Morgan. Murphy was also a director of Anaconda Copper, New York Trust, Bethlehem Steel and other companies.

69. George Sylvester Viereck, *The Strangest Friendship in History: Woodrow Wilson and Colonel House* (1932), 36.
70. *Ibid.*, 37.
71. Sutton, *Wall Street*, 71.

John D. Ryan, President, Anaconda Copper Mining Co., business partner of Percy Rockefeller, and closely connected to the Rockefellers.

Charles D. Norton, President, First National Bank and intimate associate of Henry Davison and the Morgan interests.

Cornelius Bliss, Jr., partner in Bliss, Fabyan & Co., and a Chicago textile manufacturer.

Eliot Wadsworth, *ex officio*. A partner in Stone & Webster & Co., electrical engineers, construction and stock brokers.

William Howard Taft, *ex officio*, former U. S. President.

Martin Egan, assistant to Henry Davison, chief of publicity for J. P. Morgan & Co. and head of Morgan's private intelligence network.

George B. Case, legal adviser. A senior partner in the law firm of White & Case which was connected to J. P. Morgan and other Wall Street interests.

Joseph Hartwell, legal counsel and another associate of White & Case.

Ivy Lee, publicity, chief of public relations for the Pennsylvania Railroad, and connected to Standard Oil.

When the USA entered World War I, one of the first to push for a mission to Russia was Alexander Legge, general manager of International Harvester and vice-president of President Wilson's new War Industries Board. Legge offered to put up $200,000 to fund the enterprise.[72] Mining magnate William Boyce Thompson then jumped in and offered to bankroll the entire operation. The Mission received the blessings of Wilson and House, who granted its members commissions in the U.S. Army Reserve and  the privilege of using military and diplomatic codes for communication with Washington. This naturally begs the question: Why did an ostensibly private, charitable organization need to use coded communications?

Legge

The answer is that the ARC Mission operated not only as the "operational vehicle" for American financial and commercial interests in Russia, but once again as a thinly-disguised propaganda and intelligence operation of the U.S. Government.[73] The ARC Mission sailed from Vancouver, Canada on 5 July and arrived in Petrograd on 1 August 1917. Its "commissioners" were as follows:

The nominal chief of the mission was **Dr. Frank Billings** a professor of medicine at the University of Chicago. That linked him to Crane and Harper, and Crane certainly had something to do with his appoint-

Billings

---

72. Mahoney, *American Prisoners*, 109.

73. *Ibid.*, 107-108.

ment. Under Billings were four other doctors, a food chemist, a chemist and a hygienist.[74] Billings and most of the other medical professionals left Russia after barely a month, Billings reportedly "completely disgusted" by what others in the mission were up to.[75]

The rest of the members were all connected to business and finance, and the most important of these was **William Boyce Thompson**. Just as Crane dominated the Root mission, Thompson was the leading figure in the ARC outfit until his departure in November. He was the founder and president of the Newmont Mining Co, a director of the Federal Reserve Bank of New York, New York Life Insurance, Sinclair Oil, Hayden, Stone & Co. stockbrokers, and a major stockholder in Chase National Bank.

Before leaving the States, Thompson received a private briefing from President Wilson. Thompson came away believing he had a mandate "to undertake any work necessary or advisable in the effort to prevent the disintegration of the Russian forces."[76] He saw himself as more important than the American ambassador, Francis, who he completely ignored and undercut.

Upon reaching Petrograd, Thompson not only paid for all the expenses of the ARC Mission but also dished out large sums, in effect bribes, to Russian Government officials. He made a particular friend in strongman Kerensky's private secretary David Soskice and promised the floundering Provisional Government a million dollars to fund pro-war propaganda. To direct this, Thompson recruited veteran anti-tsarist and darling of the Friends of Russian Freedom, Ekaterina Breshko-Breshkovskaya. Through ARC, Thompson also provided money for the "relief of political refugees." The $200,000 provided by International Harvester also ended up being used as "subsidies to Russian political organizations," i.e., propaganda.[77] Thompson was every inch the rich, self-important American, living in a suite in the Europe Hotel, renting the former Imperial box at the Petrograd Opera and riding around the city in a chauffeured limo. This earned him the nickname, "the American Tsar."[78]

Thompson initially backed the Kerensky regime against the Bolsheviks, but when Kerensky fell, he promptly switched gears and left the $1 million in the hands of Lenin & Co. Political ideology meant nothing to Thompson and the interests he represented; they were willing to back and deal with any Russian regime that offered to give them the access and concessions they wanted.

---

74. They were Dr. D. J. McCarthy, Prof. William S. Thayer, Prof. C. E. A. Winslow, Dr. Malcolm Grow, Dr. Wilbur E. Post, Prof. Henry J. Sherman, and Dr. Orrin S. Wightman.

75. William Hand, *Raymond Robins' Own Story* (1920), 11.

76. Herman Hagedorn, *The Magnate: William Boyce Thompson and His Time, 1869-1930* (1935), 183-184.

77. Mahoney, *American Prisoners*, 109.

78. *Ibid.*, 111.

Next in significance, and ultimately perhaps more important, was **Raymond Robins.** As mentioned, he'd made a fortune in the Alaska gold-rush and became a devout Christian and "socialist do-gooder."[79] He also became a devoted supporter of Theodore Roosevelt and Robins' appointment to the ARC Mission came at the insistence of the ex-President. With the departure of Billings, and later Thompson, Robins emerged the ARC chief in Russia. He would develop a very close relationship with Trotsky and become an outspoken champion and de facto agent of the Bolshevik regime.

The rest of the ARC crew included:

Cornelius Kelleher, personal secretary to Thompson, who later wrote that "the Red Cross component of the Mission was nothing but a mask."[80]

Henry S. Brown was a veteran journalist connected to the *New York Herald* and another friend of Thompson.

Herbert A. Magnuson was an American engineer who worked in China before joining the ARC Mission in the fall of 1917. He was recommended by John Finch, Thompson's "agent" in China.

James W. Anderson, the chief auditor of Liggett & Myers Tobacco Co., who handled the Mission's accounts.

Robert L. Barr, an officer and later vice-president of Chase National Bank and Chase Securities Co.

Frederic M. Corse (attached in Russia), vice president and longtime representative of the New York Life Insurance Co. in Russia.

Thomas D. Thacher was special assistant to Robins and a lawyer with the high-powered New York firm of Simpson, Thacher & Bartlett. Thacher subsequently became director of the William Boyce Thompson Institute. He also became a passionate advocate of normalized trade with the Bolsheviks.[81]

Thacher

Alan Wardwell was another corporate Lawyer, with Stetson, Jennings & Russell, the firm which acted as legal counsel for J. P. Morgan, U. S. Steel and other big corporations. Through his family, Wardwell was connected to Standard Oil, the Harrimans and the New York Trust Co. It's also probable that Wardwell was an intelligence officer using the ARC Mission as cover.[82] H. B. Redfield, Wardwell's assistant, was also an attorney at Stetson, Jennings & Russell.

Harold H. Swift was President of Swift & Co., Chicago, and another Crane link. So, too, was William G. Nicholson, also connected to Swift.

Henry J. Horn was Vice-president of the New Haven Railroad.

George C. Whipple and **Malcolm Pirnie** were partners in the Wall Street engineering firm of Hazen, Whipple & Fuller.

79. *Ibid.*, 93.
80. Sutton, *Wall Street,* 71.
81. "Favor Open Trade with Soviet Russia," *New York Times* (16 Feb. 1919).
82. Mahoney, *American Prisoners*, 115.

William Cochran, an executive from advertising giant McCann & Co., New York, handled public relations.

Finally, **Henry C. Emery**, Guaranty Trust's branch manager in Petrograd, served as the Mission's financial adviser. Those weren't his only jobs. Simultaneously, Emery was the American representative on the Inter-Allied Priority Board which worked with the Russian General Staff in managing war supply contracts.[83]

Clearly, the business of the Mission wasn't passing out hot meals and bandages. Behind all the boilerplate about freedom and democracy, most of the above men, and others like them, didn't much care what sort of government ruled Russia. The imperative was that any government keep the door open to American business. Keeping Russia in the war was much the same proposition; it would aid the Allied war effort, of course, but most importantly it would maintain the flow of orders to American factories, the demand for loans, and reap more profits for Wall Street.

THE "AMERICAN AMBULANCE" IN RUSSIA

Finally, there was another American mission operating in Russia, supposedly wholly private: the so-called American Ambulance. It was exactly that, a small volunteer corps of ambulances and medical personnel which operated with the Russian Army. The Ambulance was an offshoot of a larger charitable organization, the American White Cross. The latter, allegedly, was a philanthropic enterprise of the Sovereign Order of St. John of Jerusalem, a self-proclaimed branch of the infamous Knights of Malta.[84] Regardless, the American Ambulance was the brainchild of New York Progressive politician (and future U.S. Congressman) Hamilton Fish III, and its treasurer was Guaranty Trust executive William H. Hamilton. Among its directors was Morganite Willard Straight, Crane's friend Robert McCormick and Reilly's business crony and Ford Motor agent for Russia, Marcus Friede. Its headquarters was located at 120 Broadway.[85]

During the autumn of 1917, representatives of the Ambulance initiated their own secret plan to prop up the tottering Kerensky regime. Using a modest slush fund of $6,000, wired from New York, an ad hoc committee including Kerensky, U.S. Ambassador David Francis and other "leaders of the revolution," aimed to "put Russia on her feet," but the scheme was cut short by the Bolshevik coup.[86] If you don't like the revolution you've made, make another.

---

83. USDS, *Papers Relating to the Foreign Relations of the United States*, Vol. 2 (1918), 83, n.3.

84. The Sovereign Order of Saint John of Jerusalem, "After Malta: History and Lineage Charts since 1797," http://www.osjknights.com/History-After-Malta.htm.

85. "The American Ambulance in Russia," National Library of Medicine, Bethesda, MD.

86. "Tells of Aid for Kerensky," *New York Times* (28 Dec. 1917), 2.

CHAPTER NINE

BOLSHEVISM, INC.

THE BOLSHEVIKS TAKE CHARGE

We left Trotsky waiting for a train in Christiania. He soon caught one and stepped onto a platform at Petrograd's Finland Station in mid-May. That put his arrival a month behind Lenin (and Crane) and in the wake of the Provisional Government's first crisis. The latter saw the fall of Crane's darling Paul Milyukov and other liberals and the rise of Alexander Kerensky. The sole Socialist Revolutionary (SR) in the original cabinet, by July Kerensky would become prime minister and engineer a governing coalition largely composed of SRs, Mensheviks and non-party specialists.[1]

Charles Crane took a dim view of Kerensky in whom he saw a "popular revolutionary orator" possessing "no capacity whatsoever" as a real leader.[2] Crane bemoaned the fact that rabble-rousers like Kerensky and the "influence of repatriated New York Jewish East Siders" (like Trotsky) had hijacked his wonderful liberal revolution.[3] What Crane didn't grasp, and what Lenin and Trotsky did, was that the real power in Russia wasn't the teetering Provisional Government but the Petrograd Soviet of Workers and Soldiers Deputies and the hundreds of local soviets, sprouting like mushrooms across the county, that looked to it for guidance. While the Soviet imagined itself the voice of the Russian masses, it was an organization for Socialists only and initially contained no representation for peasants, overwhelmingly the largest social group. At the outset, it also contained no Bolsheviks. The Soviet possessed absolutely no *de jure* authority but it merrily passed resolutions and issued orders that the Government was compelled to recognize. The classic case was Army Order #1, issued on 14 March, which resulted in officers being stripped of almost all authority and replaced with elected "soldiers' committees." The Soviet was the horse Lenin intended to seize and ride into power. And so did Trotsky.

The political union of Lenin and Trotsky, a pair who had tossed insults at each other for years, is usually chalked up to some sort of historical kis-

---

1. The Kadets and other liberals held nine out of ten portfolios in the first cabinet and only three out of sixteen in the final one (October).

2. Saul, 149-150.

3. *Ibid.*

met. What is important to understand is that this alliance did not happen overnight. In 1911, Lenin had branded Trotsky a "Judas" and as recently as February 1917 called him a "scoundrel" and opportunistic zigzag who "twists, swindles, poses as a Left, helps the Right, so long as he can."[4] For his part, in May 1917, Trotsky proclaimed that "I cannot be called a Bolshevik ... we must not be demanded to recognize Bolshevism."[5] He would not formally become a Bolshevik until August 1917, almost three months after his arrival.

In Petrograd, Trotsky maneuvered himself into the leadership of the "Menshevik Internationalist" faction which numbered at most a few thousand. In the meantime, Bolshevik ranks swelled from little more that 20,000 in March, to 100,000 in May and 200,000 by August. Lenin was clearly at the head of a growing concern, Trotsky was not. So what did Lenin have to gain by embracing "Judas"? For one, co-opting him

Lenin, Trotsky and the Delegates of the 10th Congress of the Russian Communist Party.

eliminated a rival. For another, Trotsky possessed a brand name, charisma, and superb oratorical skills, something the Bolsheviks could not have too much of. The same, of course, can be asked of Trotsky. From his perspective, it made more sense to join forces with a successful enterprise than struggle to build a competing one selling the same product. It was logic any capitalist would understand. But no alliance has to be permanent. In the end, the Revolution could only have one master.

The turning point was the so-called July Days uprising. At the beginning of that month, Kerensky threw the Russian Army into another offensive aimed at scoring a big victory and bolstering moral. Instead, it quickly degenerated into mutiny and rout and ignited mass protests in Petrograd. Holding his finger to the wind, Lenin decided the time was right to seize power. That proved a near fatal miscalculation. Kerensky rallied loyal troops and by 18 July another would-be revolution had fizzled. To avoid arrest, Lenin fled to the Finnish woods where he would remain in hiding until November. This left Trotsky holding center stage, and he wasted no time exploiting it.

The Government at first ignored him because he wasn't a Bolshevik. To rectify this oversight, on 23 July Trotsky wrote an open letter proclaiming his total agreement with Lenin. Still, it was another two weeks before

---

4. "Judas Trotsky's Blush of Shame," *Lenin Collected Works*, Vol. 17 (1974), 45 and Lenin to Inessa Armand, *Labour Monthly*, September 1949.

5. Leon Trotsky, Mezhrayontsi conference, May 1917, quoted in Lenin, *Miscellany IV*, Russ. ed. (1925), 303.

Kerensky got around to arresting him. Once jailed for the cause, Lenin formally admitted Trotsky to Bolshevik ranks and even elevated him to the Central Committee. This did not sit well with other comrades who saw Trotsky as an interloper and opportunist. And they were right.

As an agitator and organizer, Trotsky was an asset, but was that all he had to offer? In the weeks leading up to the July crisis, the Bolsheviks mounted an aggressive propaganda campaign. In March they had no press to speak of, but by June they were flooding barracks and trenches alone with 100,000 papers per day and by early July they churned out nearly 700,000 papers, pamphlets and broadsheets.[6] The money behind this was presumably German supplied through Parvus' network and Aschberg's bank. Even before the July Days, Kerensky's Minister of Justice, Paul Pereverzev (himself a revolutionary), had gotten wind of Lenin's German connections and started to build a case against him. On 21 July, he charged Lenin and key comrades with high treason. However, Pereverzev's case was weak.[7] His main evidence was a set of intercepted cables showing transfers of funds from Stockholm to Petrograd, all disguised as legitimate business transactions. The problem was proving they weren't just legitimate business.

Provable or not, Lenin's German pipeline was exposed. He needed another, more discreet, source of funds, and he needed it right away. He apparently found one. Bolshevik propaganda temporarily slackened under the attacks of the Provisional Government, but it did not stop. In early September their main organ, *Pravda* (temporarily rebranded *Rabochy put'*, "Workers; Path") was still putting out 50,000 copies per day and by the end of the month that had doubled.[8] Was money the real price of Trotsky's admission to the Bolshevik club? Did he use his connections in New York to set funds flowing through American channels with little risk of detection? Even a small firm like Reilly's Traders, Inc., with its Petrograd office and accounts at National City and Guaranty Trust (and the help of Uncle Abram, of course), would have been an excellent conduit. As we've seen, it was hardly the only one.

Regardless, Trotsky didn't stay in jail for long. In late August 1917, an ambitious general, Lavr Kornilov, attempted a coup d'etat. Kerensky freed Trotsky and other Bolsheviks to rally the workers of Petrograd in defense of the Revolution. Maybe that had been the plan all along.[9] The coup (the "re-revolution"?) failed, but Kerensky's credibility was finished and Trotsky's star

Kornilov

6. Richard Pipes, *The Russian Revolution* (1990), 410.

7. For a full and careful examination of this case, see: Semion Lyandres, "The Bolsheviks' 'German Gold' Revisited," *Carl Beck Papers*, #1106 (1995).

8. Roger Pethybridge, *The Spread of the Russian Revolution: Essays on 1917* (1972), 121-122.

9. There is still uncertainty about just who and what was behind the "Kornilov Affair." The General's coup certainly had the backing of dethroned liberals like Milyukov, but other theories held that Kerensky himself instigated the affair in a half-baked scheme to strengthen his position. If so, it didn't work.

blazed even brighter. In early October, the Bolsheviks gained control of the Petrograd Soviet and he became its chairman. He also led the Military Revolutionary Committee which meticulously prepared a fresh coup against the floundering Kerensky. That finally came down on the night of 6-7 November. Lenin emerged from his woodland hideaway to take credit and proclaim the triumph of Soviet power. Trotsky, however, was the real architect of the "October Revolution," and he knew it.

THE WISEMAN PROGRAM

As noted in the last chapter, soon after Trotsky's departure from New York, Sir William Wiseman began to organize a secret propaganda campaign in Russia. Why Wiseman, who had no acquaintance with Russian matters, would have been so interested is another question. Perhaps Reilly encouraged him. In part, Wiseman was reacting to concerns from London, where as early as 7 April (before either Lenin or Trotsky reached Petrograd), there were worries about the nefarious influence of "revolutionary pacifists."[10] By 18 May, right as Trotsky arrived on the scene, Wiseman had his program planned out. This had to be, he emphasized, "entirely unofficial and very secretly organized."[11] "The propaganda should be organized under one head in America, who would be the only person knowing the details," he emphasized. "The other people working in the scheme," he added, "would, under no circumstances, be allowed to know of each others' existence." In other words, Wiseman would hold all the threads, and only he would know the overall plan. His idea was to dispatch "six or seven different missions to Petrograd," including revolutionaries, Czech, Polish and Jewish activists and even "Germans who are working for us among the real Germans." The avowed goal was to counteract the efforts of "German agents [who] have already been at work in the United States, and are sending Russian-Jewish Socialists back to Petrograd who are either knowingly or unknowingly working in the German cause."

What Wiseman needed to make this work, naturally, was money. Through House, he persuaded President Wilson to authorize $75,000 (about $1,500,000 in 2017) "for expenses of a confidential nature."[12] Wiseman then twisted the arm of his own government for an equal amount which was all deposited in his personal account at J.P. Morgan. Wiseman also sought help from private quarters. Through his agent Richard Gottheil, he leaned on Schiff to write Jewish bankers in Petrograd urging them to back the new government. Schiff also may have kicked in more money, possibly much more.

---

10. TNA, FO 115/2317, Balfour note, 7 April 1917.

11. WWP, 10/255, "Russia", 1.

12. William Fowler, *British-American Relations: The Role of Sir William Wiseman* (1969), 114, n.35.

Finally, Wiseman enlisted another agent, his friend and experienced British spy W. Somerset Maugham. Maugham, a well-known author, went to Petrograd under the guise of researching a book.[13] He also went armed with letters of recommendation, one of them to Charles Crane.[14] Through Gottheil, Wiseman reached out to Crane, then in Petrograd, as early as 3 May.[15] Gottheil exhorted Crane to "see some of [the] leaders of the Jewish community and advise them how strongly we Jews in America feel that their assistance should be given by all parties to the new regime." Maugham later supplied Wiseman with a report, dated 11 September, in which he mentioned meeting with Crane's man Samuel Harper. Maugham judged him "rather too sure of his information, which he gains from sources which were once reliable but now out of touch with current politics."[16]

Maugham

Most intriguing, as mentioned earlier, Maugham's report claimed that "the chief German agent in Russia is Max Warburg … brother of Paul Warburg."[17] There may have been confusion with another Warburg brother, Fritz, who indeed served as the German "financial attaché" in Stockholm and was the reputed "head of the German spy system outside of Germany."[18] Or maybe brother Max was exactly what Maugham claimed. According to information received by American Military Intelligence, even Felix Warburg, Schiff's partner in Jewish relief efforts, "handled and financed" Russian disorganization with other Germans through Stockholm.[19] Other reports held that brothers Max and Paul were somehow "at the bottom of" Bolshevism.[20] The source of the latter statement, incidentally, was Casimir Pilenas, the same man who had denounced Trotsky to Wiseman.

Wiseman's scheme was every bit as much about gathering intelligence as it was dispensing propaganda. In the latter regard it seems to have been a thorough bust. In early 1918, Wiseman, under some pressure, filed a brief report on the achievements of his "Intelligence and Propaganda Work in Russia."[21] His conclusion was that "the situation in Russia was completely

---

13. WWP, 10/255, Wiseman to Gottheil, 30 June 1917.

14. Fowler, 115.

15. WWP, 10/255, Gottheil to Crane, 3 May 1917.

16. WWP, 10/257, "Summary of Reports Received from Agent in Petrograd," 3.

17. *Ibid.*

18. MID, #10080-342, 12-24, IO-NYC, 2 July 1918.

19. MID, #10087-22, Extract of letter from U.S. Military Attaché, Stockholm, 20 Feb. 1918.

20. MID, #10058-285, 83-84, 19 Feb. 1919.

21. WWP, 10/261, "Intelligence & Propaganda Work in Russia July to December 1917," 19 Jan. 1918.

out of hand, and that no propaganda or organized support undertaken by the Allies could possibly stem the rise of Bolshevism." He also noted that "one of our agents from America is a well-known international Socialist who was at once accepted by the Bolshevics [sic] and admitted to their conferences." One could easily picture Trotsky in that role was it not for the fact that Wiseman immediately added that the same agent later "challenged Trotzky [sic] to a public discussion."

Or maybe Wiseman was just making sure that no one got the *right* idea. Remember, he was the only person who really knew who his agents were, what they were doing, and where their information went. It all comes back to the sticky issue of Wiseman's loyalties. In light of accusations that he acted contrary to British/Allied interests during the war, it raises some interesting questions. Was it merely coincidence that Wiseman's secret slush fund was in place just before Trotsky proclaimed his loyalty to Lenin and was "accepted by the Bolsheviks and admitted to their conferences?" Wiseman's post-war reward, remember, would come not from His Majesty's Government but from Kuhn Loeb. At the end of his memo, Sir William advised that in future "we ought to concentrate on some special object rather that attempt general political propaganda" and offered to put forward "new proposals." One of these would be sending Sidney Reilly back to Russia.

JOHN REED, ESTABLISHMENT REVOLUTIONARY

John Silas Reed was a rock star of American radicalism. The quintessential "romantic revolutionary," he died young, left a more or less handsome corpse and was buried next to the Kremlin. As a revolutionary he cut a familiar figure. The son of a wealthy family, Harvard man and bon-vivant, he had nothing in common with the down-trodden proletarians whose cause he championed. Fellow leftists who suspected him of self-indulgent dilettantism had their reasons, and some may have suspected him of worse. As Antony Sutton noted,

Reed

Reed was an "Establishment Revolutionary" who never lacked for rich, influential friends to come to his defense and who never lost the privileges of his class even while attacking it.[22]

On 14 August 1917, John Reed received a new U.S. passport to go to Russia. The purpose of the travel, as given in the application, was "mag-

---

22. Sutton, *Wall Street*, 137.

azine work." Given his well-known radicalism, the application generated some concern in Washington, and the file contains a couple of interesting attachments. The first was a report to the Bureau of Investigation from Richmond Levering, a Wall Street businessman with offices at the familiar 120 Broadway. Levering quoted a "confidential source" who described Reed as a "violent socialist writer" who told the informant "in absolute confidence" that the real purpose of his trip was to attend an anti-war Socialist conference in Stockholm. Levering referred the matter to the Manhattan office of the Bureau of Investigation. The question was whether Reed's application should be denied. One issue was his status under the new Selective Service law. He had registered for the draft in June but proclaimed himself a "conscientious objector to the war."[23] This resulted in the second attachment, a letter from the U. S. Army's Provost Marshal General who declared that the War Department had "no objection to the issuance of a passport to him."

The passport flap indicates three things: first, Reed was in contact with at least one Government informant who he took into his confidence; second, that informant was close to an important New York businessman; third, when queried, the Army had no reservations about his travel despite his proclaimed opposition to the war. All are worth keeping in mind in light of future developments.

After reaching Petrograd in the turbulent autumn of 1917, Reed quickly identified with the Bolsheviks and recorded their rise to power in his famous *Ten Days That Shook the World.* He jumped on the bandwagon of the Red regime and contributed his talents to its Bureau of International Revolutionary Propaganda. The latter functioned under the People's Commissariat for Foreign Affairs headed by Trotsky. Reed's fervid support of the Bolsheviks made him a pariah to some Americans in the Russian capital, Ambassador Francis among them, but not to all. Reed maintained close, and sometimes curious, connections to other U.S. officials, notably Raymond Robins, William F. Sands, and Edgar Sisson. All, to one degree or another, had links to American intelligence.

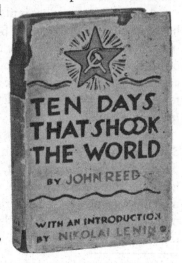

In Petrograd, left-leaning Robins put Reed on the Red Cross payroll. Robins had become another fan of the Bolsheviks, especially Trotsky who he hailed as "a four kind son-of-a-bitch, but the greatest Jew since Christ."[24] More than that, Robins surrounded himself with trio of Russian

---

23. Reed's draft registration 5 June 1917.
24. Kennan, *Russia Leaves the War* (1956), 422.

translators and secretaries, two of whom, Alexander Gumberg and Boris Reinstein were "American Bolsheviki" discussed in Chapter Five. The third, a Captain Ilovaisky, was also an avowed Bolshevik. The common view is that Reed took the job because he was hard-up for money, but there may have been more involved. Among other things, it afforded him a pipeline to Trotsky and the whole Bolshevik hierarchy.

Reed's work for Robins has been characterized as an "agent for ... gathering information."[25] Reeds wife, Louise Bryant, later testified that both she and her husband supplied Robins with exactly that.[26] There is, of course, very slight distinction between supplying information and providing intelligence. The ARC mission in Russia, recall, *unofficially* functioned as a "thinly disguised propaganda and intelligence collection operation of the United States Government."[27] Through operatives like Reed and with the blessing of Reds like Trotsky, Robins collected and disseminated intelligence; but for who, exactly? In the view of former CIA officer Harry Mahoney, Reed was an "irregular agent" and "part of a larger scheme of semi-organized irregular agents operating covertly under the tacit auspices of some part of the United States Government."[28] Of course, wherever the U.S. Government was, Wall Street was never far away.

Bryant

Another incident that hints at Robins' connection to American intelligence again involves Louise Bryant. She departed Petrograd in advance of her husband, and on 20 January 1918 Robins gave her a letter of recommendation addressed to Marine Maj. Breckenridge, U. S. naval attaché and resident naval intelligence officer in Christiania, Norway. Robins formally requested Breckinridge afford her "such special consideration as may be possible."[29]

As detailed, the ARC mission was little more than a fig leaf for Wall Street interests. This was further reflected in two documents Reed produced in Robin's employ. First, he drew up a prospectus for a new periodical in Petrograd that would push American views (i.e. propaganda) and, most importantly, boost American business and investment in Russia. Its mockup masthead openly declared that "this paper is devoted to promoting the interests of American capital."[30] As one Reed biographer put it,

25. Mahoney, *American Prisoners*, 88.

26. BI, #82787, Case of John Silas Reed, complied by Julian W. Bowes for U. S. Secret Service, 1919, Report #2.

27. Mahoney, *Ibid.*, 138, n. 151.

28. *Ibid.*, 99.

29. William M. Greene, "Louise Bryant - An Informal Biography of an Activist." http://louisebryant.com/partthree.htm

30. Eric Homberger, *John Reed* (1990), 160 and Kennan, *Russia Leaves the War*, 408.

"no revolutionary would want to have anything to do with such a tainted proposal," but Reed did.[31] Again, his need for cash, apparently, "overrode [his] scruples." Another explanation might be that Reed, like Robins, believed the absolutely essential thing was securing American recognition and assistance for the new regime and that garnering the backing of Wall Street was the best way to do it. The second document was a candid report by Reed on his conversations with Bolshevik officials on the subject of "future Russian-American commercial relations."[32] It was another odd assignment for a revolutionary Socialist.

It was during late 1917 and early 1918 that the State Department picked up information concerning financial transactions between U.S. and Russian banks. On 2 November 1917, just days before the Bolshevik coup, Guaranty Trust Co. used the Russo-Asiatic Bank to transfer 100,000 rubles ($50,000) to Libau in the German-occupied Baltic Provinces.[33] Said funds were then credited to the account of Schiff & Co. State Bank in Chicago. This Schiff & Co., just to be clear, had no connection to Jacob Schiff or Kuhn Loeb, none visible besides the name, that is. One person associated with Russo-Asiatic, of course, was Abram Zhivotovsky. On 28 January 1918, Russo-Asiatic again figured in the remittance of funds from the American Smelting & Refining Co. (Guggenheims) and Henry Heil & Co. (chemical manufacturer), through National City Bank, once again to the ultimate credit of Schiff & Co.[34] Much the same was recorded in another report dated 1 February. Others, dated 30 January and 5 February, showed Hanover National Bank using Russo-Asiatic to direct payments to Siberia.[35] On 21 June 1918, the familiar Nya Banken shows up trading with the Russo-Asiatic branch in London (formerly run by Alexander Weinstein) and using it as an intermediary with New York banks.[36] All of these may have been perfectly mundane business transactions, but they do illustrate the relative ease with which money flowed to and from Russia even during a period of acute political crisis.

Speaking of Guaranty Trust, its Russian rep, Henry C. Emery, remained in Petrograd through late February 1918. With a laissez-passer personally supplied by Trotsky, he set out for Stockholm via then Red controlled southern Finland. Unfortunately for him, he ran into German interventionist forces who interned him for the next eight months.[37] Finally returning to New York in November 1918, Emery would become a quiet but persistent advocate of the Soviet regime and a financial helping hand to its various emissaries.

---

31. Homberger, 160.

32. Mahoney, *American Prisoners*, 89.

33. USDS, #763.72112/5538, Russo-Asiatic Bank, 2 Nov. 1917.

34. *Ibid.*, #763.72112/6579, 28 Jan. 1918.

35. *Ibid.*, #763.7211/6645, 30 Jan, 1918 and /7244, 5 Feb. 1918.

36. *Ibid.*, #763.72112/9325, 21 June 1918.

37. Henry C. Emery, Emergency Passport application, American Legation, Copenhagen, 24 Oct. 1918.

Back to John Reed, his value went deeper than a mere informant and propagandist. In late 1917/early 1918, American policy (and Allied policy generally) towards the new Russian government was in limbo. Washington would not grant recognition, but simultaneously declared its willingness "to go to any honorable lengths to avoid any break with the Bolshevist regime just at this time."[38] While many Americans saw the Bolsheviks as detestable radicals and German stooges, others, like Robins and his superior, William Boyce Thompson, believed that accommodation was not only possible but also desirable. Even Charles Crane, back in DC and huddled with House and Wilson, advised that the best thing the U.S. Government could do for the present was let Russia "work out its own destiny."[39] The Red regime had proclaimed an armistice but was yet to make peace with the Germans. In this volatile atmosphere, no matter how frosty official relations became, it was practical to maintain a back channel for communication and negotiation. Men like Reed, Robins and Thompson provided that.

Sands

William Franklin Sands is another example of Reed's association with persons linked to Washington, intelligence and Wall Street. Sands was a career U.S. diplomat who acted as a troubleshooter in far-flung hot spots while simultaneously serving as the representative of American banks and firms. More simply put, he was a spy who used diplomatic posts and commercial dealings as cover. Beyond this, don't you know, he also knew Charles Crane. In 1916, the State Department tapped Sands to go to Petrograd as a "special assistant to the Ambassador" nominally tasked with overseeing American relief to Austrian and German POWs and internees.[40] Shortly after the first Russian revolution in March, Sands abruptly quit his diplomatic post and re-emerged the Russian representative of 120 Broadway's American International Corporation.

During the fall of 1917, Sands, the spy-diplomat-capitalist, became very chummy with John Reed, and Reed's new found advocacy for American business fit perfectly with AIC's agenda. However, Sands never really severed his ties to the State Department. Not only did he continue to receive classified State correspondence, but on his return to the U. S. in December 1917 he brought with him diplomatic pouches containing

---

38. "Bolsheviki Seize All Private Banks," *New York Times* (29 Dec. 1917).

39. "Francis Cowed Mob Invading Embassy," *New York Times* (27 Dec. 1917).

40. Sands' 5 July 1917 passport application, and attached 9 May 1917 letter of Ambassador David R. Francis.

copies of Russian secret treaties which he handed to Secretary of State Robert Lansing.[41] Lansing asked Sands to compile a confidential report on Russian conditions. Sands, exactly like Robins and Thompson, argued for Washington's recognition and assistance to the Bolsheviks. This, he felt, would serve the best interests of America *and* American International.

Sands also came to the defense of John Reed. After various delays, Reed finally reached American shores on 28 April 1918. Back home, he faced criminal charges for his past involvement with the allegedly seditious publication *The Masses*. Two unsuccessful prosecutions followed which made Reed one of the most famous radicals in the country. On 5 June, Sands wrote to State's Frank Polk, head of its Bureau of Secret Intelligence. Sand's ostensible purpose was to forward an appeal from Reed asking for the return of his papers seized by federal agents upon his arrival. That Reed picked Sands as his intermediary argues that he knew exactly who he was and who he worked for.

Writing from his AIC desk at 120, Sands flatly stated that "I do not believe that Mr. Reed is either a 'Bolshevik' or a 'dangerous anarchist,' as I have often seen him described."[42] Rather, he characterized Reed a "sensational journalist" with self-control issues. Most importantly, he thought Reed ought to be handled delicately because he could be – *and had been* – of great value to the Government and American interests. Sands noted "a conversation" with Reed after his return, a meeting that sounds a lot like a de-briefing. Reed "had sketched certain attempts by the Soviet Government to initiate constructive development," and expressed his desire to "place whatever observations he had made or information he had obtained through his connection with Leon Trotzky [sic] at the disposal of our Government." Moreover, once he had his papers back, Reed "voluntarily offer[ed] any information they might contain to the Government." Sands regarded Reed's recent attempt to deliver a speech in Philadelphia (where he was arrested) as "the only lecture on Russia which I would have paid to hear, if I had not already seen his notes on the subject." Sands also noted that Reed had recently supplied a memorandum on Russia to Assistant Secretary of State William Bullitt and that "I wanted him to let me see it first and perhaps edit it."

The Bolsheviki, Sands admitted, "liked" Reed and harassing him would only irritate them and make relations more difficult. In any case, he suggested, "[Reed] can be handled and controlled much better by other means than by the police." In this, presumably, Sands spoke from experience. Sands concluded by offering that it was far better to "use" Reed than to alienate him and that "unless I am very much mistaken [he is] susceptible to discreet guidance and might be quite useful." Was Sands thinking of

---

41. Sutton, *Wall Street*, 134-135, citing Morris, Stockholm to Washington, 16 Jan. 1918, and other documents in USDS #861.00.969.

42. USDS, #360-D-1121.R/25 (John Reed).

the interests of the U.S. Government or of American International, or did he make any real distinction between them?

In Petrograd, Reed forged a relationship with yet another American representative, Edgar Grant Sisson. Here, too, the diplomatic-intelligence-Wall Street nexus is evident. Sisson was a Chicago newspaper man hand-picked by the chief of the U.S. Committee on Public Information (CPI), George Creel, to head an office in Petrograd. The CPI was, without question, a propaganda agency. As such, it endeavored to mount a pro-Ally campaign in Russia and resented what it regarded as the ARC's amateurish meddling. Sisson did not arrive on the scene until after the Bolsheviks had taken power but unlike Reed, Robins and Sands, he took a violent dislike of them. His conviction that Lenin and Trotsky were German  agents eventually led him to purchase and promote a collection of mostly spurious documents purporting to prove just that, ever after known as the "Sisson Documents." This is clear evidence that Sisson and the CPI were involved intelligence-gathering; indeed, "the CPI was in the closest possible relationship to the intelligence branches of the Army and Navy...."[43] According to George Kennan, "In the little circle of American leftists in Petrograd to which Reed belonged," Sisson was "unquestionably identified from the beginning as an important American intelligence agent probably with lines leading to very high circles in Washington."[44]

Given this, some Bolsheviks must have been puzzled by Reed's association with Sisson, just as some Americans could not fathom what he saw in Reed. Sisson personally didn't seem to care much for Reed but was obeying orders from his superior, George Creel, a pal of Reed's from *Masses* days. Creel, in turn, may have acted at the urging of Crane. Sisson's main task in Russia was to oversee the production of propaganda aimed at undermining the morale of German and Austrian troops, and Reed's work for the Bolshevik Propaganda Bureau had precisely the same aim.[45] So was Reed simultaneously working for CPI? He later admitted that he "always asked advice" from American officials when it came to his "political activity" in Russia.[46]

The main point is that Reed managed to ingratiate himself with the Bolsheviks perhaps more than any other American. In January 1918, he was the warm-up act for Comrade Trotsky at the Third Congress of Soviets. The assembled multitude hailed the American as a revolutionary

43. James R. Mock and Cedric Larsen, *Words That Won the War: The Story of the Committee on Public Information, 1917-1919* (1939), 237. On CPI's relationship with Military Intelligence, see also Rhodri Jeffreys-Jones, *American Espionage: From Secret Service to CIA* (1977), 44.

44. Kennan, *Russia Leaves the War*, 409.

45. "Bolshevik Propaganda," Hearings before the U. S. Senate, Subcommittee on the Committee of the Judiciary, 65th Congress, 3rd Session, 1919, 467-468.

46. *Ibid.*, 564

hero. On 29 January, Trotsky bestowed further honor by naming Reed the new Soviet consul in New York. Thus, a bona fide American radical, but also a man linked to U.S. intelligence and Wall Street, was to be the Bolshevik's representative in America. And Trotsky arranged it.

However, Reed's diplomatic appointed was undermined by Alexander Gumberg, maybe because he was suspicious about where the American's loyalties really lay. Gumberg told his brother, Bolshevik commissar Sergius Zorin, that "I had grounds for considering this appointment undesirable and told this to Vladimir Ilyich [Lenin]...."[47] Specifically, he handed Lenin the two "pro-capitalist" documents Reed had written for Robins. Before Reed reached New York, Petrograd canceled his consular appointment.

On his way back to the States, Reed ran into difficulty in Christiania. An uncooperative American consul refused to grant him a visa for New York. The CPI's Creel promptly came to the rescue by proposing that Reed return to Russia "as a representative of the United States Government, or something of that sort."[48] The intermediary of this proposal was Lincoln Steffens. Reed's job would be to convince Lenin and Trotsky of President Wilson's sincerity and gain their cooperation with his and Col. House's grand scheme for world peace. The second ranking CPI representative in Russia, Arthur Bullard, the man Reed would work under if he returned, was also "a friend of Crane's."[49] Was the Chicago magnate's hand behind the whole thing? Reed, however, was desperate to get home and passed on the offer.

There were other games afoot. In December 1917, Trotsky suddenly announced the discovery of an insidious "American Plot" against the infant Soviet regime. It boiled down to the accusation that Ambassador Francis, definitely not a fan of Petrograd's new masters, had conspired to deliver money and vehicles to rebellious Cossack General Alexis Kaledin.[50] The accusation wasn't baseless. There were American officials who were helping Kaledin; even Charles Crane may have had a hand in it.[51] However, Trotsky's real aim was to force Washington to recall reactionary Francis and replace him with Raymond "Red" Robins.[52]

At the center of this conspiracy was a familiar name, Andrew Kolpashnikov, the very same Russian officer who had sailed with Trotsky on the *Kristianiafjord* and "helped" with his interrogation in Halifax. Kolpashnikov, recall, was linked to John McGregor Grant and Reilly and his

47. Kennan, *Russia Leaves the War*, 408. Zorin sat on the Revolutionary Tribunal of the Petrograd Soviet which worked hand in glove with the newly-formed Bolshevik secret police, the Extraordinary Commission, or Cheka.
48. "Bolshevik Propaganda," 564.
49. Saul, 156.
50. "Trotzky's American Plot," *New York Times* (28 Dec. 1917), 2.
51. David Foglesong, *America's Secret War against Bolshevism* (1995), 100-104.
52. "Raymond Robins and the Reds," *New York Times* (22 June 1920).

other friends in New York business circles included Coleman DuPont, Frederic Coudert, and Nicholas Roosevelt.[53] Francis managed to hang-on, but Kolpashnikov spent five months in prison before being set free on Trotsky's order and allowed to return to the U.S.A. When persons suspected of equal or lesser offenses against Soviet power ended up in front of a firing squad, this was kid-glove treatment. Or did Kolpashnikov merely act his designated part in Trotsky's scheme?

WILLIAM BOYCE THOMPSON: THE "BOLSHEVIK OF WALL STREET."

As mentioned, American policy towards Russia in early 1918 was in a state of utter confusion. Diplomatic personnel like Ambassador Francis and Moscow Consul General Maddin Summers despised Lenin & Co. and they were under a presidential order, dated 6 December, to refrain from any *direct* communication with the Bolshevik Government. This is what made men like Reed and Robins vital. Diplomatic relations were not formally severed. Meanwhile, in Washington, Col. House dreamed of co-opting the Bolsheviks into his plan for winning the war and creating a New World Order through the League of Nations.

The pro-Bolshevik faction on Wall Street had its most outspoken pitchman in the aforementioned William Boyce Thompson. Departing Petrograd, he arrived back in the States on Christmas Day 1917. On 18th January he sat for an interview with a representative of Dow Jones and published in the *Wall Street Journal*.[54] Despite the fact that Bolsheviks had proclaimed an armistice on the Eastern Front and opened peace negotiations with Berlin and its allies, Thompson stridently insisted that the Russians would never conclude a separate peace. He pooh-poohed reports that there was "anarchy" in Russia and said that the Russian people, who he believed the Bolsheviks fairly represented, were "trying to adopt Socialism as the basis of their government." If they were allowed to succeed, "an extremely democratic, well-managed country will emerge." In other words, an excellent business environment.

A few days later, Thompson addressed the members of New York's Rocky Mountain Club, another exclusive confab of millionaires including Thompson himself, Jacob Schiff's pal's Albert Seligman and Oscar Straus, and even Theodore Roosevelt.[55] Before this august gathering, and glowing-ly introduced by Morgan partner Thomas Lamont, Thompson set out to marshal "public support in America over to the side of the Bolsheviki." The latter, he pleaded, represented the "common people of Russia" and their re-gime was "a democracy which comes as near being representative of the soil as it would be possible to find anywhere." Kerensky failed, he argued, be-

---

53. "Col. Kolpatchnikoff Weds," *New York Times* (5 June 1919).

54. "Head of Red Cross Mission...," *Wall Street Journal*, (18 Jan. 1918).

55. "Col. Thompson Emphasizes Bolsheviki's Activities," *Wall Street Journal* (24 Jan. 918), 7.

cause he bent too far to accommodate "arrogant capital." Lenin and Trotsky, Thompson admitted, had veered completely towards labor, but he was sure a proper balance would be achieved in time. The most important thing at present, he insisted, was that the Bolsheviki had not made a separate peace, and their revolutionary propaganda was materially aiding the Allied cause by undermining the fighting spirit of German and Austrian soldiers.

Thompson even took personal credit for funding this propaganda. Recall that back in September 1917, when Kerensky was still in the saddle, Thompson put up $1,000,000 of his own money to underwrite an "educational" campaign headed by "Babushka" Breshko-Breshkovskaya. A telegram dated 9 September confirmed that J. P. Morgan & Co. had deposited the money in Thompson's account at National City Bank's Petrograd branch.[56] If nothing else, notice the ease with which a million dollars went from New York to Russia. Breshkovskaya's program never made headway, and *all or most of the million was still there* when the Bolsheviks took control. Thompson generously allowed them to use it to fund their new Bureau of International Revolutionary Propaganda, the same outfit that employed John Reed. The same one that Trotsky oversaw. Thompson took great pride that his money had made possible the "thousands of pounds of Bolshevik literature" flooding into Germany and Austria.[57]

Throughout early 1918, Thompson kept up his pro-Bolshevik campaign. He declared himself to be "in absolute sympathy with the Russian democracy as represented by the Bolsheviki at present."[58] The latter, were "not perfect but genuine democrats." "Many of their ideas are wild," he conceded, but "their democracy can only succeed by recognizing the fullness of capital as well as of labor, and that will come in time."[59] Thompson maintained his pro-Bolshevik stance even after they made a liar out of him and signed the separate Treaty of Brest-Litovsk in March. On 5 May 1918, in Washington, he joined with Senator William Borah, Oscar Straus and a bevy of other well-connected citizens to form the pro-recognition American League to Aid and Cooperate with Russia.[60]

Thompson wasn't the only Wall Street big-shot making positive statements about the Bolsheviks. On 24 January, Bethlehem Steel boss Charles Schwab told another exclusive gathering that the present war was bound "to create sweeping social changes across the globe," and as a result the worker "will be the man who will dominate the world."[61] "The

---

56. Hagedorn, 251.
57. "A Million for the Paper Bombardment," *Wilmington Morning News* [DE] (1 Feb. 1918), 4.
58. "Bolsheviki Will Not Make Separate Peace," *New York Times Magazine* (27 Jan. 1918), 74.
59. "Thompson Asking for U.S. Recognition of Bolsheviki," *The Washington Herald* (3 Feb. 1918), 1,5.
60. "Russia Must Be Saved," *The Baltimore Sun* (6 May 1918), 6.
61. "Sees New Era for Laboring Man," *New York Times* (25 Jan. 1918) and "Worker to Rule, Asserts Schwab," *Indianapolis Star* (25 Jan. 1918), 1.

Bolshevik sentiment must be taken into consideration," he added, and "like all revolutionary movements, it will probably work good." Indeed, Schwab expressed confidence that "Socialism was working for the good of mankind." "We must not fight this movement," he cautioned his audience, "but we must educate it." Schwab got his biggest applause, however, when he noted that the war effort would reward the U.S. "many times over" and that an era of American "commercial and social supremacy" lay ahead. He apparently saw no contradiction between that and the expected triumph of World Socialism.

ALEXANDER BUBLIKOV AND THE RUSSIAN ECONOMIC LEAGUE

If the Bolshevik seizure of power inspired American intrigues in Russia, it also gave rise to Russian intrigues in the U.S. One example was Alexander Bublikov, a railway engineer and former Duma member who earned the distinction of being the "man who arrested Nicholas II" back in March 1917. Apparently fleeing the new order in Petrograd, Bublikov, like Thompson, landed in New York on Christmas 1917. His destination was 120 Broadway and the person he met there was Kerensky's Ambassador Boris Bakhmetev. Bakhmetev's regular address was the Russian Embassy in Washington or, alternately, the Russian Consulate General in New York; so why were they meeting at the Equitable?

Bublikov

In early February 1918, Bublikov was guest of honor at a gathering of Mensheviks (and a few Bolsheviks) at Manhattan's Arlington Hall. Bublikov gave a brief talk and received a hearty ovation.[62] Soon after, he attended a similar meeting in Chicago, and more followed. Bublikov outwardly presented himself as anti-Bolshevik, though not anti-Soviet. For instance, in April 1919, he appeared on stage with Raymond Robins who gave a rousing address in favor of the Bolsheviki.[63] If Bublikov expressed a different view, his remarks are unrecorded. Inevitably, there were rumors that he had been sent to the States as a stealth emissary of Lenin and Trotsky with the aim of bringing the Russian Embassy other state agencies under their control.

Regardless, what Bublikov obviously did was to go into business and at 120 Broadway. During 1918 he helped incorporate an American branch of the Youroveta Home and Foreign Trading Co. He became its vice president, the head position being held by another Russian businessman, Leon Wourgaft. Originally formed in 1910 as the South Russian Company for Foreign and Domestic Trade (hence the Russian acronym, "Youroveta"), in 1915 it relocated its headquarters to Petrograd. One of its avowed goals

---

62. "'Bolshevik' Barred in Russian Meeting," *New York Times* (12 Feb. 1918).

63. "Raymond Robins Praises the Soviets," *The Butte Daily Bulletin* [MT] (2 April 1919), 6.

was to "attract American capital."[64] Another interesting rumor, duly reported to U.S. Military Intelligence in January 1919, was that Jacob Schiff had acquired a controlling interest in the firm.

Bublikov also served as vice-president of the Russian Economic League, an association of dispossessed bankers and industrialists who naturally wished to see a non-Communist government back home. Bublikov was among those pitching the creation of a new "Russian Bank" to be set up in New York with capital provided by the "Allied nations."[65] Practically, of course, that meant capital supplied by Wall Street. The latter would thus gain a dominant position in Russian finance if and when a more amenable government appeared. The timing certainly was right; in early 1919, the survival of the Leninist regime was still a rather iffy proposition. "Diversifying investments" was always good policy.

As a postscript, Bublikov moved to Paris in 1919, but returned to New York in the spring of 1922 to wind up the affairs of the now defunct Youroveta. The 1922 visit includes an odd detail. Bublikov's New York host on that occasion was Michael Oganesov, a onetime Tsarist diplomat who had also gone into business. The curious part is that in July 1919, Oganesov's then wife, Marie, died of complications of an abortion performed by none other than Julius Hammer.[66] Surely Hammer wasn't the only abortionist available in New York City, which raises the question of how he and Oganesov knew one another, not to mention how Bublikov fit in to the equation.

THE AMERICAN SPY

Back in May 1916, American businessman Xenophon Kalamatiano had returned to Russia as representative for Chicago-based International Manufacturers' Sales and Claude M. Nankivel of 120 Broadway. He simultaneously served as an intelligence asset enlisted by Charles Crane's chief agent, Samuel Harper. Harry Mahoney describes this as a "parallel intelligence organization" separate from the State's Department's Bureau but which "used the Department's support systems when needed."[67] Likewise Crane, while having no formal connection to State, had ready access to classified cables and documents.

Early on, Kalamatiano supplied mostly economic information to the U.S. Embassy's commercial attaché, William Chapin Huntington. Huntington, to no surprise, was a close friend of Harper. Huntington digest-

---

64. George Weiss, *America's Maritime Progress* (1920), 360.
65. "Proposes New Russian Bank and Currency for Russia," *Wall Street Journal* (29 April 1919), 12.
66. Epstein, 42. As Epstein notes, while Julius Hammer was tried and imprisoned for the death, the actual procedure was probably carried out by his son Armand.
67. Mahoney, *American Prisoners*, 261.

ed Kalamatiano's intelligence into reports which he passed on to Harper who in turn sent them to Crane. The latter then passed them to House and the President.[68] Huntington also distributed copies to representatives of International Harvester, New York Life, and the American-Russian Chamber of Commerce.[69]

In the fall of 1917, as the Bolshevik takeover loomed, Moscow Consul General Maddin Summers put Kalamatiano on his payroll, nominally as a vice-consul, but actually as a spy. In February 1918, Trotsky broke off peace talks with the Central Powers and simply proclaimed the war over. The Germans responded by resuming military operations and advancing on Petrograd. Fearing occupation of the city, Ambassador Francis and the American Embassy decamped to Vologda, a provincial town about 300 miles to the east. The Bolsheviks moved their capital to Moscow. The Moscow Consulate under Summers now became the center of American activity, diplomatic and otherwise.

Impressed with Kalamatiano's work, in March 1918 Summers promoted him to Chief Observer of the Information Service.[70] As such, he collected information and compiled reports which he delivered to Summers. Curiously, Kalamatiano also sent copies to New York using Nankivel's office in the Equitable Building as an apparent accommodation address.[71] Did he do this with Summers' approval or was this part of some other operation? That the Equitable was also Reilly's headquarters cannot be forgotten.

By May, Kalamatiano was a full-fledged spymaster controlling fourteen sub-observers each running a string of informants.[72] That same month, Raymond Robins finally received his recall from Washington. This was a blow to the Bolsheviks who thus lost their best advocate among the remaining Americans. The man most responsible for Robin's recall was Summers who thus became an arch-enemy of Lenin and his comrades. Mere days after Robin's departure, Summers dropped dead. Most people assumed poor health and overwork did him in, and they probably were right, yet the timing is another of those coincidences too ripe to ignore. Kalamatiano thereafter reported to the new Consul General, DeWitt C. Poole.

Poole

68. *Ibid.*, 79.

69. *Ibid.*, 79-80.

70. For a more complete version of Kalamatiano's story see Richard B. Spence, "The Tragic Fate of Kalamatiano: America's Man in Moscow," *International Journal of Intelligence and CounterIntelligence*, Vol. 12, #3 (1999), 346-374.

71. USDS, #361.1121K121/54, "Report on the So-Called 'Lockhart Trial' in Moscow, December 1918," 3.

72. USDS, #125.0061/67, "Special Employees in Russia."

In early January 1918, Sidney Reilly suddenly appeared in London wearing the uniform of a lieutenant in the Royal Flying Corps. Norman Thwaites later confessed that he, with Wiseman's approval, had secured Reilly the commission.[73] Reilly wasn't looking to be a pilot. Rather, on 19 January he applied to the War Office for a post in intelligence. This sparked a background check which dug up plenty of dirt.

Nevertheless, on 15 March the eccentric chief of the Secret Intelligence Service, and Wiseman's boss, Mansfield Cumming, approved the hiring of the "very clever-very doubtful" Mr. Reilly to go on a secret mission into Bolshevik-controlled Russia.[74] A week later, just days before his departure, MI5 intercepted a telegram from Reilly to the unofficial Soviet representative in London, Maxim Litvinov. The son of a wealthy Russian-Jewish banker, Litvinov had been a Bolshevik since 1903 and long involved in money and arms smuggling.[75] Reilly's message *regretted that Litvinov had not replied* to his previous two wires and asked "when and where I can see you tomorrow?"[76] MI5 found it all rather suspicious.

Cumming may have been eccentric, but he was no fool. So why did he hire Reilly? The deciding factor seems to have been a "favorable" report provided by William Wiseman, a report not to be found in Reilly's surviving SIS file or anywhere else. What could he have offered that would have counter-balanced the seemingly overwhelming negatives? Sir William knew, as do we, that Reilly was the intimate business partner of Trotsky's uncle and confidant, Abram Zhivotovsky. Based on his own recent experience, Wiseman could argue that Trotsky might be amenable to further collaboration, especially if that offer came from a man he knew and trusted, Reilly.

To put this into perspective, the spring of 1918 was a critical juncture for Britain and the Allies generally. Shed of the Eastern Front, the Germans concentrated their strength in the West and on 21 March launched a massive offensive that sent the British Army reeling in northern France. Defeat seemed a real possibility and any gamble that might induce Bolshevik Russia to re-enter the fray against Berlin was a chance worth taking. Trotsky was the key to any reconciliation, and he also now was chief of the infant Red Army. Trotsky, recall, had almost scuttled the peace negotiation with the Germans as and he openly opposed the harsh Brest-Litovsk Treaty. If Trotsky could be coaxed back into the Allied fold, Reilly was the man to do it. As ever, the deal would require money.

---

73. Thwaites,183.

74. Alan Judd, *The Quest for C: Mansfield Cumming and the Founding of the Secret Service* (1999), 437.

75. Among other things, Litvinov had been involved in the efforts to launder the 500-Ruble notes from the Tiflis robbery.

76. TNA, KV2/827, Copy of telegram, 22 March 1918.

Reilly's British controllers for his Russian mission were based in Stockholm. Someone else had just set-up shop there: Abram Zhivotovsky. In the wake of the October Revolution, Uncle Abram had moved to the Swedish capital where he maintained an office "closely connected with the Venya [sic, Nya] Bank," i.e. with Olof Aschberg.[77] On 16 April, Reilly sent Stockholm his first report from Petrograd which emphasized two key points. First, "money ... positively is [the] most potent factor with Bolshevik leaders."[78] He recommended that His Majesty's Government invest at least a million Pounds with the Reds to counteract German influence. Second, he assured London that this could be accomplished "with the tacit consent of certain influential Bolsheviks."[79] One of these had to be Trotsky.

Reilly's subsequent reports consistently advised backing the Bolsheviks, or rather, *some* Bolsheviks. In the same period, he reported at least eight interviews with Gen. Michael Bonch-Bruyevich, head of the Supreme Military Council and Trotsky's right-hand man in building the Red Army. The General also happened to be the brother of veteran Bolshevik and Lenin's personal secretary, Vladimir Bonch-Bruyevich. In any case, he was a perfect cut-out for confidential communication between Reilly and Trotsky. What Wiseman likely realized, but what Cumming and most other Brits did not, was that Reilly was never really working for them. He was still serving the Revolution, or at least Trotsky's Revolution.

Bonch-Bruyevich

Reilly's Russian intrigues are far too convoluted to go onto here. For our purposes, the most important thing is his interaction with Kalamatiano. Reilly somehow convinced the American to share intelligence, even informants. Exactly how is unclear, since Kalamatiano later admitted that information he gleaned about Reilly in New York and Russia was invariably "unfavorable."[80] On the other hand, someone had assured him that Reilly was a "professional." Who was that?

During this period, Reilly maintained regular cable communication with New York. His telegrams came from and went to his wife, Nadine, and seemed to deal with personal matters. Of course, they afforded an opportunity to convey other information. Mrs. Reilly remained in intimate contact with Zhivotovsky-agent Alexander Weinstein who had taken over Reilly's 120 Broadway office. U.S. Consul Poole later emphasized that evidence of Reilly's treachery was to be found in his communications with New York.[81]

77. BI, #339512, In re: Shivotovsky (Zhivotovsky), Bolshevik Activities, 8 Jan. 1919.

78. SIS, CX 2616 (Reilly SIS file), CX 027753, 16 April 1918, 5.

79. *Ibid.*, 8.

80. USDS, #361.1121K12/54, "Report on the So-Called 'Lockhart Trial' in Moscow, December 1918," 8-9.

81. TNA, FO 371/3319, #165188, Findlay to FO, 30 Sept. 1918.

By August 1918, Reilly supposedly masterminded a plot to subvert the Latvian troops guarding the Kremlin and stage a palace coup against the Bolsheviks. In reality, there was no plot, since all the principal conspirators were actually working for the Bolshevik secret police, the Cheka. That included Reilly. The real aim was to compromise Allied agents and to provide cover and context for the main event, the assassination of Lenin. That would open the door to what Reilly and those behind him really wanted, the elevation of Trotsky to the Soviet throne. On 30 August, at a factory outside Moscow, the attempt occurred; two bullets struck Lenin, but he just managed to survive.

The Cheka immediately began rounding-up every Western officer they could find. Reilly "accidentally" left a card bearing Kalamatiano's name and address, and those of all his agents, lying in plain view for them to find.[82] Kalamatiano found such carelessness inexplicable. Kalamatiano was outside Moscow when the arrests started to go down and would have been safe had he not tried to return to the Consulate, probably to recover money stashed there. Always the money. The Cheka nabbed him outside the Consulate's gate on 18 September.

The upshot was that Kalamatiano, alone among the Allied officials implicated, went on trial for his life and ended up sentenced to death. The Bolsheviks kept him alive, however, hoping to use him as a pawn in future negotiations. Like Kalamatiano, Consul DeWitt Poole was convinced that Reilly was the traitor. He told the British as much and informed them that a recently intercepted telegram from Petrograd to New York showed that Reilly was still at his old Petrograd address weeks after he supposedly had gone into hiding.[83] Even that damning bit of information the Brits chose to ignore.

Kalamatiano's case had serious implication for Bolshevik-American relations, particularly the desire of some on Wall Street to normalize those relations. The State Department was thoroughly poisoned against any accommodation with the Moscow Reds. Making deals with an unrecognized regime that held Americans prisoner became a very tricky proposition, but not an impossible one.

THE GRUZENBERG GAMBIT

While all this was going on, there was another operation underway. In the aftermath of the October Revolution, Russian officials in the U.S. had to figure out what side they were on. Not a few, either out of ideological sympathy or practical necessity, chose the Bolsheviks. One of these was Yury Lomonosov, the railway expert who had come to America as a member of the Russian Diplomatic Mission in 1917. Lomonosov was an old friend of Lenin's money-man, Leonid Krasin, and he may have been a pro-Bolshevik much

82. USDS, #361.1121K12/54, *Ibid.*
83. TNA, FO 371/3319, *Ibid.*

longer that he let on.[84] In any case, in May 1918, he let his true colors fly and entertained hope that he might become the Soviet representative in the States.

Lomonosov decided to send an emissary to Moscow to seek "instructions."[85] As mentioned, that man was Michael Gruzenberg, another of the American Bolsheviki. Traveling via Scandinavia, he reached Moscow on 20 August, just about the time Reilly's schemes were reaching their peak. Gruzenberg's declared purpose was to arrange the "purchase of goods," presumably American ones. But he also traveled as an authorized agent of George Creel and the U.S. Committee on Public Information (CPI) with a charge "to get information."[86] Gruzenberg seems to have taken the job that Reed turned down.

This arrangement likely explains why agents of the U.S. Government facilitated Gruzenberg's journey at every step, even intervening to deliver $10,000 he acquired in Moscow into Lomonosov's hands in New York.[87] The key intermediary in this curious deal was Thomas L. Chadbourne, an ex-CPI man whose real job was "Wall Street lawyer."[88] Chadbourne, one more specimen of "radical capitalist," was the chairman of the board of the International Mining Corporation, a director of twenty others, and an expert in multi-national firms. To no surprise, he was another associate of the ubiquitous Charles Crane. With the departure of Reed and Robins, this was probably another gambit instigated by Crane and Col. House with the aim of establishing a new back-channel

Chadbourne

to the Kremlin. Lenin had other ideas. He handed Gruzenberg $25,000 and sent him back to Western Europe to set up bank accounts.[89] Those accounts were then to be filled with more money. Money from where?

FURSTENBERG IN NEW YORK?

Finally, there is another incident from the summer of 1918 that deserves mention. In June, Justice Department and Military Intelligence investigators received a report from a visiting Belgian soldier, Edmond Birenweig, claiming that he had encountered Jacob Furstenberg, Parvus' accomplice and Lenin's confidant, strolling down Manhattan's 5th Ave. This

Furstenberg

84. MID, #9140-5201, "In Re: Leonid Andrejevich Dunajev," 24 Oct. 1917, 2.

85. Anthony Heywood, *Engineer of Revolutionary Russia: Iurii V. Lomonosov (1876-1952) and the Railways* (2011), 85.

86. BI, #8000-381693, "Foreign Bolshevik Agents in Norway," 3, 8.

87. Heywood, 182.

88. Specifically, the firm of Chadbourne, Babbit and Wallace, 14 Wall St.

89. Heywood, 182.

was sometime in late May or early June.[90] Birenweig had been attached to a Belgian armored car detachment on the Eastern Front and withdrew via Siberia and America following the Bolshevik-German peace. While in Russia, he claimed to have seen Furstenberg and other Bolshevik officials first hand, and he was able to describe Furstenberg accurately. Moreover, two other soldiers from Birenweig's unit attested that they, too, had run into Furstenberg in New York, and in the company of no less than John Reed.[91] Birenweig and his fellows repeatedly swore to what they had seen to the Americans and their own military superiors, but U.S. investigators were unable to find any evidence to substantiate it.

Furstenberg (alias Ganetsky or Hanecki), of course, had been the right-hand man of Alexander Parvus in the "Copenhagen Operation." After the Bolsheviks took power, Lenin made him deputy commissar of the State Bank and he became an important figure in Soviet finance. Other reports had him meeting with German, Danish and Swedish financiers (Aschberg) during May 1918, so a fast trip across the Atlantic for similar parleys would have made sense.[92] His "principal task was to send money to Russia."[93] If the Soviets were going to send a stealth financial agent to America, Furstenberg would have been an excellent choice.

There are two oddments that might link-up with this. Around this same time, U.S. Military Intelligence received a report from Stockholm that Fritz Warburg "paid Colonel Malinowsky of the Bolshevik Secret Service in the U.S.A. the sum of $600,000" sometime in the "spring of 1918."[94] Another report claimed that *Paul* Warburg was "supposed to be in touch with [the same Col. Malinowsky] in NYC."[95] Interestingly, on a 31 July cover letter attached to a Department of Justice report on the Birenweig-Furstenberg case, MID Capt. James Bruff wrote "re: Paul Warburg."[96]

The "Malinowsky" mentioned is certainly an alias and otherwise unidentifiable. That there was a functioning "Bolshevik Secret Service" in the U.S. in early 1918 seems far-fetched, but might this be a muddled reference to the secret Bolshevik network earlier set-up by Kollontai? Surely that remained functional in some form. More to the point, was "Malinowsky" really Furstenberg, and did he come to New York to confer with Paul Warburg through the mediation of brother Fritz and with the help of Wall Street-linked Reed? If so, was the $600,000 paid to him to be deposited in New York or picked up there?

---

90. MID, #10087-7/15, "Re Furstenberg alias Hanecki," 21 June 1918, 2.
91. *Ibid.*, 4.
92. USDS, #763.72119/1791, #1169, Stockholm, 15 June 1918.
93. *Ibid.*
94. RIP, "Information Gathered…," 1.
95. MID, #10080-342/38, War Trade Board report, c. Aug. 1918.
96. MID #10087-7/87W, Schaff to MID, 31 July 1918.

CRANE'S FAILED MISSION TO MOSCOW

With all the high drama playing out in Russia during the summer of 1918, it's understandable that busy-body Charles Crane would want to have a look for himself. At the end of August, he obtained a fresh passport from the Department of State, hand delivered by his son, Richard. On the application, Crane noted that he would be sailing 18 September en route to Russia via Japan and China. He would never reach his final destination. By October, Crane was in Harbin, Manchuria where he met with John Stevens, head of the earlier mentioned Railway Service Corps. Also there was another of Crane's academic agents, archaeologist Thomas Whittemore who was involved in Russian "relief work."[97] Whittemore had made a connection with the Bolshevik's new foreign commissar, George Chicherin, who he believed could get him safely to Moscow. Crane planned to tag along. In the end, the chaos spreading across Siberia made him reconsider. What did Crane plan on doing if he reached the Red capital? It certainly wasn't a sight-seeing trip.

---

97. Saul, 178-179.

CHAPTER TEN

THE DEALMAKERS

THE BULLITT AND HAPGOOD MISSIONS

In January 1919, the Great War was over, defeated Germany teetered on the verge of its own Bolshevik revolution, and President Wilson, accompanied by Col. House, arrived in Paris to negotiate peace and make the world safe for democracy. In Russia, civil war raged as the Soviet regime, defended by Trotsky's Red Army, fought for its life against an array of "White" opponents. At the same time, Allied forces, including thousands of American troops, had become embroiled in this battle by occupying Vladivostok, Archangel and Murmansk, Odessa and other ports in the Black Sea. Intervention had engaged the Allies in an undeclared shooting war with the Bolsheviks.

Wilson dreamed, and House schemed, about dragging the Russian factions into their own peace conference. This might necessitate breaking ranks with the British and French and granting recognition to Lenin's Government. In January, Wilson received near simultaneous memos from Lincoln Steffens and William Bullitt, the latter a young State Department official attached to the American Peace Delegation. Secretly egged-on by Col. House, both urged Wilson to send an American mission to Moscow to sound out the Bolsheviks.[1] Bullitt, by the way, was the same fellow who received a "Russian memorandum" from Reed in early 1918.

Through House's influence, Bullitt got the nod to head the mission. An avowed leftist sympathizer and son of a wealthy Philadelphia family (sound familiar?), Bullitt was a protégée of the Colonel, and headed the "Current Intelligence Summaries" office in Paris. Accompanying him were Lincoln Steffens, Bullitt's friend and personal secretary, Robert E. Lynch and a military intelligence officer, Walter W. Pettit. All, to one degree or another, professed pro-Bolshevik sympathies. Steffens, for instance, later made his famous quip, "I have been over to the future, and it works," based on this visit.

Bullitt and his team left Paris on 22 February and traveled via Scandinavia. In Stockholm, they met Swedish Socialist (and future communist) Karl Kilbom. Kilbom knew Aschberg and had worked closely with

1. Saul, 189.

the Bolshevik Centre in Stockholm, including Bukharin and Kollontai. The Americans reached Moscow on 11 March and returned to Helsinki five days later where Bullitt fired off a long wire to the President, House and Secretary Lansing, explaining what had transpired. After meetings with Commissar for Foreign Affairs Chicherin, his deputy Litvinov, and finally Lenin, Bullitt came away convinced that he had secured the Bolsheviks' commitment to parley with other Russian factions and "in the most straightforward, unequivocal manner the determination of the Soviet Government to pay its foreign debts."[2] As a precondition, however, Lenin insisted on full recognition and an immediate end to blockade and intervention. Capt. Pettit, meanwhile, held separate talks with Chicherin, Litvinov and "American Bolshevik" Bill Shatoff. The nature and purpose of those conversations is unknown. On 27 March, Bullitt and friends returned to Paris, but found the President had changed his mind and turned dead-set against recognition.

One person deeply disturbed by the Bullitt adventure, and perhaps significant to Wilson's change of heart, was Charles Crane. He warned that Bullitt's proposal "might ruin everything" (what was that?) and that "our people at home will certainly not stand for the recognition of the Bolshevists at the bidding of Wall Street."[3] It was an interesting comment from a man intimately acquainted with the Street. Was it a dig at Schiff, Morgan, Thompson, or all of them?

The bigger issue was that Bullitt's gambit conflicted with Crane's own scheme to reach out to the Moscow Reds. As early as the spring of 1918, he had approached House with the idea of appointing liberal journalist Norman Hapgood American minister to Denmark. While he lacked diplomatic experience, Hapgood, a member of the Friends of Russian Freedom, had the right ideological bent. He also had recently served as editor of Crane's *Harper's Weekly*. Hapgood got the Copenhagen appointment in February 1919, just as Bullitt left Paris. Delays prevented him from taking up the post until June.

Once in the Danish capital, Parvus' old stomping ground and the center of Bolshevik and anti-Bolshevik intrigues, he busied himself trying set up trade deals while acting as a diplomatic back-door to the Kremlin. His ambassadorship was over in less than six months. In mid-November 1919, the U.S. press reported his imminent return either because the climate didn't agree with him or, more ominously, because he had been "linked with Bolshevism."[4] In December, as he headed back to Washington, fresh reports claimed Hapgood had turned the American Legation into "a trading post for the Soviet Government" and "worked hand in glove" with

---

2. WWP, 9/211, Bullitt to American Mission, Paris, 16 March 1919.

3. Henry Wickham Steed, *Through Thirty Years, 1892-1922* (1925), 304.

4. "Norman Hapgood Is Coming Back Home," *Watertown Daily News* [NY] (17 Nov. 1919), 4.

Moscow's agents to help them transact business with Americans.[5] One story accused him of working "to persuade a group of Wall Street interests to finance the firm of Lenine and Trotzky [sic]" assuring them that the investment would "yield rich dividends."[6] At the State Department, Frank Polk merely offered that Hapgood had been "too lenient ... in the granting of visas to 'Russian extremists.'"[7] How much of this was true is hard to

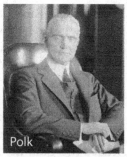

Polk

say. Hapgood vociferously denied being a "Bolshevik agent," but then he would in any case. He did admit dealing with Alexander Berkenheim, the chief of *Tsentrosoyuz*, a large Russian cooperative society that operated inside and outside Soviet-controlled territory.[8]

THE "MARTENS BUREAU"

It was also in early1919 that a secret Bolshevik courier, traveling as a sailor on a Swedish ship, landed in New York bearing a message from Commissar Chicherin. Dated 2 January, it tersely informed Ludwig Martens, Vice-President of Weinberg & Posner Engineering, 120 Broadway, that he was now the Red regime's representative in the United States. By 11 March, Martens had formed a small committee consisting of himself, former *Novy Mir* Manager Gregory Weinstein and Socialist entrepreneur Julius Hammer. Not long after, Martens appeared in Washington to present his "credentials."[9] Official Washington declined to accept them.

Martens was not easily discouraged. Back in New York, on 21 March the Socialist daily *New York Call* announced the creation of the Russian Soviet Government Bureau, thereafter commonly referred to as the "Martens' Bureau." Initially set up at 299 Broadway, the former home of Santeri Nuorteva's Finnish Information Bureau, it relocated to the World Tower Building at 110 West 40th St. where Martens leased the entire third floor. By the end of March, the Bureau already boasted thirty full-time employees.[10] Directly under Martens was Nuorteva, who functioned as general secretary and, as noted, was widely perceived as the real head of the organization. Weinstein acted as Martens' personal secretary and office manager and Nuorteva was similarly served by Kenneth Durant. The latter had an interesting background. While the Bureau was mostly staffed

5. "Hapgood Is Coming But Wasn't Called," *Pueblo Chieftain* [CO] (27 Dec. 1919), 10. Hapgood's leading critic was George Harvey, a millionaire street-car magnate, publisher and the pre-Crane owner of *Harper's Weekly*.

6. "Hapgood Returns," *Bellingham Herald* [WA] (29 Dec. 1919), 4.

7. Saul, 188.

8. "Hapgood Out," *Idaho Statesman* (31 Dec. 1919), 1.

9. *Papers Relating to the Foreign Relations of the United States: 1919* (1937), 134.

10. U.S. Senate, "Russian Propaganda," Exhibit # 10 (1920), 41-43.

by persons of Russian or Russian-Jewish origins, Durant was the blue-blood son of a Philadelphia stockbroker, a Harvard grad, a former Committee on Public Information employee and onetime personal aide to Col. House. That made him the ideal man to serve as the Bureau's unofficial connection to Washington.

K. Durant

Other notable staffers were leftist industrialist Abraham Heller who headed the Commercial Department, Evans Clark, who oversaw the Information and Publicity Department, future Soviet master spy Arthur Adams, who single-handedly ran the Technical Department, Isaac Hourwich, who directed the Legal and Economics & Statistics Departments, and Jacob Hartman, managing editor of the Bureau's main publication, *Soviet Russia*. Also attached were British-born Wilfred Humphries whose prior gigs included service with the CPI in Russia, the YMCA and the American Red Cross. Then there was Lt. Gen. Boris Tagueev Rustam-Bek, a former Russian aeronautics and intelligence officer who served as the Bureau's "military expert."

Rustam-Bek played another role. In the fall of 1920, he was the chief fund-raiser for the Soviet Russia Medical Relief Fund, a job in which he worked closely with Trotsky's former New York friend, Dr. Michael Michailovsky. While his ostensible task was raising money, Rustam-Bek boasted to comrades that he already had millions of dollars at his disposal for propaganda and other purposes. More interesting, a Bureau of Investigation report noted that Rustam-Bek was "actively connected to the *New Republic* and Willard

Rustam-Bek
387. Борисъ Тагеевъ. — Boris Tagueeff.

Straight."[11] Straight, of course, was a Morgan partner and he and his Wall Street heiress-social activist wife ran the magazine as a mouthpiece for liberal-progressive causes.

The big question is why Lenin tapped Martens for this critical post.[12] By his own admission, Martens was never a "prime mover" among the Bolsheviks.[13] There were plenty of others who knew English and had more experience in America. Edward Jay Epstein argues that Martens got the job because he was "one of the most trusted agents in [Lenin's] inner circle."[14] Harry Mahoney, on the other hand, argues that Martens wasn't

---

11. BI, #202600-189, "Re: Bolshevik Funds in America," March 1921, 11-12.

12. This wasn't the first attempt. In January 1918, the Bolsheviks chose American radical John Reed as their emissary to the U.S., but this was promptly withdrawn. In June, both journalist Albert Rhys Williams and Bolshevik activist Maxim Litvinov reportedly received the nod, but the State Department denied Williams a visa and Litvinov was a de facto prisoner in Britain.

13. Martens Testimony, 20.

14. Epstein, 39.

Lenin's man at all, but Trotsky's. By replacing Nuorteva with Martens, "Trotsky had finally succeeded in placing one of his most trusted men in America."[15] Regardless, an important factor must have been Martens' connections to American business and financial circles – connections he made at 120 Broadway. His main assignment for the Kremlin was selling Soviet Russia as a lucrative field for American trade and investment and thus rallying Wall Street's support for diplomatic recognition.

Selling Russia as an economic proposition in early 1919 was no easy task. First, the U.S. Government had no relations with the Bolsheviks and therefore could not provide American businessmen with normal diplomatic protections. Beyond that, the U.S. actively observed an economic blockade of Soviet Russia which forbade the movement of money or goods to or from Soviet-controlled territory.

Another deterrent was that the Russian economy was in complete shambles. Through the combined attrition of war, revolution and now civil war, Russian industrial production had shrunk to 26% of its 1913 level and would contract to even less in 1920.[16] Worker productivity was 22% of 1913 and import and export trade had ceased to exist. So too had real money. The mass printing of paper currency, begun under the Tsarist and Provisional Governments and continued under the Bolsheviks, had by 1921 inflated the once-solid ruble into a bubble of airy nothing. Disease and famine stalked village and city; typhus infected more that 5,000,000 during 1919-20 and cholera ravaged hundreds of thousands more.[17] A quarter of the population faced acute starvation.

Then there were the Soviet decrees which had destroyed legal private enterprise, starting with the nationalization of banking in December 1917, the nationalization of foreign trade in April 1918, and the nationalization of industry and manufacturing that commenced in June 1918. On top of this was the troubling repudiation of state debts announced in February 1918. While it technically applied only to debts contracted during the war, this included the loans backed by National City and Guaranty Trust and the unknown number of "private loans" advanced to the Russian Government by Americans. What American businessman in his right mind would want to do business with people who refused to acknowledge their debts and proclaimed their ultimate goal to be the annihilation of capitalism?

Finally, the Bolsheviks controlled only part of Russia, if arguably the most important part. The central European provinces including Petrograd, Moscow and most of the population and remaining industry were in their hands, but Siberia, the Caucasus and much of Ukraine were held by the "Whites" whose armies were then driving deeper and deeper into

15. Mahoney, *Saga*, 122.
16. Tony Cliff, "War Communism (1917-1921)." https://www.marxists.org/archive/cliff/works/1978/lenin3/ch07.html.
17. *Ibid*.

the Soviet domain. Any deals made with the Bolsheviks might be dead letters in short order.

On the other hand, a smart and somewhat unscrupulous business-man could look through these negatives and see immense potential. First, the Bolsheviks were desperate and thus willing to grant terms otherwise unacceptable. The Whites were in no less dire straits. Revolutionary cha-os and nationalization had effectively annulled ownership of Russian as-sets and left everything open to acquisition at bargain prices. The whole former Tsarist Empire was one giant fire-sale. Russians needed virtually everything, and Americans could sell it to them.

In fact, Martens had no problem finding Americans anxious to do busi-ness and even underwrite his operation. He could also promise to pay cash. Martens claimed to have $200 million in gold at his disposal which, as we will see, was basically true.[18] The rub was, it was in Russia and the U.S. em-bargo made it impossible to import *legally*. Martens simultaneously laid claim to all American goods and monetary assets belonging to the Imperial and Provisional regimes, at least $150 million and possibly double that.[19] If the Soviet regime received recognition, all of this would pass into his hands, and Wall Street "wanted to be present when the distribution began."[20]

In an early memo to Evans Clark, Abraham Heller ad-vocated using Morgan's Dwight Morrow and former head of the Columbia Law School George Kirchwey to reach out to "Wall Street money interests."[21] Evans met with National City's Frank Vanderlip and with Washington lawyers and in-fluence peddlers Amos Pinchot and Dudley Field Malone. In a 19 May 1919 letter to Congressman James P. Mulvihill, Heller emphasized that Martens was prepared to deposit $200 million in American banks.[22] Morgan, National City, First National and Kidder-Peabody were the key targets of Martens' charm campaign.

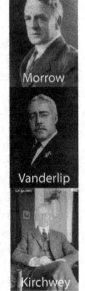

In early April, Martens and Nuorteva were the guests of honor at a "confidential luncheon" at 120 Broadway's Bank-ers Club where they met with "representatives of leading fi-nancial institutions."[23] This was set up by "a man who want-ed to give the Bolsheviks a fair hearing," most likely William Thompson. The whole thing was kept hush-hush. All Mar-tens would reveal was that National City Bank wasn't rep-

18. "Bolshevik Envoy Opens Office Here to Win U.S. Trade," *New York Tribune* (9 April 1919), 2.

19. "Reds' Envoy Wants Russia's Cash Here," *New York Times* (8 April 1919), and "Soviet Russia to Ask $300,000,000 from America," *Winnipeg Tribune* (10 May 1919), 29.

20. MID, #10110-1194/29, Trevor to Churchill, 11 April 1919.

21. "Letters Link Henry Ford with Soviet Bureau Here," *New York Tribune* (27 June 1919), 1. Kirchwey, a prominent pacifist and social causist was Evans' father-in-law.

22. *Ibid.*, 5.

23. "Reds' Envoy Wants Russia's Cash Here," *Ibid.*

resented. Sleuthing by Military Intelligence determined that Raymond Robins was present, plus Charles Sabin, Francis Sisson and Henry Emery, all officers of Guaranty Trust, and all connected to its foreign department.[24] Sisson was also a public relations expert. Other reports suggested that Sabin "in his private capacity had advanced money to [the Bureau] in some way or another which is yet unexplained."[25] Further investigation revealed that the rent for the Bureaus' World Tower offices was paid though an account at Guaranty Trust.

Another Guaranty Trust figure linked to the Soviet Bureau was Max May, the mastermind of its foreign exchange department. Indeed, the German-born May's prowess in that sphere saw him hailed as "unquestionably the greatest foreign exchange expert in the world."[26] During the war, under May's guidance, Guaranty acquired ruble accounts nominally worth several million dollars but which now, thanks to the blockade and inflation, were virtually worthless. The only way to restore their value would be for the Soviet government to back them with gold.

In January 1918, May abruptly resigned from Guaranty Trust and re-emerged as managing director of a new Foreign Trade Banking Corporation with offices at 35 Wall Street.[27] His partner in this was George Gaston of Gaston, Williams and Wigmore, a foreign trade concern with offices conveniently located in Petrograd, Archangel and Vladivostok. May also was a longtime friend of Olof Aschberg, and just a few years down the road he and Aschberg would become officers of the Roskombank, the Soviets' first "international bank."[28] Evidence showed that Gaston's original firm was only a "side issue" run by "insiders of the Guaranty Trust Co."[29] Now these same "insiders" used May to create a new side issue to handle future trade with Russia. Upon Martens' arrival they were ready and anxious to cash-in.

Martens also set up "constant consultation" in Estonia between Edward Falck of Guaranty Trust and William Coombs of Pressed Steel Car Co. with the resident Soviet representative, Isidor Gukovsky.[30] Both Americans expressed their disgust that Washington was letting its policy be guided by "sentimental rot" while American capital could be making good money and "cutting out the British."[31]

Guaranty Trust was not the only game in town. On 29 April, Martens was guest speaker at another luncheon of financiers held at the Hotel Astor. It was hosted by the newly founded Council on Foreign Relations, the

24. MID, #10110-1194/331, "Synopsis...", 10.
25. MID, #10110-1194/63, "In re: L.C.A.K. Martens," 14 May 1919, 2.
26. "Max May Retires for Period of War," *New York Times* (10 Jan. 1918).
27. *Standard Daily Trade Service*, #4 (April-June 1918), 30.
28. Solzhenitsyn, 129-130.
29. MID, #10110-1194/64. *Ibid.*
30. USDS, Diplomatic Post Records, Pt. II, Sect. A, reel 2, #187, Gade to State, 11 May 1920.
31. *Ibid.*

brainchild of Col. House. That same month, Abraham Heller arranged Martens' appearance on Charles Crane's home turf when he addressed "1,000 manufacturers, exporters and bankers" at the National Foreign Trade Convention in Chicago.[32] Martens set up a branch office of the Bureau in the Windy City, the "Central Soviet Bureau," and another soon followed in Detroit. He reached out to National City Bank, assuring them that the $100 million in Russian bonds it backed during the war were not annulled and that Moscow was open to a mutually satisfactory, if secret, settlement.[33]

By the end of 1919, Martens claimed the Soviet Bureau had 400 American companies "anxious to do business" with $7 million in contracts already executed.[34] Among the firms were giants like American and Baldwin Locomotive, American Steel Export (which employed Reilly cronies Rogovine and Orbanowsky), International Harvester, Armour and Swift meatpackers, and an array of smaller firms that counted Bobroff Engineering and Julius Hammer's Allied Drug in the mix.[35]

The potentially biggest fish was Ford Motor Co. On 9 April, Heller approached Ford representative Ernest Kanseler asking for an audience with Henry.[36] That led Ford's secretary and factotum, Ernest Liebold, to invite Heller and Nuorteva to Dearborn. Ford had been quietly selling small batches of vehicles and tractors to Soviet intermediaries in Scandinavia, probably Aschberg's Swedish Economic Co., since the fall of 1918. Most of Ford's Russian business circa 1918-1922 was "largely unrecorded by the company" to avoid political complications at home.[37] In mid-March 1919, just before the Soviet Bureau came into being, Ford inked a deal with Ivan Stakheeff and Co., owned by banker P.P. Batolin "a neutral private firm" which sold to both sides in the Russian turmoil.[38] In August, Martens proudly reported to Moscow that Ford's tractor division was willing to provide up to 10,000 machines and had written the State Department for approval.[39] During this time, Edsel Ford advised his agents in New York to "keep in as close touch with Russia through various channels as much as possible."[40]

32. Katherine A. S. Siegel, *Loans and Legitimacy: The Evolution of Soviet-American Relations, 1919-1933* (1996), 13-14.

33. Martens Testimony, 43.

34. "Tells of Contracts with Soviet Russia," *New York Times* (27 Jan. 1920) and "Firms Repudiate Martens," *New York Times* (30 Jan. 1920).

35. Siegel, 20-22.

36. Mira Wilkins and Fred E. Hill, *American Business Abroad: Ford on Six Continents* (2011), 209-210.

37. Christine White, "Ford in Russia: In Pursuit of the Chimerical Market," in John C. Woods and Michael C. Woods (eds.) *Henry Ford: Critical Evaluations in Business and Management* (2003), 75 n.36.

38. Boris M. Shpotov, "Ford in Russia, from 1909 to World War II," 509. http://beagle.u-bordeaux4.fr/ifrede/Ford/Pdf/Shpotov.pdf.

39. *Ibid.*, 511.

40. Wilkins and Hill, 209-210.

With all this going for him, Martens' mission looked to be a roaring success. It wasn't – the success was purely on paper. While he might have collected contracts worth millions, Martens visibly shipped a mere $200,000 in goods in the same period.[41] Failure is usually attributed to the blockade which made it all but impossible to pay for goods or get them into Russia. That was indeed a problem, but not an insurmountable one. For instance, Martens received at least $90,000 from Moscow through early 1920, albeit in sporadic installments.[42] Isaac Hourwich described the process by which gold or hard currency went to a Soviet agent in Stockholm who deposited it in a Swedish bank.[43] Said agent then obtained a bank draft which he transferred to an account in a New York bank like Guaranty Trust. There, another agent, who controlled that account, drew out the cash and handed it to Martens. An interesting detail was that the Soviet Bureau's expenses in this period were no more that $50,000, which raised the question of where the other $40,000 went.

Martens' real problem was bad publicity. By 1919, the Bolshevik regime had been thoroughly vilified in the mainstream American press. Most of the vilification was entirely justified, but it also stirred up fears of Red subversion at home and concern that Martens, with his extra cash, was subsidizing it. Concern that the Soviet Bureau was a wellspring of revolutionary agitation spurred New York State authorities to raid its offices on 12 June 1919. From that point on, Martens was first grilled before a State investigating body, the so-called Lusk Committee, and then, in early 1920, the U.S. Senate. The possibility that Martens might be arrested or deported and the Bureau closed or raided and all its dealings exposed was a huge disincentive to image-conscious businessmen, no matter how much they wanted a contract.

Martens and his comrades tried to counter this by cultivating friends in Washington: diplomatic recognition would solve all problems. The point men in this effort were Evans Clark and Kenneth Durant.[44] Also involved were the indefatigable Raymond Robins and his ever-present Soviet sidekick, Alexander Gumberg. They had some success in recruiting Senators William Borah and Joseph France to their cause. In October 1919, Nuorteva and Bureau attorney Charles Recht met in Washington with Senators Charles Dick and Medill McCormick, Supreme Court Justice Louis Brandeis and Sir Arthur Willard, *London Times* bureau chief.[45] The last was a close friend and wartime colleague of William Wiseman. McCormick, for good measure, was a friend of Crane's, while Brandeis was close to Schiff.

41. Siegel, 26.
42. "Martens Refuses to Give Up Papers," *New York Times* (26 Nov. 1919).
43. "Soviet Funds Sent Here Via Sweden," *New York Times* (30 Dec. 1919).
44. Siegel, 16.
45. MID, #10010-1194-299, "In re: Russian Soviet Bureau," 29 Oct. 1919, 1.

Speaking of Schiff, a curious incident occurred in February 1920. Late that month, one Dmitry Navashin arrived in New York from England. Prior to that, he had been in Copenhagen supposedly overseeing the Russian Red Cross. In truth, he was a financial expert working for the Soviets in foreign exchange and the following year he would take over the Russian State Bank branch in Paris. He was also an old friend of Furstenberg and Krasin. Navashin declared his business in New York to be Red Cross-related, but it was with Martens and his Bureau. Coincidentally or not, a few lines below him on the passenger manifest appears the name of Ernst Heinz Schiff, "stockbroker." He was Jacob Schiff's London-based nephew, who had just crossed the pond to visit his uncle, or so he claimed.

THE WALL STREET BOMB

In July 1920, Martens finally got a break: the dying Wilson Administration abandoned almost all restrictions on American-Russian trade.
However, any chance that might evolve into recognition ended with a bang. Just after noon on 16 September 1920, a wagon loaded with TNT and metal shards exploded directly in front of the J. P. Morgan offices at 23 Wall Street. Thirty-nine people, mostly employees on their way to lunch, lay dead or mortally injured. Another 200 suffered wounds. Despite

Aftermath of bomb

numerous suspects and arrests in the years following, the "Wall Street Bomb" case remained unsolved.[46] While lacking any credible evidence, investigators fixated on the notion that the dastardly crime was the work of "Reds" probably linked to Soviet Russia. The fact that this was entirely contrary to the desires of Lenin & Co. and that rival capitalist interests might be behind it never seemed to enter their heads. Martens and Nuorteva suspected the hand of the notorious Pinkerton Detective Agency and launched their own investigation. At the same time, a group of nervous and gullible Wall Streeters headed by insurance tycoon Henry Marsh hired Jacob Nosovitsky, a former comrade of Martens, turned informer, to hunt down the Red angle.[47] No one came up with anything.

---

46. The most thorough work on the case is Beverly Gage, *The Day Wall Street Exploded: A Story of America's First Age of Terror* (2010). It later became accepted wisdom that an Italian anarchist, Mario Buda, masterminded the bomb as revenge for the arrests of Sacco and Vanzetti, but that was just a popular myth.
47. "International Spy, Hired by Capitalists, Probes Wall St. Explosion," *New York American* (13 Dec. 1925), 1-2.

However, the damage was done and the jig was up. In December 1920, facing certain deportation, Martens threw in the towel and agreed to leave the U.S. voluntarily.[48] The following January, the Soviet Bureau closed its doors.

THE COMMITTEE ON THE STUDY OF BOLSHEVISM

To be sure, there were Wall Street interests that opposed recognition. They found a voice in the Committee on the Study of Bolshevism formed under the auspices of another "millionaires' club," the Union League. Crane was a member, as were Elihu Root, John D. and William Rockefeller, Herbert Hoover, Charles Sabin and Henry P. Davison. Through Davison and others, the Club was linked to the American Red Cross. Who constituted the Bolshevism Committee is uncertain, but on 10 April 1919, it offered a summary report and recommendations.[49] These attacked both the Martens Bureau and the Bullitt mission. The report came down squarely against granting recognition to a regime "committed to the proposition of the expropriation of all capitalists and the permanent destruction of the Bourgeoisie." Despite this, it noted that "many forces have been set at work to accomplish [recognition]." As for Martens, "it is hardly conceivable that such a mission would have been sent unless such encouragement had been received." Beyond this, formal recognition of the Soviet Republic, "would be to add fuel to the flame of internal disorder within our boundaries."

W. Rockefeller

While the Committee opposed *recognition*, de jure or de facto, it made no objection to *trade*. Again, from a purely commercial standpoint, the lack of diplomatic protections presented risks but also afforded distinct advantages. Without official framework or oversight, one was free to negotiate any sort of terms with the Russians. That is precisely what some had in mind.

CONCESSIONS AND THE "KHAN OF KAMCHATKA"

Before saying farewell to Wall Street, Ludwig Martens and Nuorteva managed to pull off two final deals. The first was the creation of a successor "front" to handle U.S.-Soviet trade and serve as a "nucleus for communication with Soviet Russia," the Products Exchange Corporation ("Prodexco") which became the assignee of the deals with Ford and others.

---

48. "Martens to Go in January," *New York Times* (22 Dec. 1920).
49. WWP, "Report by the Committee on the Study of Bolshevism of the Union League Club," 10 April 1919.

[50] Its incorporators were Kenneth Durant, Charles Recht, John G. Ohsol, and Julius Fox, all American citizens. Ohsol, a Latvian, had been a Bolshevik deputy in the 4th Duma. Mixed up in this behind the scenes was former Chicagoan Michael Gruzenberg, now Moscow's clandestine courier. In addition, by setting up bank accounts in Switzerland, in the fall of 1919, Gruzenberg smuggled a cache of purloined diamonds into the U.S., some of which probably went to bankroll Prodexco.[51]

The other and much bigger deal was the so-called Vanderlip Concession. Washington Baker Vanderlip was a veteran mining and oil promoter who prospected in Siberia in the late 1890s. He was no relation to National City's Frank Vanderlip, though it didn't hurt that the Bolsheviks imagined he was. In 1920 he became front-man for a syndicate of West Coast capitalists in search of Russian opportunities. Martens gave him letters of introduction to Lenin and Trotsky. The syndicate behind Vanderlip was dominated by oil men, most notably Edward L. Doheny, the kingpin of Pan-American Petroleum, William L. Stewart, President of Union Oil, and Max Whittier of Associated Oil.[52] Another leading figure was Harry Chandler, the monarch of the *Los Angeles Times*.

The heads of banks, trust and insurance companies rounded out the remainder. Looming behind them all was Standard Oil of California – though it chose to remain invisible at first.

During the summer of 1920, Vanderlip was wined and dined as best Red Moscow could provide, and in October he proudly announced to the world a 66-year lease on all of Siberia east of the 160th meridian, including the whole of the vast Kamchatka Peninsula.[53] The territory was known to hold huge reserves of oil, coal, timber and fisheries, and Vanderlip estimated its total worth at a whopping $3 billion. The catch, of course, was that the agreement only went into effect when the U.S. Government granted the Soviets full recognition. To sweeten the deal for Washington, Vanderlip advertised that the concession included two naval bases, one

---

50. U.S. House of Representatives, "Investigation of Un-American Propaganda Activities in the United States," (1939), 5157.

51. McMeekin, 224.

52. "Name Financial Group 'Grub-Staking' Vanderlip," *National Petroleum News*, #48 (Dec. 1920), 28.

53. "American Contract with Soviet Russia," *New York Times* (26 Oct. 1920).

the excellent harbor at Avacha Bay.[54] He claimed both would be made available to the U.S. Navy, which would afford it complete dominance of the northern Pacific. If that sounds like something the Japanese might object to, yes it was.

Arriving back in New York on 13 December 1920, Vanderlip dined that evening with Martens and Nuorteva, then headed for the West Coast, leaving Washington to figure out what would happen next. When the new Harding Administration still failed to grant recognition, Vanderlip headed back to Moscow in February 1921. Interestingly, during his second visit, the Cheka arrested Nuorteva on charges of misappropriating funds, behind which lay darker suspicion that he was an "American agent."[55] The man reportedly responsible for the accusation was Washington Vanderlip. Regardless, when Vanderlip again appeared in New York, he came waving a new concession, this one for 10 million acre of prime spruce forest near Archangel.[56] Still, there was no recognition.

The catch was that Lenin's Government did not actually control the property it was leasing. Nominally, Kamchatka and the adjoining regions were part of the so-called Far Eastern Republic (FER), the buffer state Moscow set up in early 1920. To make matters even more complicated, the FER leadership had granted an almost identical concession to another American syndicate, this one headed by no less than William Boyce Thompson.[57] But the FER didn't have possession of Kamchatka, either. In May 1921, a Japanese-backed White regime seized control of Vladivostok and dispatched a small garrison to the Peninsula. The Whites would remain in control until October 1922. In the meantime, Standard Oil jumped into Vanderlip's deal, acquiring a 25% stake. But without recognition Vanderlip's Siberian empire remained just a scrap of paper.[58]

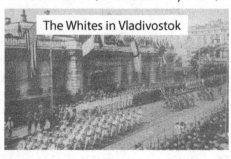

The Whites in Vladivostok

Behind this affair there was arguably something much bigger going on. Critics saw the Vanderlip and Thompson concessions as a ploy by the Bolsheviks to embroil the Americans and Japanese in a war. Kremlin policy makers did indeed believe "a clash of interests between Japan and America in the Far East would be extremely beneficial politically."[59] However, to for-

54. "Has 2 Naval Bases Says W. B. Vanderlip," *New York Times* (23 June 1921),

55. "Nuorteva Arrested in Moscow on Charge of Being American Agent," *New York Times* (24 May 1921).

56. "W.B. Vanderlip Tells of Another Big Grant," *New York Times* (19 May 1921).

57. "Two U.S. Groups Sold Same Rights in Siberian East," *Washington Herald* (7 July 1921), 1.

58. "Standard Oil Joins Vanderlip Project," *New York Times* (11 Jan. 1922).

59. Yusy Vagit, "Oil of Russia," 82. http://www.rulit.me/books/oil-of-russia-read-263258-82.html.

mer KGB officer Alexei Kirichenko, the story was more devious still.[60] In November 1920, the forces of Baron Peter Vrangel, the last White army opposing the Soviets in European Russia, abandoned their stronghold in the Crimea and evacuated to Turkey. A scheme surfaced to transfer Vrangel's 40,000 experienced soldiers to the Far East where they would reinforce the Vladivostok Whites and perhaps turn the tide of the civil war in Siberia. Initially the British, French and Japanese all backed the plan, but the Brits quickly dropped out, presumably under American pressure. Movement of the Whites to Siberia then fell entirely on Japan's shoulders. Kirichenko, in an

Vrangel

unpublished manuscript, claimed Washington issued a "serious warning" to Tokyo that it should abandon the plan and pull all its remaining troops from Russian territory. Most interesting of all, Kirichenko claimed that Trotsky, "who was the most valuable agent" for the Americans, got their cooperation by offering "lucrative concessions in the East." Concessions like Vanderlip's, presumably. If Trotsky was a "valuable agent" for the Americans when did he become one? Did the roots of this arrangement go back to early 1917?

THE WAR FOR OIL

No sooner did the Vanderlip bubble burst, than another American popped up to try his hand at the concession game. This was Henry Mason Day, a Wall Street "soldier of fortune" in the mold of William Franklin Sands. In August 1921, the U.S. press announced that Day, then president of the American Foreign Trade Organization, was in the Soviet Caucasus seeking an "American monopoly" on the region's oil.[61] Among other things, Day's outfit represented Ford, General Motors and International Harvester. He also had possession of $500,000 in gold.[62] Whose was it? In the States, Day forged an alliance with the Barnsdall Corporation, a smallish oil and mining concern run by Robert Law, Jr., a Bankers Club member and Wall Street playboy linked to Standard Oil. Together, Law and Day formed the International Barnsdall Corporation. After more dickering in Moscow, in early 1922, Day nailed down an exclusive deal for International Barnsdall to undertake the restoration and expansion of the rich Baku oil fields.[63]

60. Alexei A. Kirichenko, "Amerikantsy spasayut Sovetsuyu Rossiyu," chapter from an unpublished manuscript on Japanese-Russian relations. Thanks to Prof. Hiroaki Kuromiya for bringing this material to my attention.

61. "American a Soviet Agent," *New York Times* (23 Aug. 1921).

62. *Ibid.*

63. *Petroleum Age*, Vol. 9, #9 (1 May 1922), 86, and "Barnsdall Confirms Baku Oil Negotiations," *New York Times* (29 March 1922).

As usual, behind Day and Barnsdall was a larger presence. Mason Day happened to be the "most trusted business associate and closest friend" of Harry F. Sinclair, head honcho of Sinclair Consolidated Oil and one of the most aggressive and unscrupulous operators in an industry filled with aggressive and unscrupulous men.[64] The same Harry Sinclair was soon to be embroiled in the infamous Teapot Dome Scandal, with tentacles reaching deep into the Harding Administration. Sinclair, in turn, was backed by other powerful forces. Permanent directors of Consolidated Oil (based at 55 Liberty Street, just a block away from 120 Broadway) included William Boyce Thompson, as well as Harry Payne Whitney from Guaranty Trust, William Corey of Midvale Steel and Chase National's Albert Wiggin. They were also all directors of American International Corporation.

The Barnsdall deal sounded the alarm on the other side of the Atlantic where Sir Henry Deterding, kingpin of Royal Dutch Shell (RDS) had hatched his own plans for Russian oil. Prior to WWI, Deterding bought up big shares in Russia's Caucasus oilfields, making him the second biggest proprietor in the Empire. Only the Nobel Brothers' holdings were larger. Deterding and the Nobels, of course, then lost everything to the Bolsheviks. In 1920, Standard Oil of New Jersey bought a half-interest in Nobel. The stage was thus set for an Anglo-American battle for control of Russian oil and, more broadly, for the "future oil supply of the world."[65]

This rivalry gave the Soviets an opportunity to play the two sides against each other, and that is precisely what they did. On 10 April 1922, a general European economic conference opened at Genoa, Italy. The Moscow Reds were there in force, waving concessions in every direction. Deterding didn't attend. Instead, he headed for New York where, on 3 May, Wall Street gave him a royal reception at Manhattan's Midday Club.[66] His main hosts

---

64. Laton McCartney, *The Teapot Dome Scandal: How Big Oil Bought the White House and Tried to Steal the Country* (2009), 166.

65. "Uncle Sam and John Bull Engage in Titanic Struggle for Domination of Future Oil Supply of the World," *Brooklyn Daily Eagle* (21 May 1922), E5.

66. "Kahn and Schiff Entertain Royal Dutch Company Head," *New York Tribune* (4 May 1922), 8.

were Kuhn Loeb's Otto Kahn and Mortimer Schiff, but William Wiseman, Paul Warburg, Charles Stone, Averell Harriman and Bernard Baruch were also on hand. Deterding's aim was to enlist Kuhn Loeb and other American allies in a common front against the Bolsheviks and Standard. Back in 1919, in the spirit of "economic internationalism," Kuhn Loeb had offered Shell's common stock to American investors and in return acquired a big stake in Shell's Asiatic Petroleum subsidiary.[67] Behind the scenes, of course, Deterding desperately sought his own accommodation with Moscow.

Stalin & A. Harriman

Baruch

Most American oil men ignored Deterding's "united front." In 1922 Sinclair reached accord with the soon to be extinct Far Eastern Republic and secured an exploration concession for northern Sakhalin.[68] He ran into the same problem as Vanderlip. The Japanese occupied northern Sakhalin and would do so until 1925. So long as they were there, Sinclair's concession meant nothing.

Meanwhile, U.S. labor stepped forward to extend a fraternal proletarian hand to the embattled Bolsheviks. In 1921, Sidney Hillman, the Socialist boss of the Amalgamated Clothing Workers, made his pilgrimage to Moscow.[69] His traveling companion was Northwestern University economist and labor expert Earl Dean Howard. They returned to the States to found the Russian American Industrial Corporation (RAIC).[70] Financed by the Union's two banks, Amalgamated Bank of New York and Amalgamated Trust & Savings in Chicago, RAIC aimed to create a huge Russian clothing syndicate that would buy American cotton and wool and employ tens of thousands of Russian workers in Soviet mills. Stockholders in the enterprise supposedly included Lenin himself. Hillman boasted that Secretary of Commerce Herbert Hoover (who will feature prominently in the following chapter) had guaranteed the U. S. Government would place no obstacles in the way of the plan. By 1924, the RAIC had more than 17,000 workers laboring in thirty-four plants, but it could not turn a profit and folded the following year. While one might suppose that this was one Russian venture in which Wall Street had no skin, that wasn't quite the case. Sitting on the board of directors of the Amalgamated Bank, the RAIC's main financial prop, was none other than Paul Warburg.[71]

---

67. W. L. Randolph, "Shell Transport and Trading," *The Magazine of Wall Street and Business Analyst*, Vol. 24, #2 (May 1919), 788-789.

68. "Reds Give American Concession," *Los Angeles Times* (8 Oct. 1922), 4.

69. While pro-Soviet at this point, Hillman later became a bitter foe of the Communists in the American labor movement.

70. Georges Popoff, "U.S. Men Form Giant Trust in Russia," *The Indiana Gazette* (27 Nov. 1922), 7.

71. MID, #10110-1534, IOCD, 17 April 1920.

CHARLES CRANE RETURNS TO RUSSIA

During 1919, Charles Crane's attention had shifted to the Middle East where President Wilson dispatched him on a fact-finding mission: the so-called "King-Crane Commission." His report advocating American mandates in the region attests to Crane's continuing "special relationship" with the State Department.[72] In the Middle East, the Elephant in the Room was again oil, and Crane suspected that the British and French fully intended to keep every drop of that for themselves. His suspicions were confirmed the following year when the San Remo Oil Agreement excluded American companies from any of the ex-Ottoman petroleum assets.[73] The World War for Oil was on, and Russia and its immense reserves were a key battleground.

In early 1920, Wilson name Charles Crane the American ambassador to China. The Chicagoan, it may be recalled, had held this post once before but was obliged to resign through the obstructionism of the Japanese and Schiff. Crane took up his ambassadorial post in May 1920, but he again stepped down when the Republican Harding administration took power in Washington. In Beijing, Crane's eye was inevitably drawn to events in neighboring Siberia where the Civil War still raged. As noted, control of eastern Siberia was then split between a White government in Vladivostok and the "Pink" Far Eastern Republic headquartered in Chita. Among the leading lights of the latter were former "American Bolsheviki" Alexander Krasnoshchekoff, the Republic's first president, and "Bill" Shatoff, minister of transport. All pretense of independence aside, the FER was never more than a convenient fiction and all important shots were called in Moscow, something the canny Crane certainly realized.

In May 1921, shed of his ambassadorship, Crane initiated contact with the Beijing representative of the FER, Ignaty Yurin (Dzevaltovsky). This was directly coincidental with Washington's dispatch of two special emissaries to Chita. These were assistant military attaché Maj. J. W. Davies and acting commercial attaché James F. Abbott. Of course, as fate – or design – would have it, Crane and Abbott were old friends. Crane had consulted with him on Russian matters back in 1918 when Abbott was attached to the Military Intelligence Division. Abbott and Davies returned to Beijing in June. Crane, meanwhile, had taken a detour to Harbin, Manchuria where he outfitted a special rail carriage intended to carry him and a small party across Siberia to Moscow, and from there to Prague. That was Crane's official story. The real reasons were more complicated and, naturally, secret.

Crane's traveling companions were his younger son, John, Crane's long-time secretary Donald Brodie, newspaperman (*Chicago Daily News*)

72. Saul, 196-197. In this venture Crane once again operated as a "Presidential agent."
73. Daniel Yergin, *The Prize: The Epic Quest for Oil, Money and Power* (1993), 195.

Junius Wood, Morgan Palmer and Paul Dutko. The last two are especially interesting because they both had connections to the U.S. State Department. Dutko was a Russian-speaking Pennsylvanian who earlier had served in the American Embassy in Tokyo as a code and cipher clerk, and he later worked in Vladivostok and Harbin where he became a vice-consul. Aboard the train, Dutko sent and received coded messages to and from Washington; just a little unusual for a private pleasure trip. Morgan Palmer had served in diplomatic posts in China since 1910. During 1918-20, he worked for the American Red Cross (just like Robins and Thompson) and he was a major in the US Army Reserve.

Charles Crane's little adventure is of interest because it coincides with two other American initiatives in Russia; the first being the above Vanderlip Syndicate. The State Department had given Vanderlip a cold shoulder, publicly at least. Crane's appearance in Chita directly overlapped with Vanderlip's second return from Moscow. Crane's sometime-collaborator, sometime-competitor William Boyce Thompson, we recall, had signed a deal for an almost identical concession. He had a team of experts in Chita when Crane arrived. While Crane's political clout in Washington faded with the passing of Wilson, Thompson had positioned himself as the "financial angel" of the Republican Party and was on good terms with the new man in the White House, Warren G. Harding. Vanderlip also had connections to Harding. Some rumors held that the hidden hand behind Vanderlip was Thompson. So, were there actually two rival  American syndicates or just one? Was Vanderlip's flamboyant hucksterism a distraction from Thompson's more subtle maneuvers? In either case, was Crane now on hand to help or hinder matters? The one thing that seems certain is that Charles Crane was back in the saddle as an unofficial agent of the U.S. Government and American economic interests.

Crane and companions reached Chita in June but ran into difficulty when Moscow refused permission to proceed into Soviet territory. The necessary OK finally came on 2 July after protracted telegraphic negotiations. Meanwhile, in the FER capital, Crane connected, or re-connected, with Krasnoshchekoff and Shatoff. Among other things, Krasnoshchekoff helped Crane obtain 100,000,000 paper rubles for a mere $3,000. Crane later claimed to have "bribed" Shatoff.[74] Both men acted as Crane's intermediaries in the negotiations with Moscow, an effort which does not seem to have earned either any brownie points in the Kremlin. In the Soviet version, Crane only received permission to proceed when he guaranteed that the American Government would use its influence to force Japanese evacuation of Vladivostok and other areas of eastern Siberia. Again,

---

74. Saul, 202.

that was quite a promise to extort from a supposedly private citizen and presumes the Soviets knew he was acting on Washington's behalf. Note that this all tends to mesh with Kirichenko's story.

The Crane party pushed on, reaching Omsk on 15 July and Yaroslavl on 24 July. In the latter spot, Crane made a long overdue inspection of the still-functioning Crane-Westinghouse factory. At this point, only three foreign companies still operated in Russia and they were all American: Crane-Westinghouse, International Harvester and Singer.

Crane finally arrived in Moscow on 26 July, which brings us to a second coincidence. On that same day, Herbert Hoover's cable arrived at the Kremlin offering to put his American Relief Administration at the disposal of Russia's famine-stricken regions. We'll have more to say about that in the following chapter. The essential point here is that Hoover's offer had one absolute condition before negotiations could commence: the release of several American prisoners held in Soviet custody. One of these captives was Xenophon Kalamatiano, a man whose fateful presence in Russia likely had more than a little to do with Crane. Another, whose story we'll also encounter in the next chapter, was Weston Estes.

Kalamatiano and Estes were hermetically sealed in the Red penal system, but another American captive, Royal Keely, had been paroled and met with Crane soon after his arrival. Back in 1919, Yury Lomonosov, the Russian railway expert who worked with the Martens Bureau, recruited Keely to go to the Workers' Paradise to compile a report on commerce and industry under Soviet rule. Keely probably also went to Russia as a stealth agent for Crane and had links to U.S. intelligence.[75] The Soviet intention was that Keely's report would be a glowing endorsement to Wall Street and encourage American investment and recognition. Instead, it was harshly critical and the Cheka arrested him before he could return to the States.[76] Regarding his sit-down with Crane, Keely probably provided him with the latest information concerning the whereabouts and conditions of the other prisoners, and Crane duly passed that to Hoover's agents in Riga.

The strong implication is that the two American capitalists were working hand-in-glove and Crane's Moscow visit was an unofficial prologue to the ARA-Kremlin negotiations. This is supported by the fact that the only Soviet official Crane admitted meeting with in Moscow was Deputy Commissar of Foreign Affairs Maxim Litvinov, the same official sent to hash out the deal with Hoover.[77] Crane's train reached Riga, Latvia on 7 August. Three days later, in the same place, the ARA talks commenced.

75. Keely regularly handed over information to a known MID agent in Moscow, Marguerite Harrison, which was probably the real reason for his arrest. USDS, Telegram #111 from American Legation Vyborg, Finland to State, 20 Nov. 1920.

76. Mahoney, *American Prisoners*, 323-329. Keely (sometimes spelled Keeley) was a civil engineer.

77. Bertrand M. Patenaude, *The Big Show in Bololand: The American Relief Expedition to Soviet Russia in the Famine of 1921* (2002), 40-41.

Interestingly, in Moscow John Crane met with another Foreign Commissariat staffer, a man "from Chicago."[78] This was Michael Gruzenberg, who we last met setting up bank accounts in Switzerland and smuggling diamonds to Ludwig Martens. Notably, Gruzenberg was very close to Trotsky, the *eminence rouge* who must have been studiously observing everything from just behind the scenes.

Crane's efforts did not go unrewarded. Just after he departed Russia, in September 1921, the Soviets nationalized all remaining American enterprises. All except one, that is. The Westinghouse plant, Crane's baby, was spared, and would remain so until 1925. Its managers remained at the helm, and the Soviet Government bought everything it produced.[79]

THE RETURN OF REILLY AND WISEMAN

We last saw Sidney Reilly slipping into the shadows after the 1918 Lockhart Plot fiasco, a disaster for which he was largely responsible. He resurfaced in Stockholm that October. Despite Consul DeWitt Poole's damning evidence – that Reilly was in Petrograd openly cabling New York while supposedly being hunted by the Reds – the British took him back into the fold. One reason was his pro-Bolshevik accomplices, diplomat Bruce Lockhart and intelligence officer George Hill, who backed him up. Another was that some in London were not sorry to see the blame fall on Kalamatiano and the Americans. The masters of the City, London's Wall Street, were no slouches in economic imperialism and just as anxious to cash in on the post-Tsar bonanza as their Yankee cousins. They even felt they had a better right; Russia owed far more debts to the U.K. than the U.S.[80] Lurking behind the façade of Anglo-American alliance was a bitter economic rivalry.

After returning with Hill to Russia's Black Sea region in December, by spring 1919 Reilly was back in London. On 11 April, the U.S. Embassy received a request from the Foreign Office to grant Sidney George Reilly a visa the visit the States "on urgent government business."[81] And not just any visa – a diplomatic one. Reilly needed a diplomatic visa for a very simple reason; due to the denunciations of Poole and Kalamatiano he feared possible arrest. The passport officer complied and the result was a diplomatic kerfuffle.

In Washington, thanks to Poole, Reilly's name set off alarm bells. The secretary of the London Embassy, Edward Bell, tried to get to the bottom of it but was stonewalled by British officials who couldn't decide if Reilly was going to New York on official or "personal" business, or just to "get

---

78. Saul, 205.

79. "Soviet Has Seized American Plants," *New York Times* (12 Sept. 1921).

80. On this see: J. T. Walton Newbold, "Bankers, Bondholders and Bolsheviks," (1919).

81. USDS, #811.111/21911, Bell to Winslow, "Secret #1222," 21 April 1919, 2.

[him] out of the way for a while."[82] It seemed evident that he was on some mission for the SIS, but no one could say what. Bell found the British attitude frustrating, but told Washington it didn't seem worth making a big fuss over.

Reilly's liner was bound for New York, but during the stop in Halifax, he debarked and caught a train, crossing the U.S.-Canadian border on 21 April. He didn't travel alone. With him was his old comrade Antony Jechalski who had wormed his way into Polish diplomatic service. Note that their arrival immediately followed the establishment of the Soviet Bureau. Ensconced in the Gotham Hotel, Reilly and Jechalski rendezvoused with a third man, Jonas Lied, fresh from Siberia via Japan.

Jonas Lied was a Norwegian national and honorary Russian subject. He was owner of the Siberian Steamship and Trading Company and his business dealings in Russia and Scandinavia had brought him into contact with many men, among them Olof Aschberg, Abram Zhivotovsky and, of course, Reilly. In early 1919, he was in New York as an agent for another big Bolshevik

Lied

deal, the Hannevig Concession. In this, the Soviet Government offered an 80-year lease on 8-million acres of the finest taiga, and the right to build a rail line connecting the Siberian rivers to the Arctic ports.[83] The nominal concessionaire was Edward Hannevig, a Norwegian banker and another associate of Aschberg. However, his two brothers, and the bank they operated, Christoffer Hannevig, Inc., were located at 139 Broadway, close to the Equitable. The New York press claimed that "American capital" was behind Hannevig.[84] On 5 July 1919, Lied was back in New York for a meeting with the familiar Henry C. Emery at Guaranty Trust. Two days later, Lied registered the incorporation of a new company, the American-Russian Industrial Syndicate. As Sutton notes, the money behind this outfit came from Sinclair Oil, Guggenheim Brothers and J.G. White Engineering, all located at 120 Broadway.[85] Eventually, Sinclair assumed the controlling interest.[86] Also connected with the syndicate was Eugene Lubovitch, another ex-pat Russian banker and, as you can likely guess, past and present associate of Reilly and Zhivotovsky.[87]

Meanwhile, despite the claim that he was in New York on "official business" for the British Government, Reilly appeared to busy himself with entirely personal matters. Most notably, he arranged a suit against

---

82. *Ibid.* 3-7.

83. "American Capital in Deal with Reds," *New York Times* (2 May 1919).

84. *Ibid.*

85. Sutton, *Wall Street*, 136-137.

86. *Poor's and Moody's Manual Consolidated*, Vol. 2 (1922), 1637.

87. USDS, #861.516/84, Winslow, 2 Sept. 1919.

Remington Arms for unpaid commissions.[88] Simultaneously, his partner Alexander Weinstein was involved in a suit by the Russo-Asiatic Bank against Guaranty Trust. The apparent aim was to gain control of Guaranty's dormant ruble accounts.

However, the real purpose of Reilly's visit is revealed in his 10 May coded telegram to J. Picton Bagge, an official of the British Board of Trade.[89] Reilly related his "conversations with prominent American bankers and manufacturers" who were "fully alive to the possibilities of Russia as [an] inexhaustible market for American manufacturers and as a great field for capital." Reilly aimed to forge a "British-American combination which could assimilate and exploit" Russian firms and banks, particularly those controlled by the aforementioned Batolin and other émigré tycoons. Batolin, Reilly noted, had already made a "good impression" with American International Corp. and Ford Motor. The Wall Street point man for the transatlantic combine was to be NCB's redoubtable Samuel McRoberts, who Reilly hailed as possessing "great influence" and who "directs the foreign policy" of his and other banks. The envisioned syndicate would include American International, Armour & Co., plus "the Guggenheims, Ford, Percy Rockefeller, the Duponts, John Ryan, etc." Reilly promised a more detailed report on his return to London. Accompanied by Jechalski, he was back in England by the end of May.

Soon after, on 13 June, another familiar face returned to Manhattan, Sir William Wiseman. Over the next few months, he and Reilly maintained regular, coded communication. In London, Reilly threw himself into the so-called "Russian Banking Scheme." This used yet another front man, Russian-Polish banker Karol Yaroshinsky, to buy up stock in nationalized Russian banks from desperate émigré stockholders. Yaroshinsky's syndicate was financed by City bankers who hoped to end up owning the lion's share of the Russian banking system and all its assets. It would give them a big edge in future dickering with the Reds and sideline the pestiferous Yankees. Of course, one of Yaroshinsky's collaborators was Abram Zhivotovsky.[90]

On 19 August Reilly cabled Wiseman to inform him that the British Government had given a green light to the Yaroshinsky scheme.[91] First, he wanted Wiseman to sit on the advisory board. He also asked Wiseman to keep an eye on the activities of the above. Reilly and friends wanted Batolin squashed, a move that would help Yaroshinsky – and Martens. Wiseman agreed to both requests.[92] The following month, Reilly also sent a coded cable to Alexander Weinstein in New York telling him "to supply

---

88. Supreme Court, New York County, "Upton Dale Thomas [Reilly's secretary and factotum] against Remington Arms and Ammunition Company," 19 June 1919.

89. TNA, FO 371/4019, CXC 416, 10 May, 1919, 1.

90. E. Semenov, *Russkie banki zagranitsei i Bolsheviki* (1926), 58-59.

91. WWP, 6/176, CXP 962, 19 Aug. 1919.

92. *Ibid.*, Draft cable, Aug. 1919.

[Wiseman] with all information you possess about Batolin," especially "his transactions with American banks and companies and also with all information you have or can obtain about existing or proposed American commerce and industrial activities with regard to Russia."[93]

A curious thing is that in a 3 July letter to a British colleague, Eric Drummond, Wiseman declared that he no longer re- garded himself in His Majesty's service, which again raises the question of who he was serving.[94] In the same letter, Sir William noted that political enemies in Washington intended to attack Wilson and House "for being too friendly with the Bolsheviks." Appar- ently, they had gotten hold of "some rather indiscreet correspondence." Whose? Wiseman also mentioned "our friend Dudley Field Malone [who] has come out as a regular social- *ist revolutionary* leader. He spends his time trying to keep the Bolsheviks out of jail. He is still a most delightful companion and sends you his love." Malone, among other things, was a legal advisor to the Soviet Bureau. For a simple banker, no longer in government service, Wiseman seemed to be surprisingly well informed.

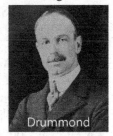
Drummond

London also tried to get a jump on the Yanks by doing what they would not – negotiate a formal trade agreement with the Bolshies. In May 1920, Leonid Krasin arrived to do just that. He at once formed a close bond with Reilly, a relationship some British officials found highly suspicious. In November of that year, MI5 discovered that Krasin had received a £5000 ($25,000 U.S.) check from Guaranty Trust.[95] He unconvincingly claimed to have no idea who it was from or for what. In any event, the trade pact negations proved successful and an agreement was signed in March 1921.

Around the same time, Reilly enlisted an old associate to take on as- signments in the States. This was Sir Paul Dukes who, like Reilly, had won acclaim (and in his case a knighthood) for espionage exploits in Russia during 1918-19. In March 1921, Dukes arrived in New York as Reilly's personal agent.[96] Over the following weeks, Dukes' diaries record lun- cheons at the Bankers Club, dinners with exiled Russian bankers and meetings with Col. House in Washington, Philadelphia and New York.[97] Given that House was now "out of power," what were these about? Later, he sat down with Raymond Robins, and Dukes made the rounds of high- end Manhattan art dealers, the very sort anxious to buy the artworks the Bolsheviks were so anxious to sell.[98]

93. *Ibid.*, CXG 484, 10 Sept. 1919.

94. WWP, 1/27, 3 July 1919.

95. TNA, KV2/573, To Serocold, 27 Nov. 1920.

96. Among other things, Dukes arranged an auction of Reilly's Napoleonic collection.

97. HIA, Paul Dukes Collection, 1921 and 1922 datebooks/diaries.

98. On this, see McMeekin.

In the same period, Reilly entered a business alliance with retired British officer Edward L. Spears, a contentious arrangement in which Spears' main job appeared to be keeping an eye on his dubious partner. In late 1921, Spears observed that Reilly's "great danger is his associates before he worked with us."[99] At the same time, British concerns about Reilly reached a tipping point and SIS discreetly severed ties. Most of them, anyway.

Wiseman returned to New York in October 1920. On the same ship was a young Wall Street attorney, William "Wild Bill" Donovan, future American spymaster and head of the OSS. Donovan's employer was J. P. Morgan, and he was returning from Europe after a months-long fact-finding (intelligence) mission for Morgan's new Foreign Commerce Corporation of America, another Wall Street ploy to outflank the British. Donovan and Morgan were very interested in the progress of Bolshevism in Russia and its chance of spreading elsewhere. It seems unlikely the presence of Wiseman and Donovan on the same liner was an accident.

Donovan

Wiseman's big opportunity came in September 1920 when Jacob Schiff died. The new dominant figure at Kuhn Loeb was his old collaborator Otto Kahn. The following year, Kahn latter invited him into the firm. Was this a reward for past services rendered? Regardless, it did not sit well with everyone. U.S. Military Intelligence received reports that Wiseman's employment "caused disquiet among British financiers, especially Jews."[100] In early 1922, Kuhn Loeb organized its own spin-off to capitalize on East European opportunities, the New York & Foreign Development Corporation. Wiseman became its head.[101] For much of that year he was in Czechoslovakia, Poland and Romania, where he employed Reilly as an agent. What were they up to? The big score was still Russia.

Among Sir William's fiercest detractors was a man who had nursed a grudge against him since 1916: Guy Gaunt. Officially retired from Naval service but still connected to intelligence, Gaunt preserved a strong connection to Kuhn Loeb's rival J. P. Morgan. On 1 July 1921, just days after Wiseman returned to New York, Gaunt landed and went straight to Morgan's offices. On the same day, but in a different liner, another British intelligence operative arrived in New York, Claude M. Dansey. Back in 1917, Dansey had raised questions about Wiseman's handling of the

Dansey

---

99. CA, SPRS 2/5, Spears diaries, entry for 23 Nov. 1921.

100. MID, #2657-D-683, Churchill to Biddle, 13 May 1922.

101. "Little Chance for War Says Sir William Wiseman," *New York Times* (1 May 1922). The same article describes Wiseman as connected to Kuhn Loeb's "London branch."

Trotsky business.[102] The simultaneous arrival of two spooks, both having issues with Wiseman, suggests they were trailing him. If nothing else, he had now clearly aligned himself with Wall Street interests against (London) City interests. And then there was his questionable relationship with the very questionable Reilly.

THE VANISHING RUSSIAN GOLD RESERVE

In 1914, The Russian Imperial Government possessed one of the world's largest gold reserves, pegged by the U.S. Commerce Department at $807,500,000.[103] During the War, the Russian Government sent some $400 million abroad, mostly to Britain, to underwrite war purchases. New production, confiscation and "safe-keeping" of the Romanian State Gold Reserve (which the Romanians would never see again), left a total of around $640 million by the time of the October revolution. The Bolsheviks ended up with about half – $308 million – in Moscow, while the remaining $332 million was stored in the Volga River town of Kazan. In early 1918, the latter fell into the hands of the Whites, who moved it to Omsk, in western Siberia, capital of the so-called Provisional All-Russian Government. In November 1918, Admiral Alexander Kolchak seized Omsk and the gold. Over the next year, he spent and/or squandered $122 million.[104]

Much of that made its way to Wall Street. In 1919, an "Anglo-American financial syndicate," essentially Morgan and his allies in the Bank of England, extended Kolchak's government $38 million in credits in return for $40 million in gold deposited in a Shanghai bank.[105] By the time Kolchak fell in early 1920, the syndicate had collected half the gold. That summer, the remainder went to New York, but instead of around $20 million there was $28,500,000. Ludwig Martens, who followed the whole thing closely, was at a loss to explain where the addition $8,500,000 came from. Any way you look at it, at least $48 million of Kolchak's gold ended up in U.S. or British banks.

In the autumn of 1919, with the Red Army closing in on Omsk, the Whites loaded the remaining $210 million on a special train headed towards Vladivostok. The train derailed, and as much as $32 million disappeared in the resulting chaos. The Reds eventually recovered about $178 million and shipped it back to Moscow. In the meantime, the Bolsheviks had turned over $160 million of their stash to the Germans as reparations under the Treaty of Brest-Litovsk. By early 1920, therefore, Lenin & Co. had managed to reassemble something like $300 million in bullion. By

102. TNA, KV2/502, CX 015649, 19 Jan. 1918.

103. United States Treasury, *Annual Report of the Director of the Mint, 1922*, 182.

104. Exact figures at any stage vary. For a basic accounting, see: William Clarke, *The Lost Fortune of the Tsars* (1994), 177-188.

105. BA, Russian Embassy files, #3532 Bullard to Bakhmetev, 7 Dec. 1920, attachment "August 1920."

February 1921, this had been reduced to $175 million, and on 10 August 1921, the reserve was a mere $1,264,000. Soon it was $0.

How did the Soviets dispose of $300 million in gold during a time when they were blockaded and unable to move it or spend it in most countries in the world? Martens had never gotten a single ounce into the U.S. – legally. The answer is the Baltic Loophole and Swedish banks. The small Baltic states, especially Estonia, were not on good terms with Soviet Russia, but they allowed just about anything to flow into and out of Bol-shevikland for a piece of the action.

The man overseeing the movement of Russian gold through Estonia to Sweden was our old friend Olof Aschberg. Max May arranged with him to buy gold directly for Guaranty Trust.[106] By April 1921, an estimated $120 million in So-viet gold had reached Sweden, $42 million since January.[107] In Stockholm it was melted down to remove all incriminating signs of origin and re-stamped. By March, at least 90 tons (almost $60 million) had received that treatment. From there, it headed to London and Paris but, above all, New York, where it commonly arrived consigned as 1st class mail.[108] The first substantial shipment of crypto-Bolshevik gold, 7 tons ($4,600,000), arrived in the U.S. on the Swedish steamer *Carlsholm* in March.[109] 70 tons of repackaged bullion, roughly $46 million, reached New York by May 1921, and much more was on the way.[110] More gold still poured in via France and Britain.[111]

American banks were in a gold-buying frenzy. In August 1921, an estimated $460,000,000 of the yellow stuff had come to the U.S. since the first of the year.[112] A mere $10,720,000 was exported. The import-ed shipments went to many receivers, but the main ones were Guar-anty Trust, Equitable Trust, J. P. Morgan and, heads above the rest, Kuhn Loeb. By August, the latter firm had imported an astounding $102,290,000, almost a quarter of the total.[113] When the Russian vaults emptied and the Swedish processing completed, this bonanza stopped.

106. McMeekin, 145.

107. "Soviet Gold in Sweden ...", *New York Times* (23 April 1921).

108. "Bolshevik Gold on Ship Due Here May 11, *Brooklyn Daily Eagle* (4 Mat 1921), 3.

109. "Tons of Soviet Gold Coming Here from Sweden," *New York Times* (23 March 1921).

110. "More Soviet Gold Coming from Scandinavia," *New York Times* (5 May 1921). In 1921 the official price of gold in the United States was $20.67 per 0z., the same as it had been since 1879. That translated to $661,440 per ton, thus the reputed 120 tons in Sweden represented roughly $80 million.

111. "Fears Soviet Gold Comes from Allies," *New York Times* (2 April 1921)

112. "$460,000,000 in Gold Imported in 1921," *New York Times* (24 Aug. 1921).

113. "$7,500,000 in Gold Imports for Banks," *New York Times* (23 Aug. 1921).

The Russian gold reserve did not vanish; it went abroad, and overwhelmingly to Wall Street.

Was this just Americans cashing in on the "Russian fire-sale"? What did the Soviets get out of exporting all their gold? The gold hemorrhage did not immediately coincide with a huge uptick in Moscow's importation of goods. However, in 1923-24, U.S.-Russian trade assumed an appreciable volume when the Soviets imported some $50 million in American products. During 1924-25, this increased to over $100 million.[114] The simple answer seems to be that the gold was a giant grubstake for future buying.

A common fear in the West was that the Soviets were stashing money abroad to bankroll Communist movements and revolutionary subversion. To some extent this was true, although the Comintern and foreign Communists never got much more than crumbs. Another possibility is that the gold, in part, was payment on a debt, or put another way, a return on past American investment in the Russian Revolution. Was that why Kuhn Loeb garnered the lion's share? Another idea is that the Bolsheviks transferred wealth abroad as a "rainy day fund" to support them in exile and finance a new revolutionary movement should the Soviet regime collapse. During late 1920 and early 1921, the Bolsheviks confronted both economic ruin and a rising tide of peasant rebellion. One, admittedly iffy, source maintained that by 1921 there was the equivalent of $90 million sequestered in U.S. and Swiss banks under accounts controlled by Lenin, Trotsky, Furstenberg, Cheka chief Felix Dzerzhinsky and others.[115] Trotsky, for instance, supposedly had $11 million in a New York Bank and Furstenberg $10 million. Any way you look at it, was Wall Street just reaping what it had sown?

---

114. Soviet Russian Information Bureau, "American-Russian Trade" (1929). https://www.marxists.org/history/ussr/government/1928/sufds/ch13.htm.

115. Valentin Katasonov, "Kak Bol'shevili garbili narod i 'otmyvali' nagrablennoe v zapadnykh bankakh," (2014). http://belomor999.livejournal.com/35695.html. The source is a supposed April 1921 memo from Lenin to two heads of the Cheka, Gleb Boky and Yosif Unshlikht, to which he appended an article from an American newspaper (presumably the *New York Times*, but no such article can be found) outlined the amounts and places of deposit.

CHAPTER ELEVEN

KREMLIN RULES

FENCING RED LOOT

For those on Wall Street (and elsewhere) who dreamed of putting the brakes on Russia's economic development and seeing its riches and resources up for grabs under a regime willing to sell anything, that dream had basically come true. From 1918 through early 1921, Bolshevik "War Communism" reduced Russia to an economy based on barter and robbery. Besides the abolition of private trade and the destruction of the monetary system, the Red regime embarked on a massive looting campaign, ransacking palaces, bank vaults, churches and museums. They expropriated every valuable they could get their hands on and stashed it all in a new "State Treasury," the Gokhran. By the close of 1921, an estimated $450 million in valuables had been sequestered there, with more to come, much of it destined to be fenced abroad for a fraction of its value in capitalist hard currency.[1]

The first known attempt to pawn some of this swag in the States occurred in May 1918, when Customs officials arrested two men, an American, Montifiore G. Kahn and a Russian, Vladimir Jogelson, on charges of smuggling jewelry and other valuables.[2] U.S. Customs initially valued the items, which included Tsar Nicholas' cigarette case and one of Tsaritsa Alexandra's necklaces, at $350,000, but in early 1920, the lot auctioned off for a tenth of that.[3] The purchaser was a fashionable Broadway jeweler, Charles A. Keene. Wall Street types were among his main clientele. In 1907, the same Keene had acquired and sold a diamond brooch that once belonged to Catherine the Great. Proceeds of the sale went to the "Russian Liberation Organization" to fund the struggle against Tsarism.[4] It seems reasonable to assume he was playing much the same role in 1920. In 1925, another news item datelined Moscow announced that *$250 million* in "surplus items" from Gokhran, including the "Czar's gems" had been slated "for sale in America."[5] If so, it was handled very discreetly.

---

1. McMeekin, 64-65.
2. Montifiore Kahn would go on to have a long career as a Soviet agent.
3. "Smuggled Gems Worth $350,000 Taken by Police," *Bridgeport Telegram* [CN] (8 June 1918), 4 and "Smuggled Goods Sold High," *Billings Gazette* [MT] (1 May 1920), 4.
4. "Catherine the Great Brooch," *New York Times* (8 Aug. 1907).
5. "Russia to Offer Czar's gems for sale in America," *Chicago Tribune* (13 Dec. 1925), 3.

LENIN'S "NEW ECONOMIC POLICY"

No "War Communism" policy created more resentment and hardship than the forced requisitioning of grain from the peasantry. Drought only added to the food shortage and general misery in the countryside. During the 1920 harvest, exasperated peasants began to rise in revolt. By the following spring, rebellions raged from western Siberia to Ukraine. By March 1921, 50,000 peasant rebels controlled a swath of territory barely 200 miles south of the Kremlin.[6] That same month, thousands of soldiers and sailors at the Kronstadt naval base, twenty miles from Petrograd, rose in mutiny against the Communist dictatorship. The Bolsheviks had won the civil war against the Whites, but now seemed to be on the verge of losing another to the Greens.

Soviet propaganda depicting the Kronstadt rebels as White agents

Almost inevitably, the Kronstadt Rebellion had an American angle. In the summer of 1921, Maryland Senator Joseph France, formerly a fervent backer of Ludwig Martens, paid a visit to Moscow. He ostensibly came to lobby for the release of American prisoners and to boost Soviet-American amity and trade. A physician by training, France also had a career in finance and was a director of the Maryland Trust Company. On 1 August 1921, in Riga, while on his way back to the States, France publicly accused the chief of the American Red Cross in the Baltic States, Col. Edward W. Ryan, of having "instigated" the Kronstadt revolt.[7] Ryan forcefully denied the accusation and painted the Senator as a Soviet dupe.

That description was probably fair, but what is most interesting about the dust-up is how quickly it vanished down the memory-hole. After a flurry of initial press reports, almost all favoring Ryan, the Mighty Wurlitzer fell silent. France never produced any proof, and Ryan acted as if the whole thing never happened. It smells like a story quickly and forcefully spiked. That Ryan masterminded the Kronstadt uprising is absurd; it didn't require his instigation. However, that he may have encouraged or abetted it is not. Indeed, the rebels openly acknowledged receiving humanitarian aid from him.[8] As we've seen, the history of the American Red Cross in

---

6. This was the so-called Tambov Rebellion.

7. "Senator France Lays Revolt to Red Cross Chief," *Chicago Tribune* (3 Aug. 1921).

8. "Ukrainian Rebels Capture Cities in South Russia," *Evening Public Ledger* [PA] (12 March 1921), 1.

Russia had not been one of apolitical charity. Besides, Ryan shows every sign of having been another of Washington's "irregular agents." In 1913, the State Department recruited him for work in revolution-torn Mexico, where Huertaist authorities arrested and nearly shot him as a spy.[9] During the war, he ran a volunteer hospital in Serbia, another excellent vantage point from which to observe and report. In the Baltic, in 1919, he aided General Nicholas Yudenich's White army and even accompanied it on its ill-fated attack on Petrograd. In 1920, in an obvious intelligence mission, Ryan went to Moscow disguised as a member of the Estonian peace delegation.[10] Keep in mind that had the Kronstadt rebels and their ilk managed to topple the Bolsheviks, it would not have meant a return to the old order. It would mean the Soviet regime under new management, precisely what some on Wall Street and elsewhere hoped for.

While the Kronstadt rebellion raged, Lenin addressed the 10th Party Congress and dropped a bomb-shell. War Communism, he argued, had to be abandoned and accommodation sought with the peasants and the hated bourgeoisie to restore order and a functioning economy. Simply put, the Bolsheviks had to make economic concessions to keep political pow-

Lenin speaking at 10th Congress

er. For the Marxist faithful, this was a bitter pill to swallow and Lenin's new course faced strong resistance. Trotsky, always ready to grandstand by taking a contrary position, became the main voice of the opposition.

The resulting New Economic Policy (NEP) most importantly turned the land and agricultural economy over to the peasants who, in exchange for a tax, were free to plant, buy and sell as they liked. Small industry and retail trade went back to the hands of previous owners or a class of new petty-capitalists, the Nepmen. The "commanding heights" of the economy, heavy industry, transport, banking and foreign trade, remained under state control. In 1922, the Soviet regime introduced a new currency. Last, but by no means least, the NEP rang the dinner bell for foreign capitalist investment by offering sweeping concessions. The afore-mentioned Barnsdall oil deal was but one example. From 1921 through 1929, the Soviet regime awarded around 340 concessions and technical assistance contracts, of which 113, about one-third, went to Americans.[11]

Lenin's NEP about-face was born of necessity, but that may not tell the whole story. Was it purely coincidental that this policy shift occurred

9. "Arrested As Spy in Mexico," *New York Times* (2 May 1914).

10. Walter Duranty, "Senator France Assails Col. Ryan," *New York Times* (4 Aug. 1921).

11. Antony Sutton, *Western Technology and Soviet Economic Development, 1917-1930* (1960), 351-383. On Barnsdall specifically, see 18-22.

immediately after Moscow began its Great Gold Migration to the West? Again, was that transfer a sign of good faith to Wall Street for the deals yet to be made? Was it a precondition for the economic assistance Russia so desperately needed? Capitalism is not philanthropy.

Consider what the Bolsheviks had achieved. In less than four years, they had expropriated the Russian economy from its former owners, run it into the ground, and stripped the country of gold and valuables, most of which ended up in the West – the lion's share in America. Russia had been turned into an economic wasteland which foreign capitalists were now being invited to rebuild.

Consider also the parallel situation of Germany. In 1919, the Reich narrowly avoided its own Communist regime, but ended up with the unstable Weimar Republic and the huge economic burden of $37 billion in war debts and an added $32 billion in reparations. In 1922, galloping hyper-inflation destroyed the mark just as it did the ruble. A resulting default on reparations payments sparked the 1923 French invasion of the industrial Ruhr and an international crisis that Wall Street rode in to

Dawes

solve. The "bailout" plan, fronted by U.S. banker, ex-Treasury official and future Vice President Charles G. Dawes, provided Berlin with a $200 million loan, floated by J. P. Morgan. This backed a new currency and provided cash to pay reparations. Essentially, the Americans loaned money to the Germans, so they could pay reparations to the French and British, so they could pay back their $7 billion in war loans to the U.S. Any way you turn it, the Yankees came out ahead. Russia was now ripe for the same treatment.

"THE GREAT HUMANITARIAN": HERBERT HOOVER AND THE ARA

It must have been a great disappointment to Herbert Clark Hoover that he was eventually best known as the president whose administration inaugurated the Great Depression. Humanitarianism aside, Hoover was a Wall Street insider whose associations included the exclusive Rocky Mountain Club, where he hobnobbed with friends like William Boyce Thompson. But he also headed a large international aid organization, an early NGO, the American Relief Administration (ARA). It says something that ARA headquarters was at 42 Broadway, close to Wall Street action. Hoover simultaneously served as U.S. Secretary of Commerce (1921-28). Beyond this, he had personal business interests in Russia.

A geologist by training, in 1897 Hoover headed off to the goldfields of Australia. Working for the British Berwick-Moreing mining company, he proved a capable manager and by 1904 he was a partner and director of Berwick-Moreing's Chinese Engineering and Mining Co. He arrived in Russia in 1911, where he took over as director of Russo-Asiatic Consolidated Corporation (also British controlled) and became a major stockholder in its Kyshtym copper and iron mines. His investments, especially in Russia, made him a millionaire several times over.

Freed from the burden of earning a living, and being a good Quaker, Hoover turned his hand to public service. During 1914-16, he oversaw Belgian Relief, and in 1917 Woodrow Wilson named him Food Administrator. In 1919, backed with $100 million appropriated by Congress and an equal amount in private (largely corporate) donations, he launched the ARA, which undertook relief efforts in war-ravaged Europe. By early 1921, those activities were winding down just as a new crisis/opportunity presented itself in Soviet Russia.

The combined effects of war, Bolshevik misrule and drought had reduced large areas of rural Russia, especially the Volga region, to a parlous state. While the Reds desperately needed outside aid to address this crisis, they refused to directly beg the Americans or any other foreign bourgeoisie for help. However, they were willing to let ever-useful comrade Maxim Gorky and Russian Orthodox Patriarch Tikhon do the begging. On 13 July, Gorky sent an appeal, addressed to fellow writers, along with Tikhon's, addressed to the Archbishops of Canterbury and New York, to Fridtjof Nansen, famed Norwegian explorer and head of the International Red Cross.[12] Nansen responded that only the Americans had the resources to render meaningful help. Soon after, unnamed "Soviet interests" published Gorky's letter in New York.[13] By 18 July, the Soviet official organ *Izvestiya* chimed in, acknowledging the "serious situation" and soliciting international assistance, although it specifically rejected any help from Washington because of the U.S. Government's refusal to extend recognition.[14]

Nansen

Fearing that Nansen or other meddlesome Europeans might seize the initiative, on 23 July Hoover jumped in. He wired Gorky offering the aid of the ARA which, he emphasized, was not affiliated with the American Government. Hoover's only condition was that the Soviets release all American captives before negotiations began. As noted, Hoover's note reached Moscow the same day as Charles Crane. Formal talks commenced in Riga on 10 August in which Moscow's Maxim Litvinov squared off with Hoover's man Walter Lyman Brown (another mining engineer). The

12. "Russian Plead for Famine relief," *New York Times* (19 July 1921), 2.

13. "Aid Asked for Starving Russian," *New York Times* (4 Aug. 1921), 2.

14. "Millions Flee Red Starvation," *Journal Gazette* [Mattoon, IL] (18 July 1921), 7.

Soviet starting position was that they wanted food, but no army of kha-ki-clad Yankees running around distributing it. Lyman insisted that there would be no aid unless the ARA handled distribution. After ten days of tough dickering, Brown and Hoover got their way.

Over the next two years, some 300 Americans labored in Soviet Russia and supervised more than 120,000 Russians, all, of course, under the watchful eyes of the omnipresent Cheka. Millions of lives were saved, and while Russian gratitude was genuine, it was mixed with suspicion. If the Americans' goal was only to give away food, why were they so intensely and officiously interested in collecting information? What was the purpose of the notebooks and ledgers they carried around everywhere?

It was the unquestioned conceit of the American side that the ARA's effort was "a 100 percent humanitarian operation."[15] The truth was more complicated. The official historian of the ARA's Russian operation, Thomas Dickerson, revealed the underlying thinking when he opined that America's policy toward Russia should be one of "moral trusteeship" that would "conserve it for great uses in the future."[16] In other words, behind all the chest-thumping self-righteousness, there were calculated economic motives. Hoover's private views reflected this quite clearly. To him, Russia represented "a vast, unconquered market," and American interests needed to position themselves "to undertake the leadership in the reconstruction of Russia when the proper moment arises."[17]

As noted by Sutton, in early 1922, Hoover approached the State Department with the scheme to use Guaranty Trust as the American agency of the Soviet State Bank (Gosbank) and a clearing house for all Soviet purchasing in the U.S.[18] The key figure on the New York end was the familiar Henry C. Emery, now manager of Guaranty's foreign department, the post previously held by Max May. Speaking of May, in 1921 he dissolved his Foreign Trade Banking Association (the outfit he formed after leaving Guaranty Trust), and in September 1922, with ARA relief at full steam, he resurfaced as vice president and foreign exchange chief of the Chicago-based National Bank of the Republic.[19] NBR, it may be recalled, counted Charles Crane among its directors and major stockholders. That's not all. In December of that year, Max May went to Moscow where he took on another job: director of a new Russian Commercial Bank (Roskombank), a joint venture of the Soviet Government and "important foreign interests, notably Swedish."[20] The latter, and May's co-director, was "Red Banker" Olof Aschberg.

---

15. Patenaude, 635.
16. *Ibid.*
17. *Ibid.*, 637.
18. USDS, #861.516/111, Hoover to Hughes, Jan. 1922.
19. B. C. Forbes column, *The Greenville News* [NC] (19 Dec. 1922), 13.
20. *Ibid.*

SAVING JOHN REED

Russia had been on Hoover's radar well before 1921, and a man who played a role in this, witting or not, was "Establishment Revolutionary" John Reed. The secret link between Hoover and Reed was a California-born dentist, turned intelligence officer, turned businessman name Weston Burgess Estes. In June 1917, Estes received a lieutenant's commission in the Army's Dental Reserve Corps and ended up at Ft. Totten, New York. There he became friends with a fellow medical man, Dr. Harris Ayres Houghton. Houghton had another job, that of post intelligence officer. He collected information on radicals suspected of conniving with German agents, and he enlisted Estes to help. On 2 January 1918, Houghton submitted a report "testifying as to the good work of Lt. Estes."[21] In July 1918, another report praised Estes as "an officer of great ability and loyal."[22]

In March 1918, Estes formally requested a transfer to intelligence. By November of that year, he was an assistant to the Department Intelligence Officer of the Eastern Division, Capt. Hamilton J. Smith. However, as far as the outside world was concerned, Estes was still just a dentist.[23] His new duties brought him "in contact with the radicals and Communists in New York City."[24] Harry Mahoney pegs Estes as "case officering penetration agents into these radical groups."[25] This is affirmed by daily expense reports which show Estes meeting "informants."[26] Estes officially left MID in January 1919, but he admitted to staying in contact with many radical acquaintances.[27] John Reed certainly was one of them. Estes later admitted that Reed "knew me, and knew that I was 'safe.'"[28]

In October 1919, John Reed slipped out of the U.S. and headed back to Russia. His avowed purpose was to represent the newly-formed American Communist Labor Party to the Comintern. Of course, that was not all there was to it. Shortly after his departure, the Bureau of Investigation interviewed a Mr. Lang, an exporter at Manhattan's 55 Liberty Street, the same address as Sinclair Consolidated Oil. Lang stated that a few weeks before Reed had approached him with a proposition to ship $50,000 in tungsten ore to Russia. When Lang fretted over legal complications, Reed

---

21. MID, #10012-57, Intelligence Office, Eastern Division, 12 Jan. 1918.

22. MID, #10080-16-20, Intelligence Office, Governor's Island, 10 July 1918.

23. Edward C. Kirk (ed.), *The Dental Cosmos* (Philadelphia: S. S. White & Co., 1918), 543.

24. Dr. Weston B. Estes. "Russian Experiences," *Long Island Medical Journal*, Vol. 15, #12 (Dec. 1921), 410.

25. Mahoney, *American Prisoners*, 241.

26. MID, #968-201/1-4, Expense Account of Captain Weston B. Estes, October 1918.

27. Estes, 410.

28. Estes, 411.

assured him that "the Department of State knew of this matter."[29] So was Reed going to Russia as an agent for the Communist Party, a business agent, an agent of the U.S. Government, or all three?

By chance or design, another American with interest in Russian trade was Dr. Weston Estes. As he explained it, his contacts with the pro-Bolshevik crowd whetted his curiosity about what was happening in Russia and the economic possibilities it offered. "I was really very anxious to do some business with the communists and their government," he claimed, and so "gathered a little company of businessmen together" who agreed to send him to Russia to get "the truth."[30] These powerful unnamed men, said Estes, were willing to sell the Russians whatever they wanted and would willingly break a blockade to do it. He also noted that "some of [the] radicals also asked me to go to Soviet Russia and they helped me to get there." Was one of them Reed? As for the Bolsheviks, "I had every reason to believe that they were anxious to get hold of me." Where did he get that idea?

In a letter attached to his passport application, Estes indicated that he intended to visit Norway, Denmark, Sweden and Finland, but made no reference to Russia. His avowed aim was to "seek markets for my manufactured dental articles" ... "obtain foreign patents and rights," and "buy or take industrial films."[31] He later confessed that this was all "something of a camouflage."[32] He also revealed that his main "partner" in the enterprise was Herman M. Suter. Suter, however, was no businessman. A journalist, until recently Suter had worked for George Creel and the Committee on Public Information. In December 1919, he and another ex-CPI man, Walter Rogers, took over management of the *Washington Herald*. Suter also became an informant for the Bureau of Investigation.[33] The most interesting point is who put Suter and Rogers in charge of the *Herald*. That happened to be the paper's new owners, Charles R. Crane and Herbert Hoover.[34]

Further evidence of a link between Estes and Hoover is found in a July 1921 letter from the vice-president of the Intercontinental Development Company to the *Washington Herald*. Written while Estes was still in Soviet captivity, it noted that "Mr. Rickard ... has inherited from Mr. Suter the responsibility" for Estes.[35] This was Edgar Rickard, longtime assistant and close friend of Herbert Hoover. Suter was never more than a cut-out for Hoover and Crane, and they were obviously working in unison.

29. BI, #182787, "In re: John Reed, Bolshevik Activities," 21 Nov. 1919.

30. Estes, 410.

31. Estes' passport was issued 12 Jan. 1921.

32. Estes, 409.

33. BI, #389705, J. E. Hoover, "Memorandum for Mr. Suter," 25 Oct.1925.

34. "Hoover and Crane Buyers of Herald," *Washington Herald* (7 Dec. 1919), 16.

35. HIA, American Relief Administration (ARA), Russian Operations, Box 342, folder 9, Edward M. Flesh to J. E. Rice, 21 July 1921.

Where Crane was concerned, Washington was never far away. Estes' friends in Military Intelligence were also aware of his mission. MID chief Gen. Marlborough Churchill supplied Estes with letters of introduction to U. S. military attaches in Scandinavia and the Baltic States, requesting they render him all necessary assistance in "a most confidential manner."[36] Churchill believed that if Estes' "business connections" panned out, "he could obtain useful information for us from Soviet Russia."[37] MID also jumped to Estes' defense when the State Department received a report that he had gone to Russia in the interest of "certain radical groups."[38] In response, Lt. Col. John Dunn of MID's Negative Division noted that his office was unaware that Estes represented radical elements and that the misconception probably arose from his personal connection to John Reed.

Estes sailed for Norway on 16 January 1920. Accompanying him was a motion-picture cameraman, John M. Flick. They reached Stockholm in February and were received by local Soviet representatives Fredrik Strom and Wilhelm Hellberg. The travelers also teamed up with a Russian-born Swedish businessman, Carl Valdemar Ruckman, an associate of the ubiquitous Olof Aschberg.[39] The Americans next hopped over to Copenhagen to see Moscow's man there, Maxim Litvinov. Estes recalled that they discussed the "possibility of selling American-manufactured goods in Russia."[40] However, Litvinov "tried to involve them in politics" which led to their leaving Copenhagen without securing entrée to the Red domain.[41]

Meanwhile, John Reed found himself under arrest in Finland and facing possible execution. Leaving Moscow, he had slipped across the Finnish border and stowed away on an outbound ship. On 13 March, customs inspectors discovered him in the vessel's coal bunker. Reed carried a cache of diamonds, various currencies and false identification.[42] Two items are especially interesting. The first was a 27 October 1919 letter of recommendation issued to Samuel Arnold, Jr. by the Committee on Public Information office in London. This declared that Arnold was going to the Baltic States "on the business of the Committee."[43] Oddly, the CPI had officially ceased to exist by that date. More interesting was a letter from Trotsky to Reed dated January 1919. In this, Trotsky promised that he would make immediate inqui-

Reed

---

36. MID, #237/23, Memo to Col. Coxe, July 1920.

37. *Ibid.*

38. MID, #10058-714, Confidential Letter 534, 8 Sept. 1920.

39. HIA, ARA, Estes to Suter, 26 April 1921.

40. Estes, 410.

41. MID, #10058-714, Confidential Letter.

42. Details of Reed's arrest and interrogation can be found in BI, #182787, including a translation of the 24 April 1920 Finnish Police report.

43. *Ibid.*

ries "regarding military films and, if possible, these films will be given to the American correspondent."[44] Did this relate to Estes' current mission? What was Reed's connection to Trotsky?

Estes next appeared in Helsinki where he "had something to do in procuring [Reed's] release...."[45] The Finns merely fined Reed for smuggling and deported him to Estonia on 5 June. He crossed back into Russia two days later. The initial plan was that Estes and Flick would tag along with him to Moscow. After they completed their "business," Reed would return with them to America. Estes even secured Reed "a false passport out of Estonia" for the return trip.[46]

Things didn't go as they planned. The Soviet passport officer in Tallinn was Adolph Guy, who had once worked at *Novy Mir*.[47] He probably recognized Estes. Denied a visa, he and Flick waited in Estonia for two months. While there, Estes reported, "I secured authentic information to the effect that John Reed's life was in danger."[48] "By use of those devious ways which, under the circumstances, people communicate," he added, Estes established communication with Reed in Moscow. Reed suspected that some of his Soviet comrades had betrayed him in Finland with the express aim of getting him killed. Estes warned him that "he would never be allowed to leave [Russia] again, alive."[49] Not without help, anyway. Reed was "eager to seek information from me and assistance in getting back home."

It was only by going directly to Foreign Commissar Chicherin, Estes claimed, that Reed finally got him a visa.[50] He and Flick crossed the frontier on 2 August and took a train to Petrograd. After an exhausting train ride, the two Americans finally reached Moscow on the 6th. By 7:00 that evening, both were under arrest.

Estes would spend the next year in cells and prison hospitals. There, he encountered another American prisoner and a former functionary of the Soviet "Foreign Office," Nathan Chabrow, who offered a clue as to how he had been betrayed.[51] It seemed "a certain Bobroff, head of the Bobroff Manufacturing Co.," had sent reports to Moscow about Americans planning to visit and had "communicated to the Bolsheviks information which ... had reference to Estes."[52]

---

44. BI, #182787, Trotsky to Reed, 21 Jan. 1919, from Finnish Intelligence Police.

45. Estes, 410.

46. Estes, 411, and BI, #182787, Young to Dept. of State, 9 June 1920.

47. *Ibid.* Estes implies that Guy went by another name in New York but does not identify it. He says Guy was the man "who took Trotsky's place" at *Novy Mir.*

48. Estes, 410.

49. Estes, 411.

50. *Ibid.*

51. MID, #2070-2119, Estes' statement, 14, and Kilpatrick, 12. Kilpatrick believed that Chabrow (or Chadbro) worked for the "Foreign Office of the Vecheka." See also Mahoney, *American Prisoners*, 231-232.

52. *Ibid.*, Estes, 14.

Bobroff, of course, is one of our American Bolsheviki. Another American businessman (and Socialist) in Russia, Jacob Rubin, made an identical accusation against him.[53] Most recently, Bobroff had been associated with Martens' Bureau and very close to Kenneth Durant.[54] An intercepted August 1920 letter from Bobroff to Durant showed the former involved in clandestine financial transactions between Russia and New York.[55] Bobroff also arranged for Americans seeking to visit Moscow. One of his issues was that Estes had not gone through him. Rubin claimed Bobroff's brother worked in the "Secret Service Department under [Santeri] Nuorteva" who then headed up the Anglo-American section of the Commissariat of Foreign Affairs.[56] For his faithful service, Bobroff had received his own minor concession under the NEP.

Estes and Flick were among the American prisoners set free through Crane's intercession in August 1921. After debriefing in Riga, Estes returned to the States via London. There, on 6 September, he gave a deposition to Hoover's American Relief Administration regarding conditions in Russia. In this, he studiously avoided any mention of Reed, which Mahoney interprets as evidence that Estes "as a case officer was protecting Reed, his agent..." even if he was dead.[57]

And dead he was. Reed, after all, had helped infiltrate Estes, an American intelligence agent, into Russia. In September, his suspicious Soviet hosts shuttled Reed off to a conference in far-off Baku where, as the official story goes, he contracted typhus. Returning to Moscow, he died on 6 October. As Estes had warned, he never left Russia alive.

Back in the U.S.A., Estes became a regular on the anti-Bolshevik speaking circuit. Three months after his homecoming, he was quoted in a news article talking about Soviet gold hoarded on Wall Street.[58] What did he know about that? The following year he published his recollections as *Prison and Hospital Life in Soviet Russia*. In 1923, however, the 46-year-old Estes simply vanished.

THE OCTOPUS

Sidney Reilly had an interesting nickname for international capitalism: the "Occult Octopus."[59] Since we last looked in on him, he had visibly kept himself occupied with business ventures that included not only Spears and Wiseman but also Abram Zhivotovsky. By 1921, the latter had resettled in Paris where he formed the *Societe Nouvelle d'Etudes pour l'Industrie en Russie* ("New Society for the Study of Industry in Russia"), a front that bought up stock in Russian companies and resold it to Mos-

53. BI, #202-600-65. Statement of Jacob. H. Rubin, 10-11.
54. USDS, #316-119-458/64, Bobroff to Durant, 3 Aug. 1920.
55. *Ibid.*
56. BI, #202-600/65, Rubin, 11.
57. Mahoney, *American Prisoners*, 351, n. 51.
58. MID, #9961-2301, IO 2nd Corps Area, 9 Nov. 1921. Reference only; the file has disappeared.
59. Gill Bennett, *Churchill's Man of Mystery: Desmond Morton and the World of Intelligence* (2007), 61.

cow.[60] In the early part of 1923, just before his return to New York, Reilly's correspondence indicated renewed contact with Uncle Abram.[61]

Reilly's other job was *consigliere*, cheerleader and babysitter to anti-Bolshevik die-hard, Boris Savinkov, himself a former anti-Tsarist terrorist. More recently, Savinkov had been an utterly disloyal deputy to Kerensky. Thereafter, he formed his own political organization, the Union for the Defense of the Motherland and Freedom, and aligned himself with the Poles, the Brits, Mussolini, or anyone else who would aid him in his struggle against the Leninites. Reilly was still secretly serving Moscow and made sure that none of Savinkov's schemes succeeded. Broke and desperate, Savinkov fell completely under Reilly's spell. As one British intelligence report put it, "[Reilly] almost is Boris Savinkov."[62] In the fall of 1921, Reilly expressly violated the wishes of the Foreign Office by finagling a visa for Savinkov to visit London.[63] There he set up  a meeting between Savinkov and Krasin, the first step in Savinkov's eventual negotiated surrender to the Bolsheviks. This "Savinkov Affair" precipitated a critical re-examination of Reilly's connection to the SIS. Doubts had always existed, and Reilly's cozy relationship with Krasin, then the Soviet trade representative in Britain, was impossible to ignore.

In January 1922, Reilly embarked on another trip to Central Europe. On 1 February, SIS wired its station chiefs in Vienna and Budapest to "be careful not to tell him anything of real importance" but also to avoid doing anything that would make him think "that he is receiving different treatment to that to which he has become accustomed."[64] The wire reassured the stations that Reilly was not anti-British and appeared to be "genuinely working against the Bolsheviks." Of course, no such reassurance would have been necessary were there not suspicions to the contrary.

The problem was that Reilly "knows far too much about our organization," and the unstated worry was that if antagonized he might take what he knew to the other side.[65] And that "other side" was Moscow. What his SIS colleagues could not bring themselves to admit, or were too afraid to say aloud, was that he had been doing precisely that for years.

60. Roger Mennevee, *Documents Diplomatiques*, fragment, c. 1923, and Semenov, 60-63.

61. GARF, Fond #5831, opis 1, delo 170, Reilly-Savinkov letters of 20 Feb. and 8 March 1923.

62. SIS, CX2616, Morton to Maw, 31 Jan. 1922.

63. TNA, FO 371/6931, #13792, 16 Dec. 1921.

64. SIS, CX2616, Maw to MVO, 1 Feb. 1922.

65. *Ibid.*

Another SIS memo admitted that "we do not know altogether what to make of him." Or, for that matter, who the hell he really was.[66] A rush began to collect information and refresh memories. On 13 February, a report from the SIS station in New York rehashed Reilly's dubious wartime activities in America, though it admitted there was no hard proof of anything.[67] The very next day, SIS's assistant director of special intelligence, Stewart Menzies, sent for Reilly's agency file. Strangely, it couldn't be located and efforts to dig it up proved fruitless.[68] Menzies confessed that he had "always distrusted" Reilly as an "extremely clever but absolutely unscrupulous person."[69] More ominously, Menzies speculated that there might be "other influences at work." As doubts about Reilly grew, they inevitably drew attention to those who had supported and abetted him – William Wiseman for instance.

Menzies

On 13 May 1923, Norman Thwaites, Reilly and Wiseman's past and present collaborator, wrote to Under-Secretary of State Leland Harrison to inform him of Reilly's upcoming trip to the States. Thwaites urged Harrison to consult with Reilly on "Russian affairs."[70] On 1 August, Reilly landed in Boston and headed straight for the familiar territory of lower Manhattan. Ensconced in the Gotham Hotel, he immediately established contact with Paul Dukes and Wiseman. SIS officer Humphrey Plowden warned the New York station of Reilly's arrival and cautioned them that he "knows a certain amount about our organization" and to keep a polite distance.[71] Nevertheless, SIS was very keen to know what he was up to. Reilly's only obvious business was half-heartedly pursuing his suit against Baldwin Locomotive over the Eddystone contract. In Late August, Reilly wrote Harrison at State, urgently requesting a meeting. Harrison ignored him.

Harris

As it happened, Reilly's 1923 return to New York coincided with the appearance of a fresh Soviet emissary, Isaiah Khurgin, who would set up a new commercial agency, the American Trading Organization, or Amtorg. Khurgin had most recently served in Berlin as an assistant to Moscow's foreign trade troubleshooter, Leonid Krasin. In the German capital, Khurgin contacted Clifford M. Carver, the local representative of Wall Street investment bankers W. A. Harriman & Co. Chasing Russian concessions, Averell Harriman, son of railroad magnate E. H. Harriman, snapped up a

---

66. *Ibid.*, Morton to Maw, 31 Jan. 1922.
67. *Ibid.*, Report on Reilly, 13 Feb. 1922.
68. TNA, KV2/827, Menzies to MI5, 2 Feb. 1922.
69. *Ibid.*
70. Library of Congress, Leland Harrison Papers, Container 9, Thwaites to Harrison, 13 July 1923.
71. SIS, CX2616, Plowden to YN0, 24 July 1923.

big share of the German-Soviet Derutra shipping company.[72] With Carver and Harriman's help, Khurgin secured a U.S. visa and on 1 June 1923 he arrived with the nominal mission of heading Derutra's American office. Khurgin had no experience in business and absolutely no acquaintance with America. Reilly did, and he would have been the ideal person to provide the newcomer with advice and contacts.

Another Soviet traveler who showed up in New York was Viktor Nogin. An old associate of Lenin, Nogin was another collaborator of Krasin. His designated mission in America was representing the All-Russian Textile Syndicate and securing contracts for American cotton. However, Nogin also happened to be head of the Communist Party's Central Auditing Commission, a body that oversaw the Party's accounts and the treasury. Nogin's secret job was arranging New York financing for Khurgin's operation. With the assistance of the ever Bolshevik-loving Raymond Robins, Nogin visited Washington and helped new President Calvin Coolidge send a cable of greetings to Moscow.[73] Another familiar

Nogin

face returning to the States at the time was Reilly crony Antony Jechalski. He was busy making contacts in the oil industry, notably Sinclair, and voiced "marked approval of [the] Soviet Government."[74]

Reilly headed back to Europe at the end of December but reappeared again in New York on 17 May 1924. This was exactly *one day* before Khurgin formally announced the creation of Amtorg. Over the next two months, Reilly huddled with Dukes and Wiseman pursuing "business" of mysterious nature. Then he hopped back across the pond in July to shepherd burned-out Savinkov back to Moscow.[75]

On 21 October 1924, Reilly was again in New York, this time just *one day prior* to Khurgin's return to Moscow. Khurgin would be gone for seven months, which raises the question of who ran Amtorg in his absence. That November, a New York judge dismissed Reilly's suit against Baldwin, a setback that supposedly left him destitute. Nevertheless, barely a month later, Reilly somehow got his hands on $100,000 (courtesy of Amtorg?) to bankroll a new import-export company, Trading Ventures, Inc. This he initially established at 115 Broadway and later moved to the Cunard Building at 25 Broadway. An SIS snoop described the office as "well-furnished" and staffed by persons who seemed to all be of German or Jewish origin, the

72. Harriman formed his investment bank in 1922. In 1931, it became Brown Brothers, Harriman. I note for the record that Averell Harriman was a Yale man and Skull & Bones member.

73. Neil Salzmann, *Reform and Revolution: The Life and Times of Raymond Robins*, 313.

74. MID, #9140-1496/363, 21 and 25 Nov. 1924.

75. Spence, *Trust No One*, 397-398.

atmosphere being distinctly "foreign."[76] Reilly's partners in this enterprise were Paul Herzog, a prominent Wall Street attorney, and Jacob A. Maller, an ex-pat Russian businessman and, to no surprise, an associate of Abram Zhivotovsky. Maller had arrived in New York back in June 1924 and worked with another export outfit, the Russian-American Commercial Agency, which had been shipping American machinery to Russia since 1919.[77]

In January 1925, Reilly wrote to ex-partner Edward Spears that "I am in excellent connection with Kuhn, Loeb & Co., the Metropolitan Trust Co., the National City Bank, Blair & Co., and several other minor banks."[78] His connection to Kuhn Loeb surely ran through Wiseman. In December 1924, precisely the time Reilly founded Trading Ventures, State Department Special Agent Sharp determined that Wiseman not only was *au courant* with Reilly's whereabouts, but also actively involved with him in various foreign business deals.[79]

The nature of one of these deals is revealed in Reilly's MI5 file. In 1924, Reilly and Sir William were mixed up in a scheme to supply Russia with 2,000,000 rifles.[80] That, of course, meant rifles for Trotsky's Red Army. Also involved were Reilly's wartime partner Charles Flint and two other Wall Street sharpers, Franklin Helm and James Slevin. Helm had links to Standard Oil and the New York investment bank of Harvey Fisk & Sons.[81] The roots of the deal went back to the fall of 1921 when Krasin, at Trotsky's urging, sought to secretly purchase arms and munitions in the U.S. His initial effort foundered on the refusal of the State Department to issue him a visa. However, in November 1921 another Reilly crony, Henry C. Manger, incorporated the China & Japan Trading Co. which bought and shipped large quantities of surplus military supplies to Manchuria.[82] Some of this bounty went to the hands of cooperative Chinese warlords, but the rest found its way to Siberia.

It was also in January 1925 that Reilly began a correspondence with two of his erstwhile British intelligence colleagues in the Baltic States, George Hill and Ernest Boyce. The story is far too complicated to detail here, but suffice to say that Boyce suddenly urged Reilly to come to Finland, and ultimately Russia, as soon as he could. What truly united Reilly, Hill and Boyce was common allegiance to Soviet intelligence.[83] Hill and

76. SIS, CX2616, YN #1215, 24 July 1925.

77. "Millions in American Machinery for Siberia," *The Walnut Valley Times* [KS] (23 May 1919), 8.

78. HIA, Lockhart Collection, Box 6, Reilly to Spears, 23 Jan. 1925.

79. USDS, CSA 215, 13 Dec. 1924, 2-3, 15.

80. TNA, KV2/502, SZ/835, Boyleston Beale, 15 Sept. 1927.

81. "New Light Shed on Helm's Career," *New York Times* (28 April 1921), 3.

82. Certificate of Incorporation of the China & Japan Trading Company, Ltd., 28. Nov. 1921, and USDS, CSA 215, *Ibid*. 1.

83. GARF, Fond #23-751 of the former Tsentral'nyi Gosudarstvennyi Istorichesky Arkhiv-Moskva, Comrade V. A. Styrne's "Explanatory Note to the File on Prisoner #73," 10 Nov. 1925. Styrne explicitly identifies Hill as a *sotrudnik* ("collaborator") of the OGPU and Boyce as an "OGPU

Reilly has been serving the Red cause since at least 1918, while Boyce, presumably, was a more recent recruit. Boyce and Reilly's letters contain cryptic references to "the recent fight for share control" among the Moscow "Board of Directors" and the position of "minority interests" who must "make up their minds to sacrifice a good portion of their original ideas ... in a manner which will be acceptable both to the internal and international markets."[84]

To understand what was going on, we need to go back to 1922 when Lenin began to suffer a series of debilitating strokes. The same year saw the elevation of Joseph Stalin to the powerful post of Communist Party Secretary. Lenin's illness, and most importantly his death in early 1924, sparked a battle for succession ("fight for share control") in the Bolshevik Politburo ("Board of Directors"), the two prime contenders being Stalin and Trotsky. By early 1925, Trotsky appeared to be losing the contest. On 15 January, under pressure, he stepped down as Peoples' Commissar for War. Hill's appeal to Reilly followed a little over a week later. The "minority interests" who Reilly was asked to help, were Trotsky and his faction. In response, he told Boyce that he was in contact with "the largest automobile manufacturer," obviously, Ford, and the latter would be willing to provide cash to fund the "minority's" campaign provided they made it worth his while.[85] They would need to compromise those "original ideas" (communist principles) to get capitalist help. Reilly and Zhivotovsky had never truly worked for Lenin and the Bolsheviks; they had always worked for Trotsky. Whether it realized it or not, Wall Street was now embroiled in a power struggle going on in Moscow. If you aren't satisfied with the revolution you made, make another – and then another.

THE DROWNED COMMISSAR

In May 1925, Trotsky took up a new post, head of the Main Concessions Committee. To hear him tell it, it was pure bureaucratic drudge work. That wasn't the whole truth. Overseeing concessions wasn't the same as overseeing the Red Army, but it did afford Trotsky the opportunity to meet and communicate with foreign capitalist agents. In his contest with Stalin, that could prove a critical advantage. Comrade Trotsky appreciated the value of sound financial backing in any revolutionary enterprise.

Later that same month, Amtorg's long-absent chief, Isaiah Khurgin, returned to New York. Since the demise of the Soviet Bureau, Russian-American commerce had been conducted through a variety of fronts. Already mentioned was the Products Exchange Corporation, or Prodex-

agent."
84. HIA, Lockhart, *Ibid.* Boyce to Reilly, 26 Jan. 1925 and Reilly reply. Both are reproduced in *The Adventures of Sidney Reilly* (1986), 172-177.
85. *Ibid.*

co. Another was the Peoples' Industrial Trading Corporation. Incorporated in 1920 and fronted by Chicago broker and businessman Emanuel F. Rosenbaum, the real powers behind the PITC were a Julius Hammer associate, Henry Kuntz and another of Olof Aschberg, Eric Lidval.[86] By 1923 both outfits were supplanted by the Allied American Corporation, or Alamerico, wholly run by Julius Hammer and his sons Harry, Armand and Victor. The elder Hammer boasted personal acquaintance with both Lenin and Trotsky and was a dedicated Communist. However, the Hammers' practical ability to run these enterprises left much to be desired.[87]

On 9 July 1923, The New York Times carried a piece by its man in Moscow, Walter Duranty, announcing a deal between the Soviet Government and Hammer's Allied American.[88] Hammer received a one-year contract to conduct import and export business "without interference of control on the part of Soviet organizations." Hammer claimed exclusive contacts with more than thirty American firms, the most important being Ford; the same Ford with whom Reilly claimed connection.

The next day, Khurgin fired off a letter to the editor "correcting" Duranty's article.[89] The arrangement with Hammer, he stressed, was a "temporary commercial agreement," and the Commissariat of Foreign Trade did not relinquish oversight of Allied American's transactions. Khurgin was correct and his letter served notice to any interested parties that the Soviet Government had not handed over its American trade to the Hammers.

Khurgin's initial task in New York was to finalize a secret pact struck in Germany with the E. H. Gary Steel Corporation.[90] The head of that concern, Elbert H. Gary, also happened to be president and chairman of the board of U.S. Steel. The preliminary agreement committed Gary and the Soviets to each put up $5 million, and the result would be a steady supply of finished rails, girders and specialty alloys to Russia. There was even talk of Krasin coming to America to sign the pact. Krasin, however, was unable to sell the agreement to the Politburo, which suddenly insisted on a renegotiation of the terms. The Yanks refused and the deal collapsed, leaving "a very bad impression on the U.S. end."[91]

Gary

---

86. State of New York, Court of Appeals, "Henry Kuntz against the People's Industrial Trading Corporation," 24 March 1922.
87. Epstein, 120-121.
88. "Soviet Concession to American Firm." New York Times (9 July 1923), 3.
89. "Trade Agreement with Soviet." New York Times (18 July, 1925), 14.
90. TNA, KV2/574, V.S.O. Report, 17 Nov. 1933.
91. Ibid.

In the fall of 1923, Krasin contacted another American businessman, Wallace Banta Phillips, who ran a rubber and chemical outfit, Pyrene Corporation, in London. As chance (?) would have it, Phillips was a good friend of William Wiseman. One of Banta's employees, and his point man with Krasin, was Wiseman's old #2 and Reilly's pal Norman Thwaites. Phillips, Krasin was assured, had "considerable influence in commercial and banking circles" in the States.[92] There was, as one might suspect, another side to Phillips. He operated an "industrial spy service" that had agents around the world and he served as an American intelligence officer in both world wars.[93] Once again, whenever American business ventured into Russia, American intelligence was never far behind.

Phillips

Speaking of spies, Khurgin did not come to America just as Krasin's man, but also as a scout for the Comintern and Soviet intelligence. Moscow never ceased reminding him that Amtorg's duties included acquiring "secret military and political intelligence."[94] This inevitably created a conflict between his responsibilities as a trade representative and the needs of the "security organs." The latter wanted their personnel posted to Amtorg and "believed that Khurgin made too little effort" to assist this.[95] Intelligence historian G. J. A. O'Toole wonders if Khurgin "may have lost sight of priorities in such matters."[96]

On 23 May 1924, Khurgin drew up the certificate that formally created the Amtorg Trading Corporation out of Prodexco and another front, Arcos-America.[97] Khurgin chaired the board of directors and Paul Ziev, former Soviet trade representative in Latvia, was president. Other officers included the familiar John Ohsol and Julius Fox, both ex-Prodexco execs.[98] To sweeten the deal, and in true Wall Street fashion, the new directors received big blocks of Amtorg stock and fat annual salaries of $12,000.[99]

The Hammers found themselves entirely cut out. The Commissariat of Foreign Trade informed Julius that Allied American's contract would be terminated and that its American business would be taken over by Amtorg.[100] Amtorg even moved into Allied American's offices at 165 Broad-

---

92. TNA, KV2/574, Intercepted letter from Basil Thomson to Krasin, 25 Oct. 1923.

93. Joseph E. Persico, *Roosevelt's Secret War: FDR and World War II Espionage* (2002), 55.

94. "V avangarde kovarno-denezhnykh otnoshenii," *Den'gi* (13 Oct. 2008). http://www.kommersant.ru/doc/1038253.

95. *Ibid.*

96. G. J. A. O'Toole. *Honorable Treachery: A History of U. S. Intelligence, Espionage and Covert Action from the American Revolution to the CIA.* New York: Atlantic Monthly Press (1991), 323.

97. "Amtorg Trading Corporation vs. New York Indemnity Company," *Supreme Court of New York County, Appellate Division, First Department* (1928), 672-677.

98. "Russia-U.S. Trade to Grow under New Co.", *Daily Worker* (27 June 1924), 3.

99. Frank Weller, "Soviet Russia's Hopes of Recognition are Vision of United States Trade." *Las Vegas Daily Optic* (26 Oct. 1933), 5.

100. Epstein, 95

way, absorbing its "lease, the bank lines of credit, the employees and the contracts."[101] Khurgin took it upon himself to inform Ford that his organization would be handling all their Russian business from now on.

Julius Hammer took his case to Trotsky. He argued that he had forged an invaluable personal relationship with the Flivver King and pleaded with Trotsky to overrule the Commissariat of Foreign Trade and leave the Ford deal in his hands. Trotsky basically agreed, and with this assurance, Hammer sped back to New York where he landed on August 5th, 1925. On the 21st Trotsky sent a confidential memo to Khurgin's superior, Deputy Commissar of Foreign Trade Moise Frumkin, in which he stressed that as an "American concessionaire-capitalist," and one familiar with Ford, Hammer was a better "scout and business propagandist" in America than a Soviet *apparatchik* like Khurgin. The latter, Trotsky advised, should embrace Hammer and use him.

Armand Hammer biographer *Edward Jay Epstein* finds it frankly suspicious that just days after Trotsky's memo, Khurgin was dead. However, there is nothing in the memo to suggest Khurgin should be replaced or eliminated; all Trotsky demanded was that the pair work together. Maybe Hammer interpreted it differently. If anyone would have wished Khurgin dead, it was him.

Meanwhile, Sidney Reilly repeatedly delayed his departure from New York. Back in January, he told Spears he would return to Europe around the "end of spring." That would have been right around the time Khurgin came back to New York. Despite constant pleading from Boyce, Reilly hung on at 25 Broadway. What was he waiting for? Or who? Maybe Efraim Sklyansky.

Efriam Markovich Sklyansky first came to Trotsky's attention in 1917 when he helped organize the toppling of the Provisional Government. From 1918 through 1924, Sklyansky was Trotsky's deputy people's commissar for military and naval affairs, vice chairman of the Revolutionary Military Council and trusted comrade.[102] Trotsky lauded him as "one of the outstanding and most meritorious organizers of the Red Army."[103] Historian Yury Fel'shtinski calls Sklyansky the "factual head and coordinator of the Red Army's campaign during the civil war."[104]

Sklyansky

Sklyansky's fall from grace began in 1924 and, as sure as night follows day, was a preface to Trotsky's own. In March of that year, Stalin and his Politburo allies pushed Sklyansky out of the military commissariat. Stalin

101. *Ibid.*, 97.
102. V. N. Ipatieff, *My Life as a Chemist*. Stanford, CA: Stanford Univ. Press (1946), 264.
103. Trotsky, "The 'Tanaka Memorial'," *Fourth International*, Vol. 2 No. 5 (June 1941), 131-135.
104. YuryFel'shtinski. *Lenin and His Comrades: The Bolsheviks Take Over Russia, 1917-1924*, New York: Enigma Books (2013), 259.

next sidelined him to the Moscow textile trust, *Mossukno*. It was suppos-edly Stalin who in May 1925 proposed sending Sklyansky to America to assume control of Amtorg.[105] For Stalin, New York seemed a convenient "place of exile" for bothersome oppositionists."[106]

There's again reason to suspect the above was not the whole story. Sklyansky's reassignment oh-so conveniently meshed with Trotsky's move to the Main Concession Committee, and the two remained as thick as thieves. Trotsky recalled that shortly before his departure, Sklyansky called to "ask advice."[107] By Trotsky's recollection, Sklyansky was "pleased" and even excited to be going abroad.[108] Is that because it was a move they had carefully plotted together?

Writer Yury Zverev claims Trotsky possessed "links with influential circles in the U.S.A." and gave Sklyansky the secret task of holding talks with them.[109] If so, was that connected to Reilly? Another source contends that once in America Sklyansky planned to connive with "anti-Stalinist" Khurgin with the aim of establishing a Trotskyite base of operations be-yond Stalin's control and just blocks from Wall Street.[110]

On 11 August Sklyansky received a U.S. visa in Berlin and sailed from Hamburg three days later. On the 24th, he landed in New York. Sidney Reilly was still in town, but barely 48 hours later, he was on a ship headed back across the Atlantic. Had Reilly been waiting for Sklyansky to arrive? Was his assignment now to arrange the Moscow end of the secret organi-zation Sklyansky planned to set up in New York? If it worked, would Wall Street start filling Trotsky's war chest?

Besides Sklyansky, there were other Soviet travelers gathering in New York. In late June, the Communist *Daily Worker* claimed that Patmagian, Krasin's "private secretary," was on his way to the U.S. on a "secret mis-sion."[111] On 25 July, Valerian Obolensky (Ossinsky) arrived. Obolensky was connected to the Soviet State Planning Office, a former candidate member of the Party Central Committee and a member of the Comint-ern's executive. He was also a member of Trotsky's Left Opposition and intensely interested in the American automotive industry, especially Ford. In New York, Obolensky made straight for Amtorg. On 24 August, the same day as Sklyansky, Boris Berlatsky and Abram Fineberg, both Moscow "bankers," landed on Broadway.[112] They, too, headed to Amtorg.

105. Bazhanov, 65.

106. Bazhanov, 65.

107. Trotsky, *My Life*, 403.

108. Trotsky, *Pravda, Ibid.*

109. Yury Zverev, "Glavnyi sekret 'Tovarishcha Konstantina.'" *Blistatel'nyi DISK*, 26-28. http://ta-leon.thewebproduction.com/taleonclub_en/ProjectImages/2396/18-29.pdf.

110. "V avangarde...."

111. *Daily Worker* (29 June 1925), 2.

112. In 1931, Berlatsky was one of the defendants in the "Menshevik Trial." See, "Jews in New Communist Purge in Russia," *Jewish Telegraph Agency* (28 Feb. 1931).

Khurgin behaved as if nothing unusual was going on. On 22nd August, he gave a widely-published interview which painted a glowing picture of U.S.-Soviet trade with the prediction of ever-expanding bounty for all.[113] He crowed that Soviet purchases in the U.S. had exceeded $30 million in the past year and predicted that it would grow five-fold in the event of American recognition.[114] Adding to this rosy picture, back in Moscow, an agreement had just been reached between Khurgin's friend Averell Harriman and Trotsky's Concessions Committee for the biggest American concession to date, a twenty-year lease on the rich Chiaturi manganese mines in Soviet Georgia.[115]

New York sightseeing was not on Sklyansky's agenda. He, Khurgin and a few other comrades almost immediately left Manhattan for the bucolic splendor and privacy of the Adirondacks. On the evening of 25 August, they boarded an overnight train and awoke early the next morning 350 miles north at the tiny hamlet of Sabattis. From there it was a bumpy twenty-mile car ride to the Sagamore Hotel on Long Lake, the most isolated spot in the whole Empire State.

Of the many resort homes, called "camps," around Long Lake, two belonged to the Durant brothers, Douglas and Kenneth.[116] By this time, "Blue-blood Bolshevik" Kenneth was American chief of the Soviet news service Rosta (later TASS). He knew Khurgin well and may have been the one to suggest Long Lake. Kenneth Durant's "camp" was on adjoining Forked Lake, just a short distance from the Sagamore Hotel. However, supposedly to evade mounting scrutiny from U.S. authorities, Kenneth sailed for England in late July 1925 and would not return until November. He visited Moscow in the interim. It was interesting timing. His deserted camp would have been just the spot for a very private meeting.

Brother Douglas had his home right on Long Lake, little more than a mile from the Sagamore. Douglas Durant was to all appearances a conservative capitalist. But appearances can be deceiving. In 1919, the Bureau of Investigation opened a file on Douglas, even before they took interest in his brother. While job-hunting in New York one day, Douglas popped in on Kenneth at the Soviet Bureau. Afterwards, claimed Douglas, he suspected that he was being followed, and assuming it must be government agents, he went to the Bureau to straighten things out. Despite assurances that he in no way shared his brother's opinions, Agent Charles Scully found Durant's behavior suspicious. Scully believed Douglas had visited

---

113. "American Trade with Soviet Russia," *Trenton Evening News* (23 Aug. 1925), 12.

114. George E. Lyndon, "Soviet Spending Millions in U. S. for Machinery," *Brooklyn Daily Eagle* (23 Aug. 1925), A-15.

115. The deal was concluded on 25 June 1925 by Harriman's agent J. Speed Elliot. Stephen D. Fitch, "The Harriman Manganese Concession in the Soviet Union: Lessons for Today." *Berkeley Journal of International Law*, Vol. 9, #1 (1991), 209-211.

116. BI, File #388529, "Kenneth Durant: Agent of Lenine [sic] and Trotzky [sic]." 6 Oct. 1920.

the BI office in order "to ascertain whether or not the Government was interested in watching the movements of Martens at this time."[117] Investigation also revealed that Douglas Durant had given them a phony address.

The Sagamore management later explained that Khurgin, Sklyansky and the other Russians had "made the trip here to enjoy a few days rest."[118] However, Soviet *Izvestiya* claimed that the Amtorg party was there to rendezvous with "senior officials of Soviet institutions in the United States."[119] Who were they? The Sagamore said *five* Russians arrived early on the 26th.[120] However, Soviet sources mention *six* men in the party.[121] The Hotel steadfastly refused to divulge anything more.[122] The Soviet press did drop the name of a third member of the group, Boris Kraevsky, Amtorg's deputy chairman.[123] Where were all the other "senior officials of Soviet institutions" staying? What were they there to discuss, and how many of them were Trotsky partisans? Was Long Lake to be the venue for a secret Trotskyist meeting?

Another possibility is that the gathering was a cover for a meeting with American business interests; Ford, perhaps? But business matters could be more easily and sensibly attended to in New York, nor was there any special need for secrecy. What was going on at Long Lake was not ordinary. Of course, businessmen weren't the only "influential circles."

What about the U.S. Government? Under Secretary of State Charles Evans Hughes (1921-25), American official policy towards Soviet Russia had been one of strict non-recognition. Part of Khurgin's (and Sklyansky's) job was to change that. In March 1925, Frank B. Kellogg took the helm at State. While he ultimately stuck with non-recognition, Kellogg was more open to the possibility. At the same time, the influential pro-recognition Senator William E. Borah had taken the chairmanship of the key Senate Foreign Relations Committee. The chances of recognition had never looked better. It's also interesting that Frank Kellogg spent his boyhood in Long Lake, had relatives there, and was a regular visitor during the 20s. That small world again.

Hughes

Kellogg

117. BI, #370947, "Douglas Durant: Anarchistic Activities." 23 July 1919 and report of S. Busha 25 Aug. 1919.

118. "Two Representatives of Soviet Govt. Lose Lives in Long Lake," *Glens Falls Post-Star* (28 Aug. 1925), 1.

119. "Podrobnosti tragicheskoi gibeli t.t.Sklyanskogo i Khurgina." *Izvestiya* (29 Aug. 1925).

120. *Glens Falls Post Star, Ibid.*

121. E.g., Sergei Nekhamkin, "Smert' s politikoi i bez: Ekho pokhoronnykh orkestrov 1925 goda," *Argumenty nedeli* (15 Sept. 2010). http://argumenti.ru/print/history/n2,55/76567.

122. *Glen Falls Post-Star, Ibid.*

123. *Izvestiya, Ibid.*

One slightly "off" visitor at the Lake that summer was Hamlet Cecil Sharp, who was staying at a small family-owned resort called the Endion. It mostly catered to couples and families. Sharp was a single, thirty-year old engineer from New York City. He also was a lieutenant in the Marine Corps Reserve. Later, he served in Naval Intelligence.[124] Did Kellogg or someone else in Washington tap him as a cut-out, a deniable intermediary, to meet with Khurgin and Sklyansky? Or, was he there to keep an eye on them?

On the afternoon of 27 August, Khurgin, Sklyansky and the rest of the gang decided to go boating. This made perfect sense, except that the day was unseasonably cool and breezy, with a strong wind whipping up the lake. It was definitely not canoeing weather. Nevertheless, Khurgin and Sklyansky piled into one canoe, Kraevsky into another and the rest grabbed a rowboat. They headed south, into the wind, sticking close to shore. After traveling a short distance, *Khurgin suddenly veered into open water* where wind and waves now hit from the side. The others sensibly turned back to shore, but Khurgin and his hapless passenger pressed on.

After losing sight of the canoe and its occupants, Kraevsky and friends located a motor launch and went in search. Twenty minutes later they came across the scene of the accident, on the opposite side of the lake, where several local boats had already gathered. Khurgin and Sklyansky were dead; drowned less than 100 yards from shore. This was directly in front of the Endion resort and right next door to Douglas Durant's camp. What a coincidence.

A local, Talbot Bissell, who claimed to have witnessed the capsizing, recollected a very curious detail. During the recovery of the bodies a briefcase was retrieved from the lake. For reasons not explained, this ended up in his hands. When the "dead men's friends" from the Sagamore appeared, Bissell handed it to them. "He had no idea who these people were," recalled his son, "and that U. S. agents would have given their right arms to have that brief case."[125] If accurate, why would anyone go on a casual canoe trip, in bad weather no less, toting a brief case? The answer surely must be that it wasn't a casual trip; Khurgin and Sklyansky were on their way to see someone, and it was worth risking their lives to do it. What kind of deal had that kind of stakes?

On 31 August, New York City witnessed its "first Soviet funeral."[126] Some 500 mourners crowded into the Campbell Funeral Home at Broadway and 66th St. to bid farewell to comrades Khurgin and Sklyansky. In Moscow, Trotsky was "stunned by the news" and a large wreath bearing

---

124. NARA, U. S. Marine Corps Muster Rolls, 1893-1958 (T-977, roll #0521, 193).

125. Talbot Bissell, "7/31/03 response to Amy Godine's article." Long Lake Archives, 2011. Thanks to Abbie Venner for this document.

126. "First Soviet Funeral Devoid of Religion Conducted Here," *New York Post* (31 Aug. 1925), 1.

his inscription was on prominent display.[127] Nearby were other wreaths and bouquets from the many, many American entrepreneurs and financiers who had done business with Amtorg. On 20 September, at Moscow's Novodevichy Cemetery, the pair's cremated remains received a final send-off. Trotsky was among those in the long procession following an elaborate catafalque.[128] Leonid Krasin delivered a speech in honor of the dead.[129] Stalin did not attend.

The immediate, and persistent, suspicion in Moscow was that Stalin had engineered Khurgin's and Sklyansky's demise. It wasn't an irrational assumption. Nevertheless, the circumstances of their deaths point strongly to an accident. The real question isn't how they died but what brought them there in the first place. Any way you look at it, things couldn't have gone better for Stalin.

THE LAST OF REILLY

Little more than two months later, another death took place in Russia that may have been a delayed echo of events at Long Lake. On 22 September, Sidney Reilly finally reached Helsinki. Three nights later he crossed the Soviet border, which is about the last thing that can be said about him with any certainty. The standard version of his demise, in both Soviet and Western sources, is that he was lured back to Moscow through the machinations of the Trust, a supposed anti-Bolshevik conspiracy that was a clever ruse invented by the OGPU (the renamed Cheka) to ensnare its enemies. It's a tale that doesn't stand up to serious scrutiny. First, Reilly was fully aware that the Trust was an OGPU operation. If nothing else, Savinkov told him so in a prison letter dated 7 Oct. 1924.[130] Of course, Dzerzhinsky's men would never have permitted Savinkov to send that letter unless they knew that Reilly *already* knew. And he did, because he was part of the Trust.

The Trust's modus operandi was that it pretended to be an opposition movement to which émigrés and foreign interests could lend political and financial support. But what if someone used the operation as a cover to channel support and funds to a *real* opposition – the Trotskyist opposition? In a 1998 interview, veteran Sovietologist Nathalie Grant correctly identified SIS officer Boyce as working for the Reds.[131] More intriguing, she insisted that "Trotsky was mixed up in [the Trust]" and that "it was used by Stalin to get Trotsky." She also noted that Trotsky sent an "emis-

---

127. "Death Causes Soviet Upset," *Macon Telegraph* 30 Aug. 1925, 14.

128. "Sklyansky and Churgin, Communists Drowned in America, Buried in Non-Jewish Cemetery in Moscow," *The Canadian Jewish Chronicle* (9 Oct. 1925), 12.

129. *Pravda* (22 Sept. 1925).

130. Spence, *Renegade*, 334-336.

131. Andea Lynn interview of Nathalie Grant, Lovettsville, VA, 14 Nov. 1998.

sary" to Reilly in Finland the night he crossed the border. On the other hand, Grant maintained that Reilly did not make the crossing willingly, but was kidnapped. That was because she could not fathom how so experienced an operative could fall into so obvious a trap. What she missed was that Reilly wasn't walking into a trap, he was walking into the arms of people he believed to be his comrades. Some of them were, but somewhere along the line the secret of Reilly's mission had been blown. What was in that brief case fished out of Long Lake?

As the standard story goes, Reilly met with the "executive committee" of the Trust at a dacha (summer house) outside Moscow on the afternoon of the 27th. Later that day, OGPU agents, who had been posing as members of the Trust, arrested him, although some adamantly opposed this. The deciding factor was Stalin, who monitored the situation closely, demanding updates every half-hour.[132] Why would he have taken such keen interest in the arrest of a single British spy? A dangerous Trotskyist agent, of course, would have been another matter. The Soviets first put out a story that Reilly had been killed trying to re-cross the Finnish border a few nights later. His actual arrest was not acknowledged until 1927, and in 1940, a semi-official source declared that he had been executed the same year.[133] Only in the 1990s, did other files come available claiming that, after interrogation, the OGPU shot Reilly on 5 November 1925.[134] In any event, Sidney Reilly, whoever he was in truth, ceased to exist. He took many secrets with him into oblivion.

---

132. HIA, B. I. Nicolaevsky Collection, 300-1, "Rasstrel' angliiskogo ofitsera Sidnei Reilli." An English translation of the same article is attached to Reilly's SIS file.
133. Spence, *Trust No One*, 440-465.
134. Igor Prelin, "Zhizn' i smert' Sidneia Reilli," Moscow, (c. 1991).

EPILOGUE

THE END OF THE BEGINNING

As 1925 came to its close, there was no obvious slackening in the ardor for accord between Wall Street and the Reds. As the late Khurgin predicted, everything seemed poised to bound onward and upwards. On 10 December, the familiar Bankers Club at 120 Broadway was the site of yet another meeting between American financiers and Soviet representatives. A 13 December *Associated Press* story originating in Moscow called the conclave "secret" and proclaimed it the "first outspoken recognition by American finance and industry of the importance of Russian trade and the stability of the Soviet Government."[1] The hosts of the meeting were Reeve Schley, Vice President of Chase National Bank, who had just returned from Moscow in September, Charles Sabin, now Chairman of the Board of Guaranty Trust, and Charles Schwab, the boss of Bethlehem Steel.[2] On the Russian side were Paul Ziev, who had taken the helm at Amtorg and Alexander Gumberg, Raymond Robins' old pal, now a vice president of the Soviet Textile Syndicate.[3] The Americans, however, quickly issued a statement vociferously denying that there had been anything secret about the gathering or anything at all out of the ordinary. It had "no political significance," they insisted, and they in no way granted their support to the Soviet regime or its recognition.[4]

Schwab

In fact, the meeting centered on the founding, or rather re-founding, of the American-Russian Chamber of Commerce (ARCC). The original ARCC had appeared during the war, sponsored by Westinghouse (i.e. Crane) and Chase National. After 1917, it fell under the control of anti-Bolshevik Russians and by 1920 became inactive. Schley and Gumberg now aimed to revive it as the centerpiece of U.S.-Soviet economic cooperation. They largely succeeded and the Chamber soon had a membership that claimed 150 of Wall Street's financial elite. During the summer

1. "New York Bankers Dine U.S. Envoys of Soviet Trade Bodies," *Chicago Tribune* (13 Dec. 1925), 3.
2. "Bankers Here Meet Soviet Financiers," *New York Times* (13 Dec. 1925).
3. "Russian Purchases Grow," *New York Times* (14 Dec. 1925).
4. "Bankers Here Deny Endorsing Soviet," *New York Times* (14 Dec. 1925).

of 1929, the Chamber sponsored a Russian junket for a select group of American bankers and businessmen, plus assorted wives, children and hangers-on. Shepherded by Schley and Gumberg, this well-heeled herd of almost a hundred persons spent a month taking in the Soviet sights from the comfort of luxury hotel rooms and rail cars. The sight of "American society women" parading around the deck of a Volga steamer in lingerie, must have been a sight to behold for the locals.[5]

In November 1933, when plump, grinning Maxim Litvinov, now Peoples Commissar for Foreign Affairs, arrived in the States to finally negotiate the terms of U.S. recognition, ARCC gave him a grand reception at the Waldorf Astoria.[6] Wall Street turned out in style. Sharing the dais with the guest of honor were, of course, Schley and Gumberg, along with executives of Chase National, National City Bank, J. P. Morgan, Ford Motor, General Motors, Chrysler, American Express, General Electric, and corporate legal-eagles like Paul Cravath and Alan Wardwell. Also in attendance were Lillian Wald, Norman Hapgood and Raymond Robins, who delivered the keynote address. To Hapgood and Wald, it must have seemed like old times when the Friends of Russian Freedom feted visiting Russian revolutionaries.

What ARCC clearly demonstrates it that Wall Street-Kremlin collaboration continued well into the 1930s and beyond. Deals were still being made, along with money. But if so, why does this book end its story in 1925? The answer to that lies on the Russian end, not the American, and what happened wasn't a cessation in economic activity but a critical shift in its balance of power.

In December 1925, the Soviet Communist Party convened its 14th Party Congress. Dubbed the "Congress of Industrialization," Stalin used it as the launching pad for a new policy, "Socialism in One Country." Instead of waiting for outsiders, be they a victorious Western proletariat or Western capitalists, to "save" Soviet Russia and guide its development, Russia would pull itself up by its own bootstraps. It would cease to be a "raw materials appendage  of World Capitalism" and an importer of technology.[7] Western technological assistance and finance would still have roles to play, significant ones, but only in a purely subordinate capacity.

14th Party Congress

Stalin had the facts and figures to back up his change in policy. During 1925, Russia's industrial output had returned to 75% of its pre-war peak,

5. H. V. Kaltenborn, *Brooklyn Daily Eagle* (3 Aug. 1929), 1.

6. "Testimonial Dinner for the Honorable Maxim M. Litvinoff," 14 Nov. 1933.

7. "Pyatnaya kolona byla i ran'she, kak Stalin reshil dannyi vopros," DAL.BY (17 Dec. 2012).

and in the following year it would meet and even exceed that level.[8] However, foreign concessions contributed less than 1% of this.[9] The reality is that most concessions were small-scale and most concessionaires simply out to make a quick buck, mark, or pound. Almost none had any real interest in building a strong, self-sufficient Soviet economy. Even Harriman's manganese concession, one of the biggest of the lot, and from which he hoped to extract $120 million in profits over its twenty-year span, failed in less than three years and ended up costing Harriman almost $5 million.[10] By 1928, only sixty-eight concessions were still in business and almost none were around two years later. In their place, the Soviets pushed "technical assistance agreements" in which foreign firms contracted to provide expertise and training but owned the rights to nothing. By the end of the 20s, Americans held more than half of these technical assistance contracts, and by the mid-30s almost two-thirds.[11] The key difference is that they were no longer partners of the Soviet Government but mere employees.

Another sign of this power shift was a 1932 proposal by "Soviet financiers" to offer American investors the chance to subscribe to "a Soviet internal loan on a gold ruble basis exclusively."[12] "The issue has no political aspects," claimed Moscow, "but will be on a purely financial basis." The big advantage to Wall Street investors, now in the full grip of the Depression, was that the Russian bonds would be "issued on a gold basis and not subject to stock market fluctuations," thus offering "a stable and highly profitable tax-exempt security as well as insurance against possible depreciation." the The *New York Times* reported, "many millions of dollars" had already been subscribed.[13]

Back in 1921, Herbert Hoover, like many others on Wall Street, still imagined a future in which U.S. interests would "undertake the leadership in the reconstruction of Russia when the proper moment arrives" and dominate Russia's "vast, unconquered market."[14] That dream was now dead, at least for the foreseeable future. There never was a Grand Unified Wall Street Conspiracy to economically dominate Russia. The likes of Crane, Ford, Harriman, Morgan, Schiff, the Warburgs and others all had their schemes and hopes, but they seldom acted to any common purpose. More often, their plans competed with and undercut one another. In addition, American capitalists seriously underestimated the ruthless resolve

---

8. Alec Nove, *An Economic History of the USSR* (1972), 94.

9. Anthony Heywood, "Soviet Economic Concessions Policy and Industrial Development in the 1920s: The Case of the Moscow Railway Repair Factory," *Europe-Asia Studies*, Vol. 52, #3 (May 2000), 549-569.

10. *Ibid.*

11. Boris Shpotov, "The Soviet and American Business: Unique Examples of Economic Collaboration, 1920s-1930s," *History Research*, Vol. 2, #3 (March 2012), 186.

12. "Moscow Tells of Plan," *New York Times* (11 Aug. 1932), 8.

13. *Ibid.*

14. Patenaude, 637.

and resilience of the Bolsheviks. Wall Streeters, who almost all hoped for the Reds' demise, and the Soviets, who likewise awaited capitalism's destruction, could never muster an authentic spirit of collaboration. It was always mutual exploitation.

Josef Stalin was a ruthless political gangster, but he was also, despite what Trotsky thought, highly intelligent and very perceptive. And there may have been another incentive for him to pull the rug from under American and other foreign capitalists. It was also at the 14th Party Congress, that he openly broke with his erstwhile anti-Trotsky allies, Leo Kamenev and Gregory Zinoviev. Trotsky, who was in attendance, watched his enemies attack each other, yet did not utter a word. Even his staunchest champions have never understood this curious inaction. The usual explanation is that he was so flabbergasted to see his foes turn on each other that he did not know how to respond. In a man always ready to seize opportunity and never at a loss for words, that hardly sounds convincing.

A better insight may have been offered by Trotsky's American admirer, and John Reed's old friend, Max Eastman, who observed that when Trotsky's "cocksureness breaks down he is nonplussed."[15] Could it be that the recent death of Sklyansky, and possibly Reilly's, had left him derailed and confused, even afraid? As Nathalie Grant suggested, did Stalin use those events to "get Trotsky," to back him into a corner, or intimidate him into silence? Did Trotsky keep quiet because he feared his machina-

Eastman

tions with American and other foreign interests might be exposed?

In any case, whether he realized it or not, Trotsky was finished. Stalin emerged from the 14th Congress with the overwhelming support of the delegates. As Uncle Joe would admit, whether that was an honest or manipulated vote hardly mattered. In 1926, Trotsky found himself booted from the Politburo, the following year from the Party, and the year after that exiled to a remote corner of Central Asia. Anyone who had hoped to see Trotsky at the head of the Soviet regime or leading a new revolution had clearly backed the wrong horse.

But that doesn't mean there weren't a few diehards still willing to try, and that brings us back to New York. While in Central Asia, Trotsky received a letter dated 3 October 1928.[16] It purported to be from an American follower who provided the Old Man with call-number information for his books in the New York Public Library. A long string of numbers followed, none of which had anything to do with library locations. Rather, the numbers none-too-cleverly concealed a coded message. It acknowl-

---

15. Max Eastman, *Great Companions* (1959), 53-69.
16. Thanks to Elena Chavchavadze and the Russian Cultural Foundation for access to this document.

edged that Trotsky's proposed plan for "active struggle" against "Kinto" (a disparaging name for Stalin) would be adopted, and that an unnamed country (the U.S.?) had guaranteed Trotsky a visa and diplomatic protection if he could secure his release from the USSR. Most intriguing, the message noted that "the material side of the project is completely secured" and "the money sent has been deposited," presumably meaning deposited in New York. The message was signed, "your Abram." Was this Uncle Abram once more coming to the assistance of his nephew?[17]

It would be another sixty-six years before Wall Street and other Western interests again saw Russia wracked by political turmoil and economically prostrate. Once again, Americans led the charge to "democratize" the new Russia and guide it into the loving arms of international capitalism. But that bid also failed, and the upshot has been a return to what is usually described as "Cold War" hostility, intrigue and mutual vilification. But as we have seen, this pattern began long before the Cold War. As an "outlier" from the Western norm, politically and economically, Tsarist Russia was reviled as an abomination and a threat, as were the Bolsheviks and, today, the Putin regime. As the saying goes, the more things change, the more they stay the same.

---

17. Abram Zhivotovsky was certainly still alive in 1928. For the record, he was resident in Paris in 1940 when it was occupied by the Nazis. He was among Jews rounded up in 1941 and subsequently transported to Auschwitz where he perished in 1942 or 1943. As for Trotsky, Stalin kicked him out of the Soviet Union in 1929. He spent several years bouncing around Turkey and Europe before landing in a villa outside Mexico City. There, in 1940, a Stalinist assassin finally struck him down, leaving the "Man of Steel" unchallenged for the absolute supremacy of a totalitarian State supposed by its founders to be a new "worker's paradise."

SELECTED BIBLIOGRAPHY

The literature of the Russian Revolution is immense, as is that relating to American business and finance, not to mention international. The following is a very selective list mostly consisting of books not cited in the notes and basically intended as a basis for further reading.

Ackerman, Kenneth D. *Trotsky in New York, 1917: A Radical on the Eve of Revolution.* Berkeley, CA: Counterpoint (2016).

Adler, Cyrus. *Jacob Schiff: His Life and Letters* (2 vols.). New York: Doubleday Doran (1928).

Ascher, Abraham, *The Revolution of 1905: A Short History.* Stanford, CA: Stanford Univ. Press (2004).

Birmingham, Stephen. *"Our Crowd": The Great Jewish Families of New York.* New York: Harper & Row (1967).

Bolton, Kerry. *Revolution from Above.* London: Arktos Media (2011).

Brachev, Viktor. *Okkul'tnye istoki revoliutsii: Russkie masony XX veka* [Occult Sources of Revolution: Russian Masons in the XX century]. Moscow: Bystrov (2007).

Bunich, Igor. *Zoloto partii* [The Party's Gold]. Moscow: Sans (1992).

Butler, Smedley D. *War Is a Racket.* Los Angeles: Feral House (2003).

Cameron, Rondo and Brovkin, V. I. (eds). *International Banking, 1870-1914.* London: Oxfprd Univ. Press (1992)

Carosso, Vincent. *The Morgans: Private International Bankers, 1854-1913.* Cambridge: Harvard Univ. Press (1987).

Chernow, Ron. *The Warburgs: The Twentieth Century Odyssey of a Remarkable Jewish Family.* New York: Vintage Books (2016).

Clarke, William, *The Lost Fortune of the Tsars.* New York: St Martin's Griffin (1994).

Davies, R. W. (ed.). *From Tsarism to the New Economic Policy: Continuity and Change in the Economy of the USSR.* Ithaca, NY: Cornell Univ. Press (1991).

De Michelis, Cesare G. *The Non-Existent Manuscript: A Study of the Protocols of the Sages of Zion.* Lincoln: Univ. of Nebraska Press (2004).

Epstein, Edward J., Dossier: *The Secret History of Armand Hammer.* New York: Carroll & Graf (1996).

Feld, Marjorie N. *Lillian Wald: A Biography.* Chapel Hill: Univ. of North Carolina Press (2009).

Fel'shtinsky, Yury. *Vozhdi v zakone* [Leaders-in-Law]. Moscow: Terra (2008).

Figes, Orlando. *A People's Tragedy: The Russian Revolution, 1891-1924*. New York: Penguin (1998).

Fleming, Thomas. *The Illusion of Victory: America in WWI*. New York: Basic Books (2003).

Foglesong. David S. *America's Secret War against Bolshevism: U.S. Intervention in the Russian Civil War, 1917-1920*. Chapel Hill: The Univ. of North Carolina Press (1995).

Futrell, Michael. *Northern Underground: Episodes of Russian Revolutionary Transport and Communications through Scandinavia and Finland, 1863-1917*. New York: Praeger (1963).

Hodgson, Godfrey. *Woodrow Wilson's Right Hand: The Life of Colonel Edward M. House*. New Haven: Yale Univ. Press (2006).

House, Edward M. *Philip Dru Administrator: A Story of Tomorrow, 1920-1935*. CreateSpace Independent Publishing (2011).

Jeansonne, Glen. *Herbert Hoover: A Life*. New York: New American Library (2016).

Kennedy, Paul. *The Rise and Fall of the Great Powers*. New York: Vintage Books (1989).

Klehr, Harvey, Haynes, John Earl and Firsov, Fridrikh Igorevich. *The Secret World of American Communism*. New Haven: Yale Univ. Press (1995).

Lieven, Dominic. *The End of Tsarist Russia: The March to World War I and Revolution*. New York: Penguin (2016).

Mahoney, Harry T. and Marjorie L. *American Prisoners of the Bolsheviks: The Genesis of Modern American Intelligence*. Bethesda, MD: Academica Press (2001).

_____. *The Saga of Leon Trotsky: His Clandestine Operations and His Assassination*. San Francisco: Austin & Winfield (1998).

McMeekin, Sean. *History's Greatest Heist: The Looting of Russia by the Bolsheviks*. New Haven: Yale Univ. Press (2009).

_____. *The Russian Revolution: A New History*. New York: Basic Books (2017).

Morris, Charles R. *The Tycoons: How Andrew Carnegie, John D. Rockefeller, Jay Gould and J. P. Morgan Invented the American Supereconomy*. New Yo4rk: Holt (2006).

O'Connor, Timothy E. *The Engineer of Revolution: L. B. Krasin and the Bolsheviks*. Boulder, CO: Westview Press (1992).

Owen, G. L., *The Betterment of Man: A Rational History of Western Civilization*. New York: Capricorn Books (1974).

Partnoy, Frank. *The Match King: Ivar Kreuger, the Financial Genius behind a Century of Wall Street Scandals*. New York: PublicAffairs (2010).

Patenaude, Bertrand M., *The Big Show in Bololand: The American Relief Expedition to Soviet Russia in the Famine of 1921*. Stanford: Stanford Univ. Press (2002).

Pipes, Richard. *The Unknown Lenin: From the Secret Archive*. New Haven: Yale Univ. Press (1996).

Poole, Dewitt Clinton (Lees, Lorraine M. and Rodner, William S., eds.). *An American Diplomat in Bolshevik Russia*. Madison: Univ. Of Wisconsin Press (2014).

Pretorius, D. M. *The Banker and the Mole: Lenin, Parvus, the German-Bolshevik Conspiracy and the Russian Revolution of October 1917.* Amazon Kindle edition (2016).

Quigley, Carroll, *The Anglo-American Establishment.* New York: Books in Focus (1981).

_____, *Tragedy and Hope: A History of the World in Our Time.* Rancho Palos Verdes, CA: GSG & Assoc. (2004).

Rosenstone, Ron. *Romantic Revolutionary: A Biography of John Reed.* Cambridge: Harvard Univ. Press (1991).

Rothbard, Murray N. *Wall Street, Bankers and American Foreign Policy.* Auburn, AL: Ludwig von Mises Inst. (2011).

Ruud, Charles A. and Stepanov, Sergei A., *Fontanka 16: The Tsar's Secret Police.* Montreal: McGill-Queen's Univ. Press (1999).

Salzman, Neil J. *Reform and Revolution: The Life and Times of Raymond Robins.* Kent, OH: Kent State Univ. Press (1991).

Saul, Norman E. *The Life and Times of Charles R. Crane, 1858-1939.* Lanham, MD: Lexington Books (2013).

Schurer, Heinz, *"Alexander Helphand-Parvus–Russian Revolutionary and German Patriot." Russian Review, Vol. 18, No. 4 (Oct. 1959).*

Spence, Richard B., *Boris Savinkov: Renegade on the Left.* Boulder, CO: East European Monographs (1991).

_____. "Englishmen in New York: The SIS American Station, 1915-21," *Intelligence and National Security,* Vol. 19, #3 (Autumn 2004).

_____. "Hidden Agendas: Spies, Lies and Intrigue Surrounding Trotsky's American Visit, January-April, 1917," *Revolutionary Russia,* Vol. 21, #1 (June 2008)

_____. "John Reed, American Spy?: Reed, American Intelligence and Weston Estes' 1920 Mission to Russia," *American Communist History,* Vol. 13, #1 (April 2014).

_____, *Trust No One: The Secret World of Sidney Reilly.* Los Angeles: Feral House (2002).

Sutton, Antony C. *America's Secret Establishment: An Introduction to Skull & Bones.* Walterville, OR: TrineDay (2004).

_____. *Wall Street and the Bolshevik Revolution.* New Rochelle, NY: Arlington House (1974).

_____. *Western Technology and Soviet Economic Development 1917-1930.* Stanford: Hoover Institution Press (1968).

Thatcher, Ian D. *Leon Trotsky and World War One, August 1914-February 1917.* New York: St. Martin's Press (2000).

Volkogonov, Dmitri (Trans. and ed. by Harold Shukman). *Trotsky: The Eternal Revolutionary.* New York: The Free Press (1996).

Yergin, Daniel, *The Prize: The Epic Quest for Oil, Money & Power.* New York: Touchstone Books (1991).

Index